PILGRIMAGE IN THE CHRISTIAN BALKAN WORLD

Pilgrimage in the Christian Balkan World

The Path to Touch the Sacred and Holy

Edited by
DORINA DRAGNEA,
EMMANOUIL GER. VARVOUNIS,
EVELYN REUTER,
PETKO HRISTOV AND
SUSAN SOREK

BREPOLS

Cover illustration:
Fragment of an Icon of the Crucifixion with
Mary Magdalene and the Virgin Mary, 1300s
https://www.clevelandart.org/art/1954.394

© 2023, Brepols Publishers n. v., Turnhout, Belgium.

All rights reserved. No part of this publication may be
reproduced, stored in a retrieval system, or transmitted, in any
form or by any means, electronic, mechanical, photocopying,
recording, or otherwise without the prior permission of the
publisher.

D/2023/0095/9
ISBN 978-2-503-60308-7
eISBN 978-2-503-60309-4
DOI 10.1484/M.STR-EB.5.131895

Printed in the EU on acid-free paper.

Table of Contents

Introduction   7
Dorina DRAGNEA and Emmanouil Ger. VARVOUNIS

Life-giving Energies and Healing   27
Emically Sensitive Ethnography of Orthodox Christian Pilgrimage in Bulgaria
Magdalena LUBAŃSKA

Christian Shrines as a Space of Ethnic and Religious Interrelations   49
Two Cases in Kosovo and Albania
Aleksandra DUGUSHINA and Alexander NOVIK

Pilgrimage Diffusion and Polycentrism in the Veneration of Saint Nicodemus of Berat   69
Konstantinos GIAKOUMIS

Visiting Saint Naum   91
Blurring Motivations and Activities of Pilgrims and Tourists
Evelyn REUTER

The Phenomenon of Pilgrimages on the East Adriatic Coast between the Middle of the Thirteenth and the End of the Fifteenth Centuries   109
Zoran LADIĆ

Holy Journey to the Monastery or at the Wonderworking Icon of the Neamț as Described by Archimandrite Andronic Popovici   131
Ion GUMENÂI

Pilgrimages and Pilgrims in the Arad County as an Expression of the Confessional, Ethnic and Socio-political Realities (1700–1939)   145
Maria Alexandra PANTEA

The Mother of God of Bistrica Shrine as Croatian National Pilgrimage Center   165
Mirela HROVATIN

TABLE OF CONTENTS

Pilgrimage in the Romanian Orthodox Church   185
Aspects of the Pedagogy of Faith
Constantin NECULA

Pilgrimage Rituals and Places in Modern Greece   201
Emmanouil Ger. VARVOUNIS

The Pilgrimage Practice in Moldova as a Medium for Displaying of the Official and Vernacular Religiosity   221
Dorina DRAGNEA

From a Local Sanctuary to the 'Ostrog of Djerdap'   239
The Role of Monasticism in Creating the Most Visited Pilgrimage Destination in Serbia
Biljana ANĐELKOVIĆ

Revitalizing Identity through Pilgrimage to an Aegean Island   257
Memory, Ritual Practice and Communal Belonging at the Annual Celebration of Saint Panteleimon's Feast in Saria, Greece
Vassiliki CHRYSSANTHOPOULOU

From Pilgrimage to Festival and Commerce   279
Changes in the Use of Space in the Pilgrimage to the Church of Saint Barbara in the Municipality of 'Aghia Varvara' in Attica, Greece
Georgios KOUZAS

Conclusion   291
Evelyn REUTER

General Index   297

DORINA DRAGNEA AND
EMMANOUIL GER. VARVOUNIS

Introduction

Approaching a Metaphor: Touching the Sacred and Holy

After the 1990s, especially in post-socialist Southeast Europe countries, the return to open exposure of religious practices and beliefs by the population, the re-sacralisation of the former religious sites, the promotion of the shrines perceived as places and emblems of national identity and the building of new ones as a result of cooperation between Church and State, led to pilgrimage revitalization. Together with pilgrimage, the old habits and practices were revived, where people either kept the traditional structures or adapted them to the contemporary contexts, needs, and expectations. In this way, pilgrimage through its multiple implications and pilgrims has captured the attention of the scholars, concerned with explaining this collective devotion in terms of the complex aspects that it accumulates. Therefore, the regional and local contributions gain value due to the consistent data they can bring for outlining the features of the pilgrimage enacted in Orthodoxy and Catholicism.

Religious pilgrimage, called *proskýnima* (Greece), *poklonnichestvo* (Bulgaria), *hodochashchye* (Serbia), *hodochashche* (Croatia), *pelerinaj* (Romania), *poklonenie* (North Macedonia) and *pelegrinazh* (Albania) can be defined as a ritual journey enacted individually or collectively by people to holy places, during on a chosen day or periods within the liturgical year. The aim of this pilgrimage is for giving thanks and respect to *sacra*, to gain the goodwill and help of the Divinity, to be healed from physical and psychological illnesses. Furthermore, the pilgrims want to improve their own spiritual life, to express devotion for holy persons (Saints, the Apostles, and Martyrs), by joining in prayer.

Pilgrimages are liturgical institutions in motion, historically consecrated, culturally articulated, arising from the spiritual need of the faithful and stimulated by the common spiritual experience transmitted between them. These acts of collective piety often subscribe to the syncretic traits similar to the religious and ethno-linguistic variety of pilgrims united on this ritual path. In them 'territorial, ritual and intellectual experiences are made, which are synthesized into one performance',[1] whether they are Marian pilgrimages, performed for worshipping holy relics and for the celebration of saints, or if the people just have felt 'the calling'. The pilgrimage is one of the most significant liturgical journeys, during which the ethno-religious crucible of a region, in our case the Balkans or, more generally, Southeast Europe, is revealed and amalgamated in all its forms. During the pilgrimage, several things can be noticed, like the individual and collective religious and ritual ways of acting, visible strategies of accepting, negotiation, and sharing of the religious site.

Leaving from the Kim Knot's assertion that the space is as a medium in which religion is situated and the spaces, in turn, are produced by religions, religious groups, and individuals,[2] respectively the path is considered to embody this space and retains its features. The 'path' from home to shrine condenses multi sensorial attempts by the pilgrims, and it is an arena for exposing the mechanisms of belonging which are the consequences of the historical events, religious education and cultural patterns of requesting, understanding, approaching, feeling, and receiving divine help. The ceremonial and ritual behaviours in this ephemeral route are reflections of putting in the scene of the doing pilgrimage patterns.

The 'touch' represents a metaphorical expression in the volume's title, representing an incidence in concrete acts of the pilgrims as well. Starting from the liturgical experience, the sensual and tactile nature of Orthodoxy[3] and the prayer-core of the Catholicism is revealed in this volume in the content structure of the worship and devotion scenarios at the miracle working icons, saints, relics and reliquaries, statues, liturgical garments, and other agents, generators of help. On the one hand, it is considered an intangible 'touch' felt by people through emotions, states, and trances, odors, gazing, and hearing, when they approach the places and items they perceive sacred and that emanates 'holiness'. On the other hand, it is about consecrated rites and solemnities as bowing, the ritual kiss, kneeling, prostrations, and lighting of candles at the icons and relics, and statues. All these acts construct the experience of the sacred and holy 'which takes man out of himself and puts him in contact with the basic life forces of the universe'.[4]

The 'sacred' is expressed by texts, prayers, Akathists, hymns, songs, Psalms, Rosary, formulas uttered as part of ceremonials that are performed in front of icons, relics, and shrines for receiving the Divine blessing. The idea of the sacred is founded on our bodily being and the mental representation of the interior and exterior spatial coordinates[5] and transcends mundane reality, even if it is mediated

---

1 Ute Luig, 'Introduction', in *Approaching the Sacred. Pilgrimage in Historical and Intercultural Perspective*, ed. by Ute Luig (Berlin: Topoi, 2018), p. 22.
2 Kim Knot. *The Location of Religion. A Spatial Analysis* (United Kingdom: Equinox Publishing, 2005), p. 3.
3 Jill Dubisch, *In a Different Place. Pilgrimage, Gender, and Politics at a Greek Island Shrine* (Princeton, New Jersey: Princeton University Press, 1995), p. 61.
4 Andrew M. Greeley, *Come Blow Your Mind With Me* (Garden City, NY: Doubleday & Company, 1971), p. 66.
5 Veikko Anttonen, 'Space, Body, and the Notion of Boundary: A Category-Theoretical Approach to Religion', *Temenos* 41(2), (2005), p. 197.

by concrete materially representations. The sacred is vivid in pilgrim conscience, and it is conveyed by acts of veneration, which are hanging on the idea that the nature of holy (numinous) 'is such that it grips or stirs the human mind with this and that determinate affective state'.[6]

The icons, statues, and pieces of vestments that visually and symbolically express and generate holiness and relics as presences of the Divine Grace are intercessors between pilgrims and God. The acts of devotion made by believers towards them are mediating acts of an archetypal transaction, which includes bodily endeavours and financial sacrifices, oaths and spiritual duties, prescribed words, and offerings. These expressions of the religious and local cultural traditions associated with the shrines, and the practices performed by pilgrims reflect the forms of ritually and symbolically touching the sacred. Therefore, in this volume, operating with the original version of the terms, like *sabor* (from Serbian, 'mass gatherings'), *blagodat* (from Bulgarian, 'bliss', 'grace'), *dătător de viață* (from Romanian, 'life giving'), *mbarësi* (from Albanian, 'well-being'), the practice of *glendi* (from Greek, 'communal or group celebrations'), *hagiasma, ayasma, agheasmă* ('holy spring', 'holy water', 'blessed water'), to make *kurban* ('ritually animal slaughtering'), etc., express their content and meanings for the representatives of the communities.

Also, in more recent contexts, religious tourists are present, who also have their specific behaviours in seeking to satisfy their own needs, and to impregnate with, or consume the sacred in their own way. Therefore, the presence of commercialization does not appear to reduce or dampen the religious or spiritual experience lived by individuals to places that are far from their place of residence yet places that are deemed to deserve reverence, giving them important spiritual benefits.[7] Attending fairs and festivals organized during pilgrimages, buying religious objects and souvenirs, visiting the picturesque places where the altar is located, as well as the main sites of worship within its perimeter are just few examples of taking the holiness and blessing in the quotidian sphere.

General and Regional Overview of Research Literature Concerning the Topic of Pilgrimage

In order to outlining the backdrop of this volume and to see if the models and perspectives proposed by the classical and new scholarships in pilgrimage studies are applicable to the Christian Balkans, or that, the region has its own models of going on pilgrimage, understanding and approaching the sacred and holy, we will

---

6 Rudolf Otto, *The Idea of the Holy. An Inquiry Into the Non-Rational Factor in the Idea of the Divine and Its Relation to the Rational*, 2-nd edition, trans. by John W. Harvey (London, New York, Toronto: Oxford University Press, 1950), p. 12.
7 Leighanne Higgins and Kathy Hamilton, 'Sacred Places: an Exploratory Investigation of Consuming Pilgrimage', in *North American Advances in Consumer Research*, Volume 38, ed. by Darren W. Dahl, Gita V. Johar, and Stijn M. J. van Osselaer (Duluth, MN: Association for Consumer Research, 2011), p. 266.

give a short review on the trajectory of the theoretical perspective in pilgrimage topic. Approaches have been outlined, moved on, and accordingly reformulated to the tendencies and multiple implications of/on the pilgrimage.[8]

Victor and Edith Turner open the discourse on the topic of pilgrimage framing it as an expression of *communitas*[9] that is a 'direct, immediate, and total confrontation of human identities which tends to make those experiencing it think of mankind as a homogeneous, unstructured, and free community'.[10] Assemble of such characteristics are suggesting a kind of social utopia in which any hierarchy is shifting. Also, the Turners have seen pilgrimage as a *rite of passage*, on which the pilgrim left the mundane word to approaching the sacred shrine, and then to return at home spiritually changed and improved. Turners' contribution is valuable in terms of the ethnographic content it offers, as well as their patterns, which can be applied to some cases, even if singularly, having in view the post-modern realities. Withal for their role in provoking anthropologically investigating pilgrimage 'as comprising all the interactions and transactions, formal and informal, institutionalized or improvised, sacred or profane, orthodox or eccentric, which owe their existence to the pilgrimage itself'.[11]

However, scholars basing on their cases analysis provided arguments for contesting and as well as re-adapting the Turners' concepts. John Eade and Michael J. Sallnow contested the paradigm of *communitas*, considering the pilgrimage as 'an arena for competing religious and secular discourses, for both the official co-optation and non-official recovery of religious meanings, for conflict between orthodoxies, sects, and confessional groups, for drives towards consensus and communitas, and for counter-movements towards separateness and division'.[12] In turn, Simon Coleman asserts that the paradigm of John Eade *contestation* just reinterprets the *communitas* paradigm of Turner.[13] Both of them are ascertained to be metaphors of revolt, or at least deconstruction, 'they have created structures of theory that run the risk of confining conversations about pilgrimage to those scholars who happen to like to talk about religion'.[14]

---

8   See more in Simon Coleman and John Elsner, *Pilgrimages. Past and Present in the World Religions* (Cambridge: Harvard University Press, 1995); Antón M. Pazos, *Pilgrims and Politics. Rediscovering the Power of the Pilgrimage* (London: Routledge, 2012); Simon Coleman, 'Pilgrimage as Trope for Anthropology of Christianity', *Current Anthropology*, 55 (10), (2014), 281 - 291; Ian Reader, *Pilgrimage: A Very Short Introduction* (Oxford: Oxford University Press, 2015); *New Pathways in Pilgrimage Studies. Global Perspectives*, ed. by Dionigi Albera and John Eade (London/New York: Routledge, 2016).

9   Victor Turner and Edith Turner, *Image and Pilgrimage in Christian Culture. Anthropological Perspectives* (New York: Columbia University Press, 1978).

10 Victor Turner, *Dramas, Fields, and Metaphors: Symbolic Action in Human Society* (Ithaca: Cornell University Press, 1974) p. 169.

11 Victor Turner and Edith Turner, 'Introduction', in *Image and Pilgrimage in Christian Culture. Anthropological Aspects* (New York: Columbia University Press, 1978), p. 22.

12 John Eade and Michael J. Sallnow, 'Introduction', in *Contesting the Sacred: The Anthropology of Christian Pilgrimage*, ed. by John Eade and Michael J. Sallnow (London: Routledge, 1991), p. 2.

13 Simon Coleman, 'Pilgrimage as Trope for Anthropology of Christianity', *Current Anthropology*, 55 (10), (2014), p. 286.

14 Simon Coleman, 'Do You Believe in Pilgrimage? Communitas, Contestation and Beyond', *Anthropological Theory*, 2 (3), (2002), p. 363.

Correlatively, the contemporary processes, condition the considering the diversity of the societies, and of the individuals, who gather on pilgrimage at the same site, that they come with different educational, religious, economic, and social backgrounds. If we take into account the influence of technology, globalization trends, tourism, and eastern-transnational migration for labor, we notice that new behaviors, experiences, attitudes, and interests and not only religious needs are built. Therefore, the trait of community and homogeneity declines, it is apparent and only temporal, with a high degree of ephemerality at its more suitable mode. It can speak about 'communitas' at the level of the microgroup, where the same ideologies are expressed and shared.

Other perspectives, advanced by John Eade and Michael J. Sallnow is that the sacred space is a 'religious void, a ritual space capable of accommodating diverse meanings and practices.'[15] This position is to some extent true, but the quality of the void should be viewed with restraint. The sacred space is pre-charged with avowals, religious memory, hagiographic evidences, or historical events, miracle occurrences. Related to these, generations of pilgrims give and transmit between them the significance and respect that is given by themselves to the place or the holy figure which consecrated it. Respectively, when the pilgrims come to the site, they have already filled it with meanings, expectancies, and intentions. Their actions are replicas of those performed in previous times by others, or of their personal past-experiences with the site.

The debate around explaining the features of the *shared* or *mixed* site is another issue that has retained attention of the specialists. Glen Bowman on his analysis of the intercommunal interactions at holy places in North Macedonia advances the term of *mixed site*. He asserts that 'mixing' is a term capable of embracing interaction ranging from antagonistic mobilisation to amicable mutuality.[16] In such sites the diverse interpretations of the significance of the same sacred things 'are means of enabling groups with various religious conception to gather, while mimicry, imitation, disavowal, and avoidance are core strategies of mixing the nominally incommensurate in and around the same place'.[17] Dionigi Albera and Maria Couroucli, together with their contributors consider ethically and contextually the qualities of a sacred site and the practices committed there through the concepts of mixed worship, sharing, hybridity, intersection.[18] While, Maria Couroucli is operating with the mixed and shared sites, where she stresses 'the religious groups interact in a highly regulated

---

15 John Eade and Michael J. Sallnow, 'Introduction', in *Contesting the Sacred: The Anthropology of Christian Pilgrimage*, ed. by John Eade and Michael Sallnow (London: Routledge, 1991), p. 15.
16 Glenn W. Bowman, 'Orthodox-Muslim Interactions at 'Mixed Shrines' in Macedonia', in *Eastern Christians in Anthropological Perspective*, ed. by Chris Hann and Hermann Goltz (Berkeley: University of California Press, 2010), p. 202.
17 Glenn W. Bowman, 'Introduction: Sharing the *Sacra*', in *Sharing the Sacra: The Politics and Pragmatics of Inter-communal Relations around Holy Places*, ed. by Glenn Bowman (New York, Oxford: Berghahn, 2015), pp. 4–5.
18 Dionigi Albera, 'Conclusion Crossing the Frontiers between the Monotheistic Religions, an Anthropological Approach' in *Sharing Sacred Spaces in the Mediteranean. Christians, Muslims, and Jews at Shrines and Sanctuaries*, ed. by Dionigi Albera and Maria Couroucli (Bloomington: Indiana University Press, 2012), p. 220.

space, where social status and rights are conferred on an individual as a member of a particular religious community.'[19]

This outlook turn to the other side of the coin, of that pilgrimage is a medium relevant for noticing how different religious groups are articulating the identity and differences between them, or is a kind of rule self in practices.[20] In fact, through these differences in the acting of religious traditions and folk practices, it can visualize and explore the unaltered cultural forms of devotional acts, religious behaviours. Such of position, unanimously respected, keeps the distance and sometimes the contamination of the religious groups' actions. In the same key, Galia Valtchinova analysing a mixed or shared site in Bulgaria states that 'far from being a purely religious experience, the devotion manifested in such places is at once a spiritual quest and an arena for affirming and negotiating identity'.[21] An interesting look at the mixed site and its status quo, Robert M. Hayden gives, according to him this 'is maintained when all parties act in accordance with shared understandings that make interactions non-confrontational'.[22] In fact, it mirrors the status quo in the secular dimension as well.

Also, Glen Bowman's awareness the fragility of inter-communalism[23] in mixed sites, assertion that is pertinent, taking into account that some ethnographic cases prove the tensions between religion-ethnic contacts in the recent history of Southeast Europe. Such approach determines to consider the antagonistic tolerance[24] of Robert M. Hayden, which reveal eradicating attempts and temporal compromises. He views the religiouscapes as markers of patterns of dominance[25] where the sharing is 'understood only as a temporal moment expressing actual processual relations rather than a fixed quality of intergroup stasis based on long-lasting difference, antagonism,

---

19 Maria Couroucli, 'Introduction. Sharing Places – A Mediteranean Tradition', in *Sharing Sacred Spaces in the Mediteranean. Christians, Muslims, and Jews at Shrines and Sanctuaries*, ed. by Dionigi Albera and Maria Couroucli (Bloomington: Indiana University Press, 2012), p. 4.
20 *Sharing Sacred Spaces in the Mediteranean. Christians, Muslims, and Jews at Shrines and Sanctuaries*, ed. by Dionigi Albera and Maria Couroucli (Bloomington: Indiana University Press, 2012).
21 Galia Valtchinova, 'The Mounth of the Cross: Sharing and Contesting Barriers on a Balkan Pilgrimage Site', in *Sharing Sacred Spaces in the Mediteranean. Christians, Muslims, and Jews at Shrines and Sanctuaries*, ed. by Dionigi Albera and Maria Couroucli (Bloomington: Indiana University Press, 2012), p. 87.
22 Robert M. Hayden. Shared Spaces, or Mixed? in *The Oxford Handbook of Religious Space*, ed. by Jeanne H. Kilde (Oxford: online edn, Oxford Academic, 21 June 2022), https://doi.org/10.1093/oxfordhb/9780190874988.013.3 (accessed on 3. 10. 2022)
23 Glenn W. Bowman, 'Orthodox-Muslim Interactions at 'Mixed Shrines' in Macedonia', in *Eastern Christians in Anthropological Perspective*, ed. by Chris Hann and Hermann Goltz (Berkeley: University of California Press, 2010), p. 214.
24 Robert M. Hayden, 'Introduction. Competitive Sharing of religious sites in Europe, the Middle East, South Asia and Latin America' in *Antagonistic Tolerance. Competitive Sharing of Religious Sites and Spaces*, ed. by Robert M. Hayden with Tuğba Tanyeri-Erdemir, Timothy D. Walker, Aykan Erdemir, Devika Rangachari, Manuel Aguilar-Moreno, Enrique López-Hurtado, and Milica Bakić-Hayden (London and New York: Routledge, 2016), pp. 10–12.
25 *Antagonistic Tolerance. Competitive Sharing of Religious Sites and Spaces*, ed. by Robert M. Hayden with Tuğba Tanyeri-Erdemir, Timothy D. Walker, Aykan Erdemir, Devika Rangachari, Manuel Aguilar-Moreno, Enrique López-Hurtado, and Milica Bakić-Hayden (London and New York: Routledge, 2016), pp. 31–34; See also Robert M. Hayden, 'Intolerant Sovereignties and 'Multi-multi'

and pragmatic acceptance'.[26] In the *Choreography of Shared Sacred Sites*, Elazar Barkan and Karen Barkey[27] draw attention to the research of sacred sites in 'diachronic historical manner and in their synchronic moments' referring to the influence of politics on the sacred site, that can conditions the shrine to be consecutively the 'locus of communal violence' or of 'peaceful coexistence'.

Jill Dubisch[28] in her gender approach applies an experimental ethnography in pilgrimage study that transcends the reflexive discourse in order for discovering of the self and the culture of the other.

The multiple implications and influences associated with to pilgrimage performing, like tourism with its related purposes (leisure, cultural visitations, and festivals), commercialization of religions catch the interests of the specialists. In the opinion of Ian Reader pilgrimage should not be seen only through the lens of its religious character, the specialists should pay attention as well to pilgrimage in various secularised contexts.[29] In the opinion of Ellen Badone and Sharon R. Roseman incidence between tourism and pilgrimage intersect in one journey.[30] Later, Ian Reader in one of his contributions asserts as well that 'the dynamics of the marketplace, the consumerism are not antithetical to pilgrimage (or to 'religion'), but crucial to its successful functioning, development, appeal and nature.'[31]

In the same direction, the political economy perspective on pilgrimage was advanced by Simon Coleman and John Eade asserting that it 'focuses attention on an expanded environment of operation that illustrates the significance for pilgrimage of national and transnational scales of planning, infrastructure and economic activity, even in relation to smaller shrines'.[32] Coleman in one of his studies maintains that 'the sacred travel frequently overlaps with tourism, trade, migration, expressions of nationalism, creations of diaspora, imagining communities'.[33] The topic attracted

---

Protectorates. Competition Over Religious Sites and (in) Tolerance in the Balkans', in *Postsocialism Ideals, Ideologies and Practices in Eurasia*, ed. by Chris M. Hann (London and New York: Routledge, 2002), p. 167.

26 Robert M. Hayden, Hande Sozer, Tugba Tanyeri-Erdemir, and Aydin Erdemir, 'The Byzantine Mosque at Trilye: A Processual Analysis of Dominance, Sharing, Transformation and Tolerance', *History and Anthropology* 22 (1), (March 2011), 1–17.

27 Elazar Barkan and Karen Barkey 'Introduction', in *Choreographies of Shared Sacred Sites. Religion and Conflict Resolution*, ed. by Elazar Barkan and Karen Barkey (New York: Columbia University Press, 2015), pp. 1–32.

28 Jill Dubisch, *In a Different Place. Pilgrimage, Gender, and Politics at a Greek Island Shrine* (Princeton, New Jersey: Princeton University Press, 1995).

29 Ian Reader, 'Introduction', in *Pilgrimage in Popular Culture*, ed. by Ian Reader and Tony Walter (London: The Macmillan Press, 1993), pp. 1–25.

30 *Intersecting Journeys: the Anthropology of Pilgrimage and Tourism*, ed. by Ellen Badone and Sharon R. Roseman (Champaign: University of Illinois Press, 2004).

31 Ian Reader, *Pilgrimage in the Marketplace* (London: Routledge, 2015), p. 15.

32 Simon Coleman and John Eade, 'Introduction. Pilgrimage and Political Economy Introduction to a Research Agenda', in *Reframing Pilgrimage. Cultures in Motion*, ed. by Simon Coleman and John Eade (London: Routledge, 2004), p. 4.

33 Simon Coleman, 'Do you Believe in Pilgrimage? Communitas, Contestation and Beyond', *Anthropological Theory*, 2 (3), (2002), p. 363.

attention to Mario Katić, who with his contributors focus their volume on how the pilgrimage, religion, and tourism overlap and dynamically interact in sacred or pilgrimage places in Southeast Europe.[34] From one of the recent Eade' papers, we can understand which role institutions and entrepreneurs play in establishing the sacrality of particular places and inventing the rituals at these places.[35]

Focusing on one of the primary purposes for doing pilgrimage, Michael Winkelman and Jill Dubisch pay attention to its healing dimension. Their premise is 'pilgrimage is a multimedia therapy that combines different kinds of healing processes […] it is a form of "biopsychosocial" and spiritual healing that addresses many levels of the human need for healing and "wholing" the person'.[36] A valuable contribution is provided by Magdalena Lubańska who applies the post-secular anthropological theory for analyzing the practices for healing performed at the Orthodox monasteries in Bulgaria, showing the hospitals and energetic attributes that the monasteries have.[37]

The first work that gives historical support for understanding the features, roots of the pilgrimage in Southeast Europe is that of Frederick Hasluck. He carried out a monumental study of the transformation in the Balkans of Christian sites into Islamic ones and the reverse, called them 'ambiguous sanctuaries', concluding that they are the consequences of population conversions.[38]

More recently, a series of book-chapters was coordinated and addressed to pilgrimage practice in Southeast Europe by editorial team with Anglophone scholars.[39]

A valuable documentary background on lived and experienced forms of the religious in Southeast Europe, especially on Eastern Orthodoxy is ensured by the volumes edited by Chris Hann and Herman Goltz.[40] The ethnographic case studies sociocultural and philosophical anthropologically focus on the continuum between *doxa* and *praxis* in religious practices.

The clash of the ethnicity and denomination on pilgrimage sites in the countries of Southeast Europe was pointed out by various scholars. For instance, Dragoljub B. Đorđević, Dragan Todorović, and Dejan Krstić with their contributors give

---

34 *Pilgrimage and Sacred Places in Southeast Europe. History, Religious Tourism and Contemporary Trends*, ed. by Mario Katić, Tomislav Klarin, Mike McDonald (Wien: LIT Verlag, 2014).
35 John Eade, 'The Invention of Sacred Places and Rituals: A Comparative Study of Pilgrimage', *Religions* (11), (2020), doi:10.3390/rel11120649.
36 Michael Winkelman and Jill Dubisch, 'Introduction. The Anthropology of Pilgrimage', in *Pilgrimage and Healing*, ed. by Michael Winkelman and Jill Dubisch (Tucson: The University of Arizona Press, 2005), p. xxxvi.
37 Magdalena Lubańska, *Praktyki lecznicze w prawosławnych monasterach w Bułgarii. Perspektywa antropologii (post)sekularnej* (Warszawa: Wydawnictwa Uniwersytetu Warszawskiego, 2019).
38 Frederick Hasluck, *Islam and Christianity under the Sultans* (New York: Clarendon Press, 1929), ed. by Margareth M. Hasluck (Istanbul: The Isis Press, 2000).
39 See more in *Pilgrimage, Politics and Place-Making in Eastern Europe: Crossing the Borders*, ed. by Mario Katić and John Eade (London: Routledge, 2014).
40 *Eastern Christians in Anthropological Perspective*, ed. by Chris Hann and Herman Goltz (Berkeley: University of California Press, 2010). See also in this matter *Religious Orthodoxy and Popular Faith in European Society*, ed. by Ellen Badone (Princeton: Princeton University Press, 1990).

useful data and interpretations on shared cults of saintly figures and cult places, transformation of religious sites, the effects of the connection between religious and secular institutions on pilgrimage between the states of Balkans.[41] The perspective of investigating the religious practices and pilgrimage performances on the borders seems to be the central approach for several contributions in academia of Southeast Europe. Dragana Radisavlević-Ćiparizović and Dragan Todorović conducted a team who investigated pilgrimage to sacred sites among Balkan space in various periods, paying attention to the sociological aspects of the pilgrimage and religious tourism nexus.[42]

Topics like rituals, the veneration of the saints and relics, the cultural memory functions of the pilgrimage, sacred places and religious tourism in Bulgaria were explored by Albena Georgieva,[43] Margarita Karamihova,[44] Vihra Baeva,[45] Petko Hristov,[46] etc. Galia Valtchinova has investigated the mixing of religious practices, focusing on a singular site or comparatively.[47] Evgenia Troeva analyses the classic traditional sites, new Christian cult centres, New Age pilgrimage places and pilgrimage performed at cult objects in post 1989 Bulgaria, asserting that during the periods of social and personal crisis, people are more likely to turn to places and objects deemed

---

41 *Cult Places on the Border*, ed. by Dragoljub B. Đorđević, Dragan Todorović, and Dejan Krstić (Niš: JUNIR, 2014); See also Dejan Krstić, 'A Contribution to the Typology of Cult Places of the Balkans', in *Pilgrimage, Cult Places and Religious Tourism*, ed. by Dragana Radisavljević-Ciparizović (Niš: Yugoslav Society for the Scientific Study of Religion, 2010), pp. 129–40.
42 Драгана Радисављевић Ћипаризовић and Драган Тодоровић, *Ходочашћа - између светог и световног* (Ниш: ЈУНИР, 2011).
43 Албена Георгиева, 'Поклонничеството – пътуване отвъд различието', in *Брегът – морето – Европа*, ed. by Мила Сантова, Ива Станоева and Миглена Иванова (София: Акад. издателство "Проф. М. Дринов", 2006), pp. 165–72; Albena Georgieva, 'From Pilgrimage to Tourism (St Joakim Osogovski Monastery)', in *Balkan Traditional and Modern Destinations and Forms of Mobility (Macedonian Case)*, ed. by Dragi Ǵorgiev and Petko Hristov (Skopje: Macedonian Academy of Sciences and Arts, 2020), pp. 97–107.
44 Margarita Karamihova and Galia Valtchinova, 'Talking War, "Seeing" Peace: Approaching the Pilgrimage of Krastova Gora (Bulgaria)', *History and Anthropology* 3 (2009), pp. 339–62.
45 Вихра Баева, 'Между енорийския живот, поклонничеството и туризма: руската църква "Св. Николай Мирликийски Чудотворец" в София', *Българска етнология*, 1–2 (2012), 19–36; Vihra Baeva, 'Parishioners, Pilgrims, Tourists. The Visitors of an Orthodox Christian Shrine in Sofia', in *Pilgrimage and Sacred Places in Southeast Europe. History, Religious Tourism and Contemporary Trends*, ed. by Mario Katić, Tomislav Klarin, Mike McDonald (Wien: LIT Verlag, 2014), pp. 79–95.
46 Evgenia Troeva, Petko Hristov, 'Sacred Geography of the Post-Socialist Balkans: Transformations of Religious Landscape and Pilgrimage', *Southeastern Europe*, 41 (1), (2017), 1–18.
47 Galia Valtchinova, 'Le pèlerinage du "Mont de la Croix" et l'apprentissage religieux en Bulgarie post-communiste', *Cahiers de litterature orale* 45 (1999), 87–110; Galia Valtchinova, '"Jérusalem des Rhodopes" vs "La Mecque des Rhodopes": deux lieux de pèlerinage entre la Bulgarie, la Grèce et la Turquie', *Chronos. Revue d'Histoire de l'Université de Balamand* 18 (2008), 55–86; Galia Valtchinova, 'Medjugorje et Krastova Gora dans la longue durée: partage et construction de frontières dans deux pèlerinages chrétiens des Balkans', *Études Balkaniques* 1 (2009), 168–95.

to be sacred, hoping for support, spiritual experience and healing, which has given rise to pilgrimages in the twenty first century.[48]

Dragana Radisavljević Ciparizović has researched the display of folk religiosity within pilgrimage, the sanctuaries and the ethno-religious contact in mixed sites in Serbia.[49] Along the same idea, it is necessary to mention recent papers written by Biljana Anđelković.[50] A series of studies focused on traditional and non-traditional religiosity, including modern forms of worship, which help to understand the facets of religious behaviour of individuals during contemporary pilgrimage, were conducted by the specialists from Belgrade and the University of Niš.[51] Biljana Sikimić gave her investigation on the Catholic shrine of Letnica.[52]

An exhaustive monograph regarding pilgrimage in Romania was written by Mirel Bănică, who based on consecutive fieldwork on about forty-four pilgrimages reveal the faith in wonders and miracles, the forms of folk religious exposure, management and socio-economic aspects of the pilgrimage, prohibitions and ritual food, etc.[53] Valentin Lucian Beloiu has provided a sociological approach to pilgrimage.[54] It is

---

48 Evgenia Troeva, Pilgrimage in Bulgaria after 1989, in *Sakralität und Mobilität im Kaukasus und in Südosteuropa*, ed. by Tsypylma Darieva, Thede Kahl and Svetoslava Toncheva (Wien: Österreichische Akademie der Wissenschaften, 2017), pp. 143–56. See also Евгения Троева, 'География на сакралната мобилност: реликви, мощи и поклонничество в началото на XXI век', in *Етнографски проблеми на народната култура*, Т. 10, ed. by Анатол Анчев (София: Акад. издателство "Проф. М. Дринов", 2013), pp. 127–80.

49 Dragana Radisavljević-Ciparizović, 'Mixed Pilgrimages in Serbia: Question of Communitas and Pilgrims' Identity', in *Pilgrimage, Cult Places and Religious Tourism*, ed. by Dragana Radisavljević-Ciparizović (Niš: Yugoslav Society for the Scientific Study of Religion, 2010), pp. 155–65; Dragana Radisavljević-Ciparizović, 'Pilgrimage in Empirical Perspective: Pilgrims' Attitudes Towards Church and Folk Religiosity and Superstition in Serbia', in *Orthodoxy from an Empirical Perspective*, ed. by Mirko Blagojević and Dragan Todorović (Beograd – Niš: Yugoslav Society for the Scientific Study of Religion, 2011), pp. 127–37; Dragana Ciparizović, 'Pilgrimage in the 21st Century: Case Studies Three Sanctuaries in Serbia', *Religija i Tolerancija*, 24 (2015), 331–48.

50 Biljana Anđelković, 'Some Basic Factors on Pilgrimage in Contemporary Serbia', in *Perspectives of Anthropological Research in South-East Europe*, ed. by Marina Martynova and Ivana Bašić (Moscow, Belgrade: Institute for Ethnology of the Russian Academy of Sciences, 2019), pp. 207–29; Биљана Анђелковић, ' Манастир Васкресење Христово између религијских и секуларних дискурса', in Етно-културолошки зборник XXII: за проучавање културе источне Србије и суседних области', ed. by Војислав Филиповић and Ивица Тодоровић Тодоровић (Сврљиг: 2019), pp. 87–102; Биљана Анђелковић, Етницитет и ходочашће: пример поклоничког путовања манастире пиротског округа, in Етно-културолошки зборник XXIII: за проучавање културе источне Србије и суседних области, ed. by Војислав Филиповић and Ивица Тодоровић (Сврљиг: 2020), pp. 91–105.

51 *Traditional and Non-Traditional Religiosity*, ed. by Mirko Blagojević and Dragan Todorović (Beograd – Niš: Yugoslav Society for the Scientific Study of Religion, 2019); *Contemporary Religious Changes: from Desecularization to Postsecularization*, ed. by Dragan Todorović, Mirko Blagojević and Dragoljub B. Đorđević (Beograd – Niš: Yugoslav Society for the Scientific Study of Religion, 2020).

52 Biljana Sikimić, 'Sveta putovanja: Letnica na Kosovu', *Glasnik Etnografskog Instituta SANU*, LXII (1), (2014), 15–32; Biljana Sikimić, 'Dynamic Continuity of a Sacred Place: Transformation of Pilgrims' Experiences of Letnica in Kosovo', *Southeastern Europe*, 41 (1), (2017), 43–58.

53 Mirel Bănică, *Nevoia de miracol. Fenomenul pelerinajelor în România contemporană* (Iași: Polirom, 2014).

54 Valentin Lucian Beloiu, *Miracolul in viața omului modern. O monografie sociologică a pelerinajului* (București: Christiana, 2015).

worth mentioning the studies signed by Constanța Cristescu,[55] Monica Grigore,[56] Ștefan Dorondel,[57] Stelu Șerban.[58]

Concerning pilgrimage practice and folk religiosity of the urban festivals in Greece it appropriate to quote the works of Jill Dubisch,[59] Manoulis Varvounis, etc.[60] In-depth research was conducted by Vassiliki Chryssanthopoulou, who explores the *hatziliki* ('the pilgrimage to the Holy Land') of Greek migrants from Kastellorizo island, in Perth, Australia. She investigated the pilgrimage as a ritual passage, of psychological and social dimension.[61] Also, the folkloric perspective of Katerina Seraidari is addressed to the religious practices and ideological conflicts between various agents in the Cyclades, having as case-focus the worships to the Virgin of Tinos.[62] The pilgrimage to Mount Athos was explored by René Gothóni.[63] In the newest valuable book-album, *Encounters on the Holy Mountain. Stories from Mount Athos*[64] there are collected narratives on the spiritual experience of various travellers or pilgrims regarding the monastic traditions, daily life, etc., of this stronghold of the Orthodoxy, providing the possibility to discover it in detail.

Gilles de Rapper wrote about sharing of religious spaces and mixed practices of Muslims and Christians in Albania.[65] The pilgrimage place-making through an examination of the construction, destruction, reinterpretation and reconstruction

---

55 Constanta Cristescu, 'Pilgrimage and Pilgrimage Song in Transylvania', *East European Meetings in Ethnomusicology*, 1 (1994), 30–43.
56 Monica Grigore, 'Tamara's Illness. Pilgrims, Fate, and Lived Religion in Post-Communist Romania', *Religion and Society in Central and Eastern Europe*, 8 (1), (2015), 39–51.
57 Ștefan Dorondel, 'Orthodoxy, Nationalism, and Local Identities: A Romanian Case Study', *Ethnologia Balkanica*, 6 (2002), pp. 117–44.
58 Stelu Șerban, 'Pilgrimage and Nationhood in a Transylvanian Village' in *Religion and Boundaries. Studies from the Balkans, Eastern Europe and Turkey*, ed. by Galia Valtchinova (Istanbul: Isis Press, 2010), pp. 167–85.
59 Jill Dubisch, 'Golden Oranges and Silver Ships. An Interpretative Approach to a Greek Holy Shrine', *Journal of Modern Greek Studies*, 6 (1988), 128–85.
60 Μανόλης Βαρβούνης, Λαϊκή θρησκευτικότητα στον ελληνικό αστικό χώρο. Μελετήματα νεωτερικής θρησκευτικής λαογραφίας (Θεσσαλονίκη: Σταμούλης, 2014); Μανόλης Βαρβούνης, Εισαγωγή στη θρησκευτική λαογραφία. Ο κύκλος του χρόνου – ο κύκλος της ζωής – ο κύκλος της λατρείας, δεύτερος τόμος (Θεσσαλονίκη: Σταμούλης, 2017).
61 Βασιλική Χρυσανθοπούλου, 'Οι χατζήδαινες της Πέρθης', *Λαογραφία* 33 (1985), 129–54.
62 Κατερινα Σεραιδαρη, 'Μεγάλη η χάρη της': λατρευτικές πρακτικές και ιδεολογικές συγκρούσεις στις Κυκλάδες (Αθήνα: Ερίννη, 2007).
63 René Gothóni, 'Unity and Universe: Understanding Pilgrimage to Mount Athos', *Scripta Instituti Donneriani Aboensis* 22 (2010), 56–70.
64 *Encounters on the Holy Mountain. Stories from Mount Athos*, ed. by Peter Howorth and Chris Thomas (Turnhout: Brepols, 2020).
65 Gilles De Rapper, 'Religion on the Border: Sanctuaries and Festivals in Post-Communist Albania', in *Religion and Boundaries. Studies from the Balkans, Eastern Europe and Turkey*, ed. by Galia Valtchinova (Istanbul: Isis Press, 2010), pp. 247–65; Gilles de Rapper, 'The Vakëf: Sharing Religious Space in Albania', in *Sharing Sacred Spaces in the Mediterranean*, ed. by Dionigi Albera and Maria Couroucli (Indiana University Press, 2012), p. 29–50.

of Christian pilgrimage in Albania was theoretically interpreted by Konstantinos Giakoumis.[66]

Marijana Belaj gives consistent studies on pilgrimage at Međugorje in Bosnia and Herzegovina, emphasizing the exploration of the individual and their experience of pilgrimage, considering that 'the place does not become a pilgrimage by any decree and institutionalization but by pilgrimages and the employment of pilgrims in that destination'.[67] Gerald E. Markle and Frances B. McCrea have studied as well the most popular Catholic shrine – Međugorje.[68]

Josip Buturac and Mirela Hrovatin explore the Shrine of Our Lady of Marija Bistrica in Croatia.[69] The Ostrog monastery in Montenegro and folk religious practice, rituals and behaviours within pilgrimage was explored by Vladimir Bakrač[70] and the topic of ecumenism related to this shrine by Rade Božović.[71]

The sacred spaces, the cults of the saints and relics in North Macedonia have been explored by Eli Lucheska,[72] Petko Hristov and Mina Hristova.[73] Evelyn Reuter discussed

---

66 Konstantinos Giakoumis, 'An Enquiry into the Construction, Deconstruction, Transubstantiation and Reconstruction of Christian Pilgrimages in Modern-Day Albania', *Ηπειρωτικό Ημερολόγιο*, 32 (2013), 267–318; Konstantinos Giakoumis 'From Religious to Secular and Back Again. Christian Pilgrimage Space in Albania', *Pilgrimage, Politics and Place Making in Eastern Europe. Crossing the Borders*, ed. by John Eade and Mario Katić (Farnham: Ashgate Publishing Limited, 2014), pp. 103–18. See also Nataša Gregorič Bon, 'Secular Journeys, Sacred Places. Pilgrimage and Homemaking in Himarë/Himara Area of Southern Albania', in *Pilgrimage, Politics and Place-Making in Eastern Europe. Crossing the Borders*, ed. by John Eade and Mario Katić (Farnham: Ashgate Publishing Limited, 2014), pp. 135–49.
67 Marijana Belaj, *Milijuni na putu. Antropologija hodočašća i sveto tlo Međugorja* (Zagreb: Naklada Jesenski i Turk, 2012), p. 8.
68 Gerald E. Markle and Frances B. McCrea, 'Medjugorje and the Crisis in Yugoslavia', in *Politics and Religion in Central and Eastern Europe. Traditions and Transitions*, ed. by William H. Jr. Swatos (London: Praeger Publishers, 1994), pp. 197–208.
69 Josip Buturac, *Marija Bistrica: 1209–1993: povijest župe i prošteništa* (Marija Bistrica: Nacionalno svetište Majke Božje Bistričke, 1993); Marijana Belaj and Mirela Hrovatin, 'Cultural Practices in Sacralisation of Place: Vows in the Shrine of Our Lady of Marija Bistrica', in *Sacralization of Landscape and Sacred Places. Proceedings of the 3rd International Scientific Conference of Medieval Archaeology of the Institute of Archaeology*, ed. by Juraj Belaj, Marijana Belaj, et al. (Zagreb: Institut za Arheologiju, 2018), pp. 343–51.
70 Vladimir Bakrač,'Religious and Folk Customs in the North-West Part of Montenegro', in *Religion, Religious and Folk Customs on the Border*, ed. by Dragoljub B. Đorđević, Danijela Gavrilović and Dragan Todorović (Niš: Yugoslav Society for the Scientific Study of Religion, 2012), pp. 129–39.
71 Rade Božovic, 'Monastery Ostrog – Above the Ecumenism', in *Pilgrimage, Cult Places and Religious Tourism*, ed. by Dragana Radisavljević Ciparizović (Niš: Yugoslav Society for the Scientific Study of Religion, 2010), pp. 151–54.
72 Ели Луческа, 'Манастирот Трескавец со црквата Успение на света Богородица', in *Święta Góra Athos w Kulturze Europy Europa w Kulturze Athosu*, ed. by Marzanny Kuczyńskiej (Gniezno: Uniwersytet IM. Adam Mickiewicza, Collegium Europaeum Gnesnense, 2009), pp. 264–74; Ели Луческа. *Култот на христијанските светци во Македонија, Историја и традиција* (Прилеп: ИСК-Прилеп, 2010).
73 Petko Hristov and Mina Hristova, 'Sacred Places and Cultural Memory on the Triple-shared Border-Pilgrimage in the Osogovo Monastery', *Etnolog*, 15 (2014), 45–61.

how discursive strategies shape and articulate the ambiguity of common religious sites, having as an empirical site the monastery of Saint Naum in Ohrid.[74]

As it was shown, the broader and more regional or local contributions on the debating of topics consist of various theoretical outlooks, and at a particular level are made up of case studies, which contribute to a better understanding of the local models of the pilgrimage.

Perspectives and Outputs of this Volume on Christian Pilgrimages in the Balkans

In Southeast Europe, the territorial changes of the Balkan Wars, the atheistic ideology of the socialist regimes installed after II World War (except Greece), and local ethnoreligious and political-economical conflicts between countries of the former Yugoslavia in the 1990s have determined throughout that time some tendencies. On the one hand, the continuity of the historical traditions and keeping of local identities, and even dissent by the faith and religious practices, the safeguarding of the symbols, and the construction of the nationhood is relevant. On the other hand, a particular contextualized form of assimilation and displaying, the building of the cultural codes having as pillars mixed elements is present. The contact between the Orthodox, the Catholic and Protestant communities in this macro ethnographic terrain shows us the coagulation around common truths such as belonging to the Christian religion, and evidence of the tolerance swinging between *de facto* and *de jure* mode, which is amplified when the Muslim community appears in play. Therefore, the autonomy, the cross-negotiation and mutual acceptance are three ways that work synchronously in the public devotional acts like pilgrimage is and should be considered.

In an area of various religious, linguistic, and ethnic contacts, such as the Balkans, the research focusing on how cultural patterns and religious ideas work in expressing veneration, respect for what generates holiness and sacredness: saints, icons, relics, altars, statues, etc. remains very topical. Pilgrimage reflects the true face of a society, the relations between people, Church institution and state, the conflicts and compromises made by the parties to legitimize practices, altars, or collective behaviours.

Also, the distinctiveness as well as the ethno-religious and linguistic heterogeneity of the region, favour our theoretical perspective on the pilgrimage topic in the Christian Balkan communities to be set on the Coleman's view of analysing and interpreting 'human behaviour through using pilgrimage'.[75] Therefore, the purpose of this volume is to explore, re-interpret and re-contextualise the various natures of practices performed by the Orthodox and Catholic pilgrims in Balkan countries in their devotional 'path to touch the sacred and holy' through the prism of pilgrimage contents, and their

---

74 Evelyn Reuter, *Die Mehrdeutigkeit geteilter religiöser Orte. Eine ethnographische Fallstudie zum Kloster Sveti Naum in Ohrid (Mazedonien)* (Bielefeld: Transcript, 2021).
75 Simon Coleman, 'Do You Believe in Pilgrimage? Communitas, Contestation and Beyond', *Anthropological Theory*, 2 (3), (2002), p. 363.

articulating, using, and handling strategies. The chapters bring together three ways of addressing the topic: investigations concerned with theoretical issues of pilgrimage; specific case studies set in a particular time, context and place, and contributions focused on ethnographic case studies as a means of addressing larger issues.

The expertise and professional background of the contributors, from the explored region (Albania, Bulgaria, Croatia, Greece, Moldova, Romania, Serbia), and outside the region (Germany, Poland, Russia) who are coming from the discipline of cultural anthropology, folklore, history, religious studies, theology, etc., constitutes a strong point for descending to the essence of the collective practices of worship, to be interpreted theoretically and critically, analysed chronologically and diachronically. Therefore, the various visions of the authors, shaped on the base of qualitative and critical analysis of primary (ethnographic and folkloric data from field interviews, archive documents, samples, etc.) and secondary sources ensure to fill a research lack in the literature on pilgrimage in Southeast Europe, and especially on pilgrimage practices in Orthodoxy, which is the largest denomination in the region.

The contributors in their inter and transdisciplinary investigation, multi-sited ethnography researches carried out in almost twenty sites, consider as well several matters. These are the transnational migration, the policies of confirmation and validation of ethnic and national identity, the slight secularization tendencies, the reconsideration and repositioning of collective values, the giving up or adapting of the local cultural models to a globalized world, the trends of transition from rural to urban life style, etc.

There are several theoretical debates and inputs of the volume's contributors, which are joining the broader classical and newer approaches to the topic of pilgrimage. The authors explore the context in which the Christian shrines in the Balkans are spaces where the ethnic and denominational patterns in pilgrimage are revealed openly on multiple folds. There are interpreted native traditions specific to a particular group, as well as inspired among religious intergroup negotiations (e.g. Christians – Muslims) and borrowed traditions among Christians (Orthodox – Catholics). Thus, the collective ceremonial performances within pilgrimage are regarded in order for following how they stimulate cohesion, social memory, and identity, and how in the same entourage the actions are manners of differentiation towards the other, of expressing dominance and legitimation. It will be noticed that religious folklore and divine intervention stories are not just individual and collective cultural and social identity, experiences, but as well expressions of political contexts of competition. The authors focus on theoretical analysis and stressing of the historically and contemporary behaviour performed by the Christian pilgrims, highlighting the fact that the motivations for going to the sacred places can weave and transgress, from the purpose of seeking and obtaining Divine help to the leisure, religious/faith tourism. In all situations, individuals acting according to their need and express their own attitude of what is important, their beliefs towards what is sacred and holy, their own acting and veneration manners.

Respectively, one concept contested in this volume is that of Turner – 'pilgrimage polycentrism'. Konstantinos Giakoumis revisits it, providing an alternative concept of 'pilgrimage diffusion', of which he explains and argues by analysing three propagated pilgrimage practices connected to the veneration of Saint Nicodemus, the neomartyr of Berat (Albania). The practices are set in spatial and time dimensions, which are performed during the pilgrimage made at the site of the saint's relics (Berat), to the place where the saint's skull was enwalled up (the house of Ilia Koçi, in Berat), and the pilgrimage at the saint's birth-place (Vithkuq).

Another re-vised concept is the Latin term *peregrinare*, used to be largely attached to the pilgrimage. Magdalena Lubańska discussing healing pilgrimage in south-western Bulgaria, structuring her theoretical discourse on the idea of energy, advances the term *poklonnichestvo*, which consider it to be more suitable. Lubańska states that it refers to the practices of veneration of icons and relics, and pertains to what happens within the space of the shrine, during a special time when the shrine is believed to be especially imbued with healing powers. In the same contents line, Biljana Anđelković analyzing the mass gatherings at the monasteries in Serbia suggests an equivalent for *communitas* feeling – *sabornost* ('togetherness').

Also worth consideration are the Muslim Roma communities in the Southeast Europe and their adherence to the Orthodox and Catholic altars and holy figures. Several chapters of this volume discuss the hallowed spaces as *mixed*[76] ones, where different ethnic and religious communities more or less 'are discreet and respect the non-spoken rules of non-interference'.[77] For example, the chapter by Aleksandra Dugushina and Alexander Novik analyse inter-ethnic (Albanians, Serbs, Macedonians, Croats, etc.) and inter-religious (Christian and Muslim) practices within pilgrimage to the Orthodox Church of Saints Cosmas and Damian in the village of Hoçisht in Devoll region of southeast Albania and to the Catholic Church of Assumption of the Virgin Mary in the village of Letnica, Vitia/Vitina region in southeast of Kosovo. The authors investigating different representations of boundaries and trajectories of inter-group contacts, the canonical and various kinds of vernacular practices (such as sacrifices and offerings) performed by the pilgrims and their ritual behaviour, outline the strategies of identity displaying and sharing.

Evelyn Reuter deconstructs the dichotomy of 'religious' – 'secular', avoiding the synonymous terms 'sacred' and 'profane'. Theoretically unfolding her discourse on Kim Knott's spatial theory[78] and empirically on the pilgrimage to the monastery of Saint Naum, in the southwest of North Macedonia, Reuter discusses the seasonal aspects of the social and ritual behaviour of Christian and Muslim pilgrims in the context of the saint's feast day and of worship at his tomb, and how they act and move in different spaces of the core monastic complex. With the same perspective, Georgios Kouzas examines the multi-facetted significance of the special cross-moving from the sacred to secular within the urban religious pilgrimage of Saint Barbara that takes place in the town of Aigaleo in Attica, Greece. The author theoretically and factually interprets the material and intangible path of passing by the pilgrims to

---

[76] Glenn Bowman, 'Introduction: Sharing the *Sacra*', in *Sharing the Sacra: The Politics and Pragmatics of Inter-communal Relations around Holy Places*, ed. by Glenn Bowman (New York, Oxford: Berghahn, 2015), pp. 1–9.

[77] Dionigi Albera, 'Conclusion: Crossing the Frontiers between the Monotheistic Religions: An Anthropological Approach', in *Sharing Sacred Spaces in the Mediterranean. Christians, Muslims, and Jews at Shrines and Sanctuaries*, ed. by Dionigi Albera and Maria Couroucli (Bloomington, IN: Indiana University Press, 2012), p. 238.

[78] Kim Knott, *The Location of Religion. A Spatial Analysis* (London, Oakville: Equinox Publishing 2005).

sacred space and to sacred time. Kouzas, in the conclusion asserts that pilgrimage is a social event, 'it is still alive, albeit admittedly not in the form that it had in traditional folk culture. It shows that cultural phenomena, rather than remaining untouched over time, change continually. Although they are moulded by contemporary social and historical changes, they do not lose sight of the reasons why they came into existence', which in his case-study is the desire to render respect to Saint Barbara.

The perceiving of the sacred sites as therapeutic service spaces[79] is the other perspective that can reveal the pilgrim's attitude and actions, which some contributors are joining. Dorina Dragnea analyses the behavior of people within pilgrimage in the Republic of Moldova, following their performance of the official and lived religiosity expressions in seeking help at the sacred site. The author characterizes the beliefs, ritualized behaviour, gestures, and formulas, ritual and ceremonial practices in pilgrimage referring to the specific prayers and their sharing practice, the divine interventions of miracle working icons and the relics of local saints, and the experiences connected with geopiety and healing. Lubańska describes and interprets the ritual gestures of the *poklonitsi* for health, their veneration shapes towards the Saint Mina's icon, and various types of *eulogiai* consecrated at the monasteries Obradovsky and Kuklen to help pilgrims. Providing an exhaustive analysis of the ethnographic field records, the author pays attention to the link between faith, physical and spiritual health, and the role of Divine energies to gain this reward. In such a way, the sacred centre, indeed, appears and it is a vessel into which pilgrims devoutly pour their hopes, prayers, and aspirations'[80] as Eade and Sallnow assert.

Ian Reader's view on pilgrimage as market place that implies the infiltration and action of economical and religious agents on the sacred site are contiguous with the few chapters in this book. Biljana Anđelković, having as an example the Tumane monastery in Serbia, gives an analysis of how a monastery and pilgrimage to it can be revived by fraternity using various strategies, like promoting the miraculous remains of Saint Zosim Sinait and Saint Jacob, and the wide instances of miraculous healings; the repair and reconditioning of the monastery complex; constructing the parallel symbolic title of the monastery 'the Ostrog of Djerdap', and increasing the feast celebrated and the invention of new traditions (e.g. the redressing of the relics), etc.

Other chapters, set in historical periods, consider several case studies emphasizing the multiple modes and interference of the religious and laic institutions in the management of the sacred sites, organizing and monitoring of the pilgrimages to them, and infiltration of these institutions into supporting, and sometimes moulding, and manipulating pilgrims' behaviours. For instance, Zoran Ladić analyses the narrative and notarial sources (especially the wills, pilgrim diaries, communal statutes, and notary deeds) recorded in the period of the second half of the thirteenth until the end of the fifteenth century, for describing and interpreting pilgrimage phenomenon of

---

[79] Leighanne Higgins and Kathy Hamilton. 'Therapeutic Servicescapes and Market-Mediated Performances of Emotional Suffering', *Journal of Consumer Research* 45 (6), 2019, pp. 1230–53.
[80] John Eade and Michael J. Sallnow, 'Introduction', in *Contesting the Sacred: The Anthropology of Christian Pilgrimage*, ed. by John Eade and Michael Sallnow (London: Routledge, 1991), p. 15.

the East Adriatic communes. The sources provide data on the financial endeavours, and the status of the testators who used to donate bequests for pilgrimages.

While Ion Gumenâi sets his chapter in Medieval and Pre-Modern Moldavia.[81] Based on the testimonies and accounts registered by Archimandrite Andronic Popovici (1820–1893), the author is trying to answer the question, what factually is the core of interest for pilgrims – the miracle working icon of the Birth-giver of God kept in the monastery of Neamț or the monastery itself as a sacred site, consider that the pilgrimage flux, addressed to both of them was sustained and became popular under the auspices of the Voivode authority.

Maria Alexandra Pantea analyses the ethnic and denominational rivalry and the sharing of the religious space between Orthodox and Catholic communities in the Arad County (western Romania) in the first four decades of the twentieth century. The author analyses testimonies, newspapers, and official documents that reveal the social and ceremonial content as mechanisms of the identity and symbols of the faith of each group; and that the organizational structures of the pilgrimages reflect the political contexts of those times and of the competition between the Churches.

Mirela Hrovatin reviewing the historical and archival data emphasizes how the shrine of the Mother of God of Bistrica in Marija Bistrica has gained national importance and became popular in the light of other Marian and some saints' shrines in Croatia and Europe. Hrovatin analyzes how the shrine was articulated as a place of worship during the conflict periods and a core, where the national and Catholic religious identity is kept. The chapter discusses the modalities of taking in, transforming and reconverting the old pre-Christian beliefs by the Catholic Church within the pilgrimage at the Marija Bistrica shrine.

Another aspect discussed in this volume is the catechetical peculiarities of the pilgrimage practice, that can be considered alternative mechanisms for religious re-educating of individuals, the markers of the past-socialist type, and guideline instruments for the young generations. In his chapter, Constantin Necula critically discusses the patterns of religious journeys articulated during the communist period in Romania and of their performance through the lens of Orthodox theology and sociological view. Also, the author provides a new type of pilgrimage, an educational-formative one, arguing it by giving example from the current pilgrimage performance. Also, Necula outlines the ecumenism character of the pilgrimage in several sacred shrines.

The link of pilgrimage with the tourism and the commercialization of the religion is another aspect retains the attention of the scholars in the recent concerns on the subject. Katharina C. Husemann et al., stress that the commercial environment 'disenchants' the pilgrimage.[82] In fact this is not disenchantment, if we look at pilgrimage from the contemporary positions, not perceiving only its archetypal image and purpose. In this

---

81 Former principality established in the fourteenth century and a historical region. Its western half is part of Romania, the eastern side is the Republic of Moldova, while the northern and southeastern parts are in Ukraine.
82 Katharina C. Husemann, Giana M. Eckhardt, Reinhard Grohs, and Raluca E. Saceanu, 'The Dynamic Interplay between Structure, Anastructure and Antistructure in Extraordinary Experiences', *Journal of Business Research*, 69 (9), (2016), p. 3365.

volume, Emmanouil Ger. Varvounis, based on fieldwork results in various parishes of Attica, Greece, rejects the supposition about the fact that in current times people doing pilgrimage only for entertainment, he is arguing that 'Greek Orthodox Christians in Greece take part in pilgrimages primarily to enjoy the blessings offered by the places that they visit and the sacred objects for which they undertake the pilgrimage, rather than to become acquainted with the place itself or to acquire new experiences.' The author explains how pilgrimage features have changed in the believers' and tourists' consciousness and what behaviour they have adopted to perform it. This approach can articulate the pattern of pilgrimage in the Balkans, considering the Varvounis' concept of pilgrimage tourism that has not vanished the authentic and newer motives and implications of the pilgrimage. The material expressions like souvenirs, objects of piety obtained during leisure entourages like festivals, and fairs organized during the pilgrimage, denote the fact that the pilgrims 'take' and 'consume' in their own way the divine blessing and power with them. All these contents reveal the manners of gazing and understanding the sacredness and holiness by believers, and their physical, economical, and emotional endeavours to encounter and touch them. The trade with blessed objects makes the pilgrimage malleable to the desires, psychological needs, preferences, and consumerism of the people; they extend the sacred into daily life. When analyzing these 'intersecting journeys',[83] it is important to consider that 'the social composition of pilgrims has broadened, as have their motives for undertaking the journey. The new ones are mixing with older ones [...] It is this malleability that enables an institution such as pilgrimage to contain different and contradictory meanings and cope with fundamental changes in religious practices.[84] On the background of the emergence of new reasons to go on pilgrimage, such as relaxation, leisure, to ask for enrichment, finding a job, spending time with family, friends, or relatives, it is worth understanding the rationality of the religious rituals but also of the non-religious ones (social, political, economic) committed during the pilgrimage, considering the general assertion that 'in ritual, logic becomes enacted and embodied – is realized – in unique ways.'[85]

The mutual impact between the migrants and pilgrimage is worth consideration that the East-West transnational migration process is a socio-economic reality for the Southeast Europe. It can express which cultural behaviours and what practices are still performed by the members of the Diaspora after they have been somehow filtered by the cultural models of the adoption society. Pilgrimage can be perceived as meeting context of emigrants due to the fact that the devotional sites express the *loci*, where the roots of the religious and spatial identity are preserved. This perspective is actual and could be a fruitful direction for future research of the scholars in the region. In this volume, Giakoumis was approached tangentially this aspect. In detail, Vassiliki Chryssanthopoulou in her chapter anthropologically explores the annual pilgrimage to the church of Saint Panteleimon on

---

83 Ellen Badone and Sharon R. Roseman, *Intersecting Journeys: The Anthropology of Pilgrimage and Tourism* (Champaign, IL: University of Illinois, 2004).
84 Ute Luig. 'Introduction', in *Approaching the Sacred. Pilgrimage in Historical and Intercultural Perspective*, ed. by Ute Luig (Berlin: Edition Topoi, 2018), pp. 30–31.
85 Roy A. Rappaport, *Ritual and Religious in the Making of Humanity* (Cambridge: Cambridge University Press, 1999), p. 3.

Saria Island, Greece, that functions as *antamómata* ('reunions') for the emigrated locals. The chapter is enriched by valuable folkloric text records of the *mantinádes* that are related to: the pilgrims' belief in the healing power of Saint Panteleimon, the perpetual connection of the Diaspora with this pilgrimage as a root way of keeping ties, the forms of orally displaying the feeling of belonging, the common or individual vow to the saint, emotional experiences and desires, the pilgrims' care for the church of Saint Panteleimon.

***

This volume is based on a project initiated and elaborated under the auspices of the Balkan History Association (BHA) from Romania, to whom we bring thanks for the logistical support. We are very grateful to Jillian Mitchell, editorial member of Hiperboreea, BHA' journal, for proofreading the manuscript of this volume.

References

Andrew M. Greeley, *Come Blow Your Mind With Me* (Garden City, NY: Doubleday & Company, 1971).

Antagonistic Tolerance. Competitive Sharing of Religious Sites and Spaces, ed. by Robert M. Hayden with Tuğba Tanyeri-Erdemir, et al. (London and New York: Routledge, 2016).

Approaching the Sacred. Pilgrimage in Historical and Intercultural Perspective, ed. by Ute Luig (Berlin: Topoi, 2018).

Contesting the Sacred: The Anthropology of Christian Pilgrimage, ed. by John Eade and Michael J. Sallnow (London: Routledge, 1991).

Ellen Badone and Sharon R. Roseman, *Intersecting Journeys: The Anthropology of Pilgrimage and Tourism* (Champaign, IL: University of Illinois, 2004).

Galia Valtchinova, 'The Mounth of the Cross: Sharing and Contesting Barriers on a Balkan Pilgrimage Site', in *Sharing Sacred Spaces in the Mediteranean. Christians, Muslims, and Jews at Shrines and Sanctuaries*, ed. by Dionigi Albera and Maria Couroucli (Bloomington: Indiana University Press, 2012), pp. 69–93.

Glenn W. Bowman, 'Orthodox-Muslim Interactions at 'Mixed Shrines' in Macedonia', in *Eastern Christians in Anthropological Perspective*, ed. by Chris Hann and Hermann Goltz (Berkeley: University of California Press, 2010), pp. 195–219.

Ian Reader, *Pilgrimage in the Marketplace* (London: Routledge, 2015).

Jill Dubisch, *In a Different Place. Pilgrimage, Gender, and Politics at a Greek Island Shrine* (Princeton, New Jersey: Princeton University Press, 1995).

Katharina C. Husemann, Giana M. Eckhardt, Reinhard Grohs, and Raluca E. Saceanu, 'The Dynamic Interplay between Structure, Anastructure and Antistructure in Extraordinary Experiences', *Journal of Business Research*, 69 (9), (2016), 3361–70.

Kim Knot. *The Location of Religion. A Spatial Analysis* (United Kingdom: Equinox Publishing, 2005).

Leighanne Higgins and Kathy Hamilton, 'Sacred Places: an Exploratory Investigation of Consuming Pilgrimage', in *North American Advances in Consumer Research*, Volume 38, ed. by Darren W. Dahl, Gita V. Johar, and Stijn M. J. van Osselaer (Duluth, MN: Association for Consumer Research, 2011), pp. 262–67.

Leighanne Higgins and Kathy Hamilton, 'Therapeutic Servicescapes and Market-Mediated Performances of Emotional Suffering', *Journal of Consumer Research* 45 (6), 2019, pp. 1230–53.

Marijana Belaj, *Milijuni na putu. Antropologija hodočašća i sveto tlo Međugorja* (Zagreb: Naklada Jesenski i Turk, 2012).

Pilgrimage and Healing, ed. by Michael Winkelman and Jill Dubisch (Tucson: The University of Arizona Press, 2005).

Pilgrimage in Popular Culture, ed. by Ian Reader and Tony Walter (London: The Macmillan Press, 1993).

Reframing Pilgrimage. Cultures in Motion, ed. by Simon Coleman and John Eade (London: Routledge, 2004).

Robert M. Hayden, 'Intolerant Sovereignties and 'Multi-multi' Protectorates. Competition Over Religious Sites and (in) Tolerance in the Balkans', in *Postsocialism Ideals, Ideologies and Practices in Eurasia*, ed. by Chris M. Hann (London and New York: Routledge, 2002), pp. 159–79.

Robert M. Hayden, Hande Sozer, Tugba Tanyeri-Erdemir, and Aydin Erdemir, 'The Byzantine Mosque at Trilye: A Processual Analysis of Dominance, Sharing, Transformation and Tolerance', *History and Anthropology* 22 (1), (March 2011), 1–17.

Robert M. Hayden, 'Shared Spaces, or Mixed?' in *The Oxford Handbook of Religious Space*, ed. by Jeanne H. Kilde (Oxford: online edn, Oxford Academic, 21 June 2022), https://doi.org/10.1093/oxfordhb/9780190874988.013.3 (accessed on 3. 10. 2022)

Roy A. Rappaport, *Ritual and Religious in the Making of Humanity* (Cambridge: Cambridge University Press, 1999).

Rudolf Otto, *The Idea of the Holy. An Inquiry Into the Non-Rational Factor in the Idea of the Divine and Its Relation to the Rational*, 2-nd edition, trans.by John W. Harvey (London, New York, Toronto: Oxford University Press, 1950).

Sharing the Sacra: The Politics and Pragmatics of Inter-communal Relations around Holy Places, ed. by Glenn W. Bowman (New York, Oxford: Berghahn, 2015).

Sharing Sacred Spaces in the Mediteranean. Christians, Muslims, and Jews at Shrines and Sanctuaries, ed. by Dionigi Albera and Maria Couroucli (Bloomington: Indiana University Press, 2012).

Simon Coleman, 'Do You Believe in Pilgrimage? Communitas, Contestation and Beyond', *Anthropological Theory*, 2 (3), (2002), 355–68.

Simon Coleman, 'Pilgrimage as Trope for Anthropology of Christianity', *Current Anthropology*, 55 (10), (2014), 281 - 291.

Veikko Anttonen, 'Space, Body, and the Notion of Boundary: A Category-Theoretical Approach to Religion', *Temenos* 41(2), (2005), 185–201.

Victor Turner, *Dramas, Fields, and Metaphors: Symbolic Action in Human Society* (Ithaca: Cornell University Press, 1974).

Victor Turner and Edith Turner, *Image and Pilgrimage in Christian Culture. Anthropological Aspects* (New York: Columbia University Press, 1978).

MAGDALENA LUBAŃSKA

Life-giving Energies and Healing

Emically Sensitive Ethnography of Orthodox Christian Pilgrimage in Bulgaria

Introduction

The present chapter discusses the religious practices and ontological assumptions of Orthodox Christians in Bulgaria regarding the relationship between pilgrimage and healing.

The phenomenon of visiting churches and monasteries with the intention of healing is presented as a variant of Christian pilgrimage that should be analyzed in accordance with the Slavic term *poklonnichestvo*, non-equivalent with the Latin word *peregrinare*.[1]

The arguments introduced in this chapter derive from ethnographic field research aimed at observing devotional practices in monasteries and churches of South-Western Bulgaria during intermittent research trips undertaken between 2012–2018.[2]

The intent of the study was to capture what practices are most important to believers, how people engage in them and how they legitimize and explain the efficacy of such practices. Most of the examples discussed in this chapter pertain to the Obradovsky monastery, which offers the believers multiple forms of contact with sacred objects and substances and which is principally focused on addressing their needs as much as possible. The practices observed therein reflect the nature of pilgrimage in many other Bulgarian monasteries. The Kuklen monastery serves as a counterbalance, as the relations between its guardians and the visitors are sometimes strained due to the differences in the two groups' approach to healing.[3]

---

1 I discuss this subject more thoroughly in the next section of this chapter.
2 Most prominently the Bachkovo, Kuklen, Hadzidimovo, and Obradovsky monasteries, the church of Holy Trinity in Asenovgrad, Plovdiv's churches of Saint Petka the Old and Saint Petka the New, and the Saint Sophia basilica in Sofia, as well as the Vanga complex in Rupite.
3 Яна Гергова, *Култът към свети безсребърници в България. Образи, вярвания и ритуални практики* (София: Гутенберг, 2015); Magdalena Lubańska, 'Healing Chains, Relationships of Power and Competing Religious Imageries in the Monastery of Saints Kosmas and Damian in Kuklen (Bulgaria)', *Journal of Ethnology and Folkloristics* 10 (1), (2016), pp. 71–99.

Magdalena Lubańska • PhD, Associate Professor at the Institute of Ethnology and Cultural Anthropology, University of Warsaw, Poland

Pilgrimage in the Christian Balkan World: The Path to Touch the Sacred and Holy, ed. by Dorina Dragnea, Emmanouil Ger. Varvounis, Evelyn Reuter, Petko Hristov and Susan Sorek (Turnhout, 2023), pp. 27–48.
BREPOLS ❧ PUBLISHERS   DOI 10.1484/M.STR-EB.5.132398

In the course of my research, I interviewed visitors coming to monasteries and churches, recorded short videos, and observed as well as participated in the healing practices including: the veneration of icons and relics, incubation (sleeping in temples in the hope of healing), bathing in healing springs (*ayasmas*[4]), and making votive offerings (e.g. of oil, wine, lamb, and clothes). It is important to note at this point that devotional practices mentioned above are of longue durée, and bear much resemblance to those popular in the early centuries of Christianity and in the religious culture of Byzantium.

Ethnographic field research has led me to the conclusion that one of the key words with which Bulgarian Orthodox Christians justify the ontological properties of healing substances and objects is 'energy'. The believers' understanding of energy indicates the existence of a connection to Eastern Christian theology, to New Age spirituality and to *dŭnovism*.[5] At the same time, while the presence of the category of energy in contemporary religious imaginations comes as no surprise to social researchers, social sciences are unduly attached to discussing it almost exclusively within the framework of the widely understood New Age spirituality and Soviet theosophy. As a result, the term's connections with Eastern Christianity (traced back to the Middle Ages) are rarely recognized. Thus, the present chapter emphasizes the Eastern Christian context in which the category of energy functions, both at the grassroots level (the language of ordinary believers) and in theologically sophisticated intellectual treatises.

In my opinion, a certain 'hint' for anthropological analysis and finding a theory commensurate with the emic ways of naming various phenomena captured in the field may be found in theological concepts.[6] Although collaboration between these social disciplines is certainly difficult, anthropologists and theologians can mutually benefit from it by inspiring one another.[7] In this chapter I try to demonstrate that drawing on Orthodox theology helps to develop an anthropological theory that corresponds with the perspective of Orthodox believers, opening the way to a less Western-centric understanding of Christian pilgrimage.

---

4 In Bulgaria, the term is adapted from the Greek word *hagiasma*, meaning a spring whose water is considered to be healing.

5 The teachings of the popular Bulgarian theosophist Petŭr Dŭnov (1864-1944). 'It was Dŭnov who propagated the belief in cosmic divine life energies among Bulgarians. In his view, obtaining these energies was necessary for leading a healthy, happy, fulfilled life. He also created his own version of theosophy, which attracted the attention of the Bulgarian intelligentsia, as it combined quasi-scientific and mystical aspects. Dŭnov conceptualized energy as a rational living force acting in multiple ways and manifesting itself in nature; a notion he deduced from the Sanskrit term *tattvas*, which means "the living energy that permeates all space and which is the source of the motion of all celestial bodies and it is also the origin of all life in the Universe."', http://petardanov.info/Knigi/angela/Pranata.pdf. Grażyna Szwat-Gyłybowa, "Dynow Petyr." In Leksykon tradycji bułgarskiej (Lexicon of Bulgarian tradition), edited by G. Szwat-Gyłybowa (Warsaw: SOW, 2011), pp. 89–91.

6 Paul Kollman, 'What Can Theology Contribute to Anthropology', in *Theologically Engaged Anthropology*, ed. by J. Derrick Lemons (Oxford: Oxford University Press, 2018), p. 91.

7 Derrick Lemons, 'Introduction. Theologically Engaged Anthropology', in *Theologically*, p. 5.

Pilgrimage as *Poklonnichestvo* and Problem with the Turner's Theory

In social studies, a *pilgrimage* is usually defined as the practice of undertaking the hardships of a lengthy journey to sacred sites, preferably on foot. The Latin word *peregrinatio*, from which the English term pilgrimage derives, originally meant 'going abroad', only later acquiring a religious connotation as 'religiously motivated travel to a *locus sanctus*'.[8] Theoretically, the range of these motivations seems vast. However, in practice, their portrayal in social sciences has long been primarily influenced by Catholic religious sensitivities. Victor and Edith Turner write that 'behind such journeys in Christendom lies the paradigm of *via crucis*, with the added purgatorial element appropriate to fallen man'.[9] Thus interpreted, the journey is meant to have a penitential character for the pilgrims, enabling them to achieve a spiritual 'transformation' associated with a state of 'extroverted mysticism'.[10]

Until recently, Turner's concept of pilgrimage was regarded as its ideal type, within which it was seen as a liminal phenomenon, creating a space between the temporal and the supernatural world, freeing its participants from their assigned social roles and daily duties and, awakening a sense of *communitas*.[11] Reproduced in the works of social scientists, Turner's model determined the criteria for evaluating, classifying and validating pilgrimages. Consequently, practices incompatible with it have often been perceived as deviations from the model. This is the principal reason why travelling to a shrine without any commitment and effort is very often considered to have no religious value and is equated with tourism.[12]

However, for some time now, anthropologists have perceived Turner's approach as not universally applicable, even to contemporary pilgrimages to Catholic shrines.[13] Simon Coleman remarks that 'some of the more influential models of pilgrimage as sacred journey are themselves problematic and must be heavily adapted if we

---

8 Gary Vikan, *Early Byzantine Pilgrimage Art*. Revised Edition (Washington: Dumbarton Oak Research Library and Collection, 2010), p. 3.
9 Victor Turner and Edith Turner, *Image and Pilgrimage in Christian Culture. Anthropological Perspectives* (New York: Columbia University Press, 1978).
10 Victor Turner and Edith Turner, *Image and Pilgrimage*, p. 33.
11 Victor Turner and Edith Turner, *Image and Pilgrimage*, p. 8.
12 Ellen Badone and Sharon Roseman, 'Approaches to the Anthropology of Pilgrimage and Tourism', in *Intersecting Journeys: The Anthropology of Pilgrimage and Tourism*, ed. by Ellen Badone and Sharon Roseman (Urbana & Chicago: University of Illinois Press, 2004), pp. 1–23.
13 *Communitas* identified as a non-mandatory component of pilgrimage by Brian Pfaffenberger as early as 1979, as well as other aspects of Turners' theory have been revised by a number of anthropologists, including John Eade and Michael Sallnow, who recognize that pilgrimage may also bring an experience of contestation, division and dissonance, see John Eade and Michael J. Sallnow, *Contesting the Sacred. The Anthropology of Christian Pilgrimage* (Urbana & Chicago: University of Illinois Press, 1991), p. 15; Simon Coleman, 'Pilgrimage as Trope for Anthropology of Christianity', *Current Anthropology* 55 (10), (2014), p. 281-291; *International Perspectives on Pilgrimage Studies. Itineraries, Gaps, Obstacles*, ed. by Albera Dionigi and John Eade (New York & London: Routledge, 2015).

are to realize the full potential of pilgrimage to point us in different theoretical and ethnographic directions'.[14]

Nevertheless, I had some initial reservations about looking at the concept of pilgrimage from a perspective not focused on *peregrinare*, and identifying it in the practices not preceded by an arduous journey and penance. With time, however, I realized that the approach of Orthodox Christians in Bulgaria to the purpose of their visit at the shrine perfectly matches the Bulgarian word for pilgrimage - *poklonnichestvo* – and that it is the semantics of that word which should serve as the guiding reference point in this case.[15] The term refers to the practices of veneration of icons and relics, and pertains to what happens within the space of the shrine.[16] Travel is not included in the meaning of the word, which is consistent with the attitude of the faithful who, wishing to minimize the effort of the journey, reach the monasteries in buses and cars, and park them as close as possible to the entrance. What is crucial is the timing of the visit, as *poklonnichestvo* is usually undertaken at the time when the shrine is believed to be especially imbued with healing powers, for example on the eve and on the day of the commemoration of the patron saint of the given shrine.

Veneration officially consists of bowing before an icon, kissing it, lighting candles, and often also leaving a votive offering, but in fact the process involves a broader spectrum of practices reflecting the conviction that blessings and miracles can be obtained through sacred objects and substances. It is worth noting at this point that within Eastern Christianity, the sensual practice of kissing of the icon is not regarded as inferior to verbal worship of God. They are all theologically approved as correct ways of veneration. The Feast of the Triumph of Orthodoxy, established at the termination of the iconoclastic dispute in 843, reminds us that 'religious faith could be expressed, not only in propositions, in books, or in personal experience, but also through man's power over matter, through aesthetic experience, and through gestures and bodily attitudes before holy images'.[17]

---

14 Simon Coleman, *Pilgrimage*, p. 283.
15 The Old Church Slavonic category of *poklonnichestvo* is an equivalent of the Greek term *proskynesis*. The present analysis deliberately disregards the type of pilgrimage associated with the term *hajilŭk*. Borrowed into Bulgarian from the Turkish language, the word refers precisely to a journey to a distant *locus sanctus* (e.g. Jerusalem or Constantinople). Usually wealthy people and members of the elite were able to afford such journeys. One of the more recent texts on the topic is Grażyna Szwat-Gyłybowa, 'Krząctactwo i droga pielgrzyma we wspomnieniach Michaiła Madżarowa', *Slavia Meridionalis*, 20 (2020), https://doi.org/10.11649/sm.2179.
16 The findings stemming from my own ethnographic research correspond to those made by Byzantinists, who also state that pilgrimage understood as *proskynesis* and pilgrimage defined as *peregrinatio* refer to different activities and predispositions: Annemarie Weyl Carr, 'Icons and the Objects of Pilgrimage in the Middle Byzantine Constantinople', *Dumbarton Oaks Papers*, vol. 56 (2002), pp. 75–92; Alice-Mary Talbot, 'Pilgrimage to Healing Shrines: The Evidence of Miracle Accounts', *Dumbarton Oak Papers*, No. 56, (2002), p. 65.
17 John Meyendorff, *Byzantine Theology. Historical Trends and Doctrinal Themes* (New York: Fordham University Press, 1987), p. 52.

With this in mind, it is worth mentioning that practices undertaken by the Bulgarian *poklonnitsi* in relation to various carriers of divine power, reveal intriguing similarities to the *sensorium* of Byzantine pilgrims.[18] This similarity stems from long-standing cultural ties, including but not limited to the subordination of the Bulgarian Orthodox Church to the Patriarchate in Constantinople during the period of Ottoman domination (from the fourteenth century to 1870).

A Sultanic *ferman* (a decree) issued in 1870 in response to the efforts of Bulgarian national revival activists, resulted in the separation of the Bulgarian exarchate (later transformed into the autocephalous Bulgarian Orthodox Church with the status of a patriarchate) and its independence from the Ecumenical Patriarchate of Constantinople (1872). Nevertheless, the Christian religious cultures in Bulgaria and in Greece still seem very closely related. Both are less susceptible to Protestant and Catholic influence than, for example, the Orthodox Church in Russia.[19]

Byzantine pilgrims, the same as pilgrims in present-day Bulgaria, usually sought sacred sites that were as close as possible to their place of residence to surrender to the divine powers manifested there. Such visits involved gazing at icons, kissing icons and reliquaries, prostrating before them, and touching them, as well as eating, drinking and collecting various kinds of *eulogiai*, namely portable tokens treated as substitutes for the divine power present at the shrine.[20] The similarity between the Byzantine and the contemporary pilgrim's *sensorium* indicates that it is worthwhile to include a diachronic perspective and an interdisciplinary approach in the anthropological study of Bulgarian Christianity.

Scholarship by Byzantinists is of particular importance in this context, as it may serve as a valuable source of inspiration to anthropologists of Eastern Christianity. It was Byzantinists who 'blazed trails' for anthropologists, pointing to alternative (with regard to Western-centric epistemology) conceptualizations of phenomena within their common sphere of interest.

---

18   Alice-Mary Talbot, 'Pilgrimage to Healing Shrines: The Evidence of Miracle Accounts', p. 65; see also Bissera Pentcheva, *The Sensual Icon. Space, Ritual and the Senses in Byzantium* (Pennsylvania: Pennsylvania State University Press, 2010); Peter L. R. Brown, *Power and Persuasion in late Antiquity. Towards a Christian Empire* (Madison: The University of Wisconsin Press, 1992).
19   Иван Снегаров, *Кратка история на съвременните православни църкви (Българска, Руска и Сръбска)*, Т. 2. (София: Университецка Печатница, 1946–8), pp. 1–91; Tadeusz Wasilewski, *Historia Bułgarii* (Wrocław-Warszawa-Kraków-Gdańsk-Łódź: Zakład Narodowy im. Ossolińskich, 1988), pp. 149–54. See also Evy J. Haland, 'The Festival Dedicated to Agios Gerasimos a Healing Saint Fighting Demons: a Case Study', *Mediterranean Review* 9 (2), pp. 17–41; Timothy Carroll, 'Im/material Objects: Relics, Gestured Signs and the Substance of Immaterial' in *Materiality and the Study of Religion. The Stuff of the Sacred*, ed. by Tim Hutchings and Joanne McKenzie (London–New York: Routledge, 2017), pp. 119–23.
20   Gary Vikan, *Sacred Images and Sacred Power in Byzantium* (Burlington: Ashgate Variorium, 2003), p. 3; Alice-Mary Talbot, 'Pilgrimage to Healing Shrines: The Evidence of Miracle Accounts', p. 65, see also Bissera Pentcheva, *The Sensual Icon. Space, Ritual and the Senses in Byzantium*, p. 23.

Anthropology, Theology and the Creation of Emically Sensitive Concepts

At present, social studies on pilgrimages seek to understand this category as inclusively as possible and adapt it to various cultural contexts. Jill Dubish notes that 'pilgrimage is a highly flexible ritual that can be adapted to a range of needs and spiritual beliefs, thus drawing a wide spectrum of participants'.[21] Orthodox pilgrimages are also subject to various cultural influences, and it would be difficult to distinguish any unified standard among them.[22]

Considering *proskynesis* as incommensurable with *peregrinatio*, the present study seeks to provide an emically sensitive theoretical anthropological approach to its interpretation. According to Martin Holbraad and Morten Axel Pedersen, the creation of concepts in anthropology involves the adaptation of ontological assumptions proper to the community under study, which often challenge epistemological findings of this discipline of knowledge.[23] Inventing such concepts often requires the need to move away from the West-centric interpretive framework rooted in post-Enlightenment and post-Reformation epistemologies, hidden in seemingly cognitively neutral definitions, often labelled as the 'mentalistic bias' of the anthropological theory.[24] Within this bias, faith as an inner experience and trust in the sacred is valorized more highly than ritual practices aimed at contact with the sacred objects and easily associated with magic or ritualism.[25] This tendency can also be seen in the Turners' study, which considers the healing practices of pilgrims to be secondary to the moral aspect of pilgrimage – spiritual transformation.[26] In order to enrich anthropological theory with an understanding of religious healing relevant to the emic categories of the Orthodox faithful, the present study turns to the works of iconophile theologians.[27]

---

21   Jill Dubish, 'Introduction', in *Pilgrimage and Healing*, ed. by Jill Dubish and Michael Winkleman (Tucson, AZ: University of Arizona Press, 2014), p. ix.
22   It seems that in Russia *proskynesis* is often preceded by an ascetically understood journey – see Inna Naletova, 'Pilgrimage as Kenotic Communities beyond the Walls of the Church', *Eastern Christians in Anthropological Perspective*, ed. by Chris Hann and Herman Goltz (Berkeley: University of California Press, 2010), pp. 256–57; Stella Rock, 'Seeking Out the Sacred: Grace and Place in Contemporary Russian Pilgrimage', *Modern Greek Studies Yearbook, "Mediterranean, Slavic and Eastern Orthodox Studies"*, 28 (29), (2012/2013), pp. 193–218.
23   Martin Holbraad and Morten Pedersen, *The Ontological Turn. Anthropological Exposition* (Cambridge: Cambridge University Press, 2017), p. 64.
24   Talal Asad, 'The Construction of Religion as an Anthropological Category', in *Genealogies of Religion. Discipline and Reasons of Power in Christianity and Islam* (Baltimore – London: The John Hopkins University Press, 1993); Birgit Meyer, *Mediation and the Genesis of Presence. Toward a Material Approach to Religion* (Utrecht: Universiteit Utrecht, 2012), pp. 8–9.
25   Keane Webb, 'The Evidence of Senses and the Materiality of Religion', *Journal of the Royal Anthropological Institute*, 14 (1), (2008), p. 124; Meyer, *Mediation*, p. 8–9.
26   Birgit Meyer, *Mediation and the Genesis of Presence*, p. 14. In the Turners' work the healing dimension of pilgrimage is associated with magic, see Victor Turner and Edith Turner, *Image and Pilgrimage*, p. 7.
27   I have been following this approach since 2007, before it was officially recognized as a distinguishing feature of the anthropology of Eastern Christianity – 'Problemy etnograficznych badan nad religijnością', in *Religijność chrześcijan obrządku wschodniego na pograniczu polsko-ukraińskim*, ed. by

The ontological presuppositions of the phenomenon of miraculous icons and relics and related ritual practices conceptualized by iconophile theologians date from the Middle Ages. However, their cognitive potential for anthropology has only been recognized in recent years. These conceptualizations are based less on the 'semiotics of representation',[28] characteristic of Western epistemology,[29] and more on the 'semiotics of presence',[30] which recognizes that devotional objects (including icons) are venerated by believers mostly because of their properties to make supernatural powers present. It is no coincidence that in Bulgarian, relics of saints are called *moshti*,[31] where *mosht* means simply 'strength, power'. At the same time, the story of the Mandylion of Edessa, an image of Christ 'not made by human hands' (Gr. *acheiropoietos*), but miraculously impressed in a towel/scarf, evokes perceiving icons not only as images, but also as relics.[32] The primary attribute of this relic is its ability to heal the person touching the fabric by transferring the miraculous powers of Jesus. The efficacy of the sacred and healing objects is identified with their ability to transfer divine powers or energies. In practice, this type of ontological conviction corresponds with Neoplatonic philosophy, which inspired the iconophile theologians, because it 'provides a retrospective theological justification for popular pious belief'.[33]

Important Orthodox Christian theologian Gregory Palamas explains that 'God in that which pertains to the essence is non-participatory, but in that which pertains to divine grace and energy, which is the glory of God, is namable, participatory, and seen by those who are worthy of it.'[34] God's divine energies are uncreated and at the same time constitute the 'manifestation of his being outside', in the world.[35] With

---

Magdalena Lubanska (Warsaw: Wydawn. DiG, 2007). A similar perspective is adopted i. a. by Gabriel Hanganu, 'Eastern Christians and Religious Objects: Personal and Material Biographies Entangled', *Eastern Christians in Anthropological Perspective*, ed. by Chris Hann and Herman Goltz (Berkeley: University of California Press, 2010), pp. 33–55; Sonya Luehrmann, 'A Dual Quarell of Images on the Middle Volga: Icon Veneration in the Face of Protestant Pagan Critique', *Eastern Christians in Anthropological Perspective*, ed. by Chris Hann and Herman Goltz (Berkeley: University of California Press, 2010), pp. 56–78.

28 The term is used here in the understanding put forward by Keane Webb, 'Semiotic and the Social Analysis of Material Things', *Language and Communication*, 23 (2003), pp. 409–25.
29 Its symbolic origins can be found in the *Libri Carolini* (in the translation of the Acts of the Seventh Universal Council) equating the word *proskynesis* with *adoratio* (the worship due to God alone), which led to a deepening rift between Western and Eastern Christian theology – John Meyendorff, *Byzantine Theology*, p. 46.
30 Magdalena Lubanska, 'Problemy', p. 17; Sonya Luehrmann, 'A Dual Quarell of Images on the Middle Volga', p. 74.
31 Елка Бакалова, *Култът към реликвите и чудотворните икони. Традиции и съвременност* (София: БАН, 2016); Мария Шнитер, *Пътища на православния ритуал* (София: Изток-Запад, 2017), pp. 27, 74.
32 Mark Guscin, *The Image of Edessa* (London–Boston: Brill, 2009).
33 Hans Belting, *Likeness and Presence: A History of the Image before the Era of Art* (Chicago: University of Chicago Press, 1994), p. 55.
34 Gregory Palamas, 'Obrona szczegółowa', in *Palamas, Bułgakow, Łosiew. Rozważania o religii, imieniu Bożym, tragedii i filozofii, wojnie i prawach człowieka*, ed. by Lilianna Kiejzik (Warsaw: Scholar, 2010), p. 136.
35 Elżbieta Przybył, *Prawosławie* (Kraków: Znak, 2006), p. 92.

respect to sacred images, theologians have always provided the theory for an already existing practice. By explicating images and regulating access to them, theologians have been able to ensure that things do not get out of their control.[36]

Theologians not only try to moderate religious experience of believers, but also provide the taxonomy for it, often retroactively justifying the needs of ordinary people.[37] However, there are some aspects of the said needs which some theologians are unwilling to name. Theological concepts reach believers in a mediated manner – through religious art, liturgical practices, prayer and religious instruction – and aim at homogenizing believers' attitudes and imaginaries with official religious interpretations. The same religious media that help in the socialization of believers are reconstructed by the faithful, creatively 'overwritten', in a process of 'vernacularization'.[38]

The imaginaries of the Bulgarian faithful are subject not only to post-Byzantine influences, but also to the impact of new religious movements, such as *dŭnovism*, theosophy, cosmism and New Age (e.g. the teachings on the memory of water, crystals and the energetic skeleton of the earth). Their propagators are mostly middle-aged and elderly women reading esoteric literature who often refer to themselves as bioenergotherapists (*extrasensi*).[39] They shun institutionalized Orthodoxy, while still considering certain sacral objects associated with Orthodox shrines to be healing. Some members of the clergy cooperate with them, while others clearly cut them off. For five centuries, the territory of present-day Bulgaria was a part of the Ottoman Empire. That is why cultural influences originating from this socio-cultural circle are also present in the imaginations of Bulgarian believers, particularly in the practice of making blood sacrifices (*kurban*).[40]

According to Holbraad and Pedersen, in order to adequately answer the question of '*why* people do what they do, they [anthropologists] must first suppose that they understand *what* these people are doing'.[41] My own observations indicate that the

---

36 Hans Belting, *Likeness and Presence*, pp. 6–7.
37 Magdalena Lubanska, 'Healing Fabrics in Contemporary Practices of Bulgarian Pilgrims and their Liturgical, Iconographic and Theological Entanglements with Byzantine Religious Sensorium', *Journal of Orthodox Christian Studies*, 4 (1), (2021), p. 50.
38 In Bulgaria, mostly pious older women respected in their local community (Bulg. *babite*) incite the performance of new healing rituals within the space of a temple. Believers seek also their advice wishing to find a remedy for their psychosomatic afflictions. When the new ritual is met with acceptance from the clergy, it may be subject to 'secondary liturgization', and thus to institutional supervision.
39 Galia Valtchinova, 'From Postsocialist Religious Revival to a Socialist Seer and Vice Versa: The Remaking of Religion in Postsocialist Bulgaria', *Working Paper*, 9 (2007), pp. 1–31.
40 The term has been imported into Bulgarian from the Turkish language and means: 'blood sacrifice', 'sacrificial animal', and 'a meal from that animal'. It is worth mentioning, that the Turkish term *kurban* derives from the old Hebrew *qorban*, transformed via Aramaic into Arabic *qurban*, see Горан Благоев, *Курбанът в традиция на българите мюсюлмани* (София: Академично Издателство Марин Дринов, 2004), p. 28. In the Christian context, this term is generally used to signify food brought to a monastery as an offering of thanks, see. e. g. Petko Hristov and Biljana Skimić, 'Editor's Introduction', in *Kurban in the Balkans*, ed. by Biljana Skimić and Petko Hristov (Belgrade: Institute for Balkan Studies, Serbian Academy of Sciences and Arts, 2017), pp. 9–15.
41 Martin Holbraad, Morten Pedersen, *The Ontological Turn*, p. 16.

way visitors behave in church or in monasteries stems primarily from non-verbalised, semantically modest, embodied knowledge, acquired primarily by imitating the actions of other people. Paul Connerton calls this phenomenon habitual memory, which corresponds to Pierre Bourdieu's observation that each group entrusts to 'bodily automatisms those principles most basic to it and most indispensable to its conservation'.[42] At the same time, the maintenance of a persistent ontological belief that healing powers are present in certain substances and objects appears to be a fundamental element of this habitual memory.[43]

Blagodat, Veneration and Health – Ethnographic Findings

Poklonnitsi who come to the monastery usually start their visit by approaching a holy spring (Bulg. *ayasmo*),[44] where they wash their heads and faces and drink the water. Many collect the water into plastic bottles to keep in their 'household first aid kit'. Particularly treasured is water that has been sanctified during the rite of *vodosvet*, which concludes the celebrations in honour of the saints, venerated in the given church. After blessing the water, priests use the water to sprinkle the patron's icons and the visitors. Where the caretakers of the monastery allow it, pilgrims may choose to spend the night[45] in the shrine, believing that they might be cured during that time. Some even claim to have experienced the presence of the saint. I also came across the story of the healing of a paralyzed child who had been taught to walk by Saint Kyriaki[46] in the chapel dedicated to this saint in Gŭrmen.

It can be said that every element constituting *poklonnichestvo* has a healing aspect for the Orthodox Christians in Bulgaria. Asked why they engage in a particular religious practice, believers invariably explained that they undertake it 'for health' (*za zdrave*) to bring healing to specific individuals. With this intent they kiss icons or relics, share food, sleep in churches (incubation), wash themselves with water from church springs and ask priests for their blessing. While using this phrase, believers also encourage one another to engage in devotional practices.

The phrase *za zdrave* initially seemed overly laconic and self-explanatory; and thus, in the first years of my research in Bulgaria, I paid little attention to it. In time,

---

42 Paul Connerton, *How Societies Remember* (Cambridge: Cambridge University Press, 1999), pp. 72, 102; Pierre Bourdieu, *Outline of a Theory of Practice* (Cambridge: Cambridge University Press, 1977), p. 218.
43 This conviction is analyzed in reference to Byzantine devotional practices and theology by Jaroslav Pelikan, 'The Images of the Invisible', in *The Christian Tradition. A History of the Development of Doctrine*, vol. II: *The Spirit of Eastern Christendom (600–1700)* (Chicago & London: The University of Chicago Press, 1974), pp. 91–145.
44 The word *ayazmo* has a clear connection to the Greek *hagiasma*.
45 Which, naturally is linked to the practice of incubation, undertaken in sanctuaries of Asklepios and later Byzantine temples which took over their functions.
46 The 3rd c. martyr Kyriaki of Nikomedia, known to Balkan Slavs as Saint Nedelya (Eng. "Saint Kyriaki"). Georgi Minczew, *Święta księga, ikona, obrzęd* (Łódź: Wydawnictwa Uniwersytetu Łódzkiego, 2003), p. 174.

however, I came to see the phrase as essential to understanding the specificity of the practices undertaken in Orthodox churches and monasteries, because of the importance attached to it by the Bulgarian faithful. The meaning of this expression, trivialized in language, can be understood more fully in relation to Orthodox theology, which emphasizes the connection between human psychosomatic well-being and salvation.

This is precisely the issue that the mystical strand of Orthodoxy (expressed in Hesychastic theology) focuses its attention on Hesychasts[47] claim that healing is not possible without the synergy of (wo) man with God's grace: 'the healing process occurs through the synergy of the energy of God's grace and man's will'.[48] While I do not suggest that the average Orthodox Christian is familiar with hesychastic theology or even knows the term *hesychasm*, I would like to indicate that certain 'splatters' of this theology reach ordinary believers in a mediated fashion, through church rituals, iconography and some explicit expressions of religious pedagogy initiated by clergy. To provide an example: an instruction for believers taped to the glass of the devotional store in the Obradovsky monastery of Saint Mina informs them how to properly make the sign of the cross, which according to the instruction imbues believers with divine grace, enhancing their physical and spiritual strength. The same note advises that when lighting candles the faithful should recite the Lord's Prayer or the following formula: 'God give health and salvation to your servant (name of person)'. When before icons, in turn, the faithful are instructed to recite a fragment of the Jesus prayer. This instruction confirms that health is identified with salvation, a notion characteristic of Orthodox theology and congruent with the attitude of believers. Every year, on 11 November on Saint Mina's day and the eve thereof, the Obradovsky monastery attracts crowds of people who wish to venerate the icon with the hope of receiving blessings for the coming year. In 2012, when I visited the site, the queue to the icon stretched for about one kilometre. Pilgrims arriving in the morning had

---

47 The name of the movement derives from the Greek word *hēsychía* (stillness, silence, rest). Hesychasts also believed that one of the best techniques for taking control of one's body and its emotions was to recite the Jesus Prayer. Adapting it to the rhythm of breathing was said to help exercise mental alertness against 'evil thoughts combined with demonic imagery', see Krzysztof Leśniewski, *Nie potrzebują lekarza zdrowi... Hezychastyczna metoda uzdrawiania człowieka* (Lublin: KUL, 2006), p. 269. The origins of Hesychasm in Bulgaria date back to the thirteenth century, when the monk Joachim, later Patriarch of Tarnovo, came to Bulgaria from Mount Athos and, together with several disciples, founded a hermitage there. Hesychasm in Bulgaria owes much of its development to Gregory the Sinaite, a fourteenth century native of Byzantium, who was 'one of the most important promoters of the Hesychast revival on Athos and in the Balkans'. See Jan Wolski, *Kultura monastyczna w późnośredniowiecznej Bułgarii* (Łódź: WUŁ, 2018), pp. 94, 39. One of his disciples, Theodosius of Tarnovo, induced the Bulgarian Tsar Ivan Alexander to found a monastery in Kilifarevo, where he himself founded a Hesychast monastic community of about fifty people. Hesychasm was also recognized as the official teaching of the Bulgarian Church by Patriarch Euthymius, a disciple of Theodosius of Tarnovo. The influence of Hesychasm was expressed both in the sphere of new psychosomatic prayer practices and in writings and theological thought, but the movement ultimately lost importance as a result of an unfavourable historical turn. See Mathew Spinka, *A History of Christianity in the Balkans. A Study of the Spread of Byzantine Culture among the Slavs* (Chicago: Archon Books, 1968), p. 117; Jan Wolski, *Kultura monastyczna w późnośredniowiecznej Bułgarii*, p. 113.
48 Krzysztof Leśniewski, *Nie potrzebują lekarza zdrowi*, p. 15.

to wait for three or four hours; the afternoon crowd was even larger. While queuing with other visitors, I learned the vernacular etymology of the saint's name: deriving from the word *minava*, meaning 'to pass, to get over', which some pilgrims referred to the situation of overcoming a disease because of the saint's miraculous intervention. Saint Mina's icon is displayed on the exterior wall of the church, in the cloister next to the chapel of Saints Kosmas and Damian. The icon is a full-body depiction of Saint Mina, portraying him as a grey-bearded man dressed in armour, with a cross and a shield in hand. Believers focused their attention on the silver elements of the work – the hand, the belt, the cross, the nimbus, and the shield. When asked how to show reverence to the icon, they answered that one should behave spontaneously, that everyone prays to the icon using their own words, following the voice of their heart, and leaves a votive offering under the icon. The pilgrims were more precise about only two things: they claimed that touching the silver cross held by the saint is good, and at the same time recommended to wish for luck and good fortune (*kismet*) for oneself: 'You have to approach the icon and put your hand on his cross and your other hand on his hand and armour. It helps because it is a holy, glorious cross'.[49]

Pilgrims indeed put their foreheads or hands on the cross and other enamelled elements of the icon and remained in this position for a while in full contemplation.

> It is touched with the hand. It is even written on some icons that if this icon is miracle-working, women should touch it with their left hand and men with their right […] But, I am old and I cannot handle it, so I touch it with my forehead, pray and kiss it.[50]

Some also rubbed the icon with a handkerchief, which they later took home. I also saw a young mother who put her child's cap to the icon. The place where the icon is touched – in this case, mostly the silver hand of Saint Mina – is not accidental.[51] It should be noted that the motif of silver or enamelled hands, distinctive for miracle-working icons, is a Christian adaptation of the motif of the healing hand of Asclepios, and reflects the belief that the saint heals through his hand.[52] The application of hands to such elements of the image as the silver belt, the cross, or the palm, arise from their obvious affordances.[53] These smooth shiny surfaces trigger a kind of a reflexive response in the faithful. The haptic, tactile aspect[54] seems to be the key form of the

---

49 P., female, ca. 78 years old, Obradovsky monastery, 2012; Magdalena Lubanska, *Praktyki lecznicze w prawosławnych monasterach w Bułgarii. Perspektywa antropologii (post)sekularnej* (Warsaw: The University of Warsaw Press , 2019), pp. 165, 174.
50 A. female, *c*. 80 years old, Obradovsky monastery, 2012.
51 Lubanska, *Praktyki*, p.174.
52 Hans Belting, *Likeness and Presence*, p. 40.
53 James Gibson, 'The Theory of Affordances', in *The Ecological Approach to Visual Perception*, ed. by James Gibson (New York–London: Psychology Press, 2015) pp. 119–36.
54 Also noticed by Марияна Борисова, 'Поклоннически практики в Обрадовския манастир "Свети великомъченик Мина" – развитие, наративи, перспективи', in *Свети места в Софийско. Култове, разкази, образи*, ed. by Албена Георгиева (София: Академично Издателство "Марин Дринов" 2013), p. 167.

Fig. 1: Woman venerating the icon of Saint Mina at Obradovsky monastery, 2012. Photograph by Magdalena Lubańska.

believers' relationship with the material carriers of the blessing. The faithful also lit candles for their relatives, both living and dead, made the sign of the cross before the icon, and kissed it. Some left votive offerings (Gr. *charisteria*) under the icon – oil, wine, new socks, or small towels. These items, imbued with the sanctity of the holy object, were also taken home as remedies for disease.

Kissing the icon, touching it directly or with a handkerchief, and finally leaving offerings are all practices that express the pilgrims' faith in the icon's causality, while also pointing to the synergy between believer and the icon. Until believers engage in these practices, the causality of the icon remains only a potentiality.[55] At the same time, they imitate each other, although they consider their gestures to be spontaneous.

Similarly, to the faithful from Byzantium, Bulgarian believers consider the carriers of healing powers to include not only icons and relics, but also the already mentioned *eulogiai*. The latter are, however, thought to be endowed with sanctity only temporarily, and to lose this property with time; thus, they are not venerated by the faithful. They have played a similar role in the practices of Christians since the end of antiquity.[56] In principle, any object or substance can gain the status of an *eulogia*, even the flowers placed on the icon. One of the more common examples is the food brought to the church and consecrated there, which is then taken home or given to other pilgrims on the spot. These generally include *pitka* (festive bread), white cheese, oil, wine and *kolivo* (a whole grain wheat dessert). At the entrance to Saint Mina's church, there was a table on which pilgrims placed oil and a pentapartite loaf of bread (in memory of the five loaves multiplied by Christ Mt 14:14–21) with candles stuck into it. In this case, the ritual of *petohlebiye* was performed with the intention of health and prosperity of a particular person. During the prayer, the priest asks for the forgiveness of sins of that person and reads the Canon to the Most Holy Mother of God, simultaneously lighting the candles in the *pitka*. In the end the *pitka* is distributed in the church.

The *poklonnitsi* may also bring lambs for consecration. At the Obradovsky monastery, a family placed a raw lamb carcass and beautiful bouquets of flowers on the table. Afterwards the priest consecrated the lamb. This practice is usually chosen by persons who had promised to present an offering of thanks (also named *kurban*) to the saint in return for saving the person's life. During the same visit, other pilgrims approached another priest and kissed the small metal cross he displayed. The priest blessed each of them individually (mentioning the person's name – invariably the one given at baptism), prayed for them, and sprinkled them with holy water. A small bouquet of basil and field flowers was used as a sprinkler. The ritual, which believers call *porŭsvane* ('sprinkling'), is often requested on behalf of a sick person who, unable to visit the monastery in person, receives a substitute of participation in the healing holiness in the form of blessed food or clothing. New clothes or towels are also brought for a similar purpose. After being sanctified with holy water and with *miro* (holy oil), the fabrics are treated as *eulogiai*. Individuals awaiting healing wear them for a specified period believing that they are being cured from their afflictions during that time. Similar properties are ascribed to the oil from the olive lamps hanging by the church icons, or in the water in which relics were immersed. The Obradovsky monastery is unique with respect to offering pilgrims a variety of healing rites performed simultaneously on the day of the saint and on the day before. The practices are abundant yet repetitive, structurally and semantically similar, and serving the same purpose (praying for health), which may lead to the

---

55 Gabriel Hanganu, 'Eastern Christians and Religious Objects', in *Eastern Christians*, p. 41.
56 Gary Vikan, *Early Byzantine Pilgrimage Art*, p. 29.

conclusion that the wide choice is the monastery caretakers' solution to the large influx of pilgrims in need. This is the only way they can 'serve' each believer as quickly as possible without turning anyone away. Pilgrims choose the form that is preferable or the most available at a given moment[57].

The believers' conviction that their bodies can be cured by the blessing is linked to the concept of the self that 'feels itself vulnerable or 'healable' to benevolence or malevolence which is more than human, which resides in (the) cosmos or even beyond it'.[58] Charles Taylor calls it 'porous'. In this sense, the self is constantly open to external influence, good or malign, and can be hurt by negative energies produced by people or locations (actions which may or may not be intentional). This influence can be construed as an 'antidote' which shields the self from negative energies that can reach a person e.g. due to someone's 'evil eye', depriving him/her of 'life force'. It can also result from someone's conscious action: 'Yes, I wear a red thread. I do. It's against charms, so that evil eyes don't catch you';[59] 'My older sister was bewitched by her friend because she was studying overseas, she was an exemplary student and her friend envied her. They did magic to her'.[60]

In the mind of believers, contact with healing items of various kinds cleanses the self of negative energies and fills it with positive ones. At the same time, any barrier, such as covering icon or relic with glass, is often believed to weaken their effect. In the following statement, a person complains that hindering access to the relics (as is the case in the Kuklen monastery) makes it impossible to surrender to the healing energies they exude:

> When the hand of Saint Kosmas was kept on the table [standing in church – M. L.], then everyone could touch it and kiss it. But since the silver has been stolen and the hand placed in a casket [a reliquary], people can only put their hands on that glass lid, from above. Is this the way to receive the energy it emits![61]

The narthex of the Orthodox Church of Saint Kosmas and Saint Damian in the same monastery houses chains, which were once used to bind people undergoing exorcism, but which the faithful now perceive as healing instruments. Believers move these chains down the afflicted parts of their body. Some see in it the liberation of negative energies from the body; others do not wonder on what principle the healing occurs:

> There's a chain there, maybe you've seen it? It's in a big Orthodox church. And there they put it on the sick place, on the head, on the leg, on the body, in the place that hurts, and people sleep by these chains with the faith and belief that this illness will be cured.[62]

---

57 Lubanska, *Praktyki*, p. 168-169.
58 Charles Taylor, *A Secular Age* (Cambridge: The Belknap Press of Harvard University Press, 2018), p. 36.
59 V., female, *ekstrasens*, ca. 60 years old, Plovdiv, 2014.
60 A., female student, 22 years old, Asenovgrad, 2013.
61 Former *klisarka* (a helper at church), ca. 80 years old, Kuklen, 2014.
62 Male, parking attendant, ca. 70 years old, Plovdiv, 2014.

LIFE-GIVING ENERGIES AND HEALING   41

Fig. 2 and 3: Healing with chains at the Kuklen monastery, 2013. Photographs by Magdalena Lubańska.

This vernacular practice was starkly opposed by the current caretakers of the monastery. In 2012 the nuns put a table with liturgical tablecloth over the chains preventing the visitors from using them. This situation led to a serious conflict with the faithful visiting the monastery because of the chains. Ultimately, the nuns removed the table. What seems applicable in the situation is Belting's observation that images (and other sacred items) quickly become undesirable to representatives of ecclesial institutions if they begin to enjoy a greater popularity among believers than the institutions themselves.[63] On the other hand, one of the monks who used to live at and managed the Kuklen monastery, and whom I met at Krŭstova Gora, perceived the chains as carriers of divine *blagodat*, and thus functions similar to *eulogiai*. He explained that they emit heat that can be transmitted through the stone to which the chains are attached. This *blagodat* is supposed to manifest itself by reddening the diseased area as a result because of contact with the chains:

> And the chains have this property that they serve as an indicator. If you put them, for example, here, on the neck, if you have a pinched nerve or some root, it immediately begins to heat up and the skin becomes red there. If you put them on your head, in mental patients, the chain becomes warm. I don't know how it happens exactly, but they get warm…, and it's a calming feeling. The divine

---

63 Hans Belting, *Likeness and Presence*, p. 304.

'blagodat', which I can't tell you where it comes from, maybe it comes through the stone from below? Maybe from below through the stone?[64]

The presence of this category in the vocabulary of Orthodox Christian pilgrims was also noticed by Jeanne Kormina, Stella Rock and Biljana Anđelković.[65] They translate *blagodat* into English as 'grace'. However, the word 'blessing' seems to be a semantically closer equivalent, as it is related to the word 'bliss', just as the Bulgarian word *blazhenstvo* is related to the word *blagodat*. At this point it is also worth noting that also the word *eulogiai* is translated by Vikan as 'material and immaterial blessings' (from the Greek *eneulogeó* – 'to bless, to give blessing'). In modern Orthodox places of worship, as once in Byzantium, the desire to receive a blessing constitutes the principal reason for visiting the site, a fact which seems to corroborate my translational intuition.

Kormina pointed to what she called '*namolennost*' – saving up/absorbing the fervent prayers of many (generations of) people, enhancing the power of a place or object. She uses the term to describe an ontological transformation of the places and objects favoured by pilgrims, who pray at the particular place or icon intensively for a long time.[66] The chains' popularity among the faithful plays a similar role; seeing how the chains are used causes other believers to imitate the gestures performed by others, in the desire to experience the same effects. Intensified contact with certain objects (either icons or chains) seems to have yet another hidden purpose: it objectifies the presence of powers, blessings or energies working through them. It should be noted that, from the perspective of many believers, the chains have the same effect as relics or icons. Thus, they cannot understand why the current caretakers of the monastery are opposed to these items, especially since the monks who previously served there displayed a different attitude, describing the chains as 'life-giving' (*zhivotvorni*):

> And the people sprinkled them with holy water. And then, as they sprinkled them, he says, this chain has life-giving power, he said so. And this man (the sick man who came to the monastery – M. L.) felt so good that when he left, he said that nothing hurt him thanks to them.[67]

The same opinion was expressed about the miracle-working icon of Bogoroditsa in the Dormition of The Virgin church in Kuklen:

> – K: There is a very old icon there in the attic. It is *zhivotvorna*.
> – M. L.: Meaning?

---

64 Father S., a monk, ca. 75 years old, Krŭstova Gora, 2019.
65 Jeanne Kormina, 'Avtobusniki: Russian Orthodox Pilgrims Longing for Authenticity', in *Eastern Christians in Anthropological Perspective*, ed. by Chris Hann and Herman Goltz (Berkeley: University of California Press, 2010), p. 267; Stella Rock, 'Seeking Out the Sacred', p. 201; Bilijana Anđelković, 'Some Basic Factors on Pilgrimage in Contemporary Serbia', in *Perspectives of Anthropological Research in South-East Europe*, ed. by Marina Martynova and Ivana Bašić (Moscow, Belgrade: Institute for Ethnology of the Russian Academy of Sciences, 2019), pp. 207–29.
66 Jeanne Kormina explains that the word *namolennost* derives from the verb *molits'sya*, see Jeanne Kormina, 'Avtobusniki', p. 276.
67 Former *klisarka*, female, ca. 80 years old, Kuklen, 2014.

- K.: One that gives strength using no water. And that is where they sleep on the night of 14 August, up there, the night just before the feast. Women go there and I also used to go there to sleep over, and at night we say prayers until midnight, and then we're already tired, and we go to sleep. Well, and then somebody dreams something, or somebody hears something. Because someone might not have fallen asleep yet. Something might be knocking at the altar. You may hear someone walking beside you. It shows that you have been welcomed in the church, if you hear something![68]

Accordingly, I treat the concept of *zhivotvornost* as an emic category which indicates the key importance of the local religious culture. Incidentally, it is also a rare example of devotees adopting a word deriving from the language of the liturgy for their own purpose. The faithful encounter the word *zhivotvornost* in various contexts, such as listening to prayer formulas uttered by a priest and recorded in the *trebnik* (a book of religious services), or celebrating the feast of Mother of God Life-Giving Spring (*Bogoroditsa Zhivonosen Istochnik*).[69] The term is also used to legitimize the miracle-working properties of *ayasma*, an interesting example of which may be found in the two plaques from various historical periods placed over the taps with the spring water of Saints Kosmas and Damian. The most recent ones date back to 1830, with inscriptions in Greek. They inform pilgrims that the spring is *zoodochos* ('life-bearing, life-giving') and bringing strength and healing to those who use it with faith and hope. The inscriptions also state that the water cleanses the impurity of all disease.[70] Although most pilgrims do not understand the content of the inscriptions, they share an ontological conviction about the *ayasmo*'s life-bearing properties. A monk who once served at the Kuklen monastery made the following statement regarding the spring:

> The water in the *ayasmo* has healing properties. It has a kind of anti-stress effect on you. When you pour cold water over someone, they experience stress, and those people who suffer from anxiety neurosis recover. Also, the water is good for blood circulation. Some people told me about a man whose feet were always cold because of bad circulation. Nothing [helped]. He took a bath in the water two or three times, and he got better.[71]

The imaginaries of the faithful are also infiltrated by cultural influences unrelated to Orthodoxy. Sometimes, narratives that identify the efficacy of the sacraments (Bulg. *svetite tainstva*) and *eulogiai* with blessings or divine energies, appear alongside

---

68 Former *klisarka*, female, ca. 80 years old, Kuklen, 2014.
69 Magdalena Lubanska, 'Life-Giving Springs and the Mother of God Zhivonosen Istochnik/Zoodochos Pege/Balŭkliyska. Byzantine-Greek-Ottoman Intercultural influence and its After Effects in Iconography, Religious Writings and Ritual Practices in the Region of Plovdiv', *Slavia Meridionalis* 17 (2017), DOI: https://doi.org/10.11649/sm.1252.
70 Information taken from the book of the former priest ministering in the monastery: Иван Щътов, *Кукленски манастир* (София: Българска книжница, 2004), p. 17.
71 Father S., a monk, Krŭstova Gora, 2014.

Fig. 4: *Vodosvet* at the *ayasmo* of Saints Kosmas and Damian in Kuklen, 2013. Photograph by Magdalena Lubańska.

explanations associated with New Age spirituality, which also includes the category of energy. An interlocutor explains:

> – Interlocutor: That is, when there is a mental and energetic confusion, the second spirit enters the body – that is schizophrenia. With epileptic fainting – the patient should be surprised; a bucket of water is poured over his back. Because negative energies do not like to be surprised. Just like cancer cells. If you get cancer, you should not eat what you like. Cancer cells don't like you feeding them bitter herbs, like bitter sage or yarrow. Bitter herbs simply force the cells to shrink, and they regain their essence that way. They throw away what they don't need. This also happens with our body when we are stressed. But also, with water, which is energetic and mindful.
> – ML: In what sense is it mindful?
> – Interlocutor: Water has memory. Since you are an ethnologist and a young person, you should know that the Japanese theory is proven. Water has memory.[72]

The presence of the category of energy in the vocabulary of Orthodox Christian pilgrims in Bulgaria was also noticed by Margarita Karamihova and Galia Valtchinova.[73] However, they did not elaborate on its meaning in the pilgrims' worldview. The

---

[72] V. dŭnovist, female, *ekstrasens*, ca. 60 years old, Kuklen monastery, 2014.
[73] Маргарита Карамихова, *Динамика на свети места. Поклонничество и религиозни пътешествия в постсоциалистическа България* (непубликуван ръкопис на дисертация, Великотърновски Университет Свети Кирил и Методий, 2013), p. 219; Галина Вълчинова, *Знеполски похвали. Локална религия и идентичност в западна България* (София: Академично Издателство "Марин Дринов", 1999), p. 129.

subject was tackled by Kormina, according to whom the fact that Russian pilgrims consider the images placed next to the miracle-working icons as equipped with energies can be explained as adaptation of a quasi-scientific metaphor to the religious field. She claims the category of energy in the pilgrims' vocabulary to have originated from Soviet urban esotericism but does not associate the term with Orthodox Christianity.

Orthodox Christians in Bulgaria usually equate veneration with healing, perceiving pilgrimage (and more precisely – *poklonichestvo*) first and foremost as exposing oneself to life-giving, life-bearing divine energies acting in the particular church or monastery. Ethnographic findings demonstrate that the term *energy* plays a crucial role in Orthodox Christians' religious imaginaries and that it is not just a 'modern' category inscribed in the theosophical discourse, but a concept strongly influenced by Eastern Christian theology. It is due to this influence that energies are described as *zhivotvorni* – life-giving.

References

Alice-Mary Talbot, 'Pilgrimage to Healing Shrines: The Evidence of Miracle Accounts', *Dumbarton Oak Papers*, 56 (2002), 153–73.

Annemarie Weyl Carr, 'Icons and the Objects of Pilgrimage in the Middle Byzantine Constantinople', *Dumbarton Oaks Papers*, 56 (2002), 75–92.

Bilijana Anđelković, 'Some Basic Factors on Pilgrimage in Contemporary Serbia', in *Perspectives of Anthropological Research in South-East Europe*, ed. by Marina Martynova and Ivana Bašić (Moscow, Belgrade: Institute for Ethnology of the Russian Academy of Sciences, 2019), pp. 207–29.

Birgit Meyer, *Mediation and the Genesis of Presence. Toward a Material Approach to Religion* (Utrecht: Universiteit Utrecht, 2012).

Bissera Pentcheva, *The Sensual Icon. Space, Ritual and the Senses in Byzantium* (Pennsylvania: Pennsylvania State University Press, 2010).

Chris Hann and Herman Goltz, 'Introduction' in *Eastern Christians in Anthropological Perspective*, ed. by Chris Hann and Herman Goltz (Berkeley: University of California Press, 2010), pp. 267–86.

Derrick Lemons, 'Introduction. Theologically Engaged Anthropology', in *Theologically Engaged Anthropology*, ed. by J. Derrick Lemons (Oxford: Oxford University Press, 2018), pp. 1–17.

Ellen Badone and Sharon R. Roseman, 'Approaches to the Anthropology of Pilgrimage and Tourism', in *Intersecting Journeys: The Anthropology of Pilgrimage and Tourism*, ed. by Ellen Badone and Sharon R. Roseman (Urbana & Chicago: University of Illinois Press, 2004), pp. 1–23.

Elżbieta Przybył, *Prawosławie* (Kraków: Znak, 2006).

Evy J. Haland, 'The Festival Dedicated to Agios Gerasimos a Healing Saint Fighting Demons: a Case Study', *Mediterranean Review*, 9 (2), 17–41.

Елка Бакалова, *Култът към реликвите и чудотворните икони. Традиции и съвременност* (София: БАН, 2016).

Gabriel Hanganu, 'Eastern Christians and Religious Objects: Personal and Material Biographies Entangled', in *Eastern Christians in Anthropological Perspective*, ed. by Chris Hann and Herman Goltz (Berkeley: University of California Press, 2010), pp. 33–55.

Galia Valtchinova, 'From Postsocialist Religious Revival to a Socialist Seer and Vice Versa: The Remaking of Religion in Postsocialist Bulgaria', *Working Paper* 9 (2007), 1–31.

Gary Vikan, *Early Byzantine Pilgrimage Art. Revised Edition* (Washington: Dumbarton Oak Research Library and Collection, 2010).

Gary Vikan, *Sacred Images and Sacred Power in Byzantium* (Burlington: Ashgate Variorium, 2003).

Grzegorz Palamas, 'Obrona szczegółowa', in *Palamas, Bułgakow, Łosiew. Rozważania o religii, imieniu Bożym, tragedii i filozofii, wojnie i prawach człowieka*, ed. by Lilianna Kiejzik (Warsaw: Scholar, 2010).

Галина Вълчинова, *Знеполски похвали. Локална религия и идентичност в западна България* (София: Академично Издателство "Марин Дринов", 1999).

Горан Благоев, *Курбанът в традиция на българите мюсюлмани* (София: Академично Издателство Марин Дринов, 2004).

Hans Belting, *Likeness and Presence: A History of the Image before the Era of Art* (Chicago: University of Chicago Press, 1994).

Inna Naletova, 'Pilgrimage as Kenotic Communities beyond the Walls of the Church', in *Eastern Christians in Anthropological Perspective*, ed. by Chris Hann and Herman Goltz (Berkeley: University of California Press, 2010), pp. 240–66.

International Perspectives on Pilgrimage Studies. Itineraries, Gaps, Obstacles, ed. by Albera Dionigi and John Eade (New York, London: Routledge, 2015).

Яна Гергова, *Култът към свети безсребърници в България. Образи, вярвания и ритуални практики* (София: Гутенберг, 2015).

James Gibson, 'The Theory of Affordances', in *The Ecological Approach to Visual Perception*, ed. by James Gibson (New York–London: Psychology Press, 2015) pp. 119–36.

Jaroslav Pelikan, 'The Images of the Invisible', in *The Christian Tradition. A History of the Development of Doctrine*. vol. II: *The Spirit of Eastern Christendom (600–1700)* (Chicago & London: The University of Chicago Press, 1974), pp. 91–145.

Jeanne Kormina, 'Avtobusniki: Russian Orthodox Pilgrims' Longing for Authenticity', in *Eastern Christianities in Anthropological Perspective*, ed. by Chris Hann and Herman Goltz (Berkeley, Los Angeles: University of California Press, 2010), pp. 267-86.

Иван Снегаров, *Кратка история на съвременните православни църкви (Българска, Руска и Сръбска)* Т. 2. (София: Университецка Печатница, 1946–8), pp. 1–91.

Иван Щътов, *Кукленски манастир* (София: Българска книжница, 2004).

Georgi Minczew, *Święta księga, ikona, obrzęd* (Łódź: Wydawnictwa Uniwersytetu Łódzkiego, 2003).

Grażyna Szwat-Gyłybowa, 'Krzątactwo i droga pielgrzyma we wspomnieniach Michaiła Madżarowa', *Slavia Meridionalis*, 20 (2020), https://doi.org/10.11649/sm.2179

Jan Wolski, *Kultura monastyczna w późnośredniowiecznej Bułgarii* (Łódź: WUŁ, 2018).

Jill Dubish, 'Introduction', in *Pilgrimage and Healing*, ed. by Jill Dubish and Michael Winkleman (Tucson, AZ: University of Arizona Press, 2014), pp. ix–xxxvi.

John Meyendorff, *Byzantine Theology. Historical Trends and Doctrinal Themes* (New York: Fordham University Press, 1987).

John Eade and Michael Sallnow, *Contesting the Sacred. The Anthropology of Christian Pilgrimage* (Urbana & Chicago: University of Illinois Press, 1991).

Keane Webb, 'Semiotic and the Social Analysis of Material Things', *Language and Communication*, 23 (2003), 409–25.

Keane Webb, 'The Evidence of Senses and the Materiality of Religion', *Journal of the Royal Anthropological Institute*, 14 (1), (2008), p. 110-127.

Krzysztof Leśniewski, *Nie potrzebują lekarza zdrowi … Hezychastyczna metoda uzdrawiania człowieka* (Lublin: KUL, 2006).

Magdalena Lubanska 'Problemy etnograficznych badan nad religijnością', in *Religijność chrześcijan obrządku wschodniego na pograniczu polsko-ukraińskim*, ed. by Magdalena Lubanska (Warsaw: Wydawn. DiG, 2007), pp. 7–32.

Magdalena Lubanska, 'Healing Chains, Relationships of Power and Competing Religious Imageries in the Monastery of Saints Kosmas and Damian in Kuklen (Bulgaria)', *Journal of Ethnology and Folkloristics*, 10 (10), (2016), 71–99.

Magdalena Lubanska, 'Life-Giving Springs and the Mother of God Zhivonosen Istochnik/ Zoodochos Pege/Balŭkliyska. Byzantine-Greek-Ottoman Intercultural influence and its After Effects in Iconography, Religious Writings and Ritual Practices in the Region of Plovdiv', *Slavia Meridionalis* 17 (2017), DOI: https://doi.org/10.11649/sm.1252.

Magdalena Lubanska, 'Healing Fabrics in Contemporary Practices of Bulgarian Pilgrims and their Liturgical, Iconographic and Theological Entanglements with Byzantine Religious Sensorium', *Journal of Orthodox Christian Studies*, 4 (1), (2021), pp. 43-68.

Magdalena Lubanska, *Praktyki lecznicze w prawosławnych monasterach w Bułgarii. Perspektywa antropologii (post)sekularnej* (Warsaw The University of Warsaw Press, 2019).

Mark Guscin, *The Image of Edessa* (London–Boston: Brill, 2009).

Martin Holbraad and Morten Pedersen, *The Ontological Turn. Anthropological Exposition* (Cambridge: Cambridge University Press, 2017).

Марияна Борисова, 'Поклоннически практики в Обрадовския манастир "Свети великомъченик Мина" – развитие, наративи, перспективи', in *Свети места в Софийско. Култове, разкази, образи*, ed. by Албена Георгиева (София: Академично Издателство "Марин Дринов" 2013), pp. 161–69.

Маргарита Карамихова, *Динамика на свети места. Поклонничество и религиозни пътешествия в постсоциалистическа България* (Велико-Търново: УИ "Св. св. Кирил и Методий"-Велико Търново, 2014).

Мария Шнитер, *Пътища на православния ритуал* (София: Изток-Запад, 2017).

Pierre Bourdieu, *Outline a Theory of Practice* (Cambridge: Cambridge University Press, 1977).

Peter Brown, *Power and Persuasion in late Antiquity. Toward a Christian Empire* (Madison: The University of Wisconsin Press, 1992).

Paul Connerton, *How Societies Remember* (Cambridge: Cambridge University Press, 1999).

Paul Kollman, 'What Can Theology Contribute to Anthropology', in *Theologically Engaged Anthropology*, ed. by J. Derrick Lemons (Oxford: Oxford University Press, 2018), pp. 83–101.

Simon Coleman, 'Pilgrimage as Trope for Anthropology of Christianity', *Current Anthropology*, 55 (10), (2014), 281 - 291.

Sonya Luehrmann, 'A Dual Quarell of Images on the Middle Volga: Icon Veneration in the Face of Protestant Pagan Critique', in *Eastern Christians in Anthropological Perspective*, ed. by Chris Hann and Herman Goltz (Berkeley: University of California Press, 2010), pp. 56–78.

Stella Rock, 'Seeking Out the Sacred: Grace and Place in Contemporary Russian Pilgrimage', *Modern Greek Studies Yearbook, "Mediterranean, Slavic and Eastern Orthodox Studies"*, 28 (29), (2012/2013), 193–218.

Tadeusz Wasilewski, *Historia Bułgarii* (Wrocław-Warszawa-Kraków-Gdańsk-Łódź: Zakład Narodowy im. Ossolińskich, 1988).

Talal Asad, 'The Construction of Religion as an Anthropological Category', in *Genealogies of Religion. Discipline and Reasons of Power in Christianity and Islam* (Baltimore – London: The John Hopkins University Press, 1993), pp. 114–32.

Timothy Carroll, 'Im/material Objects: Relics, Gestured Signs and the Substance of Immaterial' in *Materiality and the Study of Religion. The Stuff of the Sacred*, ed. by Tim Hutchings and Joanne McKenzie (London–New York: Routledge, 2017), pp. 119–23.

Victor Turner and Edith Turner, *Image and Pilgrimage in Christian Culture. Anthropological Perspectives* (New York: Columbia University Press, 1978).

ALEKSANDRA DUGUSHINA
ALEXANDER NOVIK

Christian Shrines as a Space of Ethnic and Religious Interrelations

Two Cases in Kosovo and Albania

The ethno-religious landscape across the Balkans and the Mediterranean exhibits a wide variety of sacred places visited by members of more than one religious or ethnic community.[1] The existence of shared shrines and joint pilgrimages reveals the complex centuries-old history of shifting ethnic, religious and state borders, which has resulted in long-lasting coexistence and mixed neighbourhoods, conversion of one part of a population of a region from one religion to another, periods of rebuilding or recreating shrines similar to that of Christian churches and monasteries were transformed into Islamic religious objects during the Ottoman period. Places of joint worship include not only churches, monasteries, *tekke* and mosques, but also separate graves of 'holy people' and natural shrines integrated with the geomorphological and vegetal world (such as stones, trees, water springs, etc.) with uncertain religious affiliation.[2] Often, we could observe that the notion of 'sacred' does not have anything to do with canonical religion at all. If a particular place gets a reputation of sacredness for its 'miraculous' godsent and healing power, it does not matter for ordinary visitors whether it is a Muslim or Christian shrine, despite the fact that outside the ritual space, ethnic and confessional boundaries will be respected at different levels.

---

1 Maria Couroucli, 'Sharing Sacred Places – A Mediterranean Tradition', in *Sharing Sacred Spaces in the Mediterranean*, ed. by Dionigi Albera and Maria Couroucli (Bloomington: Indiana University Press, 2012), pp. 1–9; Karen Barkey, 'Religious Pluralism, Shared Sacred Sites, and the Ottoman Empire', in *Choreographies of Shared Sacred Sites: Religion, Politics and Conflict Resolution*, ed. by Elazar Barkan and Karen Barkey (New York: Columbia University Press, 2014), pp. 33–68.
2 Frederick William Hasluck, *Christianity and Islam under the Sultans*, ed. by Margareth M. Hasluck (Istanbul: The Isis Press, 2000), originally published by (New York: Clarendon Press, 1929), pp. 454–77.

> **Aleksandra Dugushina** • PhD, Researcher at Peter the Great Museum of Anthropology and Ethnography (Kunstkamera)
> **Alexander Novik** • PhD, Head of the Department of European Studies at Peter the Great Museum of Anthropology and Ethnography (Kunstkamera); Associate Professor in Albanian Philology and Balkan Ethnology

Pilgrimage in the Christian Balkan World: The Path to Touch the Sacred and Holy, ed. by Dorina Dragnea, Emmanouil Ger. Varvounis, Evelyn Reuter, Petko Hristov and Susan Sorek (Turnhout, 2023), pp. 49–67.
BREPOLS ❧ PUBLISHERS   DOI 10.1484/M.STR-EB.5.132399

This chapter will discuss inter-ethnic and inter-religious practices placed in a historical context in two regions: the Devoll region of South-East Albania and the Vitina/Vitia[3] region in South-East Kosovo. Both areas are located within the Albanian-Slavic borderlands representing complex multi-ethnic and multi-religious landscapes. Considering different communities typical for the regions from a religious perspective (Christians (Orthodox and Catholic) and Muslims (Sunni and Bektashi[4])), as well as from an ethnic perspective (Albanians, Serbs, Macedonians, Croats, and Roma), we will focus on specific situations of Christian shrines shared by heterogeneous visitors at the Orthodox Church of Saints Cosmas and Damian in the village of Hoçisht in Albania and the Catholic Church of the Assumption of the Virgin Mary in the village of Letnica in Kosovo.

In both regions, where ethnic/religious borders and neighbourhoods have changed during different historical periods, we suggest that Christian sacred places tend to be locations for mixed pilgrimages and arenas of inter-group contacts. Based on our field materials gathered between 2012 and 2019, as well as studies on ethnically and religiously mixed pilgrimages in these regions, presented in works by Ger Duijzings, Sanja Zlatanović, Gilles de Rapper, Biljana Sikimić and Ksenia Trofimova, we will concentrate on different aspects of the establishment of alternative dialogue in multicultural communities in Albania and Kosovo. The following questions will be addressed in the paper: what motifs and practices create scenarios of inter-ethnic and inter-faith contacts? How do historical and social experiences influence the symbiosis and contradictions within the places of joint religious practices? How does the official openness of Christian mixed shrines to diverse types of visitors correlate with clergy's reflections and experiences of visitors?

Studies on sacred places shared by different religious or ethnic communities have developed a special anthropological endeavour on pilgrimage since the publication of the well-known introduction by John Eade and Michael Sallnow to the volume *Contesting the Sacred: The Anthropology of Christian Pilgrimage* (1991) in which pilgrimage was presented as an arena capable of accommodating many competing religious and secular-minded meanings and practices.[5] Exploring the plurality of contexts including social fields surrounding sacred places, political conditions, features of religions, inter-group relations, different identities of pilgrims and religious leaders has been crucial for studies on joint worship following the

---

3 Albanian *Vitia*, Serbocroation / BCMS *Vitina*. The following abbreviations are used to mark languages mentioned in the text: Alb. – Albanian; BCMS – Bosnian, Croatian, Montenegrin, Serbian; Croat. – Croatian; Rom. – Romanes; Serb. – Serbian. Issues of dialectology remain outside the scope of the study.

4 Bektashi – Sufi dervish order which is mainly found throughout Anatolia and the Balkans, and particularly widespread in Albania, where the world Bektashi community has it's headquarter in Tirana. Bektashi doctrines are considered to have combined in their order both a Shiite and pantheistic character, pre-Islamic and non-Islamic beliefs and practices originating in Christianity and antique religions as well as ancient Turkic elements. See more in Albert Doja, 'A Political History of Bektashism in Albania', *Totalitarian Movements and Political Religions*, 7 (1), (2006), 83–107.

5 John Eade and Michael J. Sallnow, 'Introduction', in *Contesting the Sacred: The Anthropology of Christian Pilgrimage*, ed. by John Eade and Michael J. Sallnow (London: Routledge, 1991), pp. 15–16.

contestation approach.[6] In our study of these two mixed sacred sites in Albania and Kosovo, we will show that the current situation of inter-ethnic and inter-religious sharing is an integral part of the historical process and a mechanism embedded in a system of everyday life, and they both have an impact on overcoming ethnic and religious boundaries.

In the following sections we will give an overview of historical backgrounds and current state of joint pilgrimages, sanctuaries' infrastructure, various motifs of visiting the shrines and scenarios of group inter-relations, firstly at Hoçisht and then at Letnica because the two cases overlap in the same ethnic and religious perspectives representing Albanian-Slavic and Christian-Muslim border areas. In the third section we will compare the two sacred locations by paying special attention to the different representations of boundaries as well as to the different trajectories of inter-group contacts and historical experiences. These observations of various configurations of shared practices will treat Christian shrines as particular illustrations of joint devotion in ethnically and religiously mixed Balkan regions.

Village Hoçist in Albania and the Sanctuary *Satrivaç*

After the fascist occupation by Italy (1939–1943) and then Nazi Germany (1943–1944) during World War II Albania began building a socialist society, and in 1967 declared itself as the 'world's first atheist state'. Such a step was possible only under the oppressive communist dictatorship ruled by Enver Hoxha, who tried to build a 'new society' following, at first, the example of the Stalinist regime and then communist China. From 1976 the regime pursued an exclusively self-supported policy.[7] They closed all religious institutions in the country (Muslim, Bektashi, Christian, Jewish) and persecuted the clergy, thus informing the indigenous population about the

---

6 Robert M. Hayden, 'Antagonistic Tolerance: Competitive Sharing of Religious Sites in South Asia and the Balkans', *Current Anthropology*, 43 (2), (2002), pp. 205–31; Dionigi Albera, 'Why Are You Mixing What Cannot be Mixed? Shared Devotions in the Monotheisms', *History and Anthropology*, 19 (1), (2008), pp. 37–59; Glenn Bowman, 'Orthodox-Muslim Interactions at "Mixed Shrines" in Macedonia', in *Eastern Christians in Anthropological Perspective*, ed. by Chris Hann and Herman Goltz (Berkeley: University of California Press, 2010), pp. 195–219; *Sharing the Sacra: The Politics and Pragmatics of Intercommunal Relations around Holy Places*, ed. by Glenn Bowman (Oxford and New York: Berghahn Books, 2012); *Sharing Sacred Spaces in the Mediterranean: Christians, Muslims, and Jews at Shrines and Sanctuaries*, ed. by Dionigi Albera and Maria Couroucli (Bloomington: University of Indiana Press, 2012); *Pilgrimage, Politics and Place-Making in Eastern Europe: Crossing the Borders*, ed. by Mario Katić and John Eade (London: Routledge, 2014); *Choreographies of Shared Sacred Sites: Religion, Politics and Conflict Resolution*, ed. by Elazar Barkan and Karen Barkey (New York: Columbia University Press, 2014); Robert M. Hayden, Tuğba Tanyeri-Erdemir, Timothy D. Walker, Aykan Erdemir, Devika Rangachari, Manuel Aguilar-Moreno, Enrique López-Hurtado, and Milica Bakić-Hayden, *Antagonistic Tolerance: Competitive Sharing of Religious Sites and Wider Spaces* (London: Routledge, 2016).
7 Нина Смирнова, *История Албании в XX веке* (Москва: Наука, 2003), p. 331.

Fig. 1: Sign of the Orthodox Church of Saints Cosmas and Damian. Hoçisht, Albania, 2012. Photograph by Alexander Novik.

crackdown of the opposition.[8] After the fall of socialism in 1990–1991, Albanian democratic transformations restored religious institutions but, because the clergy, who survived in the country during the repression, were not enough to hold church services, the local religious specialists were replaced by ones from abroad. The Greek Archbishop Anastas (Janullatos) was also appointed by the Patriarchate of Constantinople to revive the church life among Orthodox Albanians, while the Vatican sent priests and Muslims received financial and personnel support from Turkey, Saudi Arabia, Iran, and other countries. Along with establishing new religious educational centres, constructing, and restoring religious buildings, the tradition of pilgrimage to sacred places, interrupted for many decades, started to revive.[9] This process emerged spontaneously, often through the initiative of local people without the involvement of leaders, such as religious specialists or cultural influencers.

The case of the Church of Saints Cosmas and Damian, locally called *Satrivaç* in the village Hoçisht in Devoll municipality, demonstrates very well this process (Fig. 1). During communism, the sanctuary was used as army depot but in the early 1990s the church was reopened for religious devotion.[10] The restoration of the sanctuary was launched through the efforts of local people, mainly the Orthodox residents of the village and the surrounding area. For the entire region of Devoll this initiative was not only religious, but also an important public act designed to 'consecrate' the region, since during the Middle Ages the town of Bilisht, which is now a municipal centre located nearby, was an important religious hub and served as the Orthodox metropolis.

---

[8] Alexander Novik, 'The Jewish Population in Albania and Kosovo in the 20th Century: Historical Presence and Modern Situation', in *The Balkan Jews and the Minority Issue in South-Eastern Europe*, ed. by Jolanta Sujecka (Warsaw–Bellerive-sur-Allier: Faculty of "Artes Liberales" University of Warsaw; DiG; La Rama, 2020), *Colloquia Balkanica*, 7, p. 347, http://orcid.org/0000-0002-1123-1109.

[9] Nathalie Clayer, 'God in the "Land of the Mercedes". The Religious Communities in Albania since 1990's', in *Österreichische Osthefte, Sonderband 17, Albanien*, ed. by Peter Jordan et al. (Wien: Peter Lang, 2003), pp. 277–314; Mark Tirta, *Mitologjia ndër shqiptarë* (Tiranë: Akademia e Shkencave e Shqipërisë, Instituti i Kulturës Popullore, 2004), pp. 62–65.

[10] Gilles de Rapper, 'The Vakëf: Sharing Religious Space in Albania', in *Sharing Sacred Spaces in the Mediterranean*, ed. by Dionigi Albera and Maria Couroucli (Indiana University Press, 2012), p. 31.

Gradually, over the centuries of Ottoman domination, this iconic centre of Christianity was liquidated, and religious life moved to the nearest cities like Korça and Bitola. Conversion of a significant part of the region's population to Islam also played a part in the disappearance of the Christian shrines in Devoll which was completed during the period of atheistic propaganda. In contrast with the situation in Hoçisht, churches in Korça, Voskopoja and some other places were closed but preserved as cultural monuments (following the same practice in the Soviet Union) between the 1960s and 1990s. However, in Hoçisht and neighbouring villages the religious buildings were almost completely destroyed.

According to the 2011 Census the population of around 4,500 people in Hoçisht is mixed:[11] out of 350 families only 19 are Orthodox, while the others are Sunni Muslims.[12] Together with the Orthodox community of Hoçisht Muslims participated in the restoration of the sanctuary, sometimes with financial help from Muslim villagers who had emigrated from Albania.[13] Since the mosque, rebuilt by the Ottoman authorities from Saint Mitri Church and visited by Muslim dwellers of Hoçisht, was destroyed and there was no Islamic place of worship in the village, Muslim families have been visiting the Church of Saints Cosmas and Damian as an alternative to their religious site.[14] On the one hand, during the revival of *Satrivaç* in the 1990s, Muslims found themselves in a situation where their village had acquired the reputation throughout the region as the home of an exclusively iconic Christian shrine despite the Orthodox inhabitants being a minority. On the other hand, the revival of pilgrimage and the fame of the shrine has created a public image of the village that locals are proud of and inevitably attracted the state's investment in the village. For example, the growing popularity of the Saints Cosmas and Damian sanctuary and the increasing influx of visitors forced the regional authorities to construct new roads to the village and end a neglect which has lasted for a long time due to the various reasons (economic backwardness, strategic concerns of external military threat, etc.[15]).

---

11   The National Institute of Statistics of Albania (INSTAT). Census of Population and Housing 2011 in Albania, http://www.instat.gov.al/media/3065/7__korce.pdf (accessed on 29.09.2022).
12   P., male, 65 years old, Albanian, servant in *Satrivaç* and A., male, around 60 years old, Albanian, servant in *Satrivaç*), Hoçist, 2019.
13   Gilles de Rapper. 'Religion in Post-communist Albania: Muslims, Christians and the Concept of 'Culture' (Devoll, South Albania)', *Anthropological Notebooks*, Slovenian Anthropological Society, 14 (2), (2008), pp. 31–45.
14   Александр Новик, *Изучение традиционной культуры албанцев, влахов в Центральной и Юго-Восточной Албании. Полевая тетрадь. 26.08. – 24.09.2012* [in] Архив МАЭ РАН, К-1, оп. 2, No. 2115, 52 л.
15   During the socialist years there were restrictions on movement around the country based on the authorities' policy of controlling society. Everybody who left the place of residence had to obtain permission to move, and upon arrival to register at a hotel or at the house of relatives. Traveling to border areas was particularly difficult and sometimes impossible as authorities tried to prevent the possible escape of citizens abroad. In many ways, this policy also influenced the meager construction of internal transport routes: on the one hand, to prevent the possible progress of the enemy army to the hypothetically attacked homeland, on the other hand, to prevent provocations of 'internal enemies'. See also Нина Смирнова, *История Албании*, pp. 282–340.

All these circumstances overlapped with the specific context of a long-established mixed Christian and Muslim neighbourhood, which resulted in the syncretism of many beliefs and practices, and which contributed to the sharing of *Satrivaç* by different communities. Visitors to the shrine, famous for its miraculous help and healing, come from outside the local community, and include not only Orthodox and Sunni Muslim Albanians, but also Orthodox Aromanians, the Orthodox Slavic population from Bilisht, Prespa lakes and village Vërnik/Vrbnik, Muslim Roma, and those belonging to Bektashi orders. Thanks to the surviving collective memory and the growing interest in religion after the collapse of the state atheism, the tradition of visiting the sacred place, which existed before its artificial interruption and prohibition by the authorities, has been revived.

Regardless of the fact that *Satrivaç* belongs to the official Orthodox religious institution, the inhabitants of Devoll do not consider the shrine to be monotheistic because community of worshippers is not confined to any specific religion. *Satrivaç* is often defined as *vakëf* ('waqf') or *vend i shenjtë* ('holy place'). Although the term *vakëf* has Arabic roots and was adopted from the Turkish nomination *vakıf*,[16] the Albanian term can refer to Orthodox or Catholic churches and monasteries, Bektashi sanctuaries and other sacred places that do not have a clear religious orientation. In modern Albanian language, such places meeting the definition of *vakëf* are often marginal, located in small villages or peripheral territories which can be visited any time by different confessional groups without the guidance of clergy.[17]

Satrivaç has no permanent staff of religious officials. There are three local servants, who live in Hoçisht, and are called in Albanian *shërbëtorë* or *pitropë*. They take care of the shrine, meet and manage visitors. The position of *shërbëtorë* is not paid but guarantees a number of benefits related to social prestige and reputation among rural communities. The official ceremonies are conducted by a priest from the Holy Metropolis of the Albanian Orthodox Church in Korça but only during major festivals. According to the present keepers of *Satrivaç*, its official status is still poorly defined: the territory of the 'holy place' after the communist period was designated as a 'monastery' and the official documents were not changed, although there have never been nuns or monks. Presently the sanctuary comprises a one-story building with a small room containing icons and chairs along the walls, and several rooms for pilgrims' lodging, sanitary facilities and a kitchen. The main building is surrounded by a spacious field with trees and bushes, where one can find springs, sheds for storing equipment, as well as a space for performing rituals.

Besides large pilgrimages on feasts honouring the saints during 1 July and 1 November, visits can be made all year round. According to the current main keeper of *Satrivaç* who has served there more than twenty years: 'There is no day that no one comes'.[18] Most people visit the sanctuary without regard to the church calendar to heal some mental and physical disease or for some godsend: 'They healed without

---

16 Tahir Dizdari, *Fjalor i orientalizmave në gjuhën shqipe* (Tiranë: Instituti Shqiptar i Mendimit dhe i Qytetërimit Islam, 2005), pp. 1074–75.
17 De Rapper, 'The Vakëf', p. 34.
18 P., male, 65 years old, Albanian, servant in *Satrivaç*, Hoçist, 2019.

money; they healed in the name of God. Even today miracles happen. People who come with faith, those diseases can be cured'.[19] Besides the canonical religious activities (praying, lighting the candles, etc.), visitors to the church, regardless their religious or ethnic affiliation, try to 'physically' experience the shrine: to touch or kiss the icons and church's doors. People not only donate money but also leave personal votive gifts – clothes, accessories, which refers to people's bodily sensations too.[20] People, who have not been cured by professional medicine, leave numerous images of hands, feet, eyes, ears, etc. embodied in metal, wax, wood and other materials, which are supposed to correspond with the organs to be healed.

The infrastructure of the 'holy place' and participation in rituals are open to all visitors. However, regarding ritual behaviour and the organisation of space religious servants make some distinctions between Christians and Muslims. According to our Christian respondents, Muslim Albanians do not cross themselves when entering and leaving the church - they only kiss the icons of the saints after saying a prayer. At the same time, children are allowed to cross themselves. The most controversial question concerns the place within the sanctuary which is used by Muslim visitors for sacrifice (Alb. *kurban*). Located outside the main courtyard of the church near the spring, the place assigned for animal sacrifice is covered with roosterheads, sheep skins, chicken claws, traces of fireplaces, and scraps of tissue tied to the trees' branches. According to the keeper of the shrine, Christians are unfamiliar with this sacrificial practice, which Muslims perform to gain health, happiness, well-being, and success in business for themselves or their families. During our fieldwork in 2019, we observed the sacrifice of a lamb by two Muslim Albanians from Bilisht to have a 'well-being' (Alb. *për mbarësi*). They explained that after preparing a sacrifice they 'will share it with all people, with family, uncles, with neighbours'. Two young guys allowed us to take photos and videos, and after a short conversation about reasons they chose to make *kurban* in *Satrivaç*, one of the guys replied: 'I am a Muslim, I am not a Christian. But for me it does not matter, church or mosque, I go to both. I am not a racist'.[21]

Such practices are often criticised by Christian servants, who were watching making a sacrifice with us. However, the church board does not reorganize such practices, keeping to expressing its displeasure only during routine talks. Against the background of the toleration of religious differences, obviously collective identities based on religious affiliations remain strong.[22] In many respects the faith of each visitor is recognised by everyday practices. According to our respondents, they 'see very well who is Christian and who is Muslim'.[23] The Roma community is the only group that is of particular interest during the negotiation of ritual differences by Christian

---

19 P., male, 65 years old, Albanian, servant in *Satrivaç*, Hoçist, 2019.
20 Александр Новик and Ефим Резван, *Ислам на Балканах. Часть I. Обряды перехода и семейная обрядность: рождение, обрезание: учебное пособие* (Санкт-Петербург: Издательство Санкт-Петербургского университета, 2019), pp. 58–69.
21 E., male, around 25 years old, Albanian, a visitor of *Satrivaç*, Hoçist, 2019.
22 Clayer, 'God in the "Land of the Mercedes"', pp. 284–85.
23 P., male, 65 years old, Albanian, servant in *Satrivaç* and A., male, around 60 years old, Albanian, servant in *Satrivaç*, Hoçist, 2019.

Fig. 2: Traces of sacrifices in Satrivaç. Hoçisht, Albania, 2012. Photograph by Alexander Novik.

representatives at *Satrivaç*. In general, Albanians, regardless of their religious affiliation, tend to marginalise the ethnic, cultural and religious (!) otherness of Roma that underlies the economic and ideological benefits of belonging to Islam for Roma. Sunni Muslim Roma visit *Satrivaç* on certain dates (feasts, memorable days, etc.), as well as for personal needs aimed to solve health problems or other initiatives because visiting the Christian shrine is considered as '*God's work*'. Roma vernacular practices mostly focus on sacrificing a rooster or chicken and include leaving animal's heads or entrails on the branches of bushes and trees (Fig. 2). Such practices are seen as impure within the context of the sacred place and are mostly condemned by Christian pilgrims and the residents of *Satrivaç*. Nevertheless, while the practice of sacrificing chicken is seen as typical for Roma pilgrims, the ritual is equally widespread among non-Roma childless couples seeking a child.[24]

Generally, the pilgrimage to *Satrivaç* is not the most significant on the national scale, compared with the large Albanian pilgrimages sites shared by Muslims and Christians, such as the Church of Saint Anthony of Padua in Laç or Mount Tomorr near the city of Berat.[25] However, since 1990 *Satrivaç* is considered as one of the major shrines in Devoll.[26] As already noted, the influx of pilgrims occurs on 1 July and 1 November, but the average number of visitors is no more than 300–400 persons per day. Most of the visits to *Satrivaç* are indeed unorganised and not tied to any special feasts undertaken by the natives of Devoll or inhabitants from other regions. Interestingly, there are no tours for believers organised by church institutions, travel companies or private guides to Hoçisht from Tirana and other large cities of Albania. Moreover, specific trips to sacred places and historical attractions make up a negligible percentage of domestic tourism – most Albanians prefer to holiday on the Adriatic and Ionian coast. However, despite the social and economic restraints, *Satrivaç* as a sacred place represents an example of including the local tradition to the national one without any obvious strategy by the religious authorities to develop pilgrimage practices or control them.

---

24 P., male, 65 years old, Albanian, servant in *Satrivaç* and A., male, around 60 years old, Albanian, servant in *Satrivaç*, Hoçist, 2019.
25 Nathalie Clayer, 'The pilgrimage to Mount Tomor in Albania: A Changing Sacred Place in a Changing Society', in *Sakralität und Mobilität im Kaukasus und in Südosteuropa*, ed. by Tsypylma Darieva, Thede Kahl and Svetoslava Toncheva (Wien: Österreichische Akademie der Wissenschaften, 2017), pp. 125–42.
26 See also the data gathered in Bilisht by Gilles de Rapper in the late 1990s: De Rapper, 'The Vakëf'.

Letnica Sanctuary in Kosovo

Letnica is a small village located in the county of Vitia/Vitina in southeast of Kosovo on the border with North Macedonia. Before the collapse of Yugoslavia and military conflict in the 1990s, the village was one of the centres of the Croatian Catholic community (about 4,000 people), whose members lived also in the villages of Shasharë, Vërnez and Vërnakollë.[27] A small Albanian Catholic enclave exists in southeast of Kosovo, consisting of the villages of Letnica, Binça/Binač and Stublla/Stubla. Until 1990 Serbians constituted about 90 percent of those living in the city of Vitia and they also constituted the majority in the neighbouring villages.[28] According to the 1961 official census Albanians accounted for 60 per cent of the population but by 1991 their proportion of the total population had increased to 78 per cent, while by 2011 this figure had increased to 99 per cent.

After the disintegration of Yugoslavia and a series of military actions in the 1990s, Croatian Catholics were forced to leave Kosovo.[29] According to official statistics[30] and reports of OSCE[31], in 2011 there were about 40 Croats out of 267 residents in Letnica, while in 2018 there were about 24 old age Croats who refused to leave their homeland for various reasons. The villages surrounded Letnica are inhabited also by small enclaves of Serbs, Orthodox Roma and Muslim Roma, but most of them, like Croats, left Kosovo from 1999 to 2004.[32] At the same time in 2001 there was an influx of the several hundred Albanian Muslim population from the territories bordering the Former Yugoslav Republic of Macedonia because of the interethnic clashes between Macedonians and Albanian separatist groups. Serious transformations affecting the mosaic ethnic and confessional landscape inevitably influenced the process of homogenization of the region. Nevertheless, the south and southeast of Kosovo continue to represent a zone of Slavic-Albanian contacts and the co-existence of Christian and Muslim communities.

For several centuries, Letnica was an administrative, economic and religious centre of the Catholic parish due to the high status of the Roman Catholic Church of the Assumption Virgin Mary[33] and the miraculous statue of Madonna placed above the main altar (Fig. 3). The significance of the sanctuary is also evidenced by the fact

---

27 Serbocroation/BCMS Šašare, Vrnez and Vrna(v)okolo.
28 Kosovo Census, http://pop-stat.mashke.org/kosovo-census-ks.htm (accessed on 9.05.2021).
29 Ger Duijzings, *Religion and the Politics of the Identity in Kosovo* (New York: Columbia University Press, 2000), pp. 37–58.
30 Agjencia e Statistikave të Kosovës, https://ask.rks-gov.net (accessed on 9.05.2021).
31 Organization for Security and Cooperation in Europe, https://www.osce.org/sr/kosovo/83791?download=true (accessed on 9.05.2021).
32 Today only the villages of Vrbovac, Grnčar, Klokot, Mogila and Binač constitute a Serbian Orthodox enclave in Vitia/Vitina County. An extensive study on the interethnic borders around the Serbian enclave and its neighbors in the postwar South-East Kosovo was undertaken by Sanja Zlatanović, *Etnička identifikacija na posleratnom području: srpska zajednica jugoistočnog Kosova* (Beograd: Etnografski institut SANU, 2018).
33 Albanian *Kisha e të Ngrituri e Vergjës Mari në Qiell*, Serbocroation/BCMS *Crkva Uznesenja Blažene Djevice Marije*.

Fig. 3: The Catholic Church of the Assumption of the Virgin Mary. Letnica, Kosovo, 2018. Photograph by Alexander Novik.

that the First Eucharistic Congress of the Skopje Diocese was held in Letnica in 1931, designed to unite various communities in an ethnically and religious mixed region.[34] Between the end of the World War II and the 1990s this sanctuary was the main Catholic Marian shrine in Southern Serbia visited by heterogeneous worshipers. The church, locally known as the *Church of Our Lady of Letnica*[35] is a famous centre of pilgrimage not only for the Catholic communities of the region, but also a place of worship for Muslims (Albanians, Roma), Orthodox (Serbs, Roma, Macedonians) and other ethno-confessional groups from various regions of the former Yugoslavia – Macedonia, Serbia, Bosnia and Herzegovina, Montenegro, etc.[36]

In contrast with socialist Albania, the religious life in Kosovo developed completely differently. The radical transformations in politics, economy, social and cultural life, succeeded with communist power after the World War II, lead confessional associations to lose their positions in Yugoslav society. However, the official politics of Belgrade kept free activities of all religions existing in the country that was guaranteed in the constitutions of 1946, 1963, 1974.[37] Moreover, the intertwining of ethnic and religious identities of society made any manifestation of religious intolerance in multi-cultural country impossible at the risk of having immediately interethnic conflicts. The loyalty of ruling upper circles of the League of Communists of Yugoslavia suggested providing both public support and financial assistance to religious institutions, construction of temples throughout the country, restoration of monasteries, mosques, and places of worship of various

---

34 The process of creating a poly-confessional pilgrimage in Letnica as a social and cultural project of the Catholic diocese was examined in details in: Ksenia Trofimova, 'Minor Letnica: (Re) Locating the Tradition of Shared Worship in North Macedonia', *Journal of Global Catholicism*, 4 (2), (2020), 68–107.
35 Albanian *Kisha e Zojës së Letnicës*, Serbocroation/BCMS *Crkva Letničke Gospe*.
36 Frok Zefi, *Župa Letnica* (Zajednica Kosovskih Hrvata Letnica), pp. 169–75, http://www.hkm.lu/wp-content/uploads/2017/10/Zupa-Letnica.pdf (accessed on 9.05.2021); Atanasije Urošević, 'Katolička župa Crna Gora u Južnoj Srbiji (Letnička župa)', *Glasnik Skopskog Naučnog Društva*, XIII, No. 7, (1934), 159–70.
37 Марина Ю. Мартынова, *Балканский кризис: народы и политика* (Москва: Старый сад, 1998), p. 73.

denominations. The most obvious examples in the 1980s illustrate that there were about 40 religious associations, about 20,000 professional clergy in the country, 20,000 active churches, monasteries, mosques and houses of worship, numerous religious newspapers, and books.[38]

Despite the global changes affected ethnic and state borders during the collapse of SFRY, Letnica and the sanctuary of Our Lady[39] annually on 15 August, on the day of the Assumption of the Virgin Mary, is still attracting a large number of pilgrims from different local traditions. As Biljana Sikimić notes, after the sudden interruption of pilgrimages in 1999, the process of revitalization of the shrine was launched thanks to the international troops KFOR (Kosovo Force led by NATO).[40] Members of the peacekeeping mission in Kosovo began to take part in pilgrimages to Letnica, and in the following years filmed video reports that brought Letnica worldwide fame on the Internet and social media as interfaith 'peacekeeping capacity' for post-conflict country.[41]

The main object of veneration by pilgrims in Letnica is the statue of Virgin Mary that has many names in the local languages: Alb. *Zoja Cërnagore, Zoja e Letnicës, Zoja e Bekuar, Nëna e Letnicës, Zoja e Madhe*; Croat. *Letnička Gospa, Gospa, Majka Božja Crnagorska*; Rom. *Virgyuni Mari*; Serb. *Majka Božja, Slatka Majka*. Heterogeneous groups of visitors are mostly motivated to visiting the sanctuary by the believed miraculous healing of physical and psychological diseases through the power of the statue of Our Lady in Letnica, especially by fragments of her dress, and the healing water. Once a year, on the feast of the Assumption, the clothing of the Virgin Mary (Alb. *teshat e Zojës, fustan e Zojës*; Croat. *košulja, plašt*) is changed. The wide cloak made of embroidered white silk is cut by church's servants into small pieces (Alb. *petk*, Croat. *košuljica, krpica*), which are shared among visitors. For some ethnic groups – Serbs from south Kosovo, Roma and especially for displaced Kosovo Croats – visits to the shrine became a special 'memory' route to see their motherland and abandoned houses.[42] In the narratives recorded from pilgrimage participants by missionaries and researchers in the last years, as well as in our field data collected in 2018–2019, the image of Madonna is tightly associated with healing from reproductive problems.[43] Interestingly, present-day parish representatives in Letnica, a Catholic Albanian priest and nuns, interpret revitalization of pilgrimages after military conflicts as an expression of gratitude for the children by people that

---

38 Мартынова, *Балканский кризис*, p. 64.
39 Albanian *Shenjtërorja e Zojës në Letnicë*, Serbocroation/BCMS *Svetište Gospe Letničke*.
40 Biljana Sikimić, 'Dynamic Continuity of a Sacred Place: Transformation of Pilgrims' Experiences of Letnica in Kosovo', *Southeastern Europe*, 41 (2017), pp. 43–58.
41 Biljana Sikimić, 'KFOR Soldiers as Pilgrims in Kosovo: Black Madonna in Letnica', in *Military Pilgrimage and Battlefield Tourism: Commemorating the Dead*, ed. by John Eade and Mario Katić (Routledge, 2017), pp. 51–65.
42 Duijzings, *Religion and the Politics*, pp. 37–58.
43 Zefi, *Župa Letnica*, pp. 169–81; Marija Ilić et al., 'Kultna mesta Kosova i Metohije', *Baština*, 15 (2003), pp. 160–63; Biljana Sikimić, 'Sveta putovanja: Letnica na Kosovu', *Glasnik Etnografskog instituta SANU*, LXII (1), (2014), pp. 15–32; Sanja Zlatanović, *Etnička identifikacija*, pp. 279–80.

left Kosovo: 'They come mainly to thank the Virgin Mary for giving them heavenly gifts, in other words, children they could not give birth'.[44]

Besides, Letnica is also closely intertwined with the image of Mother Theresa. It is popularly believed that the world-famous Catholic nun miraculously felt her religious vocation during the pilgrimage to Letnica Church when she was seventeen.[45] The photograph of Mother Theresa is placed next to the image of Virgin Mary on the main banner welcoming pilgrims at the stage where open sermons are held. Thanks to Mother Theresa's Albanian roots and her image, currently promoted as the 'Mother of Albanians' all over Albania and Kosovo,[46] the sanctuary in Letnica noticeably attracted new pilgrims – Albanians from all regions of Kosovo: 'And this place has become more famous, more public, more visited because of Mother Teresa. In other words, it is a holy place for the Kosovars'.[47]

During the traditional pilgrimage (Alb. *shtegtim*, Croat. *hodočašće*) rituals include both canonical and various kinds of vernacular practices. Besides participation in the service, night prayer and vigil, visitors touch the statue of Virgin Mary with personal things (underwear, T-shirts, baby clothes) or with photographs belonging to the one for whom they are seeking healing, write names and prayers on the walls behind the altar. The masses are orientated mainly on Catholic Albanians and Croats, because the liturgy is celebrated in Albanian and during the three-days pilgrimage in Croatian. The large group of pilgrims and visitors who traditionally visit Letnica are Muslim Roma from different parts of Kosovo, Serbia, North Macedonia and other regions. The presence of Roma in Letnica and their special attitude to Virgin Mary was mentioned in the reports of missionaries already in the second half of the nineteenth century. The loyalty of the Catholic parish to Roma community was manifested not only in allowing them to perform traditional rituals, for example, making sacrifice (Fig. 4), but also in organizing sermons in Romanes.[48] Official attention to Roma is observed even today: there is a separate pastoral held for them on the eve of the Assumption. In addition, on the banner stretched over the main stage near the church, where public masses are held by religious leaders of the Catholic diocese, the prayer *The Virgin Mary, pray for us* is written in English, Albanian (*Zoja e bekuar e Letnicës lutu për ne*), Croatian (*Majko Božja Letnička moli za nas*), and Romanes (*Virgyuni Mari, palikerlape vash amenge*).

Despite the presence of different Muslim worshipers, the rituals practiced by Roma take special attention of the clergy. For example, the ritual of wrapping a building of the church with a red woollen thread, widespread in almost all Slavic traditions in the Balkans, is often interpreted as a typical way of expressing the prayer by Roma pilgrims.[49] A nun of the parish we talked to, explains such 'magical' rituals

---

44 A., male, around 70 years old, Albanian, church priest in the Letnica parish, Letnica, 2018.
45 David Aikman, *Great Souls: Six Who Changed a Century* (Lexington Books, 2003), pp. 199–203.
46 Cecilie Endresen, 'The Nation and the Nun: Mother Teresa, Albania's Muslim Majority and the Secular State', *Islam and Christian–Muslim Relations*, 26 (1), (2015), 53–74, doi: 10.1080/09596410.2014.961765.
47 T., female, around 30 years old, Albanian, a nun of the Letnica parish, Letnica, 2018.
48 Trofimova, 'Minor Letnica', p. 84.
49 Trofimova, 'Minor Letnica', pp. 93–94.

CHRISTIAN SHRINES AS A SPACE OF ETHNIC AND RELIGIOUS INTERRELATIONS 61

Fig. 4: Roma pilgrims with a lamb. The Catholic Church of the Assumption of the Virgin Mary. Letnica, Kosovo, 2019. Photograph by Aleksandra Dugushina.

as a practice of those who do not know how to pray in a Christian way. However, in this perception of diversity of ritual practices, ethnic and religious identities are not contrasted but interpreted as cultural differences, 'manners' that do not lead to the group's contest:

> From time to time we are asked: 'How can I pray? I'm a Muslim'. We answer them: 'Pray as your heart tells you to. Pray this way because you have already come with faith'. We don't say: 'Pray like this', because they don't know it. Let's take a prayer to the Blessed Mary. You don't know our prayer, pray as your heart tells you. This is the best prayer your heart tells you.[50]

Negotiation concerning the practices of representatives of different religions and the freedom of their ritual behaviour are often placed in the context of the humanistic views of the Catholic Church:

> The Catholic Church as a whole is open to everyone. Yes, yes, you know everything; pray in your language as you want. We are open because the Catholic Church views a person as a living creature, and then who and what you are. And then whether you are a Muslim or an Orthodox, a pagan or an atheist, this is not so important.[51]

In general, the presence of different religious and ethnic communities in a common space of Letnica is viewed by the clergy through the concept of an equally accessible miracle for all. In the context of the widespread political discourse about Kosovo as

---

50 T., female, around 30 years old, Albanian, a nun of the Letnica parish, Letnica, 2018.
51 T., female, around 30 years old, Albanian, a nun of the Letnica parish, Letnica, 2018.

a territory of inter-ethnic and inter-religious confrontation, present-day Letnica is promoted officially not only as religious object, but also as a space of local peace-making:

> There are Catholic Albanians, Catholic Croats, Muslim Albanians, and we live together in a common environment without any problems, national or religious, so to speak, more or less creating an example of co-existence. Every day someone comes from afar, no matter what faith. In practice, it is a place of inter-faith or inter-ethnic interaction.[52]

Concluding Discussion

Examining the emergence and the functioning of two Christian mixed sacred places in Albania and Kosovo it is important to consider the different historical, political, and social experiences influenced the changing of the pilgrimage landscape. The immeasurably greater degree of freedom of religious life in Letnica (as a part of the former Yugoslavia and present-day Kosovo) throughout the twentieth and early twenty-first centuries is hardly compared to *Satrivaç* in Albania, which functioning as a centre of pilgrimage had been cut for thirty years. During a complex and controversial experiment in building socialism and atheistic propaganda in the second half of the twentieth century, any religious life in Albania was totally banned: performing (even secretly) the ritual of baptism or a wedding ceremony could have led to a serious criminal prosecution or death sentence. After the democratic reforms in the country in the early 1990s, the revival of the sanctuary of Saints Cosmas and Damian affected not only the church building itself, but also the entire surrounding landscape – household buildings, rooms for visitors, eating establishments, the village Hoçisht and road networks leading to the sanctuary. *Satrivaç* in Hoçisht has enjoyed the reputation of a sacred place since the Middle Ages which is visited by Orthodox Albanians, Orthodox Slavic population of southeastern Albania, Sunni and Bektashi Muslim Albanians, Sunni Muslim Roma, and others. The long-standing tradition of a shrine being worshipped by members of various religions correlates with the enduring practices of the Pre-Christian cults, which have been preserved in the western Balkans,[53] along with the religious tolerance that many Albanians postulate as a national idea.

In contrast, Letnica did not experience throughout the twentieth century the breakdown of religious life, as it was in *Satrivaç*. The Catholic Church in Letnica was functioning and attracting pilgrims and other visitors both from all over former Yugoslavia and from abroad due to the liberal policy of movement and travel, established by officials in Belgrade. The mixed nature of the pilgrimage in Letnica is largely defined by the multi-ethnic and multi-religious landscape of Kosovo, even more variegated than that of Albania. In practice, Vitia/Vitina area and the villages, formerly inhabited by both Croatian Catholics and Albanians, were closely overseen by the religious

---

52 A., male, around 70 years old, Albanian, church priest in the Letnica parish, Letnica, 2018.
53 Mark Tirta, *Panteoni e simbolika: doke e kode në etnokulturën shqiptare* (Tiranë: Nënë Tereza, 2007), pp. 354–60.

leaders of the Roman Catholic Church. The construction of the church in Letnica and creation of the annual pilgrimage in nineteenth century was an organized project of the Catholic Diocese of Skopje to steer back the church's influence after the years of Ottoman domination.[54] Even after the dramatic transformation in 1999 when Letnica's parish passed from Croatian care to the Diocese of Prizren-Prishtina, the church in Letnica managed to survive the continuity of Catholic service. Falling out of the sacred landscape of Kosovo focused on Orthodox churches and monasteries that were partially destroyed during a period of wars and changing of religious authorities,[55] Letnica underwent a different scenario of revitalization. Obviously, promotion of Letnica as a local centre of peace building and supporting the Albanian Catholic minority in Kosovo comprises both political strategic tools and long-lasting tradition of poly-religious pilgrimage.

However, the village of Letnica, as well as the other locality nearby inhabited by Croat population, have undergone over the past two decades significant changes in ethnic composition. Almost all Croatian Catholics, fearing for their future amidst the long inter-ethnic conflict, migrated outside Kosovo. Many houses left by Croats were bought out or illegally occupied by Albanians, and this fact is still a matter of dispute for families who left the village.[56] Although the changes in the ethnic, religious, and social composition of the inhabitants have not caused a radical breakdown of the entire landscape, new tendencies have still reformatted the village, making Letnica similar to the other Albanian-speaking settlements in the area.

Compared to a long-running ethnic conflict in Kosovo, which also entails religious issues, religious institutions in Albania almost never came into conflict on ethnic grounds. Moreover, various religious communities, as well as social institutions (customary law, including blood feud, etc.), have historically contributed to developing the ability to negotiate. The situation has remained unchanged in the present days, despite the active intervention of the state into religious practices in the 1960s until the early 1990s.

Rituals practiced in Letnica by pilgrims and visitors professing both Christianity and Islam, run counter to the practices of the Roman Catholic Church. However, all these practices related to traditional and vernacular beliefs are accepted and controlled by Catholic priests and nuns as something difficult to change or prohibit. Inter-religious and inter-ethnic harmony declared in both places, *Satrivaç* and Letnica, stands only in contradictions to Roma religious practices performing sacrifices. However, whereas in Letnica the parishioners (mainly priests and nuns) try to control and supervise the arrangement of such 'atypical' practices, in Hoçisht Roma traditions remain limited to verbal criticism.

In both places, in Satrivaç and in Letnica, people and initiatives from below provide the motive power that operates the pilgrimage leaving aside the inclusion of touristic organisations in the pilgrimage activity. The sanctuary of Saints Cosmas and

---

54 Duijzings, *Religion and the Politics*, p. 88; Trofimova, 'Minor Letnica', pp. 81–82.
55 Duijzings, *Religion and the Politics*, p. 51.
56 Organization for Security and Cooperation in Europe, https://www.osce.org/sr/kosovo/83791?download=true (accessed on 9.05.2021).

Damian is visited by Albanian, Roma, and Slavic communities, which are Orthodox, Sunni Muslims and Bektashi, lifelong believers and recent atheists, both locals and travellers from afar, that all experienced the radical social, political, and ideological transformations. Letnica is a center of pilgrimage for Catholic communities including Albanians and old Croat residents who make annual pilgrimages to their homeland, Muslim Albanians and Roma, Orthodox Serbs, Roma and Macedonians, and other different ethnic and religious groups. In such a scenario, Letnica is a joint place for people who were divided by inter-ethnic conflicts, wars, and state borders in the post-Yugoslav context.

On the one hand, as point Evgenia Troeva and Petko Hristov, religion in the post-socialist Balkans remains an important factor of group, ethnic or national identity.[57] Obviously, in people's search for a way out of the political and social crisis during the period of transition, activity in religious life is inevitably followed by rethinking of identity. On the other hand, the Balkan religious landscape clearly illustrates that sacred places and activities of religious communities play a role in a new therapeutic culture for post-traumatic communities as reviewed in Albania and Kosovo.[58] Examples of *Satrivaç* in Albania and Letnica in Kosovo help to understand the phenomena of surviving spaces of sharing throughout periods of violence, religious, ethnic or national conflicts.[59]

In conclusion, the comparison of two shared Christian shrines in the Western Balkans has shown that despite different historical and social experience in Albania and Kosovo, joint attendance of Christians and Muslims, Slavs, Roma, and Albanians is still actual. By reason of the local traditions of co-existence that initially influenced on the multi-ethnic and multi-religious character of these sacred places, and permanence of visitors' search for well-being in sacred places, we can observe one of the examples of Balkan inter-group dialogue above all significant shifting of political and ideological accents.

Archival Sources

Archive of Peter the Great Museum of Anthropology and Ethnography (Kunstkamera) of the Russian Academy of Sciences (Saint Petersburg, Russia)

Александр Новик, *Изучение традиционной культуры албанцев, влахов в Центральной и Юго-Восточной Албании. Полевая тетрадь. 26.08. – 24.09.2012* [in] Архив МАЭ РАН, К-1, оп. 2, No. 2115, 52 л.

Александр Новик, *Отчет об экспедиционных исследованиях в Тоскерии (Албания) в августе-сентябре 2012 г. 27.08. – 10.09.2012* [in] Архив МАЭ РАН. К-1, оп. 2, No. 2116, 10 л.

---

57 Evgenia Troeva and Petko Hristov, 'Sacred Geography of the Post-Socialist Balkans: Transformations of Religious Landscape and Pilgrimage', *Southeastern Europe*, 41 (1), (2017), p. 11.
58 See also Nebi Bardhoshi, Olsi Lelaj, Ervin Kaçiu, Blerina Hankollari, *Shoqëri në kufi. Një raport studimor* (Tirana: Qendra e Studimeve Albanologjike, Instituti i Antropologjisë Kulturore dhe Studimit të Artit, 2020), p. 32.
59 Karen Barkey, 'Religious Pluralism', p. 35.

References

Alexander Novik, 'The Jewish Population in Albania and Kosovo in the 20th Century: Historical Presence and Modern Situation', in *The Balkan Jews and the Minority Issue in South-Eastern Europe*, ed. by Jolanta Sujecka (Warsaw–Bellerive-sur-Allier: Faculty of Artes Liberales University of Warsaw; DiG; La Rama, 2020), *Colloquia Balkanica*, 7 pp. 341–58, http://orcid.org/0000-0002-1123-1109

Albert Doja, 'A Political History of Bektashism in Albania', *Totalitarian Movements and Political Religions*, 7 (1), (2006), 83–107, doi:10.1080/14690760500477919

Александр Новик and Ефим Резван, *Ислам на Балканах. Часть I. Обряды перехода и семейная обрядность: рождение, обрезание: учебное пособие* (Санкт-Петербург: Издательство Санкт-Петербургского университета, 2019).

Atanasije Urošević, 'Katolička župa Crna Gora u Južnoj Srbiji (Letnička župa)', *Glasnik Skopskog Naučnog Društva*, XIII, No. 7, (1934), 159–70.

Biljana Sikimić, 'Sveta putovanja: Letnica na Kosovu', *Glasnik Etnografskog instituta SANU*, LXII (1), (2014), 15–32.

Biljana Sikimić, 'Dynamic Continuity of a Sacred Place: Transformation of Pilgrims' Experiences of Letnica in Kosovo', *Southeastern Europe*, 41 (1), (2017), 43–58.

Biljana Sikimić, 'KFOR Soldiers as Pilgrims in Kosovo: Black Madonna in Letnica', in *Military Pilgrimage and Battlefield Tourism: Commemorating the Dead*, ed. by John Eade and Mario Katić (Routledge, 2017), pp. 51–65.

Cecilie Endresen, 'The Nation and the Nun: Mother Teresa, Albania's Muslim Majority and the Secular State', *Islam and Christian – Muslim Relations*, 26 (1), (2015), 53–74, DOI: 10.1080/09596410.2014.961765

Choreographies of Shared Sacred Sites: Religion, Politics and Conflict Resolution, ed. by Elazar Barkan and Karen Barkey (New York: Columbia University Press, 2014).

David Aikman, *Great Souls: Six Who Changed a Century* (Lexington Books, 2003).

Dionigi Albera, 'Why Are You Mixing What Cannot be Mixed? Shared Devotions in the Monotheisms', *History and Anthropology*, 19 (1), (2008), 37–59, doi: 10.1080/02757200802150026

Frederick William Hasluck, *Christianity and Islam under the Sultans*, ed. by Margareth M. Hasluck (Istanbul: The Isis Press, 2000), originally published by (New York: Clarendon Press, 1929).

Evgenia Troeva and Petko Hristov, 'Sacred Geography of the Post-Socialist Balkans: Transformations of Religious Landscape and Pilgrimage', *Southeastern Europe*, 41 (1), (2017), 1–18.

Ger Duijzings, *Religion and the Politics of the Identity in Kosovo* (New York: Columbia University Press, 2000).

Gilles de Rapper, 'Religion in Post-communist Albania: Muslims, Christians and the Concept of 'Culture' (Devoll, South Albania)', *Anthropological Notebooks, Slovenian Anthropological Society*, 14 (2), (2008), 31–45.

Gilles de Rapper, 'The Vakëf: Sharing Religious Space in Albania', in *Sharing Sacred Spaces in the Mediterranean*, ed. by Dionigi Albera and Maria Couroucli (Indiana University Press, 2012), pp. 29–50.

Glenn Bowman, 'Orthodox-Muslim Interactions at 'Mixed Shrines' in Macedonia', in *Eastern Christians in Anthropological Perspective*, ed. by Chris Hann and Herman Goltz (Berkeley: University of California Press, 2010), pp. 195–219.

John Eade and Michael J. Sallnow, 'Introduction', in *Contesting the Sacred: The Anthropology of Christian Pilgrimage*, ed. by John Eade and Michael J. Sallnow (London: Routledge, 1991), pp. 1–26.

Karen Barkey, 'Religious Pluralism, Shared Sacred Sites, and the Ottoman Empire', in *Choreographies of Shared Sacred Sites: Religion, Politics and Conflict Resolution*, ed. by Elazar Barkan and Karen Barkey (New York: Columbia University Press, 2014), pp. 33–68.

Ksenia Trofimova, 'Minor Letnica: (Re)Locating the Tradition of Shared Worship in North Macedonia', *Journal of Global Catholicism*, 4 (2), (2020), 68–107, doi: 10.32436/2475-6423.1076

Maria Couroucli, 'Sharing Sacred Places – A Mediterranean Tradition', in *Sharing Sacred Spaces in the Mediterranean*, ed. by Dionigi Albera and Maria Couroucli (Bloomington: Indiana University Press, 2012), pp. 1–9.

Marija Ilić, Jovanović Vladan, Milosavljevič Bojana, Ratković Dragana, Sikimić Biljana, and Čirković Svetlana, 'Kultna mesta Kosova i Metohije', *Baština*, 15 (2003), 153–74.

Mark Tirta, *Mitologjia ndër shqiptarë* (Tiranë: Akademia e Shkencave e Shqipërisë, Instituti i Kulturës Popullore, 2004).

Mark Tirta, *Panteoni e simbolika: doke e kode në etnokulturën shqiptare* (Tiranë: Nënë Tereza, 2007).

Марина Ю. Мартынова, *Балканский кризис: народы и политика* (Москва: Старый сад, 1998)

Нина Смирнова, *История Албании в XX веке* (Москва: Наука, 2003).

Nathalie Clayer, 'God in the "Land of the Mercedes". The religious communities in Albania since 1990's', in *Österreichische Osthefte, Sonderband 17, Albanien*, ed. by Peter Jordan et al. (Wien: Peter Lang, 2003), pp. 277–314.

Nathalie Clayer, 'The pilgrimage to Mount Tomor in Albania: A changing sacred place in a changing society', in *Sakralität und Mobilität im Kaukasus und in Südosteuropa*, ed. by Tsypylma Darieva, Thede Kahl and Svetoslava Toncheva (Wien: Österreichische Akademie der Wissenschaften, 2017), pp. 125–42.

Nebi Bardhoshi, Olsi Lelaj, Ervin Kaçiu and Blerina Hankollari, *Shoqëri në kufi. Një raport studimor* (Tiranë: Qendra e Studimeve Albanologjike, Instituti i Antropologjisë Kulturore dhe Studimit të Artit, 2020).

Pilgrimage, Politics and Place-Making in Eastern Europe: Crossing the Borders, ed. by Mario Katić and John Eade (London: Routledge, 2014), doi: 10.4324/9781315600505

Robert M. Hayden, 'Antagonistic Tolerance: Competitive Sharing of Religious Sites in South Asia and the Balkans', *Current Anthropology*, 43 (2), (2002), 205–31, doi: 10.1086/338303.

Robert M. Hayden, Tuğba Tanyeri-Erdemir, Timothy D. Walker, Aykan Erdemir, Devika Rangachari, Manuel Aguilar-Moreno, Enrique López-Hurtado, and Milica Bakić-Hayden, *Antagonistic Tolerance: Competitive Sharing of Religious Sites and Wider Spaces* (London: Routledge, 2016).

Sanja Zlatanović, *Etnička identifikacija na posleratnom području: srpska zajednica jugoistočnog Kosova* (Beograd: Etnografski institut SANU, 2018).

Sharing Sacred Spaces in the Mediterranean: Christians, Muslims, and Jews at Shrines and Sanctuaries, ed. by Dionigi Albera and Maria Couroucli (Bloomington: University of Indiana Press, 2012).

Sharing the Sacra: The Politics and Pragmatics of Intercommunal Relations around Holy Places, ed. by Glenn Bowman (Oxford and New York: Berghahn Books, 2012).

Tahir Dizdari, *Fjalor i orientalizmave në gjuhën shqipe* (Tiranë: Instituti Shqiptar i Mendimit dhe i Qytetërimit Islam, 2005).

Online Sources

Agjencia e Statistikave të Kosovës, https://ask.rks-gov.net (accessed on 9.05.2021).

Frok Zefi, *Župa Letnica* (Zajednica Kosovskih Hrvata Letnica), http://www.hkm.lu/wp-content/uploads/2017/10/Zupa-Letnica.pdf (accessed on 29.09.2022).

The National Institute of Statistics of Albania (INSTAT). Census of Population and Housing 2011 in Albania, http://www.instat.gov.al/media/3065/7__korce.pdf (accessed on 29.09.2022).

Instituti i studimeve për krimet dhe pasojat e komunizmit, http://www.iskk.gov.al/?lang=en (accessed on 9.05.2021).

Kosovo Census, http://pop-stat.mashke.org/kosovo-census-ks.htm (accessed on 09.05.2021).

Organisation for Security and Cooperation in Europe, https://www.osce.org/sr/kosovo/83791?download=true (accessed on 9.05.2021).

KONSTANTINOS GIAKOUMIS

Pilgrimage Diffusion and Polycentrism in the Veneration of Saint Nicodemus of Berat

Introduction

In the present chapter, I revisit the concept of 'pilgrimage polycentrism', first introduced by Victor and Edith Turner[1] and elaborate it alongside another term I bring to pilgrimage scholarship: pilgrimage diffusion. To this end, I delve into three distinct pilgrimage sites all related to the veneration of Saint Nicodemus, the neomartyr of Berat. As I will demonstrate, the connecting bond between these pilgrimage sites remains the same, i.e. Saint Nicodemus of Berat. However, as pilgrims move from one site to another, the pilgrimage centre gets diffused to additional foci (i.e. from the neomartyr Nicodemus of Berat to the known or unknown martyrs of faith in the course of Albania's communist regime and to the place of origin), thereby establishing what I term as 'pilgrimage diffusion and polycentrism'.

For the effective treatment of this argument, this chapter is divided in three sections. The first section deals with the terms under discussion, pilgrimage and pilgrimage polycentrism, to set the theoretical frame of this chapter. The second section analyzes the vita of Saint Nicodemus and its various sources, utilizing them to also reveal what historical accounts exist for his veneration and pilgrimage. In the third section of the chapter, I will present the three pilgrimage practices associated with the saint: *1. The pilgrimage on the feast-day of the saint*: celebrated initially at the church of the Dormition of the Virgin of Shumbull (Stromboli in the sources), Berat, where his relics were kept, after its 1943 destruction by the Italians the saint's relics and pilgrimage moved to the church of the Archangel Michael. *2. The pilgrimage to the house of the faithful individual who hid the saint's skull* on his own to save it. *3. And the pilgrimage on the saint's feast day at his birthplace village of Vithkuq*. Finally, in the concluding remarks of this chapter, I relate the three different sections to each

---

1 Victor Turner and Edith Turner, *Image and Pilgrimage in Christian Culture. Anthropological Perspectives* (New York: Columbia University Press, 1978), pp. 189, 233.

Konstantinos Giakoumis • PhD, Associate professor, LOGOS University College, Tirana, Albania

Pilgrimage in the Christian Balkan World: The Path to Touch the Sacred and Holy, ed. by Dorina Dragnea, Emmanouil Ger. Varvounis, Evelyn Reuter, Petko Hristov and Susan Sorek (Turnhout, 2023), pp. 69–90.
BREPOLS PUBLISHERS   DOI 10.1484/M.STR-EB.5.132400

other, for the purpose of re-capping the terminological proposition in the context of this case study.

In my inquiry, I have implemented a mixed methodological design. I have used historical research (archival work and hermeneutics) to trace the background of the veneration and pilgrimage of the saint. Participant observation fieldwork was selected as a method of getting close to pilgrims to observe and record information about their pilgrimage experience without resistance or behavioural changes.[2] The method allows for the assemblage of a number of qualitative data: field notes, photographs, as well as video and audio recordings. Fieldwork involved three different roles: complete participant, observing participant or participating observer and complete observer. The method under discussion[3] has been considered as appropriate for the study of pilgrimage, while multiple visits and alternate roles in observing were selected for the purpose of combining random and non-random samples and time, thereby enhancing the internal and external validity of findings.

Theoretical Premises

Before delving into the terms at the core of this chapter, the meaning of pilgrimage requires some explanation. Pilgrimage is defined as the visit to a place with a conviction that both the journey and its destination empower individuals or groups to create bonds with a higher state of being and contemplate on matters of life, death, and beyond.[4] Eade and Sallnow have identified the triad of 'person', 'place', and 'text' to be the centre of pilgrimage as realm of conflicting discourses,[5] while Coleman and Eade have later added 'movement' as a fourth element to pilgrimage's centre.[6] Studying a variety of cases in modern Albania, I have elsewhere demonstrated that various combinations of 'person', 'place', 'text' and 'movement' construct the centre of Christian and Communist pilgrimages.[7]

At the premises of this theoretical discussion is the perception that pilgrimage has a centre, from which its appeal springs. Such is certainly the case of the Holy

---

2 Konstantinos Giakoumis and Christopher C. Lockwood, 'Death Proximity, Group Cohesion & Mountainous Pilgrimage in Albania', in *Landscape in Southeastern Europe*, ed. by Lena Mirošević, Gregory Zaro, Mario Katić, and Danjela Birt (Zürich: Lit Verlag, 2018), p. 99.
3 Harvey Russell Bernard, *Research Methods in Anthropology. Qualitative and Quantitative Approaches*, 4th edition (Lanham, New York, Toronto, Oxford: Altamira Press, 2006), pp. 342–86.
4 Konstantinos Giakoumis, 'An Enquiry into the Construction, Deconstruction, Transubstantiation and Reconstruction of Christian Pilgrimages in Modern-Day Albania', *Ηπειρωτικό Ημερολόγιο*, 32 (2013), pp. 268–69; Konstantinos Giakoumis, 'From Religious to Secular and Back Again: Christian Pilgrimage Space in Albania', in *Pilgrimage, Politics and Place-Making in Eastern Europe: Crossing the Borders*, ed. by John Eade and Mario Katić (London: Ashgate, 2014), p. 103.
5 John Eade and Michael J. Sallnow, 'Introduction', in *Contesting the Sacred: The Anthropology of Christian Pilgrimage*, ed. by John Eade and Michael J. Sallnow (London and New York: Routledge, 1991), p. 5.
6 Simon Coleman and John Eade, *Reframing Pilgrimage. Cultures in Motion* (London and New York: Routledge, 2004), p. 17.
7 Giakoumis, 'From Religious to Secular and Back Again', pp. 103–18.

Land, where there is an undisputable centre in the person of Jesus Christ. Yet, to satisfy those who wish, but cannot undertake the pilgrimage journey, a number of substitute objects, places, rituals and practices have been introduced, whose role is to accomplish the mission of the original pilgrimage to new locations. 'Pilgrimage diffusion', defined as the process by which the appeal of a pilgrimage destination is transferred to another place, is often facilitated by objects whose provenance is from the original pilgrimage site. A recent volume titled *Natural Materials of the Holy Land and the Visual Translation of Place, 500–1500* focuses precisely 'on the way in which matter itself carries the power of the holy',[8] dealing with natural materials carrying the spirit of place from the Holy Land elsewhere. The outcome of this process of carrying the power of the Holy Land elsewhere is the multiplication of pilgrimage sites, termed by Victor and Edith Turner as 'pilgrimage polycentrism':

> The pilgrimage complex of the Holy Land, made up of sites traditionally connected with the life, teaching, and death of Jesus, was in effect transferred piecemeal to Europe in the form of shrines dedicated to different aspects of Jesus and Mary and often reputed to be of miraculous or apparitional origin. The result was pilgrimage polycentrism, in a multilingual Europe. In other words, many shrines were founded, in many linguistic and cultural regions, as though to compensate for the lost compact shrine cluster in Palestine, where Jesus' life and death had been mapped on a limited cultural space.[9]

Although nowhere defined, it is contextually clear that what the Turners meant by 'pilgrimage polycentrism' was merely 'the multiplication of shrines',[10] as indicated in a Muslim context in which they used this term.[11] It is precisely in the sense of multiple pilgrimages that the term 'pilgrimage polycentrism' has been used by other scholars both in European[12] and non-European contexts.[13] Pursuant Eade and Sallnow's identification of a 'person' as the pilgrimage centre, whose sites extend both in the Holy Land and beyond, I suggest that the use of the term 'pilgrimage polycentrism' is unfit for use. For it refers to different pilgrimage sites centred on the person of Jesus in the context of Holy-Land-related pilgrimages, thereby constituting multiple shrines and many pilgrimage sites with the same pilgrimage centre. If we equate 'pilgrimage polycentrism' with different pilgrimage sites with the same pilgrimage centre, then there is no term to describe the sort of pilgrimage whose centre diffuses, after processes of resignification, to alternative or additional centres to the original

---

8   Caroline Walker Bynum, 'Foreward', in *Natural Materials of the Holy Land and the Visual Translation of Place, 500–1500*, ed. by Renana Bartal, Neta Bodner, and Bianca Kühnel (London and New York: Routledge, 2017), p. xix).
9   Turner and Turner, *Image and Pilgrimage*, p. 233.
10 Turner and Turner, *Image and Pilgrimage*, p. 233.
11 Cf. 'Islam's … tolerance of pilgrimage polycentrism', Turner and Turner, *Image and Pilgrimage*, p. 189.
12 Jan Van Herwaaden, *Between Saint James and Erasmus. Studies in Late-Medieval Religious Life*, trans. by Wendie Shaffer and Donald Gardner (Leiden-Boston: Brill, 2003), pp. 249, 267.
13 Knut A. Jacobsen, *Pilgrimage in the Hindu Tradition. Salvific Space* (London and New York: Routledge, 2013), pp. 142, 144–45.

one. By the term 'resignification' I refer to the process of acquisition of a new meaning to something. I therefore suggest that the term 'pilgrimage polycentrism' should not be used as a synonym for multiple shrines with the same centre, as used by the Turners and Herwaaden, or multiple decentred pilgrimages, as in Jacobsen. The term should rather be used to describe the process by which a pilgrimage originally with a single centre diffuses to other centres, directly or indirectly related to, yet, distinct from the centre this pilgrimage had at the first place.

The Case of Saint Nicodemus of Berat

The Vita of the Saint

In this section, I reconstruct the *vita* of Saint Nicodemus of Berat on the basis of diverse sources that are contradictory. Three are the main primary sources of the saint's life; yet, the divergences between the earlier and the later versions of his vita are such, as to compel Eleutheria Nikolaidou to state that: 'Nicodemus got martyred in Berat on 11 July 1722 and should rather be identical to the neomartyr Nicodemus from Elbasan, because the events related to their return to Christianity are almost identical.'[14]

Eulogios Kourilas was the first to undertake the arduous task to synthesise the *vita* of the saint on the basis of three manuscripts kept at various cells of the Skete of Saint Anne, also alluding to the existence of a fourth manuscript that was already lost in his time.[15] He was unaware of another manuscript, *acoluthia* to the saint, compiled by a certain Nikolaos, dated 1709 on the basis of an inscription on folio 1ʳ.[16] The information provided in this manuscript is not different to some of the manuscripts he had access to, as well as an *acoluthia*, which was printed in Venice in 1781 at the expense of two noblemen of Berat.[17] Kourilas was

---

14 Ελευθερία Ι. Νικολαΐδου, 'Οι Κρυπτοχριστιανοί της Σπαθίας' (Διδακτορική Διατριβή: Πανεπιστήμιο Ιωαννίνων, 1978), p. 62.
15 Κουρίλας Ευλόγιος Λαυριώτης, *Ιστορία του Ασκητισμού. Αθωνίται*, τόμος Α´ (Θεσσαλονίκη: Ακουαρόνης, 1929), pp. 85–86; for a brief and incomplete description of some of these manuscripts, cf. p. 71. Also, see Φώτιος Οικονόμου, *Η Εκκλησία εν Βορείω Ηπείρω από της Πρώτης Διαδόσεως του Χριστιανισμού μέχρι των καθ' Ημάς Χρόνων* (Αθήναι: [χ.ἐ.], 1969), pp. 108–09.
16 National Library, Tirana, DRH 1/E1, Nikolaos, *Μηνὶ Ἰουλίῳ δεκάτῃ μνήμιν ἐπιτελοῦμεν του αγίου οσίου μάρτυρος Νικοδήμου τοῦ νέου*, 1709, letter, 23.5 X 17 cm. In spite of its presentation as a holding bought by Elli Popa (Violeta Viso, 'Biblioteka Private, Pjesë e Trashëgimisë Kulturore Kombëtare', in *Komferenca Kombëtare e Bibliotekonomisë "Biblioteka dhe Kujtesa Kombëtare (Edicioni II) 20–22 nëntor 2007"*, vol. 2 (Prishtinë: Biblioteka Kombëtare dhe Universitaree Kosovës, 2008), pp. 203–04), what is known is that in January 1978, the military prosecution of Albania's communist regime broke into the house of Theofan Popa and confiscated this manuscript and a printed *akolouthia* of the saint; cf. Βασίλειος Μ. Κασκαντάμης, *Θεοφάνης Πόπα. Ένας Σύγχρονος Ιεραπόστολος* (Αθήνα: Έλαφος, 2001), pp. 175–82; cf. Andrea Llukani, 'Dosja e Teologut Theofan Popa', *Global Challenge*, VI (2), (2017), pp. 95–96.
17 Νικόλαος, *Ἀκολουθία τοῦ Ἁγίου Ὁσιομάρτυρος Νικοδήμου τοῦ Νέου, ὅς ἐμαρτύρησε κατὰ το αψιδ´ ἔτος τὸ σωτήριον. Ἐν μηνὶ Ἰουλίῳ δεκάτῃ. Νεωστὶ τυπωθεῖσα καὶ διορθωθεῖσα ἐπιμελῶς, τῇ σπουδῇ καὶ δαπάνῃ τῶν τιμιωτάτων καὶ φιλοθέων εὐπατρίδων πόλεως Βελαγράδων κυρίου Κωνσταντίνου, Νικολάου, καὶ Δημητρίου Τζεκούρε* (Venice: Antonio Bortoli Press, 1781).

also unaware of the biography of the saint published for didactic purposes by Nektarios Terpos in 1732.[18] The brief *acoluthia* dedicated to the saint, compiled in 1742 by Gregory of Moscopole (Alb. Voskopoja),[19] does not contain a *vita*, while the hymns dedicated to Nicodemus seem to follow details from both, the aforementioned *acoluthia* from 1709, as well as two of the manuscripts used by Eulogios Kourilas. Earlier on, these manuscripts became sources on which Saint Nicodemus of Mount Athos drew data for his *New Martyrologion*, including the life of his homonym saint of Berat.[20] It seems that there are three principal narrative variants of the saint's life, the first to be encountered in the 1709 manuscript of Tirana's National Library and the Saint Anne's Skete manuscripts, the second is in the book of Nektarios Terpos, while the third variant is to be found in at least one manuscript from the Skete of Saint Anne on Mount Athos. I assume that the first and second variants, used in regions of modern-day Albania and/or written by scholars from the same regions are better informed of the saint's life in Albania. In contrast, the version followed by Kourilas and Saint Nicodemus of Mount Athos is rather more informed about his conduct while living on Mount Athos. Building on these assumptions, I reconstruct his life.

Saint Nicodemus of Berat was born of faithful parents and was raised as a Christian. Following the 1709 source, written and used in regions of modern-day Albania, I suggest that his place of origin was the village of Vithkuq, South Albania, although Nektarios Terpos claims he was from Berat,[21] while Saint Nicodemus of Mount Athos records that he was from Elbasan, central Albania.[22] While all sources agree that Nicodemus was his monastic name, the 1709 manuscript informs us that his name before ordination was Dede.[23] He migrated to Berat to undertake the profession of a tailor either with his parents, who were also tailors,[24] or on

---

18 Νεκτάριος Τέρπος, Βιβλιάριον Καλούμενον Πίστις. Ἀναγκαῖον εἰς κάθε ἁπλοῦν ἄνθρωπον βεβαιωμένον ἀπό προφῆτας, Εὐαγγέλιον, Ἀποστόλους, καὶ ἄλλους σοφοὺς διδασκάλους. Εἰσὶ δὲ καὶ ἄλλοι ἐκλεκτοὶ εἰς ὠφέλειαν τῶν ἀναγινωσκόντων, ὡς φαίνεται ἐν τῷ πίνακι, μεταγλωττισθέντες εἰς ἁπλῆν φράσιν. Συναχθέντες παρὰ τοῦ ἐν Ἱερομονάχοις Νεκταρίου Τέρπου Ἐκ τῆς Θεοφρουρήτου Χώρας Βοσκοπόλεως συνεργείᾳ δὲ τοῦ ἐντιμωτάτου Κυρίου Χατζῆ Μιχάλη Γκούστα Ἐκ τῆς αὐτῆς πόλεως Νῦν πρῶτον τύποις ἐνδοθέντα καὶ ἐπιμελῶς διορθωθέντα παρ' Ἀλεξάνδρου Καγκελλαρίου. ενετίησι, 1732 παρὰ Νικολάῳ τῷ Σάρῳ, αψλβ΄. Con Licenza de΄ Superiori, e Privilegio (Venice: Nikolaos Saros, 1732), pp. 127–31.
19 Γρηγόριος Μοσχοπολίτης, Ἀκολουθία τοῦ ἁγίου ὁσιομάρτυρος Νικοδήμου, τοῦ μαρτυρήσαντος ἐν τῇ πόλει Βελεγράδων, κατὰ τὸ ΑΨΘ΄ ἔτος Ἰουλίῳ ι΄ (Μοσχόπολη: Moschopolis Press, 1742).
20 Νικόδημος ὁ Ἁγιορείτης, Νέον Μαρτυρολόγιον, ἤτοι Μαρτύρια τῶν Νεοφανῶν Ἁγίων τῶν μετὰ τὴν Ἅλωσιν τῆς Κωνσταντινουπόλεως κατὰ διαφόρους καιρούς, καὶ τόπους Μαρτυρησάντων. Συναχθέντα ἐκ Διαφόρων Συγγραφέων, καὶ μετ' Ἐπιμελείας ὅτι Πλείστης Ἐκδοθέντα (Βενετία: Νικόλαος Γλυκύς ἐξ Ἰωαννίνων, 1799), pp. 139–41.
21 Νεκτάριος Τέρπος, Βιβλιάριον Καλούμενον Πίστις, p. 128.
22 Νικόδημος ὁ Ἁγιορείτης, Νέον Μαρτυρολόγιον, p. 139.
23 National Library, Tirana, DRH 1/E1, 25ᵛ–26ʳ; cf. Nikolaos, Ἀκολουθία, 27. Hereafter, I cite only the 1781 edition. The adjective 'dede' in Albanian means 'guileless'.
24 Κουρίλας Εὐλόγιος Λαυριώτης, Ἱστορία, p. 85.

his own.[25] In Berat, he got married three times and was thrice widowed.[26] While it is most likely that he had children,[27] their number is not known. The reason of Dede's apostasy to Islam is not certain either. Nektarios Terpos gives no reason.[28] Saint Nicodemus of Mount Athos mentions without further explanation that Saint Nicodemus of Berat was deceived by a few Muslims.[29] Finally, his 1709 service provides a more plausible explanation, after which, in his desire to marry a young servant of a Muslim in a fourth marriage, Saint Nicodemus of Berat was forced by her Muslim lord to convert to Islam.[30] The element of coercion is also questionable, as, contrary to the Islamic law, the Orthodox Church does not bless a fourth marriage.

The saint's path towards remorse and repentance is equally complex and uncertain. The 1709 *acoluthia* mentions that, after reflecting on his actions he became remorseful and had his son sent to Mount Athos as a first step towards his own departure to Mount Athos,[31] while Nektarios Terpos adds that a significant role to his remorse concerned both his Christian wife, as well as some Christian fellows of his acquaintance, but omits the episode related to his son.[32] The reason and the setting of his remorse in the third *vita* of the saint is entirely different: accordingly, some Christians abducted the only son whom he did not turn to Islam and had him sent to Mount Athos. Filled with rage, Dede departed for Mount Athos aiming to retrieve his child and damage the monastery where his son was a monk of, but, instead, he himself repented on Mount Athos.[33] All three sources agree that he travelled to Mount Athos, where he was ordained a monk, while the sources from 1709 and from 1799 also mention that he spent three years in strict asceticism and prayer. There he encountered spiritual fathers at the Skete of Saint Anne,[34] Father Savvas after the 1709 source,[35] Saint Acacius, the new ascetic, Kausokalyvites, according to the 1799 source,[36] and possibly the elder Philotheos, after one of the manuscripts consulted by Kourilas.[37] The culmination

---

25 Νικόλαος, Ἀκολουθία, p. 26. The version by Saint Nicodemus of Mount Athos mentions neither a migration to Berat, nor his profession. Considering that, if scholars follow this version, then, they ought to accept the city of Elbasan as his place of martyrdom, i.e. a place where no particular veneration of the saint has been reported, I believe this version is not as informed as the others on the saint's early life. No mention of the saint's profession is made in Terpos' *vita*, too, cf. Νεκτάριος Τέρπος, Βιβλιάριον, p. 128.
26 Νικόλαος, Ἀκολουθία, pp. 26–27. According to Nektarios Terpos (p. 128) and Saint Nicodemus of Mount Athos (Nicodemus of Mount Athos, Νέον Μαρτυρολόγιον, p. 139), he appears to have been married only once.
27 Νεκτάριος Τέρπος, Βιβλιάριον, p. 128, however, makes no mention of children.
28 Νεκτάριος Τέρπος, Νεκτάριος Τέρπος, Βιβλιάριον Καλούμενον Πίστις, p. 128.
29 Νικόδημος ὁ Ἁγιορείτης, Νέον Μαρτυρολόγιον, p. 139.
30 Νικόλαος, Ἀκολουθία, pp. 26–27.
31 Νικόλαος, Ἀκολουθία, pp. 27–28.
32 Νεκτάριος Τέρπος, Βιβλιάριον Καλούμενον Πίστις, p. 128.
33 Νικόδημος ὁ Ἁγιορείτης, Νέον Μαρτυρολόγιον, p. 139.
34 Νεκτάριος Τέρπος, Βιβλιάριον Καλούμενον Πίστις, pp. 128–29.
35 Νικόλαος, Ἀκολουθία, p. 29.
36 Νικόδημος ὁ Ἁγιορείτης, Νέον Μαρτυρολόγιον, pp. 139–40.
37 Κουρίλας Εὐλόγιος Λαυριώτης, Ἱστορία, pp. 85–86.

of Saint Nicodemus' repentance, according to two of his life's sources, was his vision of the Virgin informing him that Christ accepted his repentance and blessed him to go for martyrdom, according to the 1709 source,[38] or of Christ, who, after the 1799 source, showed him details of his future martyrdom.[39]

The saint's return to his home city and his martyrdom, present significantly less divergences in his life's sources. Back in Berat, he returned to his workshop conducting a Christian life,[40] or simply went back and presented himself as a renegade from Islam and a re-convert to Orthodox Christianity.[41] All sources agree that he was arrested, brought forward before the local ruler, put on trial and tortured in order to be coerced to return to the Islamic faith. One of the tortures quoted in all sources in detail was that he was thrown from the mansion of the administrator, from a height hard to survive, but, against all odds, he stood up again intact.[42] Two out of the three sources considered in this section claim that, in the course of his defence, he made audacious and very offensive remarks against Islam and the Prophet Mohamed,[43] something which justifiably enraged the local Muslim element of the city, which demanded his conviction to death, according to the Islamic law for apostasy. Saint Nicodemus of Berat's way to martyrdom was by beheading, after being tortured and mocked on his way to the place of his execution.

With regards to the date of his martyrdom, the sources under consideration and data mentioned in one of them cause much confusion to the critical reader. Nektarios Terpos places the date of his martyrdom on a Sunday, 10 July 1709,[44] date, without mention of day, also stated in Gregory of Moscopole's *acoluthia*.[45] Although the manuscript from 1709 mentions no year, its 1781 print publication states the date of his martyrdom to be on 10 July 1714.[46] Finally, the version of the saint's *vita* by Saint Nicodemus of Mount Athos from 1799[47] and its sources[48] record 11 July 1722 to be the date of Saint Nicodemus of Berat's martyrdom. The date given in the earliest sources, 1709, is rather unlikely, as it is hard to believe that a neomartyr from the ranks of the renegades from Islam would be recognized as a saint with a dedicated *acoluthia* within the same year of his martyrdom, especially if his anti-Islamic public statements were part of his history rather than legend.

---

38 Νικόλαος, Ἀκολουθία, pp. 30–32.
39 Νικόδημος ο Αγιορείτης, Νέον Μαρτυρολόγιον, pp. 140–41.
40 Νικόλαος, Ἀκολουθία, pp. 32–33.
41 Νεκτάριος Τέρπος, Βιβλιάριον Καλούμενον Πίστις, p. 129; Νικόδημος ο Αγιορείτης, Νέον Μαρτυρολόγιον, p. 141, who mentions, though, that the saint returned 'to his fatherland', thereby implying Elbasan and not Berat.
42 Νικόλαος, Ἀκολουθία, pp. 33–36; Νεκτάριος Τέρπος, Βιβλιάριον Καλούμενον Πίστις, pp. 129–31; Νικόδημος ο Αγιορείτης, Νέον Μαρτυρολόγιον, p. 141.
43 Νικόλαος, Ἀκολουθία, p. 34; Νεκτάριος Τέρπος, Βιβλιάριον Καλούμενον Πίστις, p. 130.
44 Νεκτάριος Τέρπος, Βιβλιάριον Καλούμενον Πίστις, pp. 127, 131.
45 Γρηγόριος Μοσχοπολίτης, Ἀκολουθία, p. 1.
46 Νικόλαος, Ἀκολουθία, p. 2.
47 Νικόδημος ο Αγιορείτης, Νέον Μαρτυρολόγιον, pp. 139, 141.
48 Cf. Κουρίλας Ευλόγιος Λαυριώτης, Ιστορία, p. 86.

The name of the local ruler mentioned by Nektarios Terpos,[49] Hussein Pasha, seems to provide some support for the suggestion that the saint's martyrdom must have occurred a few decades earlier than 1709. This ruler might be identified with Hussein Pasha Vlora, i.e., a ruler of the Berat branch of the Vlora family. He was much admired for his public works in Berat by Evliyya Çelebi, who visited the city in the early 1670s. A patron of letters and learning, Hussein Pasha Vlora was killed in the siege of Kamieniec Podolski, in the context of the Polish-Ottoman war in 1672.[50] His luxurious palace was also much acclaimed.[51] I am not aware of any list of Ottoman administrators of the city of Berat after the said Hussein Pasha Vlora to determine whether there was another Hussein who existed at a later date, closer to our earliest source (dated 1709). However, a date close to 1670 is more plausible to me for the martyrdom of Saint Nicodemus of Berat's to have taken place, since an interval of almost four decades would be sufficient for bitter memories to fade out and the veneration of a martyr to acquire the critical mass necessary, before a structured pilgrimage and feast day is consecrated. Such a date is also not incompatible with other facts related to his life on Mount Athos.

Pilgrimage Practices in Veneration of Saint Nicodemus the Neomartyr of Berat

The Christian inhabitants of Berat asked[52] or bribed[53] the local governor to retrieve and bury the body of Nicodemus. The *acoluthia* of the saint indicates that his religious festival had already been established by 1709:

> They received the rich in blessing and martyred relic with hymns and songs and placed it in a chest inside the church of the Mother of God called Sroumbouli (Alb. Shumbull), as a treasure, unplundered for the faithful, where they celebrate his annual holy feast on the tenth of the month of July.[54]

In his contribution to the conference celebrating 2000 Years of Christianity in Albania, the late Anthony Bryer sharply observes that '[i]n their commemoration, martyrs too have a developing identity in their after-lives, which reflect secular as well as spiritual circumstances'.[55] To trace this developing identity, the next section investigates three distinct practices associated with the diffusion and pilgrimage of Saint Nicodemus of Berat's veneration.

---

49 Νεκτάριος Τέρπος, *Βιβλιάριον Καλούμενον Πίστις*, pp. 127, 129.
50 Gentjana Abazi-Egro, 'Literary Patronage of the Albanian Vlora Dynastic Family, 1670–1764', *POLIS*, 18 (2019), pp. 12–13, 17, 21.
51 Ferit Duka, *Shekujt Osmanë në Hapësirën Shqiptare (Studime dhe Dokumente)* (Tiranë: UET Press, 2009), p. 359.
52 Νεκτάριος Τέρπος, *Βιβλιάριον Καλούμενον Πίστις*, p. 131.
53 Νικόλαος, Ἀκολουθία, p. 36; Κουρίλας Εὐλόγιος Λαυριώτης, *Ἱστορία*, p. 86.
54 Νικόλαος, Ἀκολουθία, p. 36.
55 Anthony Bryer, 'People Get the Heroes and Martyrs They Deserve', in *2000 Years Church Art and Culture in Albania*, ed. by Pirro Thomo and Gaqo Busaka (Tirana: Orthodox Autocephalous Church of Albania, 2005), p. 61.

Pilgrimage at the Site of the Saint's Relics

The *acoluthia* of Saint Nicodemus of Berat from 1709 mentions that in that year the saint had already been recognized as such and that his feast day was celebrated annually at the church of the Dormition of the Virgin of Shumbull (Fig. 1). Synthesizing the various presented sources one can form a rather fair view of how this pilgrimage and the associated rituals were conducted. The relics of the saint were believed to be myrrh-bearing, could cure from diseases, burn demons and emanate grace.[56] The second canon of the *Paraklesis* (Supplication Service) to the saint, Ode in Sound 6, provides evidence on the practice of pilgrimage frequency: 'You provide God's grace, o wise, blessed attendant, to those who turn to your relics with longing profusely requesting it. Hence, swiftly provide remission of faults to those who now carry out your memory.'[57]

The passage indicates that veneration and pilgrimage of the saint's relics was an ongoing practice and was thus not confined to the saint's feast-day. I suggest that the excerpt 'ἐν τῷ σῷ τεμένει, περικυκλοῦντες νοερῶς' ('mentally surrounding your relics') of the first *sticheron prosomoion* of the *Lite* in Sound 4[58] refers to liturgical practices, whereby priests and faithful stand around the relics of the saint in procession honouring him in songs, odes and hymns. The enhancement of the saint's veneration in the nineteenth century is demonstrated not only by the mention of his service, memory, and relics in later sources,[59] but also by the gradual appearance of artworks bearing the saint as their subject not only in regions where the saint lived, but also elsewhere (Table 1).

#	MONUMENT AND DATE
1.	Hristofor Žefarović, *Saints Naum of Ohrid and Nicodemus of Berat*, 1741, engraving from his stematographia.[60]
2.	Constantine and Athanasios the painters from Korça, *Saint Nicodemus the Neomartyr*, 1750, arch of the side window of the northern wall, ossuary chapel of Saints Kosmas and Damian, Saints Peter and Paul monastery, Vithkuq, Korçë, southeastern Albania.[61]
3.	Unknown artist, *Reliquary of many saints*, 1774, repoussé silver, originally holding of the monastery of Saints Peter and Paul Vithkuq. Kept in: Museum of the Bank of Albania (fig. 2).

---

56 Νικόλαος, Ἀκολουθία, first and third sticheron in Sound 2 of Vespers; first hymn of the *Lite*; second canon of the Matins' Ode 4 and Ode 6 in Sound 6, pp. 6, 11, 13, 21, 25, 41, 47, 48 and 49; cf. Γρηγόριος Μοσχοπολίτης, Ἀκολουθία, second *prosomoion* in Sound 2, p. 3.
57 Νικόλαος, Ἀκολουθία, p. 47.
58 Νικόλαος, Ἀκολουθία, p. 13.
59 From the many examples one could quote, I am indicatively citing Ἄνθιμος Ἀλεξούδης, *Σύντομος Ἱστορική Περιγραφή τῆς Ἱερᾶς Μητροπόλεως Βελεγράδων καὶ τῆς ὑπό τὴν Πνευματικήν Αὐτῆς Δικαιοδοσίαν Ὑπαγομένης Χώρας* (Κέρκυρα: Ἰονία, 1868), pp. 112–13, 119.
60 Cf. Цветан Грозданов, *Свети Наум Охридски* (Скопје: Матица, 2015), p. 242, Plate 3.
61 Karin Kirchainer, 'Das Ossuarium des Petrus- und Paulus-Klosters in Vithkuq (Nordepirus) und seine Freskendekoration (1750)', *Μακεδονικά*, 34 (2004), pp. 166, 168–69, 197, and Fig. 19 on p. 207.

#	MONUMENT AND DATE
4.	Constantine and Athanasios, the painters from Korça, *Saint Nicodemus the Neomartyr*, 1779, Chapel of Saint Savva, Hilandar monastery, wall painting, fresco, Mount Athos.[62]
5.	Constantine and his son Terpo from Korça, *Saint Nicodemus*, 1782, fresco, Church of Saint George at Libofshë, Fier, central Albania.[63]
6.	Constantine and Athanasios the painters from Korça, *Saint Nicodemus*, 1783, fresco, arch of side window of the exonarthex of Xeropotamou monastery, Mount Athos.[64]
7.	George and John Tzetiri from Grabova, *Saint Nicodemus*, 1795, fresco, Church of Saint Nicholas at Vanaj, Fier, central Albania.[65]
8.	Unknown artist, *The Dormition of the Virgin and Saint Nicodemus the Younger*, 29.06.1805, engraving printed in Berat, kept in the Chapel of Saint George in Konitsa, northwestern Greece.[66]
9.	John Tzetiri, *Saint Nicodemus*, 1806, Church of the Annunciation, wall painting, fresco, Kozare, Berat.[67]
10.	Terpos, son of painter Constantine from Korça, *Saint Nicodemus*, 1810, catholicon of the monastery of Saint Naum, wall painting, fresco, Ohrid.
11.	Unknown artist, *Reliquary of Saint Nicodemus of Berat's skull*, 1815, *repoussé* silver, currently kept at the Metropolitan Mansion, Berat (fig. 3).

Table 1: List of eighteenth to early nineteenth-century artworks bearing Saint Nicodemus of Berat as their subject.

As is evident from the table above, veneration of the saint spread quickly both in the regions of the (as of 1746 former) Archdiocese of Ohrid, including his home village, as well as on Mount Athos. One should note that the veneration of the saint and his relics spread both in the Slavic world, as well as locally, in Berat, as evidenced by the engraving of a copperplate with two registers, portraying the Dormition of the Virgin,

---

62 Цветан Грозданов, *Портрети на светителите од Македонија: од IX–XVIII век* (Скопје: Републички завод за заштита на спомениците на културa, 1983), Fig. 93; Sotiris Kissas, 'Representations of Greek and Slav Saints from the Central and Western Balkans from the Ninth to the Eighteenth Century', *Cyrillomethodianum*, XI (1987), pp. 250 and Fig. 2 on p. 253); Γεώργιος Τσιγάρας, 'Οι Ζωγράφοι Κωνσταντίνος και Αθανάσιος από την Κορυτσά. Το Έργο τους στο Άγιον Όρος 1752–1783' (Διδακτορική Διατριβή: Αριστοτέλειο Πανεπιστήμιο Θεσσαλονίκης, 2003), pp. 217, 314 and Fig. 183.

63 Ралица Русева, 'Нови данни за изобразителния култ към Светите Седмочисленици през XVIII–XIX в. на територията на съвременна Албания', *Проблеми на изкуството*, 4 (2013), 20–28; Ралица Русева,'Композицията на светите седмочисленици в паметниците от XVIII–XIX век на територията на съвременна Албания', Ongül 8 (2014), pp. 83–84, 87–92, 96, 99 and 101, http://www.spisanie.ongal.net/broi8/10.RR.pdf (accessed on 20.05.2021).

64 Γεώργιος Τσιγάρας, 'Οι Ζωγράφοι', pp. 217, 314 and Fig. 183; Γεώργιος Τσιγάρας, *Μελέτες Ιστορίας της Μεταβυζαντινής Τέχνης* (Θεσσαλονίκη: Σταμούλης, 2013), pp. 157, 165 and Fig. 30 on p. 184.

65 Rousseva, 'Novi danni', pp. 20–28, Rousseva, 'Kompozitsiyata', pp. 83–84, 87–92, 96, 99 and 101.

66 Μίλτος Γαρίδης, Αθανάσιος Παλιούρας, "Συμβολή στην Εικονογραφία Νεομαρτύρων", *Ηπειρωτικά Χρονικά*, 22 (1980), pp. 201–02 and Fig. 30.

67 Ралица Русева, 'Нови данни', pp. 20–28; Ралица Русева,'Композицията', pp. 83–84, 87–92, 96, 99 and 101.

above, and Saint Nicodemus of Vithkuq below, printed in Berat and bearing the date 29 June 1805.[68] A few days before the annual festival of the saint, the church where his relics were kept issued impressions of the kind to give out to pilgrims in the form of blessings.

The saint's relics remained in the same church until its destruction by the Italians in 1943 for the purpose of extending the road leading to Berat. At that time, the church's belongings were transferred to the neighbouring church of the Archangel Michael, where the veneration of the saint's relics and the annual feast and pilgrimage were also translated. The translation of the saint's relics effected changes in the way his feast was celebrated. Contrary to the lower level of the church of the Dormition of the Virgin, the church of the Archangel Michael is situated high up to the knoll where Berat Castle is. Hence, the number of pilgrims following the procession of the saint's relics was significantly reduced. Yet, his veneration and pilgrimage continued until all religious activities were officially banned in Albania (1967). Celebrations in honour of the saint resumed soon after the fall of communism.

Today the feast-day of the saint is celebrated on two consecutive days. On the eve of the feast day (9 July) celebrations start with vespers and the blessing of five breads, to be followed on the next day (10 July) by Matins and Holy Service. On the evening of 10 July, after the Vespers service, attendants receive a piece of cotton from the saint's relics, to be replaced by fresh cotton to be given out the following year. The service is attended by a handful of pilgrims and curious visitors and tourists, mostly young and old people of Berat, the generation of 40s to 60s being rather lesser in number. Few foreigners now make their way to the saint's feast-day. Interestingly, the saint's veneration crosses ethnic, lingual, racial, and even religious barriers, as one also encounters a fair number of devout Romani Muslims from the city, who visit the chapel. The absence of the relics, which are currently kept in the Metropolitan mansion of Berat, and only come out on the feast-day of the saint or on other marked occasions, has certainly reduced the number of spontaneous pilgrims to that spot, who are now heading to the local Metropolis' mansion to venerate the relics of the saint at times other than his feast day. I have witnessed many groups of visitors from neighbouring Orthodox countries (Greece, North Macedonia, Bulgaria, and Serbia) who request access to the relics while visiting Berat in other periods. The focus of this pilgrimage practice is thus undoubtedly the saint and his relics, thereby classifying this pilgrimage under the category 'relics pilgrimage'.[69]

The Pilgrimage to the Place where the Saint's Skull was Enwalled

During the second half of the 1990s a strange sort of pilgrimage started emerging, originating in the diffusion of the saint's veneration and pilgrimage at times of harsh religious persecution. As briefly mentioned above, on 27 February 1967, a letter of the Central Committee of Albania's Labour Party instructed all local Party committees

---

68 Μίλτος Γαρίδης, Αθανάσιος Παλιούρας, 'Συμβολή στην ' Garidis and Paliouras, pp. 201–02 and Fig. 30.
69 Konstantinos Giakoumis, 'From Religious', p. 104.

to rise against religion, religious superstitions and related customs.[70] This marked a decisive communist blow against religion in Albania. The following day, a wave of violent persecution of all remaining religious elements by force of 'voluntary' actions was launched. A report of the Central Party Committee summarizes that a total of 2169 religious institutions were attacked, among which 740 mosques, 608 Orthodox churches and monasteries, 157 Roman-Catholic churches and monasteries, as well as 530 *tekkes* (building complex accommodating a Bektashi brotherhood), *türbes* (tombs of important persons after the Bektashi faith), *mekames* (tombs of prominent saints after Bektashism), etc. The same report also records the landed properties confiscated, cash deposits, as well as '6,000,000 Albanian lek worth of holy utensils and commodities'.[71]

In spite of the coercive might of these purges threatening to sweep any reactionary initiative, movements of the sort faced some resistance, especially in the provinces, as secret police operative accounts report to the capital centre. Some refused to remove religious objects from their homes and hid them in the hope the anti-religious frenzy would not last too long. The bravest and most firm believers dared to keep and hide objects retrieved from their religious shelters, before the destructive wave of the 1967 anti-religious communist rage would sweep. These devout practitioners were now to be treated as dissidents by the *Sigurimi* (Albania's secret police); hence, religious activities now had to go underground, while the state would closely keep them under surveillance. Those who kept a part of their religious cultural heritage at home were aware that they were defying strict state orders and that they were to serve long sentences if caught with religious objects at home.

In this context, keeping at home one of the most palpable religious artworks (Fig. 3), as the silver reliquary with the skull of Saint Nicodemus of Berat was, saved and preserved by Ilia Koçi, was an almost insane act, as the calibre of the object could put its holder in danger not only for religious agitation and propaganda, but also for theft of cultural heritage.

The silver reliquary of the saint's skull is an artwork inspired by the saint's *acoluthiae*. Placed in an octagonal silver frame in repoussé resembling a round-plan church, its top resembles a drumless dome, decorated with interlinked plants with leaves and fantastic flowers of the *rosaceae* family associated with Christ's Passion through the Cross[72] and also the saint described in hymnography as a rose.[73] A lid placed above the skull's front part permits direct contact with the relic. The circular dome ends with a flat, octagonal lid, in whose corners eight composite domed, belfry-like structures are cast. Each of them stands on the top of modular pseudo-columns. At their base, eight sitting-lion-shaped stands, the lion being another hymnic reference to the saint

---

70 Enver Hoxha, *Vepra (Shkurtër-Qërshor 1967)*, vol. 35 (Tiranë: '8 Nëntori', 1982), pp. 103–13.
71 Central Archive of the State, Tirana, F. 14 (Central Party Committee), D. 190 (1967), pp. 16–18, 32.
72 *Flora in Arts and Artefacts of the Korça Region. Twelfth Century B.C. to Twentieth Century A.D.*, ed. by Konstantinos Giakoumis (Tirana: PEGI, 2018), passim.
73 Γρηγόριος Μοσχοπολίτης, Ἀκολουθία, Lite Service, second *katavasia* of the Second Canon to the Saint, Ode 7 in Sound 8, p. 9.

in the context of his return to Berat presented to be as fearsome a lion's roar in the fashion of an angel of the Revelation,[74] allow the reliquary to stand slightly elevated above the bottom (ground) level, in the air, thereby symbolically rendering the glorious status of the saint. The inscription at the bottom of the reliquary records its date and the weight of silver used: 'ΕΤΙ + 1815 + ΑΠΡΗΛΙ 14 Ι² ΔΡΑΜ[ΙΑ] 755' (Year 1815, April 14, 755 drams, ca. 2.42 kg).

The space between these columns is taken up by eight panels, seven of which bear identical decorative patterns. The central panel, covering the skull's front, bears the figure of Saint Nicodemus. He stands frontally on low vegetated ground dressed with a cassock and a sleeved coat with sawn edges, tied at the chest. He bears a halo with a cross at the top of his head with hands elevated to the level of the shoulders, raising the right in blessing and bearing a rosary with his left. The saint is flanked by two churches, the left one identified as the church of the Dormition of the Virgin, where once his relics reposed, on account of the cypress tree at the church's side (cf. Fig. 1), while the other could be the main church (*kyriakon*) of the Skete of Saint Anne, Mount Athos, where he became a monk. At the side of the saint's head, an inscription reads 'Ο ΑΓΙΟΣ ΝΙΚΟΔΗΜΟΣ' (Saint Nicodemus). The saint and the churches are inscribed in a space marked by two columns and an arch above them. The arch is crowned by a rose, with two flying cherubim at the saint's sides. The remaining seven panels (Fig. 3) replicate the arched space, replacing the saint with flora patterns with such flowers like lilies and roses and the rose overarching the central panel with a cherub, thereby indicating the celestial place of Paradise.

There is no doubt that this was a well-known object of religious veneration coated in a finely cast silver reliquary. Holding this reliquary illicitly at any time would be a felony for suspected trafficking of an artwork. Doing so at times of harsh religious persecution equals, in a way, some sort of suicidal risk. In the words of his son,[75] Ilia Koçi, the person who assumed the risk of saving the saint's skull and reliquary, was born in 1914 and, as he grew up, he got trained and worked as a tailor until 1937, when he travelled to Italy with his fiancée and learnt the art of photography. This enabled him to switch profession and pursue a career as a photographer. Simultaneously, he served as churchwarden and cantor. Considering that photography was strictly controlled by the Albanian state both in terms of who could own a camera and where one could develop films, there were very few professional photographers in Berat during the communist regime, which enabled him to have some contacts with the local Party officials.

Ilia Koçi is described by his son, Llazar (b. 1945), as a man of faith, married to a faithful woman. Before the banning of religious activities in 1967, the family held an icon stand with a lid next to their fireplace in their house. After 1967 the icon stand

---

74 Γρηγόριος Μοσχοπολίτης, Ἀκολουθία, *Lite* Service, first *sticheron* in Sound 8, p. 4 (page numbers 4 and 5 are repeated twice in the print; the number cited here refers to the second of the pairs); cf. Revelation 10:3.
75 Llazar Koçi, 'Si Babai Im Shpëtoi Kokën e Shën Nikodhimit', Interview by Konstantinos Giakoumis and Heikki Hanka (Berat, 4 June 2019).

would be empty, however, the icons were kept together with other religious objects at the bottom of a wooden chest. In spite of the banning of religious hymns' rehearsal, his son remembers that his father not only prayed regularly before and after lunch and supper, but he also would sing chants, while working in the laboratory of his house. Note that maintaining even a private, low religious profile was by no means without perils. The communist regime strove to acquire information on the private life of individuals in any way they could extrapolate. Llazar recalls that once, at a young age, i.e., before 1967, yet, in the course of increasing compulsion against religious practices, he was caught with dyed eggs, which local informers would publicly display. As they lived close to families of communists also known to serve as voluntary informers, the Koçi family were aware that an eye was kept on them, on account of the former quality of its head, Ilia, as churchwarden and cantor.

Only due to this background information, can one grasp the gravity of the audacious task of Ilia Koçi, when, upon news of the raids in churches instigated by the Party instances and implemented mostly by 'voluntary' actions of Youth groups, Ilia Koçi and a few other former churchwardens decided to go to the church of the Archangel Michael and retrieve as many religious objects as they could to save them from the destructive frenzy of the times. They approached the church before dawn, according to his son's account, each following a different path, to avoid being seen walking together in the same direction.[76] Llazar Koçi approached the church from a hardly accessible path mostly used by shepherds to come down to the church. He got the skull of Saint Nicodemus and a few liturgical books; other churchwardens would take holy vestments and utensils. The remaining relics from the body of the saint were burnt or otherwise destroyed by youth groups the following day. Llazar Koçi brought these items home, hid liturgical books at the bottom of a wooden chest and walled the relic and its reliquary in the basement of his home, where the reliquary remained until churches re-opened in 1990. Until the early 1990s nobody except for Llazar's wife knew of the religious objects kept in their own house.

Even when religious activities resumed, the relic of the saint was not immediately handed to the local Metropolis. The holders of the relic, members from the Koçi family, would eagerly give the reliquary with the relic to the Church at the saint's feast day or on other occasions. They would even eagerly present the relic and its reliquary to groups of pilgrims from Albania, Greece and elsewhere that would come to his house to venerate the saint's relic and hear the story of how it survived communism. Some of the most zealous pilgrims would cross themselves and venerate the spot in which the saint's relics were walled in. Ilia died in 2004 and left instructions to his son Llazar, who continued to keep the relic until 25 October 2014. Then, upon the inauguration of a chapel in the name of the saint, he handed it over to the local metropolis where (i.e., in the Metropolis) it is currently kept. Memories of how the relic of the saint survived communist anti-religious frenzy, enriched with stories of how the saint appeared in vision to Ilia's wife and her sister demanding that his relic

---

76 Llazar Koçi, Interview.

be removed from the wall in which it was hidden have been part of the transformation of the saint's pilgrimage ever since the restitution of religious activities in Albania.

Curiosity and awe about the life of underground religious communities combined with narratives about martyrs and confessors of faith in communist Albania,[77] not only confined to Orthodox Christianity,[78] were framed in wider discussions about martyrdom and communion in modern times.[79] As a result, an additional pilgrimage centre was developed alongside the mainstream pilgrimage of Saint Nicodemus' relics. I have accompanied two such groups, one from Greece and another group of young pilgrims who were university students from Albania and had the opportunity to witness this pilgrimage diffusion. Having triangulated findings with discussions with other guides, I sensed that pilgrims thereafter developed a keen interest in underground spirituality in communist times, which promulgated feverish discussions about sainthood in modern times, especially in the course of Albania's communist regime.

This case is an example whereby diffusion of the veneration and pilgrimage of Saint Nicodemus of Berat developed an additional centre on underground spirituality in communist times. Hence, alongside the typical 'relics pilgrimage', the new pilgrimage centre shifted to the type of a 'place of a miracle',[80] whereby, through diffusion of the saint's veneration and pilgrimage, this place became a spot where pilgrims would now also venerate the grace of modern martyrs and confessors of faith, who risked their lives for their faith and to save holy objects.

The Pilgrimage at the Saint's Birth-Place

Saint Nicodemus' veneration and pilgrimage were not confined in Berat. Thus, on the saint's feast-day, while some pilgrims from Vithkuq leave their village to undertake the pilgrimage in veneration of the saint in Berat, others take the road to Vithkuq to venerate and celebrate the saint in his birthplace. Two pieces of evidence indicate

---

77 Cf. Βασίλειος Μ. Κασκαντάμης, *Θεοφάνης Πόπα*; Kristofor Beduli, ed., *Dhimitër Beduli, 'Bir i Zgjedhur dhe i Përkushtuar i Kishës Sonë' Vartholomeu i Kostandinopojës* (Tiranë: Botim i Kishës Orthodhokse Autoqefale të Shqipërisë, 1999); Kristofor Beduli, *Episkop Irine Banushi. Martir i Kishës Orthodhokse Autoqefale të Shqipërisë* (Tiranë: Botim i Kishës Orthodhokse Autoqefale të Shqipërisë, 2000); Spiro Bulika, *Bariu i Mirë (Episkop Kozmai)* (Tiranë: Botim i Kishës Orthodhokse Autoqefale të Shqipërisë, 2005).
78 Cf. Zef Pllumi, *Rrno Vetëm për me Tregue* (Tiranë: 55, 2006); Zhuljeta Grabocka-Çina, *Një Jetë me Biblën. Kujtime* (Tiranë: Expo Vision Albania, 2016).
79 Cf. Tatiana A. Chumachenko, *Russian Orthodoxy from World War II to the Khrushchev Years*, ed. and trans. by Edward E. Roslov (New York: M. E. Sharpe, 2002); Gheorghe Florin Hostiuc, 'Romania and the Orthodox Church Under the Communist Regime', *Acta Universitatis Danubius. Relationes Internationales*, 7 (1), (2014). Available at https://journals.univ-danubius.ro/index.php/internationalis/article/view/1889/2819; Ralena Nikolaeva Gerasimova, 'Religious Identity in Bulgaria During the Communist Regime. The Case of Orthodox Christianity and Islam', *Rhetoric and Communications E-Journal* 27 (2017). Available at http://journal.rhetoric.bg/; Daniela Kalkandjieva, 'Martiri e Confessori nella Chiesa Ortodossa Bulgara sotto il Comunismo', in *Martirio e Comunione. Atto del XXIV Convegno Ecumenico Internazionale di Spiritualità Ortodossa, Bose, 7–10 Settembre 2016*, ed. by Luigi d'Ayala Valva, Lisa Cremaschi and Adalberto Mainardi (Comunità di Bose: Qiqajon, 2017), pp. 263–81.
80 Konstantinos Giakoumis, 'From Religious', p. 104.

that this pilgrimage is not a new practice and that a 'relics-type pilgrimage' was also developed in the saint's place of origin since the eighteenth century. The first is a reliquary from 1774, originally from the monastery of Saints Peter and Paul at Vithkuq, which contains multiple relics including a few pieces from Saint Nicodemus of Berat. The second is the 1750 representation of the saint at the ossuary chapel of Saints Kosmas and Damian, in the same monastery. Such is the extent of this pilgrimage practice in modern times, as to voice claims that the relics once kept by Ilia Koçi should be returned to his birthplace.[81]

Since the restitution of religious life in Albania in 1990, i.e., after the fall of the communist regime, on July 10 pilgrims from Albania, Greece and other countries celebrate the memory of the saint in his birthplace, Vithkuq. This feast is also significant for other reasons, as it provides a motive for immigrants from Vithkuq to visit their own village and bond with their place of origin. The feast of Saint Nicodemus of Berat is thus also the feast-day of the Association 'The Vithkuq Brotherhood'. This is an organization established in Southbridge, Worcester County, Massachusetts, U.S.A., from members of the village's diaspora as early as 1910, for the purpose of bonding together, lobbying for the interests of the village and Albania. Remembering their roots and celebrating their identity on the same day as the feast of a neomartyr from their village provided the impetus for establishing an additional pilgrimage centre to the land of Vithkuq immigrants' fathers and mothers, a pilgrimage to their roots, so to speak. This visit, strictly viewed, is not religious; yet, the definition of pilgrimage provided at the start of this chapter leaves room for non-religious pilgrimage, also.

The pilgrimage of the saint in Vithkuq, his birthplace, and the pilgrimage of the Vithkuq diaspora to the village of their origin is thus another case whereby diffusion of Saint Nicodemus' veneration and pilgrimages established an additional pilgrimage centre, different to the initial one. The potential of this latter pilgrimage centre for economic development is recognized in the social and economic development plans of the local authorities in Vithkuq,[82] thereby indicating processes of institutionalist transformation of this latter pilgrimage centre. In 2001, the Orthodox Church of Albania built a church dedicated to Saint Nicodemus of Berat, the neomartyr from Vithkuq, where celebrations and the pilgrimage currently take place to maintain and enhance the place of the saint's life type of pilgrimage.[83]

Concluding Remarks

This chapter observed three distinct pilgrimage sites, two in Berat and one at Vithkuq, whose connecting bond remains the veneration of Saint Nicodemus of Berat. While

---

81 Andrea Llukani, 'Nikodhimi i Beratit, një shenjt shqiptar', *Rrënjët/Le Radici*, Anno 11, Nr. 2 (May 2013), p. 11.
82 Komuna Vithkuq, *Agroturizmi, Sektorë të Tjerë Ekonomik, Mjedisi, Infrastruktura, Trashëgimi Kulturore-Historike … Drejt Zhvillimit të Integruar të Territorit Vithkuq 2012–2020*. http://www.adadmalore.al/wp-content/uploads/2016/06/vithkuqi-alb-prevew.pdf (accessed on 19.05.2021).
83 Konstantinos Giakoumis, 'From Religious', p. 104.

in the first of these practices, the pilgrimage to the saint's relics, especially on the occasion of his feast day (10 July) the principal centre of the pilgrimage, in spite of its transformations and translations, remains virtually unaltered, the same does not go for the other two pilgrimage practices. Indeed, once the veneration of Saint Nicodemus and his relics led people to the (nowadays demolished) house of Ilia Koçi, the person who saved the skull of the saint in its reliquary from the communist anti-religious frenzy by walling it in the basement of his house, an additional pilgrimage centre emerged. This centred on underground spirituality and sainthood. While this second pilgrimage practice stopped once Ilia Koçi's son delivered the saint's relic to the local ecclesiastical authorities, and while the subsequent destruction of the house where the saint's relics were kept removed any material to serve any sort of pilgrimage, the third pilgrimage practice is still active. After this third pilgrimage practice, the feast-day pilgrimage held on 10 July, formerly celebrated at the local monastery, is currently held at the church dedicated to the saint at his birthplace, the village of Vithkuq. This village gradually developed into an alternative pilgrimage centre, especially for their fellow-villagers in the diaspora, by diffusion of the one that existed at the first place. Now, Vithkuq immigrants gather together to celebrate their origins and re-bond with the village of their ancestors and fellow-villagers.

These cases allowed an investigation to a terminological overarching research question: How to name the phenomenon by which a pilgrimage's centre after processes of re-signification diffuses to others, alterative or additional to the original one? In this chapter, I have shown that an initial pilgrimage centred in the veneration of Saint Nicodemus of Berat and his relics gradually diffused to two additional centres: 1. underground spirituality, martyrs and confessors of faith of the communist period's religious persecution; 2. and Vithkuq as the village of ancestry of its diaspora. I have thus argued that the most appropriate term to be adopted in describing this phenomenon is that of 'pilgrimage diffusion and polycentrism'. I am thus shifting away from the Turnerian connotation of the term, which should be simply called multiple shrines.

Archival Sources

Central Archive of the State, Tirana, F. 14 (Central Party Committee), D. 190 (1967).
National Library, Tirana, DRH 1/E1, Nikolaos, *Μηνὶ Ιουλίω δεκάτη μνήμιν ἐπιτελοῦμεν του αγίου οσίου μαρτῦρος Νικοδήμου τοῦ νέου*, 1709, letter, 23.5 X 17 cm.

References

Andrea Llukani, 'Nikodhimi i Beratit, një shenjt shqiptar', *Rrënjët/Le Radici*, Anno 11, Nr. 2 (May 2013), 11.
Andrea Llukani, 'Dosja e Teologut Theofan Popa', *Global Challenge*, VI (2), (2017), 92–99.
Anthony Bryer, 'People Get the Heroes and Martyrs They Deserve', in *2000 Years Church Art and Culture in Albania*, ed. by Pirro Thomo and Gaqo Busaka (Tirana: Orthodox Autocephalous Church of Albania, 2005), pp. 61–65.

Άνθιμος Αλεξούδης, *Σύντομος Ιστορική Περιγραφή της Ιεράς Μητροπόλεως Βελεγράδων και της υπό την Πνευματικήν Αυτής Δικαιοδοσίαν Υπαγομένης Χώρας* (Κέρκυρα: Ιονία, 1868).

Βασίλειος Μ. Κασκαντάμης, *Θεοφάνης Πόπα. Ένας Σύγχρονος Ιεραπόστολος* (Αθήνα: Έλαφος, 2001).

Caroline Walker Bynum, 'Foreward', in *Natural Materials of the Holy Land and the Visual Translation of Place, 500–1500*, ed. by Renana Bartal, Neta Bodner, and Bianca Kühnel (London and New York: Routledge, 2017), p. xix–xxii.

Цветан Грозданов, *Портрети на светителите од Македонија: од IX–XVIII век* (Скопје: Републички завод за заштита на спомениците на култура, 1983).

Цветан Грозданов, *Свети Наум Охридски* (Скопје: Матица, 2015).

Daniela Kalkandjieva, 'Martiri e Confessori nella Chiesa Ortodossa Bulgara sotto il Comunismo', in *Martirio e Comunione. Atto del XXIV Convegno Ecumenico Internazionale di Spiritualità Ortodossa, Bose, 7–10 Settembre 2016*, ed. by Luigi d'Ayala Valva, Lisa Cremaschi and Adalberto Mainardi (Comunità di Bose: Qiqajon, 2017), pp. 263–81.

Dhimitër Beduli, 'Bir i Zgjedhur dhe i Përkushtuar i Kishës Sonë' Vartholomeu i Kostandinopojës, ed. by Kristofor Beduli (Tiranë: Botim i Kishës Orthodhokse Autoqefale të Shqipërisë, 1999).

Enver Hoxha, *Vepra (Shkurtër-Qërshor 1967)*, vol. 35 (Tiranë: '8 Nëntori', 1982).

Ελευθερία Ι. Νικολαΐδου, 'Οι Κρυπτοχριστιανοί της Σπαθίας' (Διδακτορική Διατριβή: Πανεπιστήμιο Ιωαννίνων, 1978).

Ferit Duka, *Shekujt Osmanë në Hapësirën Shqiptare (Studime dhe Dokumente)* (Tiranë: UET Press, 2009).

Flora in Arts and Artefacts of the Korça Region. Twelfth Century B.C. to Twentieth Century A.D., ed. by Konstantinos Giakoumis (Tirana: PEGI, 2018).

Φώτιος Οικονόμου, *Ἡ Ἐκκλησία ἐν Βορείῳ Ἠπείρῳ ἀπὸ τῆς Πρώτης Διαδόσεως τοῦ Χριστιανισμοῦ μέχρι τῶν καθ' Ἡμᾶς Χρόνων* (Ἀθῆναι: [χ.ἐ.], 1969).

Gentjana Abazi-Egro, 'Literary Patronage of the Albanian Vlora Dynastic Family, 1670–1764', *POLIS*, 18 (2019), 5–21.

Gheorghe Florin Hostiuc, 'Romania and the Orthodox Church Under the Communist Regime', *Acta Universitatis Danubius. Relationes Internationales*, 7 (1), (2014). Available at https://journals.univ-danubius.ro/index.php/internationalis/article/view/1889/2819

Γεώργιος Τσιγάρας, 'Οι Ζωγράφοι Κωνσταντίνος και Αθανάσιος από την Κορυτσά. Το Έργο τους στο Άγιον Όρος 1752–1783' (Διδακτορική Διατριβή: Αριστοτέλειο Πανεπιστήμιο Θεσσαλονίκης, 2003).

Γεώργιος Τσιγάρας, *Μελέτες Ιστορίας της Μεταβυζαντινής Τέχνης* (Θεσσαλονίκη: Σταμούλης, 2013).

Γρηγόριος Μοσχοπολίτης, *Ἀκολουθία τοῦ ἁγίου ὁσιομάρτυρος Νικοδήμου, τοῦ μαρτυρήσαντος ἐν τῇ πόλει Βελεγράδων, κατὰ τὸ ΑΨΘ΄ ἔτος Ἰουλίῳ ι΄* (Μοσχόπολη: Moschopolis Press, 1742).

Harvey Russell Bernard, *Research Methods in Anthropology. Qualitative and Quantitative Approaches*, 4th edition (Lanham, New York, Toronto, Oxford: Altamira Press, 2006).

Jan Van Herwaaden, *Between Saint James and Erasmus. Studies in Late-Medieval Religious Life*, trans. by Wendie Shaffer and Donald Gardner (Leiden-Boston: Brill, 2003).

John Eade and Michael J. Sallnow, 'Introduction', in *Contesting the Sacred: The Anthropology of Christian Pilgrimage*, ed. by John Eade and Michael J. Sallnow (London and New York: Routledge, 1991), pp. 1–29.

Karin Kirchainer, 'Das Ossuarium des Petrus- und Paulus-Klosters in Vithkuq (Nordepirus) und seine Freskendekoration (1750)', *Μακεδονικά*, 34 (2004), 149–208.

Konstantinos Giakoumis, 'An Enquiry into the Construction, Deconstruction, Transubstantiation and Reconstruction of Christian Pilgrimages in Modern-Day Albania', *Ηπειρωτικό Ημερολόγιο*, 32 (2013), 267–318.

Konstantinos Giakoumis, 'From Religious to Secular and Back Again: Christian Pilgrimage Space in Albania', in *Pilgrimage, Politics and Place-Making in Eastern Europe: Crossing the Borders*, ed. by John Eade and Mario Katić (London: Ashgate, 2014), pp. 103–18.

Konstantinos Giakoumis and Christopher C. Lockwood, 'Death Proximity, Group Cohesion & Mountainous Pilgrimage in Albania ', in *Landscape in Southeastern Europe*, ed. by Lena Mirošević, Gregory Zaro, Mario Katić, and Danjela Birt (Zürich: Lit Verlag, 2018), pp. 89–128.

Knut A. Jacobsen, *Pilgrimage in the Hindu Tradition. Salvific space* (London and New York: Routledge, 2013).

Komuna Vithkuq, *Agroturizmi, Sektorë të Tjerë Ekonomik, Mjedisi, Infrastruktura, Trashëgimi Kulturore-Historike … Drejt Zhvillimit të Integruar të Territorit Vithkuq 2012–2020*. http://www.adadmalore.al/wp-content/uploads/2016/06/vithkuqi-alb-prevew.pdf (accessed on 19.05.2021)

Κουρίλας Ευλόγιος Λαυριώτης, *Ιστορία του Ασκητισμού. Αθωνίται, τόμος Α΄* (Θεσσαλονίκη: Ακουαρόνη, 1929).

Kristofor Beduli, *Episkop Irine Banushi. Martir i Kishës Orthodhokse Autoqefale të Shqipërisë* (Tiranë: Botim i Kishës Orthodhokse Autoqefale të Shqipërisë, 2000).

Μίλτος Γαρίδης, Αθανάσιος Παλιούρας, "Συμβολή στην Εικονογραφία Νεομαρτύρων", *Ηπειρωτικά Χρονικά*, 22 (1980), 169–203 with 33 black-and-white illustrations and 8 colour illustrations.

Νεκτάριος Τέρπος, *Βιβλιάριον Καλούμενον Πίστις. Ἀναγκαῖον εἰς κάθε ἁπλοῦν ἄνθρωπον βεβαιωμένον ἀπὸ προφῆτας, Εὐαγγέλιον, Ἀποστόλους, καὶ ἄλλους σοφοὺς διδασκάλους. Εἰσὶ δὲ καὶ ἄλλοι ἐκλεκτοὶ εἰς ὠφέλειαν τῶν ἀναγινωσκόντων, ὡς φαίνεται ἐν τῷ πίνακι, μεταγλωττισθέντες εἰς ἁπλῆν φρᾶσιν. Συναχθέντες παρὰ τοῦ ἐν Ἱερομονάχοις Νεκταρίου Τέρπου Ἐκ τῆς Θεοφρουρήτου Χώρας Βοσκοπόλεως συνεργείᾳ δὲ τοῦ ἐντιμωτάτου Κυρίου Χατζῆ Μιχάλη Γκούστα Ἐκ τῆς αὐτῆς πόλεως Νῦν πρῶτον τύποις ἐνδοθέντα καὶ ἐπιμελῶς διορθωθέντα παρ᾽ Ἀλεξάνδρου Καγκελλαρίου. ενετίῃσι, 1732 παρὰ Νικολάῳ τῷ Σάρῳ, αψλβ΄. Con Licenza de ́ Superiori, e Privilegio* (Venice: Nikolaos Saros, 1732).

Νικόδημος ο Αγιορείτης, *Νέον Μαρτυρολόγιον, ἤτοι Μαρτύρια τῶν Νεοφανῶν Ἁγίων τῶν μετὰ τὴν Ἅλωσιν τῆς Κωνσταντινουπόλεως κατὰ διαφόρους καιρούς, καὶ τόπους Μαρτυρησάντων. Συναχθέντα ἐκ Διαφόρων Συγγραφέων, καὶ μετ᾽ Ἐπιμελείας ὅτι Πλείστης Ἐκδοθέντα* (Βενετία: Νικόλαος Γλυκύς ἐξ Ιωαννίνων, 1799).

Νικόλαος, *Ἀκολουθία τοῦ Ἁγίου Ὁσιομάρτυρος Νικοδήμου τοῦ Νέου, ὅς ἐμαρτύρησε κατὰ το αψιδ΄ ἔτος τὸ σωτήριον. Ἐν μηνὶ Ἰουλίῳ δεκάτῃ. Νεωστὶ τυπωθεῖσα καὶ διορθωθεῖσα ἐπιμελῶς, τῇ σπουδῇ καὶ δαπάνῃ τῶν τιμιωτάτων καὶ φιλοθέων εὐπατριδῶν πόλεως Βελαγράδων κυρίου Κωνσταντίνου, Νικολάου, καὶ Δημητρίου Τζεκούρε* (Venice: Antonio Bortoli Press, 1781).

Ралица Русева, 'Нови данни за изобразителния култ към Светите Седмочисленици през XVIII-XIX в. на територията на съвременна Албания', *Проблеми на изкуството*, 4 (2013), 20–28;

Ралица Русева,'Композицията на светите седмочисленици в паметниците от XVIII-XIX век на територията на съвременна Албания', *Ongŭl* 8 (2014), pp. 83–84, 87–92, 96, 99 and 101. http://www.spisanie.ongal.net/broi8/10.RR.pdf (accessed on 20.05.2021).

Ralena Nikolaeva Gerasimova, 'Religious Identity in Bulgaria During the Communist Regime. The Case of Orthodox Christianity and Islam', *Rhetoric and Communications E-Journal* 27 (2017). Available at http://journal.rhetoric.bg/

Simon Coleman and John Eade, *Reframing Pilgrimage. Cultures in Motion* (London and New York: Routledge, 2004).

Sotiris Kissas, "Representations of Greek and Slav Saints from the Central and Western Balkans from the Ninth to the Eighteenth Century", *Cyrillomethodianum*, XI (1987), 249–55.

Spiro Bulika, *Bariu i Mirë (Episkop Kozmai)* (Tiranë: Botim i Kishës Orthodhokse Autoqefale të Shqipërisë, 2005).

Tatiana A. Chumachenko, *Russian Orthodoxy from World War II to the Khrushchev Years*, ed. and trans. by Edward E. Roslov (New York: M. E. Sharpe, 2002).

Victor Turner and Edith Turner, *Image and Pilgrimage in Christian Culture. Anthropological Perspectives* (New York: Columbia University Press, 1978).

Violeta Viso, 'Biblioteka Private, Pjesë e Trashëgimisë Kulturore Kombëtare', in *Komferenca Kombëtare e Bibliotekonomisë "Biblioteka dhe Kujtesa Kombëtare (Edicioni II) 20–22 nëntor 2007"*, vol. 2 (Prishtina: Biblioteka Kombëtare dhe Universitaree Kosovës, 2008), pp. 199–205.

Zhuljeta Grabocka-Çina, *Një Jetë me Biblën. Kujtime* (Tiranë: Expo Vision Albania, 2016).

Zef Pllumi, *Rrno Vetëm për me Tregue* (Tiranë: 55, 2006).

Figures

Fig. 1: Edward Lear, *The Church of the Dormition of the Virgin at Shumbull, Berat*, 15 October 1848, Watercolour and Chinese white over graphite on grey paper, 29 x 20.9 cm. Kept in Harvard University Houghton Library.

Fig. 2: Unknown artist, *Reliquary of Many Saints*, 1774, repoussé silver, kept at the Museum of the Bank of Albania.

Fig. 3: Unknown artist, *Reliquary of Saint Nicodemus of Berat's Skull*, 1815, *repoussé* silver, kept at the Metropolitan Mansion, Berat. Photograph by the author.

EVELYN REUTER

Visiting Saint Naum

Blurring Motivations and Activities of Pilgrims and Tourists

Introduction

'Visiting Saint Naum' (Macedonian *Poseti Sveti Naum*) and 'Going to Saint Naum' (Albanian *Shkoj te Shën Naumi*) are the most common expressions in the local languages meaning to visit the monastery of Saint Naum that is located in the southwest of North Macedonia close to the border of Albania. Today the monastery is a destination for locals and one of the most famous tourist attractions in North Macedonia. Thus, the monastery is frequented by the local Christians and Muslims as well as by international tourists. Especially during the feasts of the saint on 3 July, pilgrimages and sightseeing tours overlap. All visitors behave similarly, e.g. they go the tomb of the saint in the chapel within the church and spend their time in other parts of the monasterial complex with several leisure activities and recreation.

This chapter aims to discuss pilgrimage and touristic sightseeing as two perspectives on visiting religious places, and focusses on how motivations and activities of pilgrims and tourists blur. With this aim my research connects a theoretical framework on pilgrimage and tourism with the spatial concept of the monastery that divides the complex in an inner and an outer area. These areas are connected to different motivations and activities of visitors. The visitors' behavior changes when moving between these areas.

This micro-study is based on ethnographic fieldwork that I conducted between 2016–2018. During my fieldwork, I conducted interviews and conversations, participated in and observed several activities. The sample included among others, Macedonians and Albanians, Christians and Muslims, clergies, laypersons, and international tourists. Overall, I recorded 66 interviews and talks in English (1), Macedonian (40), and Albanian (25).

Drawing on this data, I deconstruct the dichotomy of 'religious' – 'secular' because these dimensions merge at the monastery.[1] Moreover, I distinguish the dimensions

---

1 I use 'religious' and 'secular' referring to the meta level of religion as cultural pattern, and avoid the synonymous terms 'sacred' and 'profane' because of their problematic and constructed character that refers to the object level of religion; cf. Evelyn Reuter, *Die Mehrdeutigkeit geteilter religiöser Orte. Eine ethnographische Fallstudie zum Kloster Sveti Naum in Ohrid (Mazedonien)* (Bielefeld: transcript, 2021), p. 51.

Evelyn Reuter • PhD, Collaborative Research Fellow at Sophia University Tokyo, Japan

Pilgrimage in the Christian Balkan World: The Path to Touch the Sacred and Holy, ed. by Dorina Dragnea, Emmanouil Ger. Varvounis, Evelyn Reuter, Petko Hristov and Susan Sorek (Turnhout, 2023), pp. 91–108.
BREPOLS PUBLISHERS   DOI 10.1484/M.STR-EB.5.132401

that the term 'secular' includes. Thus, the monastery occurs as an ambiguous place. For this purpose, first I differentiate several visits by considering motivations. Then, I analyze how visitors negotiate the meaning of the monastery referring to their motivations and activities, and considering the spatial structure, i.e. the inner and outer area of the monasterial complex.

Motivations of Visiting Religious Places

Despite the obvious blurred boundaries, the differences between pilgrimage, spiritual search for meaning and hiking are hard to distinguish.[2] Nevertheless, visitors cannot be generally characterized as pilgrims, because they may not consider themselves as such. Differentiating visits to religious places is necessary in order to cope with the perspectives of the actors. The classification of visitors based on their reasons for visiting is difficult because they can have several motivations for visiting religious places.

Pilgrimages can be defined as visits to meaningful places, i.e. to a '"threshold", a place and moment "in and out of time"'.[3] Pilgrimages are non-ordinary events, because the participants hope 'to have direct experience of the sacred, invisible, or supernatural order, either in the material aspect of miraculous healing or in the immaterial aspect of inward transformation of spirit or personality'.[4] In contrast to holiday trips, pilgrimages can shape the individual and collective self-conception.[5] Pilgrimages are not necessarily religious, because the interpreting authority can also be a state system or a political group.[6] Pilgrimages to meaningful places can be defined as political if they were explicitly established without reference to a religious community, but to implement the state ideology.

The terms that are used in the dominant local languages, i.e. Macedonian and Albanian, provide an insight in the language history, and show which aspects are important for visiting religious places. Both languages use two different terms as synonyms: *adžilak* and *poklonenie* in Macedonian; *haxhillëk* and *pelegrinazh* in

---

2 Cf. Markus Gamper and Julia Reuter, 'Pilgern als spirituelle Selbstfindung oder religiöse Pflicht? Empirische Befunde zur Pilgerpraxis auf dem Jakobsweg', in *Doing Modernity - Doing Religion*, ed. by Anna Daniel et al. (Wiesbaden: Springer Fachmedien, 2012), p. 228.
3 Victor Turner, 'The Center out There. Pilgrim's Goal', in *History of Religions*, 12 (1973), p. 214.
4 Victor Turner, *Dramas, Fields, and Metaphors: Symbolic Action in Human Society* (Ithaca, London: Cornell University Press, 1974), p. 197.
5 Cf. Polina Tšerkassova, 'Sterilization and Re-Sacralization of the Places of Secular Pilgrimage. Moving Monuments, Meanings and Crowds in Estonia', in *Pilgrimage, Politics and Place Making in Eastern Europe. Crossing the Borders*, ed. by John Eade and Mario Katić (Farnham: Ashgate Publishing Limited, 2014), p. 119.
6 Cf. *New Pathways in Pilgrimage Studies. Global Perspektives*, ed. by Dionigi Albera and John Eade (London/New York: Routledge, 2016); Konstantinos Giakoumis 'From Religious to Secular and Back Again. Christian Pilgrimage Space in Albania', *Pilgrimage, Politics and Place Making in Eastern Europe. Crossing the Borders*, ed. by John Eade and Mario Katić (Farnham: Ashgate Publishing Limited, 2014), pp. 103–18.

Albanian.⁷ Although *adžilak* and *haxhillëk* derive from the Arabic *hajj*, that marks the pilgrimage to Mecca, both terms can describe Christian and Muslim pilgrimages. The same applies for *poklonenie* and *pelegrinazh*, even though their derivations are different. The Albanian *pelegrinazh* derives from the Latin *peregrinus* and has the same etymology as Western European equivalents.⁸ The Macedonian *poklonenie* from the verb *pokloni* has two meanings, first 'to bow to someone or something', and second 'to give a present'. Thus, the term *poklonenie* refers to the humility of visitors towards the saint which they express with respectful behavior. In Macedonian the verb is constructed with 'to go on' (*odi na*), and in Albanian, with 'to make' (*bëj*). Especially the Macedonian expressions focus not on the way to a certain place, but on the veneration practices at the place. This perspective is evident in other languages of Orthodox-influenced countries in Southeastern Europe too.⁹ Nowadays, even in practice only few religious places are connected with a long pathway that has to be mastered on foot. In contrast to these observations in Southeastern Europe, in Western Europe, for many people the journey itself and the self-initiated, non-denominational a search for meaning the main goals.¹⁰

The distinction between pilgrims and other visitors is based on the motivations of travelers because external appearance and actions hardly allow any differentiating conclusions. In general, pilgrims are travelers who also may have motivations like other tourists.¹¹ These motivations include recreation, pleasure, and holidays for the purpose of education or physical compensation. Thus, the boundaries between pilgrimage and tourism blur. In consequence, the common expression 'religious tourist' includes pilgrims and those travelers that are interested in religion but are not religiously motivated. In general, '[r]eligious tourism' is a term that has come to define a movement towards places understood as religious heritage, a cultural construct framed by space and by time, an idea, an image, a building or landscape, a route: in sum, objects of memory and devotion'.¹²

Due to the strongly overlapping characteristics, a differentiation of visitors at a religious place requires a working definition that refers to their motivations. As 'religious tourists' implies the risk of misunderstanding by emphasizing the travelers'

---

7   In Macedonian, there are further expressions to describe religious motivated travels like *verski, religiozni* and *poklonički turizam*, or *odočestie*; cf. Ацо Гиревски, *Верски Туризам* (Скопје: Менора, repr. 2008). However, these terms and Albanian pendants will not be considered here because they cannot be found in my data.
8   Cf. Dionigi Albera and John Eade, 'Pilgrimage Studies in Global Perspective', in *New Pathways in Pilgrimage Studies. Global Perspektives*, ed. by Dionigi Albera and John Eade (London/New York: Routledge, 2016), pp. 5–9.
9   Cf. Vihra Baeva, 'Parishioners, Pilgrims, Tourists. The Visitors of an Orthodox Christian Shrine in Sofia', in *Pilgrimage and Sacred Places in Southeast Europe. History, Religious Tourism and Contemporary Trends*, ed. by Mario Katić et al (Wien: LIT Verlag, 2014), p. 82.
10 Cf. Markus Gamper, Julia Reuter, 'Pilgern als spirituelle', pp. 211, 228–29.
11 Cf. Walter Freyer, *Tourismus. Einführung in die Fremdenverkehrsökonomie* (Berlin et al.: De Gruyter Oldenbourg, repr. 2015), pp. 81–89.
12 Jose Eduardo Chemin, 'Pilgrimage in a secular Age. Religious and Consumer Landscapes of Late-Modernity' (unpublished doctoral thesis, University of Exeter, 2011), p. 56.

religiosity, I use the term 'religion tourists' for visitors interested in religions and religious phenomena as part of cultures such as art, architecture, and religious history. Thus, religion tourists can be classified as a sub-form of educational and sightseeing tourists and representatives of holiday and leisure tourism.[13]

Holiday and leisure tourists mostly have more than one motivation for their trip such as relaxation, sport activities, exploring culture and nature.[14] All tourist types are rarely found in pure form, the same applies to pilgrims. That is why researchers also have 'to consider [the visitors] inner heterogeneity, the zones of diffusion and the dynamic fuzzy margins between them'.[15] Instead, the category of religion tourists is mixed with other types of holidays and leisure tourism.[16] Pilgrims and religious tourists differ in terms of their motivation to visit religious places but are quite often interested in similar non-religious leisure time activities.

The encounter of different motivations, interests and activities becomes evident at the Saint Naum monastery taking its spatial arrangement into account: While the religious core of the site is primarily characterized by the motivations of pilgrims and religious tourists, the rest of the monasterial complex is dominated by non-religious travel motives. Moreover, the religious core and the tourist leisure area of the monastery complex are recognizable as two spatially separate areas.

The Saint Naum Monastery and its Visitors

The Orthodox monastery Saint Naum is one of the most famous religious places in North Macedonia close to the Albanian border. Due to its location, the monastery is connected especially to two cities: first, to Ohrid (North Macedonia) located to the north of the Lake Ohrid that is the traditional centre of the Orthodox Church in this region; second, Pogradec (Albania), a smaller city just beyond the border that some citizens claim to be the first place where Naum landed after crossing the lake in a small boat.[17]

Naum started to build his monastery around AD 900. Due to Saint Naum's reputation as miracle worker and healer, the monastery has been a goal for Christians and Muslims in the Archdiocese of Ohrid since medieval times. Even some Ottoman officers went to the monastery, stayed there overnight, spent leisure time, and contributed to the monastery's reconstruction in the seventeenth century after its destruction.[18] After the Balkan Wars, the monastery became an important reference point in the demarcation process between Albania and Serbia, later Yugoslavia.[19] In

---

13 Cf. Stefan Gatzhammer, 'Aspekte des religiös motivierten Tourismus in Europa heute. Motivationen, Ziele, Trends', in *Pilgern. Innere Disposition und praktischer Vollzug*, ed. by Johann Ev. Hafner et al. (Würzburg: Egron Verlag, 2012), pp. 253–54; Freyer, pp. 102–04.
14 Cf. Freyer, pp. 84–85.
15 Vihra Baeva, 'Parishioners, Pilgrims', p. 91.
16 Cf. Walter Freyer, *Tourismus. Einführung*, pp. 103–04.
17 Cf. Krenar Zgjani, personal communication (Pogradec, January 26, 2017).
18 Cf. Цветан Грозданов, *Свети Наум Охридски* (Скопје: Матица, 2015), p. 73.
19 Cf. Цветан Грозданов, p. 290.

1925, the issue was solved, and the monastery became part of Yugoslavia due to its meaning as cultural heritage for the Slavic Orthodox churches.

In 1950, the state expropriated the monastery, declared it as cultural heritage, and turned it into a museum.[20] Several new constructions like a restaurant, archeological excavations at the saint's tomb, and asphalting the street at the east coast of the lake boosted the change into a tourist destination. Moreover, monastic life was banned in favour of tourism: without monks no liturgies were celebrated, and lightning candles was forbidden. Instead, visitors had to pay entrance fee for visiting the museal church. However, according to several interlocutors the religious character has never vanished completely.

Fig. 1: The map gives an overview of the monasterial complex: (1) market and souvenirs, (2) toilets, (3) restaurant 'Drim', (4) restaurant 'Ostrovo', (5) hotel and restaurant 'Saint Naum', (6) monastery 'Saint Naum', (7) church 'Saint Petka', (8) springs of Black Drin, (9) church 'Saint Bogorodica', (10) church 'Saint Atanasij'. A stone wall marked red includes 5 and 6, and separates the inner and the outer area of the complex. The campground, the boat landing stage and the fair are not marked, 2016. Photograph by the author.

---

20 Cf. Стојан Ристески, *Чудата на свети Наум* (Охрид: Канео, 2009), p. 21.

After the state returned the monastery to the Macedonian Orthodox Church – Archdiocese of Ohrid (MOC) in the early 1990s, the MOC again emphasized the previous Christian character of the place. However, the touristic influence is still recognizable, because the administration of the monastery also kept the inventions of the Yugoslavian time and complemented them with some more measures. Furthermore, even monastic life is quite low, because only one monk has served in the monastery since 1991. In consequence, visitors can perceive the monastery as both, a pilgrimage as well as a tourist destination.

During my fieldwork, vacationers came from the Yugoslav successor states, from Bulgaria and Turkey, as well as from Western Europe. Especially, Orthodox people from the Balkan states or their descendants who had emigrated to Western Europe visited the monastery with stronger religious motivation. Most of them traveled individually and spend part of their holidays with relatives. There is also a large number of individual travelers from Western Europe without roots in the Balkans. Organized international travel groups come mainly from Turkey and the Netherlands. Like many Western European individual travelers, they are mostly religious and cultural tourists.

The Tomb as the Target of Pilgrimages and Religious Tourism

Historically and according to the inner spatial concept, Naum's tomb is the religious core of the monastery, and the main target for all visitors. As the tomb is located inside the monastery church, visiting the tomb can hardly be separated from visiting the church. The visitors' interests in the tomb and the church depend on their religious background and origin. Consequently, the clearest distinction between religious tourism and pilgrimage can be made in this part of the monastery.

Religious motivations for visiting the monastery and Christian Orthodox actions appear with varying intensity during Naum's summer and winter feasts. On Naum's winter feast, as well as its eve, the religious motivations and actions are more evident than in summer. On 3 July, religious motivations and actions mix with touristic ones. There are two reasons for this mixing: First, the summer feast marks a peak in the general tourist season from April to September, while the winter feast in January is outside the general tourist season. Secondly, 5 January is also the anniversary of Naum's death and the original feast.

Comparing both feasts, the visits on 5 January obviously are motivated by Christian Orthodox ideas, because all leisure activities that can be pursued in summer are missing. At the winter feast, all actions and objects are connected to the monastery church and are part of the symbolic tradition of the Christian Orthodox interpretation of the place. At the winter feast, only some people from the surrounding area especially Orthodox Macedonians visit the monastery to celebrate the feast day Divine Liturgy. On the eve of the feast, the abbot invites the visitors of the vespers for dinner. The dinner is served in the restaurant of the hotel that is usually closed in the winter season like the other parts of the monastic areal. The dinner is made according to the strict rules of the Lenten season before Christmas celebrated on 6 January.

On 5 January, most of the visitors of the liturgy are from North Macedonia, especially from Ohrid and some from larger cities like Skopje. In addition, there are also some guests from Albania. They can not speak Macedonian, but have to communicate with gestures and facial expressions to buy for example candles. In front of the courtyard, the visitors light candles before they enter the burial chapel to deposit money, oil and clothes and to hear the heartbeat of the saint. Afterwards, people crowd into the worship space, which is too small to accommodate all the guests. Those who reach the Naum icon also place money or a small, dried bunch of basil there. The fragrant scent of basil will honour the saint. The clergy also uses dried basil during the consecration of the water at the conclusion of the service in front of the church. After the consecration of water, blessed bread (Mac. *nafori*) and boiled wheat (Mac. *pčenica za slava*) are distributed among the participants. The breads were cut in the shape of a cross, and a sip of wine was poured into them. The participants filled bottles with consecrated water to take home.

The activities, which are oriented towards the ritual sequence of the church services, clearly show the religious motivations of the visitors, but only in the feast context. In contrast to the summer feast, no alternative leisure activities are offered that would suggest other motivations. Consequently, the visitors of the winter feast can be claimed to be believers (Maz. *vernici*) and pilgrims. Although the number of Orthodox people in North Macedonia statistically has increased, the number does not refer to 'convinced believers, but the number of traditional believers'.[21]

Furthermore, the assumption that the visits are mostly religiously motivated is encouraged by the attitude of the local population towards the weather conditions. The majority of the local population prefer not to leave their homes in cold, ice and snow. Even the introduction of the summer feast in 1727 was justified to protect the pilgrims from the bad weather conditions in winter.[22] Nevertheless, a couple from the neighbouring village of Peštani who visited the Naum monastery for the Eve Divine Liturgy on the winter feast said that neither the weather conditions nor the distance to the monastery posed insurmountable obstacles for them. In the past, when there were no buses or taxis, and many families had no car, they walked to the monastery in winter. They started the four-hour walk around midnight and reached the monastery around 5 am. This was in socialist Yugoslavia, when the monastery was used as a museum, and there was no clergy or Divine Liturgy. They emphasized that they walked at that time 'to honour' (Mac. *za čest*) the saint.

The few people who visited the monastery under difficult conditions can be interpreted as 'convinced believers'. Contrary to the etymological explanation of the Macedonian term *poklonenie*, the interlocutor's argumentation emphasizes the path to be overcome as relevant in order to reach the tomb. The path is not the goal, but its mastery has been part of the practice of veneration.

---

21 Zoran Matevski, 'Revitalization of monasticism in the Republic of Macedonia after the fall of communism', *The Sociological Review*, 12 (2011), p. 121.
22 Cf. Грозданов, p. 267; Max Demeter Peyfuss, *Die Druckerei von Moschopolis, 1731–1769. Buchdruck und Heiligenverehrung im Erzbistum Achrida* (Wien et al.: Böhlau, repr. 1996), p. 170.

During the winter feast, the visitors focus on the Christian Orthodox practices. Nevertheless, in the recent past, the tourist dimension increased slightly for this feast, because two boats cross the lake to the monastery on 5 January, although the boat traffic is suspended during the winter period.

The orthodox feast acts in July is identical to those in January. The festivities differ mainly in terms of the number of visitors. In addition, the main focus is even more on the tomb than in winter. The Divine Liturgy could hardly be attended by all visitors because the church is too small. More people attend the distribution of cooked wheat, bread and consecrated water after the Divine Liturgy in the larger courtyard. The distribution of these items is a short act which involves single visitors. Thus, it enables individual and sensual experiences alike at the tomb.

During the summer feast, there are more religiously interpreted activities inside the monastery complex, which deviate from the official perspective of the church representatives. For most visitors, the focus is on visiting the tomb that is connected with making votive offerings to the saint. Joan Pelushi, the Metropolitan from Korçë, explained that

> it's a [*sic!*] old belief like you offer something to God. Although it's not something Christian in the sense that we don't do sacrifice to, the blood is sacrifice. [...] So, the true offering at the Christian church is the holy Eucharist, the bloodless, without blood. [...] the people want to offer something. But [it is] not part of our Liturgy.[23]

A special type of votive offering is the offering of lambs. Although they are not slaughtered afterwards, the hegumen Nektrarij said, the lamb offering are remnants of Old Testament and pagan sacrificial rituals, or a Muslim influence.[24]

Those who give a lamb to the saint interpret their act as part of the worship practice, which has become a tradition over the centuries. For example, an interlocutor from Bitola who brought several lambs to the monastery every year emphasized that he considers this act as an expression of gratitude.[25] His statement is proven by the fact that he only came for this act. Although he identifies himself as an Orthodox Christian, he left the monastery grounds without having taken part in the Divine Liturgy. He feared that he and the lambs would become a tourist attraction if he got caught up in the mass of festival visitors.

Apart from the fact that walking around the church with the lambs may seem exotic to visitors from Western European countries, this practice gained additional tourist appeal through the musical accompaniment by a Roma band. Sometimes spectators spontaneously decide to lead a lamb around the church. The possibility to rent a lamb exists for all visitors, no matter if they come to the monastery for religious reasons or as religion tourists. Sometimes only the Roma musicians and their instruments in the monastery courtyard arouse the interest of the tourists.

---

23 Joan Pelushi, personal communication (Korçë, 4 August, 2016).
24 Cf. Otec Nektarij, personal communication (Saint Naum, 7 July, 2016).
25 Cf. Anonymous from Bitola, personal communication (Saint Naum, 2 July, 2016).

Then, the musicians play only for fun and people start dancing and donating money like at a wedding. Thus, in the inner area of the monastery, the interests of the religious and religion tourists overlap with the pleasure motivation of the holiday and leisure tourists.

The Yugoslavian efforts to transform the monastery into a tourist destination also affected the motivations for visiting the monastery among the Muslim population. An older Albanian Bektashi from a village near Resen, recalled that he had visited the Naum monastery with his family for the summer feast in his childhood. Then, the Bektashis perceived the monastery as their own. Those who did not go to the monastery could not afford it financially. Because of the distance between the Resen villages and the monastery, most of them stayed overnight at the monastery. Beyond the pragmatic argument the interlocutor emphasized the religious quality of staying overnight as 'good for the soul'. This reason clearly proves a religious motivation recognizable in further actions and interpretations that are in some points similar to those of the Christians.

The target of the Bektashis has also been the tomb inside the church. For venerating, they touched the tomb three times with their mouths. The interlocutor interpreted the green cloth on the tomb as a sign for a Bektashi grave. Unlike the Christians, the Bektashis did not walk around the church with lambs, but they gave money to the monastery. That Bektashis still visit the monastery is also known among some Christians. Stojan Risteski states in his book *Čudata na Sveti Naum* that the Bektashis put their shoes down before entering the monastery, go bowed into the church, and come out backwards facing the church.[26]

In general, less is known about the behaviour and motivations of Sunnis, especially among the Albanians of North Macedonia. According to Christians, Turks from North Macedonia call Naum 'our father'.[27] In contrast, the Turkish minority have their own legend identifying Naum with a pre-Ottoman missionary called Sarı Saltuk. Furthermore, there are some miracle stories about Turks and Albanians who were healed by Naum.[28] During the research, I rarely met anyone from these two groups who claimed to have come to the saint or the monastery for religious reasons. One was a Turkish-Albanian Sunni from Bitola who is married to a Macedonian Christian woman. Besides religious activities at the monasterial church, the couple primarily sold clothes and jewellery at the fair.

Sunni Roma from North Macedonia come with different motivations that are evident in stories from the local population.[29] In comparison, several Roma declared that they came to Naum because they have faith in him. Many lit candles and visited the grave, but only a few circled the church with a lamb. Thus, Roma can be ascribed clearer religious motivations than other Sunnis. In general, Romas are attributed with religious indifference and flexibility, but there are limits with regard to unambiguous

---

26 Cf. Ристески, *Чудата на свети Наум*, pp. 87–88.
27 Cf. Ристески, *Чудата на свети Наум*, p. 88.
28 Cf. Ристески, *Чудата на свети Наум*, p. 104.
29 Cf. Ристески, *Чудата на свети Наум*, pp. 77, 87.

Christian practices: None of the Sunni groups attended the feast liturgies nor did they make the sign of the cross.

The reasons given by Sunni visitors from Albania are even more complex. Among them, especially women married to Christians said that they visit churches, light candles, take part in the Divine Liturgy, and cross themselves. The majority of Sunni Albanians defined their visit as a pleasurable tradition that they continue to maintain. Even an imam from Pogradec emphasized that Muslims visit the Naum monastery because of curiosity and pleasure.[30] Two employees of the city administration in Pogradec said, Sunni people visit the monastery because of their religious tolerance.[31] Moreover, the monastery is located in a beautiful place and the feast with its fair is an attraction worth seeing.

While the main motivation for visitors from Southeastern Europe is to visit the tomb inside the church, international tourists are more often interested in art-history and architecture of the monastery. They mainly visit the monastery because it is mentioned in their travel guide as one of the most beautiful sights. This minimal information that international tourists have about the monastery influences their expectations. A family from Eastern Germany visited the monastery one day after the summer feast. Accommodated in Ljubaništa, the neighbouring village, they noticed that on the day before a crowd went to the monastery, but did not understand why. While visiting the church, they focused on the icons and frescoes. Due to the darkness and the damaged frescoes, they concluded that the entrance is not suitable for people with deteriorating eyesight.

These tourists associated a monastery with tranquillity and relaxation, and expected to experience authentic religious cultural heritage. One of the family members characterised the monastery as 'not so touristically overrun' and 'untouched', although the complex was 'overrun with tourists' during the feast – mainly by local tourists with religious interests and not by international cultural tourists. In addition, 'untouched' emphasizes the authenticity of the site that was preserved because of the lack of influence of western standards. However, the expressions referred to the historically grown cultural part and to the natural surroundings.

The information about the monasterial church that travelers get from travel guide books and groups get from their tour guides can vary greatly. A couple from Vienna travelling alone were very surprised about the celebrations on 2 and 3 July. They got information about the monastery from their travel guide that mentions only feasts in September and January. In other travel guides, even this information is missing.[32] Instead, the book offers a historical overview of the monastery, legends about the saint, and short information on how to get there, about accommodations, and restaurants.

In contrast, guided tour groups enjoy the advantage of receiving further information from the tour guide. Especially the guides of Turkish groups who inform

---

30 Cf. Dritan Shahu, personal communication (Pogradec, 31 July, 2016).
31 Cf. Arian Merolli and Avdulla Cana, personal communication (Pogradec, 26 January, 2017).
32 Cf. Philine von Oppeln, *Mazedonien. Unterwegs auf dem südlichen Balkan* (Berlin: Trescher Verlag, repr. 2018), pp. 134–35.

about the history of the monastery and about the legends from local Turkish people that creates a trans-national collective feeling linked to the Ottoman past, and an emotional-nostalgic relationship with the place. In addition, during the Yugoslavian period, parts of the Turkish minority emigrated to Turkey.[33] Now, some of their descendants are searching for traces of their origins.

In addition to the cultural motivations, especially the behaviour of international travelers reveals religious interests when visiting the monastery church. Even if they do not attend the Divine Liturgy, some put their ear to the grave out of curiosity. International travelers without roots in Southeastern Europe also take the opportunity to light candles. Probably, this act is founded in the well-known tradition of commemorating the dead in the Catholic Church.

The Place of Recreation and Leisure Activities

The outer area of the monasterial complex is perceived less religious than the inner core, although it is a historically established part of the monastery. The perception as a non-religious area for leisure time activities, is founded in the transformation of the monastery into a tourist destination in the second half of the twentieth century. Being turned into a museum, the religious dimension of the monastery was suppressed. However, the festivities at the beginning of July could persist as part of the local tradition. The state could hardly ban them without interfering too obviously with the self-determination and free creative power of the visitors. Due to the long absence of monks at the monastery, the feast lost its religious character and the outer area of the monasterial complex lost its religious significance as a festival area. Already during the Yugoslav period, the Saint Naum monastery was one of the 'most popular destinations of the Ohrid people and the numerous local and foreign tourists who come here from all sides every year'.[34] This process can be referred to as 'desacralisation' of religious places boosted by certain tourist activities 'such as partying'.[35] Consequently, the perception of the place and the activities are mutually dependent, and the outer area of the complex became more touristic.

The outer area consists of a natural and an artificial field for tourist activities. These fields are connected to the monastery core but are mainly an attraction for leisure and cultural tourism in summer. The natural field relates to the environment

---

33 Cf. Nathalie Clayer and Xavier Bougarel, *Europe's Balkan Muslims. A New History* (London: Hurst & Company, 2017), pp. 133–34.
34 Cf. Милчо Балевси, *Балканските политички прилики и дипломатските битки за манастирот Свети Наум* (Скопје: Македонска Книга 1984), p. 13.
35 Cf. Nataša Gregorič Bon, 'Secular Journeys, Sacred Places. Pilgrimage and Homemaking in Himarë/ Himara Area of Southern Albania', in *Pilgrimage, Politics and Place-Making in Eastern Europe. Crossing the Borders*, ed. by John Eade and Mario Katić (Farnham: Ashgate Publishing Limited, 2014), p. 148.

of the monastery.[36] This field includes for example the rock on which the monastery is built, the underground springs of the river Black Drin, the sandy beach. The monastery administration interferes insignificantly with the nature of the complex by mowing the lawn in the entrance area and planting single bushes in the green areas. The intervention in nature is especially evident in the garden that is separated from the outer area of the complex by high walls, and directly adjoins the buildings of the monastery and the monastery hotel.

This garden connects the inner religious and outer touristic areas in many ways. Due to the wall, the garden spatially belongs to the inner area, although no obvious religious activities take place in it. The garden serves as a recreational area, where vacation and leisure time tourists enjoy the waterfall installation, while visitors from the surrounding area use this site for picnic, a midday rest or an overnight stay during the feast. Furthermore, the peacocks roaming around the area between the entrance and the monastery church are another attraction.

This garden has a religious dimension too. Peacocks, a religious symbol originating from India, have become very popular in early Christian art and refer to paradise.[37] Etymologically, 'paradise' means enclosed park or garden, and was always associated with nature as an orderly creation in Christianity.[38] In addition, according to the legends, the surroundings of the monastery have been called paradise by God.[39] Even today, authors refer to the surroundings of the monastery as 'one of the biblical landscapes'.[40] This suggests that the monastery drew its religious character from the natural environment.

In nature outside the garden, attractions from the leisure time sector increase. The southern shore of the Lake Ohrid invites visitors to fish, and despite the low temperatures to swim because of the sandy beach. However, swimming at the monastery is not welcomed by strict Christian Orthodox believers for various reasons. They argue that not presenting someone's half-naked body is a matter of reverence and decency towards God, the saint and the monk at the monastery. Moreover, these believers argue that no one should go swimming on the saint's day because the danger of drowning is very high on this day. Another attraction linked to water are the boat trips to the springs of the Black Drin, which flows through Lake Ohrid. Bathing is not allowed there for safety reasons. There are strong currents where the water flows into the lake, the muddy ground near the springs or precautionary?, and

---

36 Cf. Sebastian Kempgen, 'Die Säulen in der Klosterkirche von Sveti Naum. Ein Projektbericht zur Digitalisierung des sprachlichen Kulturerbes in Makedonien', in *Wiener Slawistischer Almanach 83*, ed. by Bernhard Brehmer, Aage A. Hansen-Löve, and Tilmann Reuther (Berlin et al.: Peter Lang, 2019), p. 63.
37 Cf. Helmut Lother, *Der Pfau in der altchristlichen Kunst. Eine Studie über das Verhältnis von Ornament und Symbol* (Leipzig: Dieterich'sche Verlagsbuchhandlung, 1929), pp. 33–34, 84–85.
38 Cf. Daria Pezzoli-Olgiati, 'Paradies. I. Religionswissenschaftlich' in *Religion in Geschichte und Gegenwart. Handwörterbuch für Theologie und Religionswissenschaft* (N-Q) ed. by Hans Dieter Betz et al. (Tübingen: Mohr Siebeck, 2003), p. 909.
39 Cf. Ристески, *Чудата на свети Наум*, p. 56.
40 Cf. Грозданов, p. 10.

the risk of collisions with the boats. Bathing in connection with boat trips to another small monastery on the east coast of Lake Ohrid is less problematic, because there are no more monks to be disturbed.

Another place, whose significance shimmers between tourist and religious motivations, is the meadow to the left of the Saint Petka church. A musician from the Roma band recalled, in 2012, that there were tables and chairs in the meadow for eating, and music for dancing. However, the church forbad the 'spectacle' because drunks often started fights there. This meadow was called *ǵupana*, referring to *ǵupci* a common term for Roma in Macedonia, because they mainly stayed there in the past. During my field research, the meadow only served as a wild camping site for the Roma who ran stalls at the fair. In contrast to these statements and observations, which suggest less religious than economic motivations, there is also a Christian perspective that assumes the Roma had religious reasons for their actions: Like other groups, Roma once had their own shelter (Mac. *konak*) at this place.[41] They came to the Naum monastery mainly for the summer holiday, not for business, but to honor and respect Saint Naum. Roma helped with the feast preparations and cooked the food; they had committed themselves above all 'to health and progress'. They behaved like other believers, as it had been customary to commit oneself to a self-chosen church for certain services at a certain time. This self-commitment relates to a desire that people hoped would be fulfilled.

Thus, Roma have been considered to be an important part of the fair: 'without them, it does not look like a fair. With their music, song and dance they add a special beauty to the festivity and especially with their reverence for Sveti Naum'.[42] Music and dance vanished with the ban of the festivities on the *ǵupana* meadow. While the Roma band played mainly in the monastery courtyard and only occasionally made a little music at the fair, traditional music was played to invite people into the restaurant on the island. In the dining room of the hotel restaurant, neither a live band nor dance options were offered during the feast for reasons of piety.

The campground is an area of the outer monastic complex that has completely lost its religious connotation and has become part of the created touristic field. The campground was built during the time of Yugoslavia as a recreation centre for military staff. After Macedonia became independent, a part of the military recreation centre was made accessible to Macedonian citizens. The other part of this area is left for the recreation of military staff. Motivations for staying at this ground are not religious, although campers visit the monastery during their stay. The main purpose for staying at the campsite is relaxation which includes other leisure activities too. Nevertheless, entering the campsite on 2 and 3 July is linked to religious motivations, when it serves as a shortcut to the monastery for visitors from Albania. As many Albanian visitors, focus especially on having fun, crossing the campsite is not religiously motivated, therefore the campsite lacks any religious significance.

---

41 Cf. Ристески, *Чудата на свети Наум*, p. 170.
42 Cf. Ристески, *Чудата на свети Наум*, p. 171.

Fig. 2: The annual fair at Naum's feast in 2016. Photograph by the author.

Even other touristic activity fields in the outer area of the monastic complex lack religious motivations. Instead, the desire for fun (Mac. *kef*; Alb. *qejf*) becomes visible. The annual fair for the summer feast (Mac. *panagur*; Alb. *panair*) takes place in the square between the bridge over the Black Drin and the entrance to the inner area of the monastery, and between the landing stage of the boats and the *gupana* meadow. The location illustrates that the fair forms an intersection between religious and tourist motivations and activities. Apart from the offered non-religious goods, the fair has long been associated with the abovementioned exuberant celebrations of the *gupana* meadow.

For the local population, these details about the summer feast at the monastery are taken for granted. For travelers without roots in Southeastern Europe, who may visit the monastery coincidentally during their vacations, the festivities are big surprise: Tourists from Vienna stayed in the hotel of the monastery around the summer feast but were not prepared for the festivities. They had booked a few nights there and expected a quiet atmosphere, but not to find themselves in the middle of *Ohrider Wies'n* when they arrived on 2 July. The expression *Ohrider Wies'n* refers to the obvious parallels with folk festivals in Southern Germany and Austria such as the famous *Oktoberfest* in Munich. When they arrived from Albania, they were already surprised at the border by many people with their plastic sacks to carry their purchases from the fair home. Around 500-metres walk from the entrance of the complex to the hotel, it took thirty minutes by car, and almost ran over a bride's dress. The impression of the outer area named *Ohrider Wies'n* supports the thesis of the inner spatial order: The monastery has a religious core, and an outer area where religion is irrelevant. The festivities are more like a kermis with a religious core and all kinds of non-religious offerings than a devotional pilgrimage in honour of the saint. In contrast to some kermis festivals in German-speaking countries, only amusement rides are missing.

The artificial touristic field also includes the restaurants, the hotel and the year-round souvenir booths at the entrance of the complex. These buildings were created mainly during the Yugoslavian period, after the monastery was turned into a museum. The construction of the *Ostrovo* restaurant and hotel supported the transformation into a tourist destination, as did the development of the roads between Ohrid and the remote monastery. The MOC continued with the tourist trend and shaped tourism into a form acceptable for the religious context.[43]

Crossing the lake from Ohrid to the monastery by boat is an experience that especially international tourists enjoy. Sometimes tour operators use this route for big quite homogeneous groups, which then determine the events. Nevertheless, there are even religious motivated groups who choose the boat trip across the lake. In 2002, five clerics accompanied a group of 120 believers to the monastery as part of a faith course.[44] When the ship was caught in a storm, the passengers were frightened, and the clerics began to pray for the passenger's salvation. After the storm, the tour group spotted the Naum monastery, and one of the clerics reported, 'filled with sweet peace and deep joy, we offered gifts and a gift of the lips – appreciative songs to Saint Naum, because with his intercession before God we were saved from the terrible storm.' Thus, even the more touristic connotated lake crossing, can be claimed for Christian Orthodox motivations.

Travelers often combine a visit to the Naum monastery with a tour to the Galičica National Park, i.e. the mountain area between Lake Ohrid and Lake Prespa.[45] Some claim that this area had belonged to the monastery.[46] International tourists rarely know about this, and are more interested in hiking tours and the international nature protection project in which other countries besides North Macedonia and Albania are involved.

Conclusion: Between Pilgrimage and Sightseeing

The chapter has revealed an interplay of different motivations for visiting the monastery and linked the motivations with the spatial concept of the monasterial complex. The

---

43 Cf. Kempgen, p. 63.
44 Cf. Стојан Ристески, 'Шест записи за чуда на свети Наум', *Светиклиментово Слово* (2012), pp. 96–97.
45 Cf. Kempgen, p. 63.
46 Cf. Ристески, *Чудата на свети Наум*, pp. 115–16.

types of motivations and activities are assigned to one of the areas of the complex. In the focus of the inner area are religious interests and interests in religion as part of culture. In the outer area, the focus is on recreation and entertainment for the local population and international tourists. Almost all visitors can move effortlessly between the different areas because their manifold motivations match with the opportunities.

However, each visitor group in terms of their faith or origin has its own main motivations. Especially, the visitors from former Yugoslavia, Bulgaria and Albania cannot be clearly assigned to one category. On the one hand, referring to their nationality they belong to the international visitors. However, international guests especially from Western Europe pursue touristic motivations when visiting the monastery. On the other hand, the visitors from Southeastern Europe are emotionally connected to the monastery because of the shared history. For them, the monastery belongs to a homeland from the past. Orthodox Christians and Muslims from Southeastern Europe are religiously and touristy motivated for visiting the monastery and may have political-nostalgic feelings.

The complex results of the chapter oppose a mostly monochrome representation of the monastery. Perception and characterization of the monastery depends on the origin of the descriptors and show a broad variance. Contrary to the perception of Western travelers that the Saint Naum monastery is one of the most important sights, the monastery is considered a place of worship frequented by believers, especially on the saint's feast day. The feast is regularly and mostly anonymously reported in Macedonian newspapers. Rarely, the articles give new information, but quite often ignore the fair and tourists.

Various non-religious activities during the summer feast enrich the meaning of the monastery. However, the site never lost its religious significance. In the past, Saint Naum's reputation as a miracle worker and healer attracted pilgrims from the region, and nowadays the nature, the history, the architecture, and the art of the monastery increasingly attract international tourists. In addition, local people visit the monastery because of the feast and the annual fair as a trans-regional and nationally well-known event.

While the religious perspective emphasizes the miraculous healing power of the saint in his monastery as a 'holy place', the tourist perspective focusses on the relaxing effect of nature. Both perspectives have the idea of recreation in common. However, the understanding of what is considered recreative differs. While locals and Southeastern European visitors tend to prefer doing nothing, international tourists often aim for a varied holiday. Phases of physical activity and rest are just as much a part of such a holiday as the intellectual preoccupation with the history and culture of the travel region, which includes food, music, and dance.

The perception of the monastery influences the behaviour of visitors who reproduce their image of the place. Examining only the religious interpretation of visiting the monastery ignores its touristic dimension that is significant for a comprehensive analysis. Furthermore, the trans-religious and trans-ethnic contacts imply that there is a political dimension of visiting Saint Naum even today. Furthermore, the motivations and activities of visitors refer to the economic dimension of the monastery. This merging of the religious and the touristic, economic and political, therefore secular dimensions make the monastery an ambiguous place.

References

Ацо Гиревски, *Верски Туризам* (Скопје: Менора, repr. 2008).

Стојан Ристески, *Чудата на свети Наум* (Охрид: Канео, 2009).

Стојан Ристески, 'Шест записи за чуда на свети Наум', *Светиклиментово Слово* (2012), 96–99.

Daria Pezzoli-Olgiati, 'Paradies. I. Religionswissenschaftlich', in *Religion in Geschichte und Gegenwart. Handwörterbuch für Theologie und Religionswissenschaft* (N-Q) ed. by Hans Dieter Betz et al. (Tübingen: Mohr Siebeck, 2003), pp. 909–11.

Dionigi Albera and John Eade, 'Pilgrimage Studies in Global Perspective', in *New Pathways in Pilgrimage Studies. Global Perspektives*, ed. by Dionigi Albera and John Eade (London/New York: Routledge, 2016), pp. 13–29.

Evelyn Reuter, *Die Mehrdeutigkeit geteilter religiöser Orte. Eine ethnographische Fallstudie zum Kloster Sveti Naum in Ohrid (Mazedonien)* (Bielefeld: transcript, 2021).

Helmut Lother, *Der Pfau i der n altchristlichen Kunst. Eine Studie über das Verhältnis von Ornament und Symbol* (Leipzig: Dieterich'sche Verlagsbuchhandlung, 1929).

Jose Eduardo Chemin, 'Pilgrimage in a secular Age. Religious and Consumer Landscapes of Late-Modernity' (unpublished doctoral thesis, University of Exeter, 2011).

Konstantinos Giakoumis 'From Religious to Secular and Back Again. Christian Pilgrimage Space in Albania', *Pilgrimage, Politics and Place Making in Eastern Europe. Crossing the Borders*, ed. by John Eade and Mario Katić (Farnham: Ashgate Publishing Limited, 2014), pp. 103–18.

Markus Gamper and Julia Reuter, 'Pilgern als spirituelle Selbstfindung oder religiöse Pflicht? Empirische Befunde zur Pilgerpraxis auf dem Jakobsweg', in *Doing Modernity – Doing Religion*, ed. by Anna Daniel et al. (Wiesbaden: Springer Fachmedien, 2012), pp. 207–31.

Max Demeter Peyfuss, *Die Druckerei von Moschopolis, 1731–1769. Buchdruck und Heiligenverehrung im Erzbistum Achrida* (Wien et al.: Böhlau, 1996).

Милчо Балевси, *Балканските политички прилики и дипломатските битки за манастирот Свети Наум* (Скопје: Македонска Книга, 1984).

Nataša Gregorič Bon, 'Secular Journeys, Sacred Places. Pilgrimage and Homemaking in Himarë/Himara Area of Southern Albania', in *Pilgrimage, Politics and Place-Making in Eastern Europe. Crossing the Borders*, ed. by John Eade and Mario Katić (Farnham: Ashgate Publishing Limited, 2014), pp. 135–49.

Nathalie Clayer and Xavier Bougarel, *Europe's Balkan Muslims. A new History* (London: Hurst & Company, 2017).

New Pathways in Pilgrimage Studies. Global Perspektives, ed. by Dionigi Albera and John Eade (London/New York: Routledge, 2016).

Philine von Oppeln, *Mazedonien. Unterwegs auf dem südlichen Balkan* (Berlin: Trescher Verlag, repr. 2018).

Polina Tšerkassova, 'Sterilization and Re-Sacralization of the Places of Secular Pilgrimage. Moving Monuments, Meanings and Crowds in Estonia', in *Pilgrimage, Politics and Place Making in Eastern Europe. Crossing the Borders*, ed. by John Eade and Mario Katić (Farnham: Ashgate Publishing Limited, 2014), pp. 119–33.

Sebastian Kempgen, 'Die Säulen in der Klosterkirche von Sveti Naum. Ein Projektbericht zur Digitalisierung des sprachlichen Kulturerbes in Makedonien', in *Wiener Slawistischer Almanach 83*, ed. by Bernhard Brehmer, Aage A. Hansen-Löve, and Tilmann Reuther (Berlin et al.: Peter Lang, 2019), pp. 61–79.

Stefan Gatzhammer, 'Aspekte des religiös motivierten Tourismus in Europa heute. Motivationen, Ziele, Trends', in *Pilgern. Innere Disposition und praktischer Vollzug*, ed. by Johann Ev. Hafner et al. (Würzburg: Egron Verlag, 2012), pp. 253–70.

Цветан Грозданов, *Свети Наум Охридски* (Скопје: Матица, 2015).

Victor Turner, 'The Center out There. Pilgrim's Goal', in *History of Religions*, 12 (1973), 191–230.

Victor Turner, *Dramas, Fields, and Metaphors: Symbolic Action in Human Society* (Ithaca, London: Cornell University Press, 1974).

Vihra Baeva, 'Parishioners, Pilgrims, Tourists. The Visitors of an Orthodox Christian Shrine in Sofia', in *Pilgrimage and Sacred Places in Southeast Europe. History, Religious Tourism and Contemporary Trends*, ed. by Mario Katić et al. (Wien: LIT Verlag, 2014) pp. 79–95.

Walter Freyer, *Tourismus. Einführung in die Fremdenverkehrsökonomie* (Berlin et al.: De Gruyter Oldenbourg, repr. 2015).

Zoran Matevski, 'Revitalization of monasticism in the Republic of Macedonia after the fall of communism', *The Sociological Review*, 12 (2011), 115–27.

ZORAN LADIĆ

The Phenomenon of Pilgrimages on the East Adriatic Coast between the Middle of the Thirteenth and the End of the Fifteenth Centuries

Introduction

The contours of the phenomenon of pilgrimaging in Croatia may be traced several centuries before Croats settled in their contemporary homeland. The first written document related to pilgrimaging in the Holly Land through the continental Croatia (Slavonia) comes from the late Antique Period as testified by the anonymous pilgrim from Bordeaux in the first extant West European written pilgrim diary from 334–335.[1] The practice of pilgrimaging through Croatia continued in the Medieval Period and reached its peak in the Late Middle Ages. From the aspect of pilgrimaging, the entire medieval Kingdom of Croatia, Dalmatia, and Slavonia was situated on a very important geographical and strategic position. Some of the most important pilgrim European land routes led through medieval Slavonia (e.g. *via Danubia, Via Militaris*). The antique Roman land route leads from Senj through Croatian and Dalmatian hinterland towards the city and port of Durrës in Albania where it joined with *via Egnatia*. All of these land roads lead to Constantinople, Palestine, and Saint Catherine on Sinai. Yet, much more frequently *palmieri* used naval routes leading from Venice to Palestine ports of Jaffa, Acre, and some other in order to visit pilgrim shrines in *Terra sancta*, Jerusalem, Constantinople, and Saint Catharine on Sinai. In the High and Late Middle Ages, besides Rome as old pilgrim centre, many new pilgrim shrines were established on the Apennine peninsula next to the

---

1 That diary is important for the research of pilgrim land roads, stations, and mansions in the continental part of Croatia that is in medieval Slavonia. The East Adriatic coast is never mentioned in that travelogue. For the published version of itinerary see *Itinerary from Bordeaux to Jerusalem. The Bordeaux pilgrim (333 A. D.)* (London: ADAM Street Adelphi 1887), https://archive.org/details/cu31924028534158/page/n11/mode/2up (accessed on 21.02.2021).

Zoran Ladić • PhD, Research Coordinator in tenure at Department for Historical Sciences of the Croatian Academy of Sciences and Arts in Zagreb, Croatia

Pilgrimage in the Christian Balkan World: The Path to Touch the Sacred and Holy, ed. by Dorina Dragnea, Emmanouil Ger. Varvounis, Evelyn Reuter, Petko Hristov and Susan Sorek (Turnhout, 2023), pp. 109–129.
BREPOLS PUBLISHERS   DOI 10.1484/M.STR-EB.5.132402

new cult of saints such as Saint Francis in Assisi or Saint Anthony in Padua, as well as Marian shrines such as Loreto and Recanati. Naval routes from East Adriatic to pilgrim shrines on the Apennine peninsula started in the ports of Senj, Zadar, and Split. The both naval routes, those from Venice to the Holy Land and those from East Adriatic ports towards West Adriatic ports (Brindisi, Bari, Manfredonia, Fano, Ancona, Pesaro, and Rimini) were used by many Western European, Central European, and domestic pilgrims.[2]

Sources

There are many written proofs (in diaries, chronicles, and travel accounts written by educated Western European pilgrims) describing urban, social, ecclesiastical, cultural, intellectual, economic, and artistic contacts between European pilgrims and East Adriatic inhabitants. Such contacts, most often expressed through peaceful communication and exchange of constructive ideas, influenced the growth in the number of East Adriatic pilgrims to Jerusalem as *locus sanctissimus* among all Christian pilgrim shrines. Yet, these narrative sources usually do not give testimonies on pilgrimages of East Adriatic pilgrims traveling neither towards the oriental pilgrim sites nor towards the Apennine peninsula or some other West European pilgrim centre such as Santiago in Compostela, Aachen, and so on.[3] Regrettably, until the first half of the sixteenth century, there is no extant Croatian narrative source (chronicle or diary) related to pilgrimages of pilgrims originating from the eastern Adriatic coast.[4]

For the purpose of the analysis of pilgrimage of inhabitants of the East Adriatic communes as a form of religious spatial mobility to various late medieval pilgrim

---

2 There was a third *via* used by the late medieval Western and some of Central European *romei* travelling to Rome usually by *via Francigena* (more western land road beginning in Canterbury) or by *via Allemagna* (more eastern road towards the Apennine peninsula). These two roads joined near Venice. From there went *via Apia* leading *ad limina apostolorum Petri et Pauli* in Rome and even further to Otranto. There, some pilgrims travelled on Venetian galleys to *Terra sancta*. See Luigi Oliva, 'The Apian via', in *The Way to Jerusalem*, ed. by Anna Trono (Lecce: University of Salento Lecce – Department of Cultural Heritage, 2013), pp. 33–38.

3 However, some East Adriatic narratives and legal sources provide very valuable information regarding the phenomenon of pilgrimaging in medieval East Adriatic urban and rural settlements. It will be shown in the chapter that this is particularly the case with local statutes and foreign travelogues.

4 The first extant travelogue in Croatia was written by Georg Husz from the village of Rasinja near the city of Varaždin, who was taken into Turkish captivity after Suleyman's siege of Kőszeg in 1532. 'Descriptio peregrinationis Georgii Huszthii', ed. by Petar Matković, *Starine JAZU*, vol. 13 (1881), pp. 1–38; *Opis putovanja Jurja Husa. Descriptio peregrinationis Georgii Huszthii*, ed. by Mario Kolar, trans. by Zrinka Blažević, foreword by Irena Radej Miličić (Koprivnica: Društvo hrvatskih književnika. Podravsko-prigorski ogranak 2017). In the middle of the sixteenth century, Dubrovnik's pilgrim Bartol Đurđević wrote second oldest Croatian pilgrim diary *Specchio della peregrinatione delli più notabili luoghi della Terra santa di Promessione, Et delle processioni, et cerimonie, che nella città di Hierusalem si sogliono celebrare*. Irena Miličić, 'Teoretičari, hodočasnici, činovnici: tri vrste renesansnih putopisnih tekstova', in *Povijesni prilozi* 38 (2010), pp. 45–53.

shrines as mirrored I will examine another type of sources – last wills. I have examined a few thousand of late medieval last wills from Istrian and Dalmatian communes recorded by communal public notaries. The main reason for using the last wills as primary source in researching of that problem is in the fact that in the period from the second half of the thirteenth until the end of the fifteenth century last wills give most information regarding the practice of pilgrimaging from the East Adriatic coast. It was a consequence of the fact that the recording of these types of private legal documents became habit accepted by male and female inhabitants in East Adriatic communes (*communa*) from all social layers starting from the middle of the thirteenth century and flourishing during the fourteenth and the fifteenth century. Due to their formulaic content and several types of data found in almost all of them, last wills are known as serial type sources. These include name and surname, social status, profession, place of origin, and gender. Consequently, quantitative analysis can be applied when dealing with a substantial number of wills. In addition, since wills of the examined period were equally structured in all East Adriatic communes as private-legal documents, a comparative analysis of them is also applicable. They were composed equally for men and women settled within the city walls (*civitas*) and for those living in the villages in the communal countryside (*districtus*). The manner of writing of last wills was legally confirmed and corroborated by numerous decrees in the statutes of all Istrian and Dalmatian communes. According to these statutory decrees the habit of composing of this type of documents was allowed equally to male and female communal denizens. For that reason, the number of last wills composed for male and female testators in East Adriatic communes was almost equal. Another important factor was in the appearance of the institution of communal notaries and notarial chancelleries in the beginning of the thirteenth century as well as in the gender and social democratization in recording of last wills in the late medieval East Adriatic communes. Finally, it should be underlined that the number of last wills of denizens of the East Adriatic communes increased from decade to decade and for almost all communes there are extant hundreds (Šibenik, Trogir, Rab), and sometimes thousands of late medieval wills (Zadar, Dubrovnik).

The East Adriatic Pilgrimages from the Middle of the Thirteenth until the End of the Fifteenth Century

The First Known Data about Croatian Pilgrims from East Adriatic

In the early Medieval Period, the Croatian pilgrims to *loca sacra* were the members of the elite class of medieval lay and spiritual Croatian society (rulers, their wives, and members of their nuclear families, magnates, and some members of clergy) pilgrimaging to Cividale on the Apennine peninsula in the ninth and the tenth centuries, and personally signed their names in the Evangeliarium from Cividale.[5]

---

5   *Hrvati i Karolinzi. Dio prvi. Rasprave i vrela*, ed. by Ante Milošević (Split: Muzej hrvatskih arheooškich starina, 2000), p. 100.

Their signatures were written in the well-known *Codex Aquileiensis*. On fol. 5^v of the *Evangeliarium* from Cividale signature of the Croatian duke *Tripimiro* was written. On fol. 23^r the signatures of his son Peter and Presila, most probably the member of Trpimir personal suite (*† Presila. Petrus, filius domno Tripemero*), and on the fol. 102^v there were written the signature of duke Branimir and his wife Maruša (*† Brannimero comiti. Mariosa cometissa*).[6] Naturally, Cividale (Aquileia) should be observed as one of the centres from which Christianity spread among Croats. In that period there is still no extant data regarding the pilgrims from the lower strata of Croatian society. Pilgrimages led by rulers during that time had deep symbolic, political, and religious significance. Same, pilgrimages performed by Croatian rulers and members of their courts and families can be considered a practical move to confirm the state's belonging to *universitas Christiana*. The earliest Dalmatian data related to the pilgrimage to the one of three West European *peregrinationes maiores* – Jerusalem – was recorded by Ragusan chronicler Junius Restić and dated back in 843 when a certain priest John (*nominato Giovanni*) *Arbanese* (i.e. Albanian) returned from a pilgrimage in Jerusalem and Egypt on *una galera Veneziana, tornando d' Eggito*.[7] According to Junius Restić, priest John brought to Dubrovnik a certain relic in *una cassettina piccola e ben serrata*. Restić wrote that a small chest was kept in the church of Saint Blaise and from 1040 in the palace of the archbishop of Dubrovnik. Then the chest was opened and, as reported by Restić, it kept *il Pannicello, nel quale fu involto dalla B. Vergine Christo, Nostro Signore, bambino, con tutte le autentiche necessarie*.[8] That relic was later *riposto nel tesoro pubblico, dove le altre reliquie si conservavano*.[9] Unfortunately, Restić's information is the only one from Dalmatia, besides the above mentioned *Codex Aquileiensis*, related to the early medieval East Adriatic pilgrimages to Jerusalem.

Research of East Adriatic Pilgrimage Phenomenon based on the Data from Last Wills, Codicils, and breviaria testamentorum

Until the middle of the thirteenth century, there are no extant data in the last wills regarding the pilgrimages from the eastern Adriatic coast. Only after the establishment of communal public notary offices from the middle of the thirteenth century did the practice of recording private-legal documents spread among denizens of East Adriatic communes, first among the inhabitants of cities and soon after among the villagers from communal districts. In that period appeared the most important type

---

6 *Hrvati i Karolinzi*... ed. by Ante Milošević, p. 100.
7 Natko Nodilo, 'Chronica Ragusina Junii Restii (ab origine urbis usque ad annum 1451) item Joannis Gundulae (1451–1484)', *Monumenta spectantia historiam Slavorum Meridionalium*, vol. XXV, *Scriptores*, vol. II, (Zagrabiae: In taberna libraria eiusdem societatis typographicae 1893), p. 21.
8 Natko Nodilo, 'Chronica Ragusina', p. 21.
9 Natko Nodilo, 'Chronica Ragusina', p. 22.

of sources for the research of the phenomenon of pilgrimages – last will,[10] codicil,[11] and *breviarium testamenti*, first in Zadar, Trogir, Dubrovnik, and Kotor, and from the beginning of the fourteenth century in all other communes.[12] Like the wills of other communal and urban societies on the shores of the North Mediterranean (e.g. France, Italy), East Adriatic last wills are useful sources for the investigation of many historical issues, particularly those related to everyday life. Among other things, the East Adriatic last will make possible the study of different aspects of the religious life of the citizens, both in the urban as well as in the rural societies.

There are two forms of pilgrimages appearing in the last wills, not only East Adriatic but generally European, in the period from the middle of the thirteenth until the end of the fifteenth century: personal and substitutionary pilgrimages. While testators' departures on personal pilgrimages were the main reason for recording the last wills, substitutionary pilgrimages were usually mentioned as legacies in the wills of sick persons unable to go on a personal pilgrimage for the salvation of their souls, of the souls of their parents, children, and some other members of their nuclear family.[13]

---

10 Late medieval Eastern Adriatic communal statutes contain many decrees related to last wills and in some of the statutes even separate books were recorded concerning juridical aspects of last wills (so called *Libri testamentorum*). The common features of all East Adriatic statutes were the prohibition of recording the last wills for psychically or mentally ill (*mentecaptus*) or drunken persons. The composing of last wills was forbidden by the decrees from all statutes to underage boys and girls (so-called *illegitime aetatis*; girls became of mature age between 12 and 14 and boys between fourteen and sixteen).

11 In short, codicils were afterward supplemented or modified last wills following the wish of testators.

12 *Breviarium testamenti* was the last will most often composed in the villages of communal districts. They were recorded by local priests or chaplains as the only literate persons in the presence of two witnesses (male or female). According to the statutory decrees, the priest and witnesses were obliged to bring that document to the communal notary in the period between 15 and 30 days. In the notary office, they swear in front of the notary and the examinator as a representative of the communal authorities that the document is recorded according to the last wish of the testator. The copy of the *breviarium testament* was also written and kept in the chancellery of the communal procurator. The *breviarium testament* was usually written for inhabitants of the villages in the communal districts which were sick at the moment of composing their wills (*iacens in lecto, corpore infirmus/infirma, senectute grauatus/grauata*, and so on). Therefore, the testators were not able to personally come to the notarial chancellery in the city.

13 Substitutionary and *ex-voto* pilgrimages were taken very seriously in the Medieval Period. Only occasionally and in certain extraordinary circumstances they were not performed. Some examples, such as that from the commune of Hvar in 1430, show the seriousness of substitutionary pilgrimages. In the above mentioned year certain Dobroslav *Cethcutouich* from Hvar, by invoking the testimonies of two witnesses – Mikšin Utišinović and Mladin Utišinović, proved before the communal court, that he executed the legacy of his wife Jera and performed a pilgrimage to Rome. Above mentioned witnesses confirmed that they saw Dobroslav in Rome 'with their own eyes'. See Mirko Zjačić, 'Regeste pergamena XV vijeka Kaptolskog arhiva u Hvaru', *Bilten Historijskog arhiva Komune hvarske*, god. (VI–VII), br. (7–8), (1965), p. 14. We might note the same thing about Nicholas Chauzeuich, a member of Dubrovnik's merchant colony in Novo Brdo on Kosovo, who took a vow to make the pilgrimage to Jerusalem, but was unable to do so. For that reason, in one written document he asked Pope Paul II to resolve him from the given vow, and Pope fulfilled Nicholas 'request. Jadranka Neralić, *Put do crkvene nadarbine – rimska Kurija i Dalmacija u 15. Stoljeću* (Split: Književni krug, 2007), p. 365.

On Religious Destinations of High and Late Medieval East Adriatic Pilgrims

The first East Adriatic pilgrims who broke the above mentioned narrow social frame characteristic for the early medieval pilgrimages were the members of the wealthy layers of patricians from the communes on the East Adriatic coast. One of the first known East Adriatic personal pilgrimages is mentioned in the last will from 1291 and recorded for Thomas de Penaço, the patrician of Zadar.[14] Thomas composed his last will in the same year when the last Christian fort in the Holy Land – Acre – fell under the dominion of the Seljuks. In 1295 another patrician of Zadar, Vid, son of Črne de Galellis, recorded his last will *per Dei gratiam conpos mentis et corporis, intendens domino Iesu Christo concedente me cum tribus galeis Venetis ad longinquas partes transferre*, that is because of personal pilgrimage or maybe because of the crusade on the Venetian galley to the Holy Land.[15] As a consequence of the fall of all Christian forts in the hands of Seljuks, the papal curia regularly invited rulers, magnates, noblemen, patricians, and all other believers to join the crusaders in their goal *ad liberandum Terra sancta*. Thomas' last will is likely the reflection of these historical circumstances not only because of the date of recording of his will but also because he was *sanus corpore* and because he indicated his main testamentary wish – *intendens ire ultra mare*[16] – probably to join crusader army as a *miles Christi* which was expected in Holy Land in that period. Crusades in *Terra sancta* from the end of the eleventh until the end of the thirteenth century was almost regularly named as *peregrinatio in subsidium Terre sancte, expeditio ad Terram sanctam i.e. Palestinam liberandam, bellum militum Cruce signatorum* or *passagium de ultra mare contra infideles*. At the same time, crusaders were called *milites Christi* and *peregrini cruce signati*, and crusade army *militia Christi*. Same as other pilgrims, crusaders received eternal indulgences from all their sins.[17] Even later, during the Ottoman raid in South-Eastern Europe in the fifteenth and the sixteenth century, appeared

---

14   *Spisi zadarskih bilježnika Henrika i Creste Tarallo 1279–1308*, ed. by Mirko Zjačić (Zadar: Državni arhiv u Zadru, 1959), doc. 32, 66.
15   Serđo Dokoza, 'Inventar fonda don Kuzme Vučetića u Državnom arhivu u Zadru', *Prilozi povijesti otoka Hvara*, vol. (XI), (2002), 256–60.
16   Ibid., 256–60.
17   Roberto Lopez, *Rođenje Evrope: stoljeće V–XIV* (Zagreb: Školska knjiga, 1978), p. 230; Petar Skok, *Tri starofrancuske hronike o Zadru u godini 1202* (Zagreb: JAZU, 1951), p. 47. For example, Andrew II Árpád, the King of Hungary-Croatia went on *peregrinatio ad liberandum Terre Sancte* participating in the Fifth crusade (1217–1221). The king and his army, composed of most powerful Hungarian and Croatian magnates, started their *peregrinatio* in Hungary near the lake of Balaton and after that, the army travelled by so-called *via exercitualis* passing through Zagreb, Bihać, Knin finally arriving in the port of Split as the last station of this ancient land road. From Split, the crusader army went to the Holy Land after King Andrew chartered ten Venetian galleys and around forty other ships for the transport of his army to Palestine. See Krešimir Kužić, 'Kojim su brodovima 1217. godine prevezeni križari kralja Andrije II', *Radovi Zavoda za povijesne znanosti HAZU u Zadru*, (46), (2004), pp. 96–102; Zoran Ladić, 'Odjek pada tvrđave Accon 1291. u Hrvatskoj. O križarskoj vojni kao vidu hodočašća', *Zbornik Odsjeka za povijesne znanosti Zavoda za povijesne i društvene znanosti HAZU*, (16), (1998), pp. 43–56.

the same idea of crusades *contra infideles Turchos*.[18] Prior, and especially after the fall of the Kingdom of Bosnian 1463, Croatia and Dalmatia were threatened *de manibus impiorum*, i.e. from the Ottoman military units called *akinjdis*. It is interesting that all West European pilgrim diaries from that period testify and warn about the Ottoman threat in the East Adriatic. They also testify that the period understood as *pax Christiana* and *cultura religionis Christiane*, the ideals of Western Christianity from the eleventh until the thirteenth century, irrevocably passed. In the late Medieval and the Early Modern Period the new ideas in western Christianity – the ideas of newly divided ethnic kingdoms, states, and smaller political units were deeply rooted instead of one universal Christian Empire.[19]

In the same 1291 year, the first female last will mentioning personal pilgrimage was recorded in Zadar. In that year Zadar citizen Mary, wife of the late John and mother of the late Nicholas, a priest in the cathedral church of Saint Anastasia in Zadar, wrote her will intending to personally *uisitare limina beatorum apostolorum Petri, Pauli et Iacobi de Galicia*.[20] Thus, Mary had decided to go on a rather long voyage to distant Rome and then even farther to St James in Compostela in Spain to visit two of the most popular late medieval Christian shrines and pilgrim destinations in addition to Jerusalem.[21] Mary's last will also witnesses the beginning of the process of

---

18 During the fifteenth century, numerous last wills were recorded because the testators decided to join the Venetian or Croatian armies against the Ottoman *akindjias*. For example, in April 1463 Radoslav, *famulus magistri cerdonis Petri Clum*, from the city of Rab, composed his last will *desponens se ire contra Turchos et infidelles pro fide Christiana et pro salutis anime sue*. Državni arhiv u Zadru (henceforth: HR-DAZd); fond Rapski bilježnici (henceforth: RB), Toma Stančić (henceforth: TS), kut. 2, sv. XI, fol. 37a. On the same date certain George, *filius Vlatchi Belotich de Scrixa* (i.e. Karlobag) *desponens se ire contra Turchos et infidelles pro fide Christiana et pro salutis anime sue*, composed his last will. HR-DAZd, RB, TS, kut. 2, sv. XI, fol. 37ᵃ. There are several other last wills recorded by Rab's and by Šibenik's notaries for young immigrants from Croatia on the island of Rab and in the commune of Šibenik during the second half of the fifteenth century.
19 On the early medieval ideas of *pax Christiana* and *cultura religionis Christiane* see Tomaž Mastnak, *Križarski mir. Kršćanstvo, muslimanski svijet i zapadni politički poredak* (Zagreb: Prometej, 2005), pp. 104–24.
20 *Maria Iadratina, uxor condam Iohannis … in(ten)dens (uisi)tare limina beatorum apostolorum Petri et Pauli et Iacobi de Galicia. Spisi zadarskih bilježnika Henrika*, doc. 33, p. 66.
21 It is worth mentioning that pilgrimages to the shrine of Saint James in Compostela were particularly popular among the denizens of the commune of Šibenik and Zadar. Namely, St James played important role in the religious life of these two communes. He was the saintly protector of Šibenik (*patronus et protector commune et civitatis Sibenici*), the cathedral church in Šibenik was consecrated to Saint James the Apostle, and the fraternity of Saint James in Compostela was one of the most important fraternities in the late medieval commune of Šibenik. The first East Adriatic Confraternity dedicated to Saint James the Apostle in Spain was founded in Zadar at the beginning of the thirteenth century. Therefore, many denizens of the late medieval Šibenik and Zadar communes travelled to his saintly shrine in distant Compostela in Spain. The first recorded data on Zadar's pilgrimages comes from 1291 in the will of Mary, wife of the late John and mother of the late Nicholas, a priest in the cathedral church of Saint Anastasia. Mirko Zjačić, *Spisi zadarskih bilježnika Henrika i Creste Tarallo 1279–1308., Spisi zadarskih bilježnika* 1. Zadar: Državni arhiv u Zadru, 1959, doc. 33, pp. 66–67. Mary wrote her will with the intention to *uisitare limina beatorum apostolorum Petri, Pauli et Iacobi de Galicia*. Ibid., p. 66. Thus, Mary had decided to go on a rather long voyage to distant Rome and then even farther to Saint James de Compostela in Spain in order to visit two of the most popular late medieval Christian shrines and pilgrim destinations in addition to Jerusalem. Andrew Tičić,

growing of female personal spatial mobility from eastern Adriatic communes under the cloak of piety and new legal provisions (based on communal statutory law and the decrees of Canon law). Another Zadar's will from that period also testifies to the custom of going on pilgrimages to some other, in that period less important, pilgrim centres.[22] Yet, in contrast to the first two recorded personal pilgrimages, this one was substitutionary. In her will from 1292, the Zadar's patrician Dominica, daughter of the late Simon de Mauro, bequeathed money to be given by the executors of her will to a person willing to go on pilgrimage for the salvation of her soul *ad sanctam Mariam de Angelis* (i.e. *Portiuncula*) in Assisi which was the pilgrim shrine of one of the most popular high and late medieval saints – Saint Francis as well as popular Marian pilgrim center.[23] This is the first recorded mention of a pilgrimage to Assisi in Zadar's sources and also indicates the opening point of the growing popularity of the cult of Saint Francis among East Adriatic believers only a few decades after his canonization. These three examples tell us about the main pilgrimage directions of Zadar's pilgrims in the specific historical and religious circumstances at the end of the thirteenth and the beginning of the fourteenth centuries.

According to the data from Zadar's last wills during the fourteenth and in the very beginning of the fifteenth century there were 110 personal and substitutionary pilgrimages from Zadar to various saintly shrines. The most popular pilgrim centres among the denizens of the commune of Zadar were *limina apostolorum Petri and Pauli* in Rome, primarily because of proclamations of Jubilees in 1300, 1350, and 1400. Almost equally popular were the pilgrim centers in Jerusalem and the Holy Land as well as Saint James in Compostela. There were 50 personal and substitutionary pilgrimages to Rome. The number of pilgrimages to Assisi, *ad sanctam Mariam de Angelis*, also increased (two personal and nine substitutionary) which illustrates the growing popularity not only of the cult of Saint Francis but also of mendicant orders among the inhabitants of East Adriatic cities and their idea of 'laic and social' Christianity expressed in religious and moral categories of *caritas et misericordia*.

---

the citizen of Šibenik, composed his last will in 1452 *corpore sanus prefecturus uisitatum ecclesiam sancti Iacobi de Galicia*, see HR-DAZd, Spisi šibenski bilježnika (henceforth: SŠB), Karatus Vitale (henceforth: KV), kut. 16/II, sv. 15.Iva, fol. 15ʳ. Kate Radinović, the citizen of Šibenik, recorded her will in 1456 *sana corpore* and because she decided to *uisitare limina ecclesie sancti Iacobi de Galicia*, see HR-DAZd, SŠB, KV, kut. 16/II, sv. 15.Iva, fol. 88ᵛ. There are many other mentions of pilgrimages to the shrine of Saint James the Apostle in late medieval Istrian and Dalmatian communes, illustrating the popularity of that pilgrimage site among the people who live in East Adriatic settlements.

22   In the Late Medieval Period, the number of pilgrim centres significantly increased. After the first Jubilee, the market of saintly relics in Rome reached the peak of its productivity. The growing market of relics and their importance in everyday life significantly supported the economic development of many European late medieval urban settlements. This caused the creation of a network of numerous European pilgrim centres and caused the change in the meaning of *peregrinationes minores* and *peregrinationes maiores*. Late medieval pilgrim centres such as Assisi, Mariazell, Aachen, Loreto, Recanati, Bari, the monastery of Saint Catherine on the mount of Sinai, and some other pilgrim shrines were also considered as *peregrinationes maiores*. See Bernhardt Schimmelpfennig, 'Die Regelmässigkeit mittelalterlicher Wallfahrt', in *Wallfahrt und Alltag im Mittelalter und früher Neuzeit*, Band XIV, ed. by Harry Kühnel (Wien: Verlag der österreichischen Akademie der Wissenschaften, 1992), pp. 81–94.

23   *Spisi zadarskih bilježnika Henrika*, doc. 36, pp. 69–70.

The pilgrimages to Assisi from other East Adriatic communes in the late medieval period also significantly increased. In the period between 1346 and 1348, there were 88 testators from Dubrovnik donating monetary legacies for pilgrimages to various pilgrim centres. The centres where Dubrovnik testators went on personal pilgrimage or bequeathed legacies for substitutionary ones may be divided into three main groups according to their distance from Dubrovnik. In the first group are the most distant places such as Saint James in Compostela and Rome. In the second group are those pilgrim centers located in Italy that were more easily accessible than Rome, such as Assisi, Bari, and *Mons Sancti Angeli* in Apulia. Pilgrim centres belonging to the third group were established on the eastern Adriatic coast in the neighborhood of Dubrovnik, for instance, Saint Blaise in Kotor and Saint Mary in Ulcinj. The reason that Rome was the most popular as a pilgrimage centre among the Dubrovnik testators (thirty-three legacies) from the middle of that century was in their expectation of the *pardono grande* for all sins in the year 1350. For example, Ann, wife of Junio de Lucari, bequeathed ten ducats *una bona persona che uada per l'anima mia alo pardono grande de Roma*.[24] Near to Rome in terms of their popularity were three other Italian pilgrimage centers, Saint Nicholas in Bari (seventeen legacies), *Mons Sancti Angeli* (twenty-two legacies), and the shrine of Saint Francis in Assisi (seven legacies). One of the obvious reasons that these three centres were so popular was in the fact they were relatively close pilgrim shrines to Dubrovnik. While Saint Francis was generally one of the most popular saints in late medieval Europe, Saint Nicholas was popular among the Dalmatians because of his central role as the protecting saint of mariners which was one of the most frequent and important professions of the East Adriatic denizens. Many of the Dubrovnik testators, keeping in mind the proximity of pilgrim shrines in Bari and *Mons Sancti Angeli*, bequeathed one legacy to be given to a person wanting to go on pilgrimage to both of these places during the same voyage.[25] The greater distance of Saint James in Compostela and the high cost of travel were the main reasons for a relatively small number of bequests donated for the pilgrimages to this centre (three legacies). Even so, these legacies testify to the popularity of the cult of Saint James the Apostle in Compostela among the late medieval Dubrovnik testators.[26] Besides these international pilgrimage centers, two regional centers were mentioned in the wills of Dubrovnik testators from that period. But, pilgrimaging

---

24 Državni arhiv u Dubrovniku (henceforth: HR-DADu), Testamenta notarile (henceforth: TN), vol. 5, fol. 66'-67. On the influence of Jubilees on the growth in the number of pilgrims see Ludwig Schmugge, 'Deutsche Pilger in Italien', *Kommunikation und Mobilität im Mittelalter. Begegnungen zwischen dem Süund der Mitte Europas (112.-14. Jahrhundert)*, ed. by Siegfrid W. de Rachewiltz and Josef Riedmann (Sigmaringen: Jan Thorbecke Verlag, 1995), pp. 104–09. See also Ludwig Schmugge, Kollektive und individuelle Motivstrukturen im mittelalterlichen Pilgerwesen, in *Migration in der Feudalgesellschaft*, ed. by Gerhard Jaritz and Albert Müller (Frankfurt – New York: Campus Verlag, 1988), pp. 266–67, 272–73, and 275–76.

25 For instance, patrician Nicholas, son of Paul de Gondola, bequeathed two and a half ducats to a person wishing to go on pilgrimage *ad sancto Angelo et a sancto Nichola de Bari*. HR-DADu, TN, vol. 5, fol. 63-63'.

26 Nicholas de Gondola bequeathed 25 ducats to a person wishing to go on pilgrimage *ad sancto Jacomo de Galicia* for his soul. HR-DADu, TN, vol. 5, fol. 63-63'.

from Dubrovnik pilgrimages to Saint Mary in Ulcinj and to Saint Blaise in Kotor were mentioned only once each, although they were located on the East Adriatic coast only a little bit southern from Dubrovnik.

In the commune of Rab in Northern Dalmatia in the period between 1450 and 1500, there were eighty testators (thirty seven males and forty-three females) personally performing pilgrimages to a certain shrine or donating legacies for substitutionary pilgrimages. According to the types of pilgrimages, only twelve were personal and sixty-eight substitutionary pilgrimages. As it was already discussed, the great domination of substitutionary over personal pilgrimages in East Adriatic communes was a typical feature in the commune of Rab in the examined period as well. The reason was, same as in the other communes, in the physical or mental weakness and oldness of most of the testators. Still, some new features related to pilgrimages appeared in Rab samples of pilgrimages. During the fifty years, there were only two, one personal and one substitutionary, pilgrimage to *Terra sancta*. In 1450 Rab patrician Peter *de Zaro* bequeathed three legacies to three pilgrims ready to pilgrimage in four late medieval *peregrinationes maiores: vna persona ad sanctum sepulcrum et vna alia persona ad ecclesiam sancti Jacobi de Galitia et vna persona Romam et vna persona ad Assisium pro anima sua*.[27] In 1452 Rab's canon *Thomas de Cancarella, prior sancte Catherine de Cancario predicatorum*, recorded his last will *sanus mente, intellectu et corpore sed prefecturus ad sanctum sepulcrum domini et timens naufragia que inde euenter possent*.[28] The sample of last wills from Rab follows very similar patterns as the sample of wills from Dubrovnik. Thus, one may observe the appearance of some new pilgrim shrines popular among the testators from Rab whose fame to a great extent originated upon the spatial closeness from Rab. Of course, *peregrinationes maiores* remained equally popular except for the Holy Land (only two pilgrims) because of the already mentioned danger caused by the presence of Ottoman military forces. Rab's last wills between 1450 and 1500 also confirm the significant increase in the variety of pilgrim destinations among all late medieval East Adriatic testators. Besides the Holy Land, Rome, Saint James in Compostela, Rome, and Assisi as the most popular pilgrim shrines of that period, there appeared many other international, but also regional and local saintly shrines which became popular in the Eastern Adriatic, in this case among believers from Rab. Because of the relative closeness and proclamations of Jubilees, Rome was the most popular pilgrim shrine among Rab testators and there were twenty-seven of them personally making a pilgrimage to Rome or donating bequests for substitutionary pilgrimages. Rab's patrician Mary, wife of *nobilis viri ser Petri de Zaro*, composed her last will in 1450 wanting to make a pilgrimage *ad limina apostolorum Petri et Pauli* during the Jubilee in that same year.[29] Next to Rome, the most popular shrine among Rab testators was that of Saint Francis in Assisi. There were twenty-four personal and substitutionary pilgrimages *ad limina beati seraphici sancti Francisci* in Assisi recorded in Rab's last wills from the period examined. For instance, in 1496 Diminča, *vxor*

---

27 HR-DAZd, RB, TS, kut. 2, sv. 4; fols 1168–1169a.
28 HR-DAZd, RB, TS, kut. 2, sv. 6; fol. 55a.
29 HR-DAZd, RB, TS, kut. 2, sv. 4; fols 1176–1176a.

Antonii Uuich, a citizen of Rab requested that her husband *Anthony iusit miti post annos tres sui decessu personam vnam in Asisio ad sanctum Franciscum et alteram ad sanctum Antonium de Padua pro anima sua.*[30] The pilgrim shrine of Saint Anthony in Padua was a destination of only two substitutionary pilgrimages while that of Saint Mary in Recanati reached the peak of popularity among Rab's believers in the second half of the fifteenth century (nine pilgrimages). So it is obvious that in the fifteenth century, same as in the other European regions, Marian's devotion known as *compassio Christi* grew, together with the increasing devotion to Saint Francis, amongst the most popular forms not only concerning pilgrimages but to the whole Christian piety. Thus, in September of 1496, during the plague epidemic in the commune of Rab, *honestisima iuvenis nobillisque domina Cipriana, filia quondam ser Christofori de Cernotis oppressa epidemiali febre*, a hardly mature patrician girl being infected by that plague, composed her last will and bequeathed certain monetary legacies to the executors of her will to *iusit miti ad sanctum Antonium de Padua personas duas pro anima sua,*[31] *ad sanctam Mariam de Rechanati personas duas, ad sanctum Franciscum de Asisio personas quatuor et Roma personas tres pro anima quondam partis sui, matris sue et ipsius testatricis.*[32] Thus, Cipriana left monetary donations to eleven male or female persons willing to go on pilgrimage to four different pilgrim shrines on the Apennine peninsula. Following contemporary characteristics of West Christian piety, Cipriana left most of the pilgrim bequests, four of them, for pilgrimages to the shrine of Saint Francis. Regarding other pilgrim destinations recorded in Rab's last wills from the examined period, one may observe further growth in the popularity of the Marian cult and consequently of Marian shrines. Besides above mentioned, there were fourteen other pilgrimages to various local, regional, and international Marian shrines – ten to the most popular international Marian shrines in Recanati and Loreto (nine in Recanati and only one in Loreto), two to the famous regional pilgrim shrine of Saint Mary in Trsat near Rijeka,[33] and two to a newly founded local pilgrim shrine in Zažično in the hinterland of Šibenik in Dalmatia.[34] Three Rab pilgrims in that period visited the pilgrim shrine in Saint James in Compostela, two of them travelled to Saint Anthony in Vienne in France, and one to the old pilgrim shrine of Saint Bernard in Aquileia.

---

30 HR-DAZd, RB, Juraj Šegota (henceforth: GS), kut. 5, sv. II, 9/II, fol. 11^v.
31 HR-DAZd, RB, GS, kut. 5, sv. II, 9/II, fols 15–15^v. Interestingly, Cipriana was the only testator donating monetary bequests for two pilgrimages to the shrine of Saint Anthony in Padua. From her will as well as from the wills of other Rab testators recorded in 1496 we know about the terrible plague epidemic raging in the commune of Rab in that year. Cipriana was, as it is mentioned in her will, one of the victims of that plague. The possible reason for bequeathing legacies for pilgrims to the shrine of Saint Anthony donated by juvenile Cipriana (although perhaps of legitimate age of 12) might have been in the fact that Anthony was considered as the saintly protector of children.
32 HR-DAZd, RB, GS, kut. 5, sv. II, 9/II, fol. 15^v.
33 Since its founding at the end of the thirteenth century, the patrons of the Marian pilgrim shrine in Trsat have been members of the powerful Croatian magnate family of Frankapan.
34 Robert N. Swanson assessed the position of the Virgin Mary within the late medieval *communio sanctorum* and among believers by following words: 'Among saints Virgin Mary was untouchable'. Robert N. Swanson, *Religion and Devotion in Europe c. 1215 – c. 1515* (Cambridge: Cambridge University Press 1995), p. 144.

On Social and Gender Democratization of High and Late Medieval East Adriatic Pilgrims

The considerable variety of pilgrim shrines visited by East Adriatic pilgrims was the reflection of the late medieval pious trend among believers from the entire East Adriatic coast. That trend may be recognized in other East Adriatic communes, e.g. in the Istrian commune of Poreč in the middle of the fifteenth century. Although most of the notarial deeds from Poreč in the period from the fourteenth and the fifteenth century vanished during the previous centuries, there are sixty-one extant last wills and codicils recorded by a public communal notary of Poreč Anthony de Teodoris[35] in the period between September of 1464[36] and September of 1487.[37] In twenty-seven last wills (44.6 per cent out of all last wills) the pilgrimages are mentioned in forty cases which shows that the phenomenon of going on pilgrimage in the late medieval commune of Poreč was, same as in the other examined East Adriatic communes, rather broadly accepted by communal believers. In contrast to other East Adriatic communes, in last wills from the commune of Poreč the personal pilgrimage was not even once performed. In all of the extant last wills from Poreč, the testators bequeathed various types of legacies for *ex voto* pilgrimages or pilgrimages for the salvation of the souls of testators or their close relatives. In Poreč, same as in the other East Adriatic communes and other urban settlements, the share of male and female testators bequeathing donations for pilgrimages was roughly equal – 15 male or 55.6 per cent and 12 female or 44.4 per cent. As shown on the sample of examined Poreč and other East Adriatic communal wills, the process of democratization in spatial religious mobility of women started during the fourteenth century when females for the first time appeared in larger number as donators for pilgrimages (e.g. Zadar, Dubrovnik, Trogir) but they still relatively seldom appeared as pilgrims. From the beginning of the fifteenth century, the democratization in religious spatial mobility of females reached its peak as obviously indicated in the last wills from Poreč, Rab, and Šibenik.[38]

---

35 Državni arhiv u Pazinu (henceforth: DAPa), Istarski bilježnici (henceforth: IB), Antonius de Teodoris (henceforth: AT), sign. HR-DAPA-8.
36 HR-DAPA, AT, fol. 151^r–151^v.
37 HR-DAPA, AT, fol. 181^r–181^v.
38 Thus the same process of democratization in female spatial religious mobility may be observed in the sample of the examined last wills from Rab. There, out of eighty Rab testators personally performing pilgrimages or bequeathing legacies for substitutionary pilgrimages (which might have been performed by both male and female pilgrims) there were 37 or 46.3 per cent males and 43 or 53.7 per cent females. A similar process may be observed in the other fifteenth-century East Adriatic communes and urban settlements. In the commune of Šibenik between 1415 and 1488 the number of female last wills bequeathing legacies for pilgrimages or those leaving on personal pilgrimages was 38 (52.8 per cent) while the number of male last wills was 34 (47.2 per cent). Even more, that process of democratization in pilgrimaging among women spread among females from the citizen class and from villages in the communal districts. Even the spatial distances became greater and East Adriatic females travelled to pilgrim shrines in Saint James in Compostela and Holy Land. On the one hand, that process was enabled because of financial and material improvement not only of citizens but also of peasants in the communal districts. Another impetus that influenced the growing number of

The sample of wills from the commune of Poreč also indicates another type of democratization which is characteristic for the Central and Late Medieval Period – social diversification of testators donating bequests for pilgrimages as well as social diversification of pilgrims performing pilgrimages themselves. As recorded at the beginning of each of Poreč last wills, they were composed by the testators belonging to all communal social layers – *nobiles cives* ('one female'), *cives et incole* ('five males and five females'), *habitatores* ('three males and three females'), *forenses* ('four males and four females'), and *presbiteri* ('two priests'), following the above-mentioned process of democratization in the practice of going on pilgrimage.

The above-mentioned twenty-seven testators distributed altogether forty bequests for pilgrimages. The greater number of pilgrimages than that of testators and pilgrims is usual for all eastern Adriatic communes because in many cases when pilgrimages were substitutionary, the testators left legacies not always for one, but sometimes two, three, or even more pilgrimages to be performed for the salvation of their souls or of the souls of their relatives and friends. Same as in the other East Adriatic communes in the fifteenth century the greatest number of bequests donated for substitutionary pilgrimages in Poreč were those given for pilgrimages *ad limina apostolorum Petri et Pauli* in Rome (19 pilgrims or 47.5 per cent) which show the domination of Rome as the main pilgrim center of the East Adriatic pilgrims in the Late Middle Ages. For example, in her last will from 1467, Poreč's patrician Olivia, *filia condam ser Marci Longo et vxor Petri de Andronico*, being sick and *sedens super lecto*, donated one legacy to the pilgrim wanting to travel *ad visitandum indulgentiam sanctorum apostolorum Petri et Pauli de Roma* within the one year after her death.[39] In her last will from 1474 *Sanctucia, filia ser Alegreti Pedote et vxor Dominici de Perasto* in present-day Montenegro, the inhabitant of Poreč (*habitatrix Parentii*), requested from her husband Dominic to organize one pilgrimage to Rome for her soul within two years after her death.[40] The pilgrimage had to be financed from her dowry and certain *animalia* which belonged to Sanctucia, and had to be sold for pilgrimage.[41] Although not equally popular in all East Adriatic communes to the same degree, the shrine of Saint Mary in Loreto was from the fourteenth century desirable pilgrim destination among pilgrims from that region. There were 12 legacies (or 30 per cent) donated by Poreč testators to pilgrims wanting to travel to that Marian pilgrim shrine.[42] Thus, Francis, the son of late *ser* James *maioris* and the citizen of

---

female pilgrimages was in the fact that local communal ecclesiastical authorities (usually bishops or archbishops), following Canon law decrees regularly allowed female pilgrimages. Of course, after the confession which was obliged for men and women.

39   HR-DAPa, AT, fol. 151ʳ.
40   HR-DAPa, AT, fol. 152ᵛ.
41   HR-DAPa, AT, fol. 152ᵛ.
42   Loreto had particular pious significance for the late medieval Croatian pilgrims. Namely, according to the thirteenth century legend, on 10 December 1294 the *Santa Casa* was transferred from Trsat near Rijeka for a short period to Recanati and then to Loreto. Soon Loreto became local and regional, and from the fifteenth century international Marian pilgrim shrine. Nikola Mate Roščić, 'Hrvatska hodočašćenja u Loreto', *Croatica Christiana periodica*, (VII), (1983), pp. 88–96.

Poreč (*civis Parentii*), in his last will from 1479 bequeathed one legacy so that the executors of his will *iubsit mitti personam vnam ad visitandum ecclesiam domine sancta Marie delo Redo (!) pro anima sua.*[43] Following pious popularity among the believers from other East Adriatic communes, testators from Poreč also donated four legacies (10 per cent of all bequests to pilgrims) for pilgrimages to the church of Saint Mary *de Angelis* (*Portiuncula*) in Assisi. For instance, in 1482 *dona Maria, uxor relicta magistri Bernardi barberii* and the citizen of Poreč, *iacens in lecto infirmitate grauata*, donated one monetary legacy to be given to person wanting *visitatum ecclesiam sancti Francisci de Assixio pro anima sua*.[44] Although the rest of pilgrimages to other pilgrim shrines from Poreč were mentioned only once each, they confirm the diversity of choice of pilgrim destinations of the inhabitants of all East Adriatic communes according to the geostrategic position of these communes. Thus, testators from Poreč left donations for pilgrimages to the *peregrinationes maiores* to Jerusalem[45] and Saint James de Compostela[46] and pilgrimages to Aquileia,[47] Ljubljana,[48] and Trsat[49] near Rijeka as popular Marian shrine.

Conclusion

Based on the examination of narrative and notarial sources (pilgrim diaries, communal statutes, and notary deeds, in the first place, last wills) from a few communes, in this paper, I have tried to present a short overview of the phenomenon of pilgrimaging in the medieval East Adriatic communes as well as urban and rural settlements to various medieval pilgrim shrines. As presented in the paper, already from the Early Middle Ages, Croats accepted the phenomenon of pilgrimaging as one of the main

---

43   HR-DAPa, AT, fol. 174^r.
44   HR-DAPa, AT, fol. 177^r–177^v.
45   Certain *dona Cusmica*, daughter of late ser Michael from Gračišće and *vxor ser Nicolai condam Dominici* from Rovinj in Istria, in her last will from 1466 bequeathed one monetary legacy to be given by her husband Nicholas to one pilgrim willing to perform pilgrimage *ad indulgentias in Ierusalem*. HR-DAPa, AT, fol. 155^r–155^v.
46   In his last will recorded in 1479 ser Lazar *Scorzonus* from Novigrad in Istria, the inhabitant of Poreč, requested from his son Anthony to send one person *ad visitandum ecclesiam sancti Iacobi de Galizia pro anima sua*. See HR-DAPa, AT, fol. 172^r.
47   The above-mentioned Cusmica also donated one bequest for one pilgrimage *ad indulgentiam Aquilegie pro anima sua*. See HR-DAPa, AT, fol. 155^r–155^v.
48   The citizen of Poreč John, *filius condam ser Marci de Marse*, in his last will from 1475 requested from the executors of his will to *send personam vnam ad visitandum ecclesiam sancti Leonardi in partibus Lubiane pro anima sua*. See HR-DAPa, AT, fol. 172^r.
49   In his last will recorded in 1479, *ser* Lazar Scorzonus from Novigrad in Istria, the inhabitant of Poreč, requested from his son Anthony to *teneatur ire aut mittere personam vnam visitandum ecclesiam domine sancta Marie de Flumine et debeat vigilare per dies octo ad ecclesiam domine sancta Marie de monte et ibi celebrare faciat misam vnam personam in dicta ecclesia in satisfactionem uotorum suorum pro anima sua*. See HR-DAPa, AT, fol. 172^r. It means that Anthony had to perform personal pilgrimage or to send a certain person on pilgrimage for the soul of his father Lazar to the Marian shrine in the church of Saint Mary on the mountain of Trsat to satisfy Lazar votive promises.

reflections of worshiping of the cults of saints and their relics. The creation of *communio sanctorum*, which in the late Medieval Period consisted of more than 6000 saints, had a crucial influence on the popularization of the phenomenon of pilgrimaging in the entire Western Christian oecumene and the East Adriatic coast as well. The belief of medieval Christians in supernatural powers of saints and their relics *in vita* and *post-mortem* had significant importance in the establishment of so called *loca sacra* or saintly shrines as the basic precondition for practicing pilgrimages among a growing number of Christians all over Western Christianity. The period from the middle of the thirteenth century in the region of East Adriatic is marked by the foundation of many local and regional saintly shrines in addition to universally popular Christian pilgrim shrines such as Palestine, Rome, and Compostela. Almost all of the communes, urban and rural settlements in the East Adriatic region established their local pilgrim centres visited mainly by the local or regional population. Towards the end of the Middle Ages, the pilgrims from the eastern Adriatic coast were accompanied by thousands and thousands of pilgrims from all over Europe during their travelling in the most famous pilgrim centres in *Terra sancta*, Rome, Saint James in Compostela, and other shrines. Even though pilgrimages were a habit performed already in the Late Antique and Early Middle Ages, they became particularly popular after the extremely perceptive decision of Pope Boniface VIII and his proclamation of the first Jubilee in 1300. The analysis of last wills, similar to the researches of some other types of sources, points out that from the first Jubilee started a new era of medieval European pilgrimages promising forgiveness of all sins of pilgrims and of persons who supported his/her pilgrimage. It was a most significant impetus for performing the pilgrimages not only to Rome since the practice of indulgences soon spread in almost all other international, regional, and even local saintly shrines. There are numerous extant papal charters addressed to monasteries, churches, or bishoprics on the East Adriatic testifying about papal privileges given to monasteries, churches, bishoprics, or shrines as *loca sacra* where pilgrims could have been forgiven of all or some of their sins. Since that papal decision coincided with the sustained economic growth of European urban settlements including the East Adriatic communes and with the increase of European urban and rural population, the number of pilgrims during the fourteenth and the fifteenth century significantly grew. Even during the horrible plague and other epidemics raging continuously between 1347 and the end of the fifteenth century their number increased.

Of course, almost all pious phenomena which reached great popularity among medieval believers inevitably assumed some undesirable individual or group behaviour. The same was with pilgrimages, especially in the period examined in this paper in which the phenomenon of pilgrimaging flourished. The immoral behaviour of pilgrims was considered by many European and Croatian central and late medieval intellectuals such as Dominican Augustin Kažotić, bishop of Zagreb and well known Humanist John of Čazma (*Janus Pannonius*). Their voices *contra peregrinatio* were not only expressed through the theological and philosophical discussions but also advised, for example, concerning superstition, prostitution, shuffling, drunkenness, and some other forms of immoral behaviour of pilgrims in all international or regional pilgrim centres.

Caused by spatial closeness, Rome and some other Apennines urban societies greatly influenced the phenomenon of going on pilgrimage from the eastern Adriatic coast to Apennine saintly shrines. There are also, although weaker similarities between pilgrimages from the eastern Adriatic coast and from Central European regions as far as pilgrims' destination are concerned. Yet, only a few of the East Adriatic pilgrims travelled to Aachen or Mariazell as the most important pilgrim shrines in Central Europe.

Due to the various perils occurring on travels, dangerous historical circumstances, sicknesses, expensiveness of voyages or family reasons most of the pilgrimages were substitutionary. The personal voyages to these international pilgrim centres were rather expensive and therefore unavailable to many of believers. For instance, the coast of pilgrimage from Zadar or Dubrovnik to Rome was between 5 and 10 golden ducats. The similar prices were for the voyages to Assisi, Loreto, and Recanati. The pilgrimage to Jerusalem was more expensive and some of pilgrims spent 50 or even 60 golden ducats. Having in mind that one stone house in good condition in Zadar in the fourteenth century cost 40 golden ducats and that the price of one fine horse was between 5 and 6 ducats, it appears that pilgrimages were the privilege of elite classes of communal societies. But, it was not so. Namely, many testators donating monetary or other types of legacies for closer or distant pilgrimages chose one and the same person wanting to perform pilgrimage for a group of testators. It was a very well-organized strategy that enabled not only the members of the social elite but also the persons from all communal social strata. The growing popularity of Marian devotion among European believers also caused the foundation of local and regional Marian pilgrim shrines in almost all East Adriatic communes or their close hinterland, for instance in Drid near Trogir, in Zažično near Šibenik, and Trsat near Rijeka.

One of the important aspects in the research of the medieval East Adriatic pilgrimages is the geographic and strategic importance of that region. Due to the fact that the entire East Adriatic coast was rather early incorporated into the Roman empire, the East Adriatic coast had a long tradition of naval and land connections with the Apennine peninsula. For that reason, pilgrimaging from Zadar, Split or Dubrovnik to numerous Apennine pilgrim centres was pretty fast and relatively cheap, at least in comparison to the prices of voyages of pilgrims from other European regions. Equally important for the East Adriatic pilgrims was the position of Venice as the main port on Adriatic for pilgrims from all over Europe travelling to *Terra sancta*. Due to the good indentation of the East Adriatic coast, because of the existence of numerous and well-organized ports, because of the good ability of manoeuvring, and navigation safety, the East Adriatic coast (from the port of Poreč to the port of Durrës) became one of the most secure sections on the naval route from Venice to Palestine. In that way, the denizens of East Adriatic coastal and island communes and urban settlements frequently came into contact with the European pilgrims who used to spend the night in communal or city hospitals, patrician palaces, convents, or monasteries. A great number of East Adriatic men served on the Venetian pilgrim and other galleys as crew members, oarsmen, and ships' pilots, and most of them spoke Croatian, *Veneto*, and sometimes other languages such as Albanian, Greek, and Turkish.

As confirmed on visual sources the outer appearance of East Adriatic pilgrims did not differ from the other European pilgrims. Pilgrims, and especially males, were easily recognizable because of their 'uniform' outfits visualized in many pictures, frescoes, icons, sculptures, books, and other places. As witnessed on the fresco in the church of Saint Mary in Škriline near Beram done by the famous fifteenth-century painter Vincent from Kastav in Istria, the greatest number of pilgrims wore similar dresses and the difference in the dressing was only visible after the comparison of pilgrims from different social classes. Most of the male pilgrims wore almost equal types of pilgrim 'uniforms'. They wore simple mantels, cheap woollen overcoats, long wooden sticks, shoulder bags for personal belongings, and simple sandals or leather shoes. Many of them pinned the badges on their hats connected to the pilgrim centers they have already visited. Of course, all pilgrims obligatory carried the bishops' or permission written by other ecclesiastical authorities which were used as passports while traveling through various European, Middle Eastern, or Egyptian regions.

It may be concluded that the phenomenon of pilgrimaging had a very important role in the daily and particularly in pious life of denizens of East Adriatic coastal and island communes. As far as East Adriatic is concerned, pilgrimages were one of the most effective ways of establishing cultural, artistic, intellectual, scholarly as well as social and economic connections and of peaceful learning about various aspects of different cultures and civilizations, not only within Western Christian but also within the Eastern Christian oecumene and various Islamic countries and regions. Of course, on the personal level of medieval East Adriatic testators, pilgrimages presented one of the most efficient ways to obtain redemption of their sins and consequently the salvation of their souls in eternity.

Primary Sources

Itinerary from Bordeaux to Jerusalem. The Bordeaux pilgrim (333 A. D.) (London: ADAM Street Adelphi 1887), https://archive.org/details/cu31924028534158/page/n. 11/mode/2up (accessed on 21.02.2021).

Mirko Zjačić, 'Regeste pergamena XV vijeka Kaptolskog arhiva u Hvaru', *Bilten Historijskog arhiva Komune hvarske*, god. (VI–VII), br. (7–8), (1965), 12–26.

Natko Nodilo, Chronica Ragusina Junii Restii (ab origine urbis usque ad annum 1451) item Joannis Gundulae (1451–1484), *Monumenta spectantia historiam Slavorum Meridionalium*, vol. xxv, *Scriptores*, vol. ıı (Zagrabiae: In taberna libraria eiusdem societatis typographicae 1893).

Petar Skok, *Tri starofrancuske hronike o Zadru u godini 1202* (Zagreb: JAZU, 1951).

Serđo Dokoza, 'Inventar fonda don Kuzme Vučetića u Državnom arhivu u Zadru', in *Prilozi povijesti otoka Hvara*, vol. (XI), (2002), 256–60.

Spisi zadarskih bilježnika Henrika i Creste Tarallo 1279–1308, ed. by Mirko Zjačić (Zadar: Državni arhiv u Zadru, 1959).

Archival Sources

State Archives in Dubrovnik ('Državni arhiv u Dubrovniku'); Testamenta notarile, vol. 5.
State Archives in Pazin ('Državni arhiv u Pazinu'), Fund: Istarski bilježnici, notary Antonius de Teodoris, sign. HR-DAPA-8.
State Archives in Zadar ('Državni arhiv u Zadru'), Fund: Rapski bilježnici, notary Juraj Šegota, kut. 5, sv. II.
Državni arhiv u Zadru, Fund: Rapski bilježnici, notary Toma Stančić, kut. 2, sv. XI.
Državni arhiv u Zadru, Fund: Šibenski bilježnici, notary Karatus Vitale, kut. 16/II, sv. 15.Iva.

References

Bernhardt Schimmelpfennig, 'Die Regelmässigkeit mittelalterlicher Wallfahrt', in *Wallfahrt und Alltag im Mittelalter und früher Neuzeit*, Band XIV, ed. by Harry Kühnel (Wien: Verlag der österreichischen Akademie der Wissenschaften, 1992), pp. 81–94.
Harry Kühnel, *Wallfahrt und Alltag im Mittelalter und früher Neuzeit*, Band XIV (Wien: Verlag der österreichischen Akademie der Wissenschaften, 1992).
Krešimir Kužić, 'Kojim su brodovima 1217. godine prevezeni križari kralja Andrije II.?', *Radovi Zavoda za povijesne znanosti HAZU u Zadru*, vol. (46), (2004), pp. 93–107.
Jadranka Neralić, *Put do crkvene nadarbine – rimska Kurija i Dalmacija u 15. Stoljeću* (Split: Književni krug, 2007).
Ludwig Schmugge, 'Deutsche Pilger in Italien', in *Kommunikation und Mobilität im Mittelalter. Begegnungen zwischen dem Süund der Mitte Europas (112.-14. Jahrhundert)*, ed. by Siegfrid W. de Rachewiltz and Josef Riedmann (Sigmaringen: Jan Thorbecke Verlag, 1995), pp. 97–113.
Ludwig Schmugge, 'Kollektive und individuelle Motivstrukturen im mittelalterlichen Pilgerwesen', in *Migration in der Feudalgesellschaft*, ed. by Gerhard Jaritz and Albert Müller (Frankfurt – New York: Campus Verlag, 1988), pp. 263–89.
Luigi Oliva, 'The Apian via', in *The Way to Jerusalem*, ed. by Anna Trono (Lecce: University of Salento Lecce – Department of Cultural Heritage, 2013), pp. 33–38.
Migration in der Feudalgesellschaft, ed. by Gerhard Jaritz and Albert Müller (Frankfurt – New York: Campus Verlag, 1988).
Nikola Mate Roščić, 'Hrvatska hodočašćenja u Loreto', *Croatica Christiana periodica*, (VII), (1983), 88–96.
Robert N. Swanson, *Religion and Devotion in Europe c. 1215 – c. 1515* (Cambridge: Cambridge University Press, 1995).
Roberto Lopez, *Rođenje Evrope: stoljeće V–XIV* (Zagreb: Školska knjiga, 1978).
Siegfried W. de Rachewiltz, Josef Riedmann, eds, *Kommunikation und Mobilität im Mittelalter. Begegnungen zwischen dem Süund der Mitte Europas (112.-14) Jahrhundert* (Sigmaringen: Jan Thorbecke Verlag, 1995).
Tomaž Mastnak, *Križarski mir. Kršćanstvo, muslimanski svijet i zapadni politički poredak* (Zagreb: Prometej, 2005).

Zoran Ladić, 'Odjek pada tvrđave Accon 1291. u Hrvatskoj. O križarskoj vojni kao vidu hodočašća', *Zbornik Odsjeka za povijesne znanosti Zavoda za povijesne i društvene znanosti HAZU*, vol. (16), (1998), 43–56.

Figures

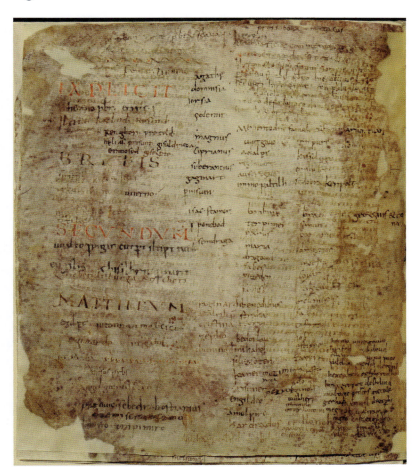

Fig. 1: The folio of *Evangeliarium* from Cividale with the signatures of Croatian pilgrims belonging to the ruling class dated to the ninth and the tenth century. Copyright: *Hrvati i Karolinzi. Dio prvi. Rasprave i vrela*, ed. by Ante Milošević (Split: Muzej hrvatskih arheoških starina, 2000), p. 100.

Fig. 2: Pilgrim presented on the fresco with presentation of the sacral program Dance of Death from the church of Saint Mary on Škrilinah. That fresco from 1474 was the product of the artistic manufacture of painter Vincent from Kastav in Istria. Among various figures represented on the fresco there is also the figure of the late medieval Istrian pilgrim. The badges on his hat enable the identification of pilgrim shrines visited by that pilgrim – *limina apostolorum* in Rome, the Marian shrine in Loreto, and the shrine of Saint Anthony in Padua. Photograph: Private collection by Zoran Ladić.

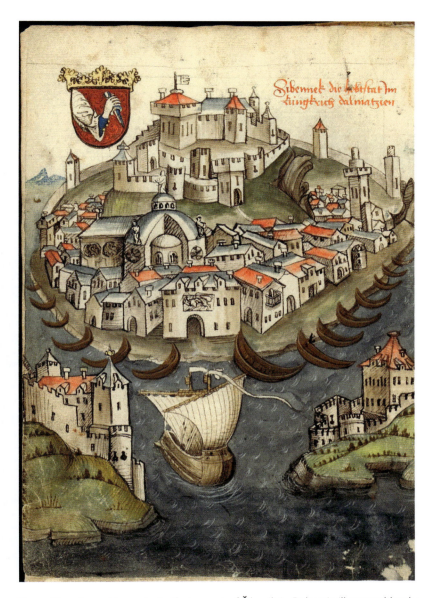

Fig. 3: The city and important pilgrim port of Šibenik in Dalmatia illustrated by the pilgrim Conrad von Grünemberg in his pilgrim diary from 1487 in which Šibenik is entitled "Sibennech die Hobstat im Küngchrich Dalmatzien", in *Beschreibung der Reise von Konstanz nach Jerusalem*, fol. 11ᵛ. Source: https://digital.blb-karlsruhe.de/blbhs/content/pageview/3853529.

ION GUMENÂI

Holy Journey to the Monastery or at the Wonderworking Icon of the Neamț as Described by Archimandrite Andronic Popovici

Introduction: Specifying the Objective and the Context

The research problem, that I intend to discuss, is to establish the essence of the pilgrimage to detect the core point of attraction – the monastery of Neamț from Moldavia[1] or the wonder working icon of the Virgin Mary known for the eighteen miracles, which is housed there. The empirical materials used for my investigation are the data recorded and related by the Archimandrite Andronic Popovici (1820–1893), who was for a long time a monk at this monastery, holding important offices and having access to manuscripts and documents. His works are of interest, because they are still relatively unknown and an interesting account about the coalition between the Church and State in encouraging the pilgrimage. My research was oriented towards this topic, because it puts into circulation new archival information with reference to the phenomenon of pilgrimage in this territory of modern Romania.

The methodological perspective of my research was drawn on classic methods like documentation and collection of data in monastery and state archives,[2] comparative analysis of the sources, critical interpretation of the testimonies.

---

1 Moldavia was a state formed in medieval Europe in 1362. Its territory includes the eastern part of today's Romania and the Republic of Moldova, while the Moldavian northern and southeastern parts are territories of Ukraine. Its western borders were the Carpathian Mountains, bounded on the north by Poland, on the east it bordered the Dniester River (although its population reached the Bug River), and on the south it bordered Wallachia and the Black Sea. The capitals of this state were consecutively Baia, Siret, Suceava and Iași. In 1812 the territory between the Dniester and the Prut was annexed by the Russian Empire. In 1859, following the unification of Moldova between the Carpathians and Prut with Wallachia, the Romania State was formed.
2 Republic of Moldova, National Archives Agency.

> **Ion Gumenâi** • PhD, Dr., Habil., at the State University of the Republic of Moldova and Senior Scientific Researcher at the Institute of History, Republic of Moldova

Pilgrimage in the Christian Balkan World: The Path to Touch the Sacred and Holy, ed. by Dorina Dragnea, Emmanouil Ger. Varvounis, Evelyn Reuter, Petko Hristov and Susan Sorek (Turnhout, 2023), pp. 131–144.
BREPOLS ❧ PUBLISHERS   DOI 10.1484/M.STR-EB.5.132403

In my chapter, initially I briefly note and contextualize the main holy figures – the Saint John the New and Saint Pious Paraskeva – that historically attracted the devotional practices of the people in Moldavia and outline my general context of analysis. Then, I focus my attention on analysing of the mechanisms and medium in transformation of the monastery of Neamț into a popular pilgrimage site in Moldavia and of the divine interventions' nature related to the miracle working icon of the Virgin Mary from the monastery.

As other post-Byzantine pilgrimages, the research of the history of pilgrimage attendance in the Romanian Principalities in the pre-modern period is at its early stage. The first known pilgrim is the Hieromonk Joachim of Wallachia,[3] attested in 1510 as the hegumen of the monastery of Saint Catherine on Mount Sinai. Given the long tradition of this phenomenon throughout the Christian world, it is unlikely that such pilgrimages to the Middle East had not happened before. Since the end of the sixteenth century, people who are called 'hagi' or 'hagiu' are frequently attested. The earliest mentioning of 'hagiu' in Romanian Principalities dates back to 15 February 1590, when a certain 'hagiu' named Dumitru was cited as a witness in a deed of sale from a store in Bucharest. A toponym, 'Hagiești' (today, Belciug, Teleorman county), was recorded even earlier, in 1580.[4]

The 'hagii' were remembered as church builders and philanthropists as well as importers and distributors of books, supporters of printing of the books or as collectors of books. For instance, in the first part of the eighteenth century 'The Geography of Europe, Asia and Africa' was bought by a priest from Craiova, Pavel the Hagi. 'The Book of Wisdom' by Sindipa the Philosopher was translated into Romanian in the monastery of Neamț in 1784, with financial help from a certain *hagi* called Ioan of Piatra. A replica of the Greek novel 'Philaret and Arethusa', translated in Romanian was in the possession of Gavriil hagi Ciurcu from Brașov, in 1813. At Iași, Enachi 'sin hagi Fragul ot Tighine', duplicated in 1777 a rich compendium of folk literature 'in the house of boyar Theodor Dorăbăț'. On the front page of the manuscript a certain hagi Georgi Lepădatu (1790) left his signature and Dimitrie, the son of a merchant from Craiova, hagi Nicolau had a copy of a Greek comedy 'Alexander' published in 1785. 'The Letters of Synesius of Cyrene' and 'The Pan-Athenian Speech of Isocrates' were copied owing to money provided by Simeon the Hagi, in 1786. At the end of the eighteenth century 'Lady Maria, the wife of hagi Constantin', member of the Budișteni family, donated a precious replica of the Gospel, in Romanian, published in 1688[5] in the church from Budeasa.

The results of the research revealed that in the Romanian Principalities merchants and artisans were the people who went on pilgrimages, whilst the local boyars rarely, if ever, took part in such endeavours. The monks were in second place. The analysis

---

3   Elisabeta Negrău, 'Pelerini din Țările Române la Ierusalim. Profiluri sociale și culturale (secolele XVI–XIX)', in *Călători și călătorii. A privi, a descoperi*, vol. I, ed. by Cristina Bogdan, Silvia Marin Barutcieff (București: Editura Universității din București, 2016), p. 15.
4   Elisabeta Negrău, 'Pelerini din Țările Române la Ierusalim' …, p. 16.
5   Elisabeta Negrău, 'Pelerini din Țările Române la Ierusalim' …, p. 26.

of documents showed that the number of pilgrims in Moldavia was higher than in Wallachia, especially in the second half of the eighteenth century. The researchers link this to the presence in Moldavia of the monk and theologian Paisius Velichkovsky and his work of translation and dissemination of spiritual texts later included in Philokalia.[6] However, the historian Liviu Pilat shows that if in the western world and Byzantium, there is an account of journeys and guides for pilgrims, in the case of Medieval Moldavia, there is not any knowledge of any Moldavian pilgrim travelling to Jerusalem or at least to Chersonese, geographically the closest holy land.[7]

Saint John the New and Saint Pious Paraskeva – Protector Saints

Before continuing the analysis it is necessary to pay attention to *Sfânta Cuvioasă Parascheva* ('Saint Pious Paraskeva') and *Sfântul Ioan cel Nou de la Suceava* ('Saint John the New in Suceava'), whose relics were brought to Moldavia, giving a similar circumstantial and temporal background for my study. These material representations of holiness, generators of the thaumaturgical energies together with the wonder working icon of Mother of God in the monastery of Neamț became during the centuries the most important *sacra* for pilgrimages.

Saint Pious Paraskeva,[8] known as Saint Pious Paraskeva of Epivates or Paraskeva of the Balkans (Saint Petka) was born in the first half of the eleventh century in Epivates, in the Byzantine Empire (today the town Boyados or Selim Pasha in Turkey), on the shores of the Marmara Sea. Saint Paraskeva died in the middle of the eleventh century, at twenty seven years old, being buried on the seashore, near Kallicrateia.

The tomb was forgotten until the end of the twelfth century, when, following the miracles performed here, the entire and untouched relics of the saint were discovered. Proving to be a miracle worker, Saint Paraskeva was soon canonized by the Patriarchate of Constantinople at the time.[9] After 1230, at the request of the Tsar of Bulgaria, John Asen II (r. 1218–1241), the Latin Emperor of Constantinople sent her relics from Epivates to (Veliko) Tarnovo. In 1395, after the Ottoman occupation of Tarnovo, the relics of Saint Paraskeva were transferred to Vidin, from where, in around 1397, they were moved to Belgrade. In 1521 they were brought back to Constantinople, and from here, at the request of the Moldavian Prince Vasile Lupu

---

6   Elisabeta Negrău, 'Pelerini din Țările Române la Ierusalim' …, pp. 26–30.
7   Liviu Pilat, 'Pelerinaje și penitenți în Moldova secolelor XIV–XV', in *Spectacolul public între tradiție și modernitate. Sărbători, ceremonialuri, pelerinaje și suplicii*, ed. by Constanța Vintilă-Ghițulescu and Mária Pakucs Willcocks (București: Institutul Cultural Român, 2007), p. 233.
8   Emil Dragnev, 'Sfinții Cefalofori: text și imagine în spațiul creștinătății orientale', in *In honoriem Răzvan Theodorescu*, ed. by Dana Jenei (București: Editura Oscar print, 2019), p. 114. See also Sorin Iftimi, 'Moaștele Cuvioasei Parascheva și rolul lor în istoria Moldovei', *Teologia și Viața*, Revista Mitropoliei Moldovei, XI (LXXVII), 8–12, (2001), 39–50.
9   Ion Vicovan and Cătălin Adumitroaie, *Cuvioasa Parascheva, sfânta populară a Ortodoxiei, în istoria și în evlavia poporului român* (Iași: Ed. Doxologia, 2011), pp. 12–15.

(r. 1634–1653), with the permission of the Ecumenical Patriarchate, they were brought to Iași in 1641 and placed in the church of the 'Three Hierarchs'. Where, the devotion of the parishioners wake her up from two centuries' 'sleep', according to the testimony of the priest Synadinos. Thus, an explicit and mutual relationship is established between popular veneration and the mediating intervention of the saint. The holy relics of Pious Paraskeva remained in the Church of the 'Holy Three Hierarchs' until 1884. On 9 January 1889,[10] the relics were transferred into the new Metropolitan Cathedral of Iași. The popularity and the role played by Saint Paraskeva in the moral-spiritual life of the people can also be seen in the number of Orthodox places of worship dedicated to her. Thus, in the fifteenth century, five churches dedicated to Saint Paraskeva were built, in the sixteenth century – six, in the seventeenth century – thirty-two, in the eighteenth century – ninety-two, and in the nineteenth century – ninety-nine churches.[11] In 1950, at the meeting of 28 February, the Holy Synod of the Romanian Orthodox Church decided the canonization of some Romanian saints and the generalization of the veneration, in all the country, of the foreign saints who had and have relics in Romania, among them was Pious Paraskeva. Her feast, celebrated on October 14, is the largest religious pilgrimage in the country.

Saint John the New was probably born at the end of the thirteenth century in Trebizond. His father was a merchant and John followed in his footsteps. In 1330 or 1332 he went from Trebizond to Cetatea Albă (Akkerman)[12] on the ship of a merchant named Reiz, a Catholic from Venice or Genoa. On the way, they had disputes on over their faiths, and John firmly upheld the truths of Orthodoxy. As a result of the intrigues insinuated by the Catholic merchant, and following the discussions with the leader of the citadel regarding the abandonment of the Orthodox faith and the acceptance of the other religion, he was tortured, thrown in jail, dragged by a horse through the streets of the city, and finally, one of the executioners drew his sword and cut off his head. Thus the blessed John received death as a martyr.[13] The fame of the martyr and the miracles reached the ears of the Prince of Moldavia, Alexander I (1400–1432), who, with the advice of Metropolitan Iosif I, brought the relics to the capital city in Suceava and placed them in the church of Mirăuți, titling John the New as *the patron saint of his country*.[14]

After repeated forced peregrinations (1686 – Żółkiew in Poland, 1783 – Rădăuți, Moldavia, during the First World War – Vienna) because of political and war conditions, in 1918 the relics were brought finally into the country and the Saint again became

---

10   Ion Vicovan and Cătălin Adumitroaie, *Cuvioasa Parascheva...* , pp. 52, 59.
11   Ion Vicovan and Cătălin Adumitroaie, *Cuvioasa Parascheva...* , pp. 52, 59.
12   Florin Grigorescu, *Sfântul Ioan cel Nou de la Suceava în viața credincioșilor* (Suceava: Editura Arhiepiscopiei Sucevei și Rădăuțului, 2003), pp. 4–5.
13   Florin Grigorescu, *Sfântul Ioan cel Nou de la Suceava...* , pp. 10–15.
14   Ștefan S. Gorovei, 'Mucenicia Sfântului Ioan cel Nou. Noi puncte de vedere', in *Închinare lui Petre Ș. Năsturel, la 80 de ani*, ed. by Ionel Cândea, Paul Cernovodeanu, and Gheorghe Lazăr (Brăila: Editura Istros, 2003), p. 557.

'the protector of the whole country of Moldavia'.[15] All Romanian believers – but especially those from northern Moldavia, the eastern parts of Transylvania and Maramureş – appropriately worship this chosen martyr of Christ.[16]

The feast day of Saint John the New in Suceava has been described by Petro Mohyla (Rom. Petru Movilă) (d. 1647), the Metropolitan of Kyiv, Halych and All Rus'. The information is taken from the Metropolitan of Moldavia Varlaam Moţoc (d. 1657), where it is noted: 'In 1620, on the Wednesday after the Descent of the Holy Spirit, when the memory of Saint John the New is celebrated in the metropolis in Suceava, as usual, the people coming from many and distant places, bring many gifts and when they kiss reliquary, they leave a lot of money … '.[17] The feast was set for Wednesday and Thursday after the Descent of the Holy Spirit. The second day of celebration of Saint John the New in Suceava was established due to one of the miracles he performed. The event took place in 1621, during the Hotin War. In the summer of that year, a detachment of Cossacks went to Suceava to rob and plunder the city. All the townspeople had taken refuge in the Metropolitan Church, praying to Saint John the New and his relics. And, when the Cossacks tried to cross a stream, which previously could have been crossed 'by foot', its waters rose increasing more and more, so that the inhabitants of Suceava were saved.[18] Also, the importance and popularity of the cult of Saint John the New from Suceava is confirmed by the many versions of his hagiography that circulated in the Romanian area and the Balkans in general,[19] by the murals in Moldavian churches,[20] and by the churches consecrated to him.[21]

The Transformation of the Monastery of Neamţ into a Pilgrimage Centre in Moldavia

The pilgrimage becomes more interesting when it is analysed from the political perspective, taking into account the authorities' desire to get closer to the sacrosanct. Towards the end of the Middle Ages, a journey to Jerusalem or Rome becomes the exclusive privilege of the wealthy. Therefore pilgrimages, which were made within the borders of the Principality, were extremely popular. It is the case, mainly, of the significant *peregrinationes secundariae*, which were focused on ancient places of importance but also where miracles had been reported.[22]

Liviu Pilat's assertion is pertinent when he refers to the covering of the void of sacred in the Principality of Moldavia, only by the fact that Prince Alexander I

---

15 Mircea Păcuraru, *Sfinţi daco-romani şi români* (Iaşi: Trinitas, 1994), p. 111.
16 Mircea Păcuraru, *Sfinţi daco-romani* … , pp. 110–11.
17 Florin Grigorescu, *Sfântul Ioan cel Nou de la Suceava*… , p. 88.
18 Ştefan S. Gorovei, *Mucenicia Sfântului Ioan*… , pp. 567–68.
19 Florin Grigorescu, *Sfântul Ioan cel Nou de la Suceava*… 2003.
20 Mircea Păcuraru, *Sfinţi daco-romani*…, p. 111.
21 Ştefan S. Gorovei, *Mucenicia Sfântului Ioan*… , pp. 568–69.
22 Liviu Pilat, 'Pelerinaje şi penitenţi în Moldova secolelor XIV–XV' … , pp. 233–34.

brought the relics of Saint John the New to the Principality.[23] Despite the absence of direct witness accounts, I consider that beginning with the sixteenth century such small pilgrimages, were made including to the Neamț monastery too, as to be the first monastic settlement in Moldavia, as it was shown by Andronic Popovici.

He noted in the first volume of his work '*Istoria sfintelor mănăstiri Neamț și Secu*' (The History of the Holy Relics of Neamț and Secu Monasteries) that the first Metropolitan of Moldavia Iosif Mușat founded the first monastery south of Târgu Neamț, an hours walking distance in the Boiștea forest, near Boiștea town. There, Iosif had his residence before he was appointed as Archbishop he built for himself several living quarters and auxiliary buildings. He gifted his proprieties, alongside the forest, all the income and all the old documents to the abbot and brethren of the monastery of Neamț. And 'they had given also the Wonder working Icon of Our Most-Holy Lady, the Birthgiver-of-God and Ever-Virgin Mary, which in the background has the Martyr Saint George, the bringer of victory and miracle worker, which had been given as a gift from the Byzantine Emperor, John VIII Palaiologos, to the Holy Neamț monastery for its and the entire nations eternal remembrance, to the strong and never defeated eternal cover of this holy and godly place and brethren for healing of souls and body of every man with unyielding diligence and belief in God and for prayers'.[24] This account confirms that Neamț is the oldest monastery in Moldavia, otherwise the Metropolitan would not have gifted it to the monastic settlement he founded, and he would not have installed it here as a precious relic for the Orthodox faith as is the wonder working icon of Virgin Mary. I consider that the monastery of Neamț is the first monastic settlement as the holder of holy remains, the relics of Saint John the New, which had been a point of attraction for pilgrims, especially from Moldavia.

Even though Andronic describes the phenomenon of pilgrimage from a later period, the intensity of this process shows it was happening for a long time. Thus, according to the accounts collected by the Archimandrite from earlier periods, at the beginning of spring, the ordinary folk even from the farthest areas of the country were readying themselves to travel to the Neamț monastery to celebrate 'The Ascension of Our Lord and Savior Jesus Christ'. The feast was considered the special time for the miracle working of the icon of the Mother of God. These future pilgrims told their relatives and friends about their intention, in order to entice them to join. In case these people could not go, they donated money to monks to make this journey for them and to do some services, for instance to mention them at the Liturgy, to read the Akathist for their sake, to receive their share of holy water, to read from the Psalter and light candles at the icons. Also, pilgrims could buy icons, books, crosses, etc.

Before embarking on their pilgrimage, the parishioners had to go to the local church where they prayed to the Virgin Mary, asking for protection and health, to

---

23   Liviu Pilat, 'Pelerinaje și penitenți în Moldova secolelor XIV–XV' ..., pp. 238–40.
24   Arhimandrit Andronic Popovici, *Istoria Sfintelor mănăstiri Neamț și Secu*, vol. I, ed. by Ion Gumenâi (Chișinău: Lexon Prim, 2016), pp. 101–02. The biography of Andronic Popovici gives the information that he was a *hagi*, he undertook many pilgrimages, including at Mount Athos, Jerusalem, Constantinople, and Kyiv Pecherska Lavra.

keep their households safe from any evils. More so, the parish priest was asked to read the prayer for those who embarked on a journey, to bless them with the cross, to sprinkle them with holy water. Afterwards, they said goodbye to their relatives and friends who accompanied them to the exit from the village, where the pilgrims turn towards the village church to bow and pray as blessing.

The sources registered these preparatory acts 'they forgave those who had accompanied them, and so, beginning their long journey, they met other pilgrims with the same desire, who were coming from other places in the country. They seemed to have wings, being elated by the godly love, ran, one faster than the other, towards the monastery. I heard these accounts from such people, who thought of themselves as being simple-minded, and others too, I heard when I was still a child, and kept them hidden all to myself'.[25] Andronic continues his account inserting his own recollections from the time when he was a 'canonarch' of the monastery of Secu and ecclesiarch of the monastery of Neamț. He recounts that once the pilgrims arrived at the monastery, they left their belongings and bowed in reverence at the gate of the monastery and from there they headed towards the main church 'and to the holy and wonder-working icon of the Most-Holy Lady, the Birthgiver-of-God and Ever-Virgin Mary, who is the reason for their journey, their primary aim'.[26] Then, after these acts of devotion, they prepared themselves for confession and Communion. At the same time, the pilgrims bowed to the crosses, parts of the relics of saints, and other things that they considered as sacred. They wrote their names on the papers, and checked them for to be read at the Akathist, Paraklesis, water blessings, Holy Unction, etc. They walked with lit candles in their hands, which they placed at those sacred places, reciting the following prayer: 'The Most Holy Lady, the Birthgiver-of-God absolve me the sinner'. On the day of the Ascension of Our Lord and Savior Jesus Christ, according to the custom of the holiday, the road, on which the wonderworking icon of the Virgin Mary was taken to the main church and to the holy water basin, where the water was blessed, it was decorated with sprigs of fir, arranged temporarily. After the icon was passed by the monks in a procession, it was returned to the church. The pilgrims took sprigs of fir tree for blessing, after which they bought small icons, crosses, books, and other objects made by monks, as gifts for themselves or their friends and relatives. After that, they worshipped at sacred places and began their journey back home, on the same route they came to the monastery.

Referring to the journey back, one thing bothered Archimandrite Andronic, specifically the untrue stories showing that: 'sitting like that pilgrims ask one another, what they have seen at the monastery, in churches and in the monks' cells and the monastic life, etc. And if anyone among them was wiser and smarter, who read stories about such holy settlements, comforted them with a word or two, showing them what significance these holy settlements have. And if there was none such, pilgrims told stories they may have heard from others, that the

---

25 Republic of Moldova, National Agency of Archives ('Republica Moldova, Agenția Națională a Arhivelor'), Fond 2119, inventar III, dosar 72, fols 4–4ᵛ.
26 Agenția Națională a Arhivelor…, fol. 5.

Moldavian Prince, Stephan III (r. 1457–1504) known as Stephan the Great, built this monastery. Or other such things like the holy icon on the feast day came to that holy water basin to bow to the Well of the Sheep Herder (this was the name of the fountain – a.n.). Or the monastery of Neamț was built by Bogdan I up to the windows and because the monks refused to bury his wife in the monastery's foundation, he did not want to finish building the monastery. Such interpretations and half-truths were told by the simple-minded folks, concerning the building and founding of the monastery of Secu. Some of them, I am embarrassed to write, as said by those who did not know any better. I frequently heard these stories. I pitied these worshipers since they were worried, spend a lot of money and exhausted themselves without measure, and at home rarely could tell anything credible to their children, relatives, friends, about what they had seen or heard in these holy monasteries'.[27] All these stories that have been shared among the flock on their return 'is usually selective and interpretive, and in numerous retellings the pilgrim is likely to edit and elaborate upon the journey's stories. Retelling is thus an important part of the return, allowing one to reinterpret the experiences simultaneously'.[28]

This description of the phenomenon from the outside is made by Andronic Popovici, describing a visit to the monastery of Neamț when Paisius Velichkovsky was its Hegumen.[29] Indeed, the Archimandrite shows that the majority of people were at the monastery during the celebration of the Ascension of our Lord. The author of the histories of Neamț and Secu monasteries shows that at this holiday people of all ages took part, men and women, rich and poor, not only from Moldavia and Wallachia but also from distant lands that came to worship at the icon of the Most-Holy Lady, the Birthgiver-of-God and Ever-Virgin Mary. After they likened the hegumen with Patriarch Avraam, they note that Paisius received all comers in his cell and after giving his blessings, he assigned them to the guest house or other cells. Because of the high number of visitors, during the celebration of the holiday, several older and more experienced monks were selected for supervising the young monks to keep them from being tempted into sinning.[30]

One thing that must be noted about this holiday is that its scale is due as well to the financial support of the Phanariote Prince of Moldavia, Constantin Moruzi (r. 1777–1782). For instance, in 1780, he accepted all the exemptions granted to the monastery, as well as all the gifts and taxes collected from the royal customs and mine, donated 52 lei to the monastery of Neamț for the holiday of Assumption of our

---

27 Agenția Națională a Arhivelor' ..., Fond 5^v–6. Archimandrite Andronic, thus emphasizes the folkloric way of transmitting the tradition among pilgrims. However, the negative side of this phenomenon is also reflected, through which some incorrect and harmful historical and orthodox information are passed on among the pilgrims of the literate people.
28 Nancy Frey, *Pilgrim Stories: On and Off the Road to Santiago* (Berkeley, CA: University of California Press, 1998), p. 186.
29 The head of an Orthodox monastery; abbot in the Latin Church.
30 Arhimandrit Andronic Popovici, *Istoria Sfintelor Mănăstiri Neamț și Secu*, vol. III–IV, ed. by Ion Gumenâi (Chișinău: Lexon Prim, 2020), pp. 205–06.

Lord.[31] The donations made by the Prince to the monastery were not random, since during the holiday dedicated to the monastery, all strata of society could take part.

One such example is given by the Andronic Popovici, even before Paisius Velichkovsky's tenure, stating that: 'also, it is necessary to show that in the year of 7241 (since the creation of the world) the good-believer Prince of Moldavia Grigorie Ghica, during the holiday of the Assumption of our Lord Jesus Christ to the Heavens, out of true Christian love came with many boyars to the holy monastery and after the reading of the Akathist and Paraklisis as was the custom, alongside the Hegumen Teofil and all brethren from the monastery's courtyard, with Litany took out the holy and wonderworking icon of our Most-Holy Lady, the Birthgiver-of-God and Ever-Virgin Mary. He bowed down to the icon, and surprised Grigore Voivode's men and the Turks that accompanied him, and the monks said that no one had ever bowed to the holy icon as impressively as he did'.[32]

In other his papers, Andronic Popovici[33] showed that before arriving at the monastery of Neamț, this icon was named 'Românca' or 'Lidanca', because the homeland of Saint Holy Martyr George was Palestine and the fortress of Lida, where he was buried, according to Simeon Metafrast's account. Germanus I, the Patriarch of Constantinople (d. 740), is credited as the author of both icons. Andronic, trying to make an analogy, writes that during the time of the Byzantine Emperor Leon III the Isaurian (r. 717–741), when right-believers were persecuted, the icon was brought from Constantinople to Rome, and when the Romans turned away from orthodox teaching, the icon was brought back to Constantinople. By the mid-fifteenth century the icon has been transferred to Moldavia, thus saving it from the Ottomans, who were ready to conquer Constantinople.[34]

Divine Interventions Related to the Miracle Working Icon from the Monastery of Neamț

Historical sources record that the wonder working icon of our The Most-Holy Lady, The God-Bearer and Ever-Virgin was given as a gift to the monastery by the first archbishop of Moldavia, Iosif I. Andronic Popovici[35] mentions that Iosif I came into

---

31   Library of the Romanian Academy ('Biblioteca Academiei Române'), MS 1270, fols 126–35.
32   Arhimandrit Andronic Popovici, *Istoria Sfintelor Mănăstiri Neamț și Secu*, vol. I, ed. by Ion Gumenâi (Chișinău: Lexon Prim, 2016), p. 209.
33   *Istorie pentru Sfânta Icoană cea Făcătoare de Minuni a Preasfintei și Prea Binecuvântatei, Slăvitei Stăpânei Noastre de Dumnezeu Născătoarei și Pururea Fecioarei Maria, care se afla in Sfânta Mănăstire Neamțul și pentru minunile cele mai presus de fire ce a făcut Preacurata Maica lui Dumnezeu aicea, după vremi* ('History of the Holy Wonder Working Icon of the Most Holy and Most Blessed Lady the Birthgiver-of-God and Ever-Virgin Mary, which is kept at the Holy Neamț monastery and of the miracles made there by the Most Immaculate Mother of God') see in Agenția Națională a Arhivelor a Republicii Moldova, Fond 2119, inventar III, dosar 45.
34   Agenția Națională a Arhivelor…, Fond 2119, inventar III, dosar 45, fols 5–5ᵛ.
35   Arhimandrit Andronic Popovici, *Istoria Sfintelor Mănăstiri Neamț și Secu*, vol. I, ed. by Ion Gumenâi (Chișinău: Lexon Prim, 2016), pp. 102–03. Also, it is necessary to mention that the monastery of Neamț had under its administration the Oancea estate, where, the church houses 'the holy wonder

possession of the icon during the reign of John VIII Palaiologos (r. 1425–1448). The Byzantine emperor was on a journey and passed Moldavia, where he was met by Prince Alexander I (known as *Alexandru cel Bun*, c. 1375–1432) along with the boyars and Archbishop Iosif I, together with other church officials with the same high status. They all accompanied the Prince on his path to the port of Chilia. The Emperor was impressed by the reception he received and stated that he had never seen or heard of such a territory with so many gifts, traditions, words of wisdom and love of country. As a result of this pleasant reception and other political discussions, John VIII sent to Alexander I, the Act of Proclamation of the Orthodox Church of Moldavia as a Synodal (autonomous) Church. To Iosif I, the Emperor sent gifts, amongst which was this wonder working icon with two faces, on one side was depicted the Mother of Jesus Christ, and, on the other the Holy Martyr George slaying the dragon. This data confirmed that at the time of arriving in the Principality of Moldova, the icon was already known as a wonder working icon.[36]

Archimandrite Andronic Popovici, in his manuscript, describes eighteen miracles of the wonder working icon of the Birthgiver-of-God, narratives that reflect the ways in which the flock frame the image of the divinity and its intervention. The analysis of the miracles performed by the icon of the Most Holy Birthgiver-of-God at the monastery of Neamț, described by Andronic Popovici, includes a miracle that happened in the fifteenth century, two from the seventeenth century, four from the eighteenth century and the rest from the nineteenth century, the last one being described by the author as his own eyewitness account. The analysis of the works by the Hegumen of the monastery of Chițcani[37] prove that these miracles are mentioned in 'Istoria sfintelor mănăstiri Neamț și Secu', that one is described in volume I, four in volume IV and ten in volume VI, so only three were included in the thematic compilation. From the thematic point of view, nine miracles refer to the miraculous recovery of sick people; four are related to the wonder working icon and Paisius Velichkovsky, four with the levitation of the icon and one is related to the punishment of an Ottoman citizen. Also, the narratives give an argument

---

working icon of Saint Great Martyr Varvara. It is clad in silver and gilded with gold at certain places. The Holy Icon sits forever on a beautiful and delicately crafted wooden box polished with gold, offering healing to all faithful and accomplishing the request of those who arduously are praying to her …,' p. 283. Also, in Secu monastery, neighbour to the monastery of Neamț, there was a wonder working icon of the Holy Mother of God, about which, Andronic, writes in volume II of his work: 'Also, during this time, this holy monastery got in possession other holy objects: a reliquary made of gilded silver containing the foot of Saint Great Martyr Theodor Tiron; smaller parts of relics belonging to other saints; a gilded silver reliquary with a golden chain which held parts of many saints; and a wonder working icon of Most Blessed Lady the Bearer of God and Ever-Virgin Mary, clad in silver and polished with gold, which was decorated all around with parts of relics of many saints', p. 62.

36 It is interesting to note that in all ten volumes of the 'Istoria Sfintelor Mănăstiri Neamț și Secu', Archimandrite Andronic Popovici begins with the image of this icon, with the following inscription 'The holy wonder working icon of the Mother of God, named 'Nemțana', offered as a gift by the Greek Emperor, Joan Palaiologos, to Alexander, the Prince of Moldavia, alongside many precious objects and estates to Holy Neamț monastery in the year of 1401'.

37 Today in Republic of Moldova.

for assigning a *miracle habituel*[38] character to this icon, as most of the miracles were performed on the feast day of the Ascension of Jesus Christ.

As regards the wonders that happened at the monastery of Neamț, the first is dated back to the year 6999 from the creation of the world or AD 1491. It is reported that in this year from the birth of Christ, the icon of the Most Holy Birthgiver-of-God, when it was moved by chief priests and monks, it stood up as if it was freeing from their arms. This occurrence was interpreted as the icon bowing down to God.[39]

Archimandrite Andronic says that the Moldavian scribe Nicolae Grămăticul (d. 1708) came to the monastery of Neamț because of this miracle, he was searching through state and patriarchal documents to know more about this icon. Exactly in the year of his arrival, the second miracle happened, namely: 'Once, during a litany service when the icon was paraded around the monastery (as I have shown in the first miracle example – a. n.), when they took the icon back to the church, the holy icon freed itself from the people's hands and lifted itself up and levitated above the pulpit. And from there, it moved towards the imperial doors, it entered the altar and making a lap around the altar, it exited through other doors, and sat in its usual place, where it is to this day. Let this be known too, that the angels, who are near the Mother of God and serve her, lifted her icon in the air. This happened during the reign of Ștefan Gheorghiță'.[40]

Another miracle has a 'violent' component, revealing that the wonder working icon has also a 'dispenser of justice', feature credited by Andronic to Paisius Velichkovsky. Archimandrite described the case of a Turkish merchant who arrived at the monastery of Neamț during the holiday of Ascension of Our Lord, and seeing an opportunity to sell his merchandise, but also deriding the Orthodox folks, who, according to him, worshiped a plank of wood, said: 'I wonder at your poor judgement, because you believe in such fairytales'. As a response, one servant from the monastery proposed to him that he should take part in the holiday and be present when the icon would be taken out of the monastery. On the following day, when the holy icon was brought out, he asked the Turkish merchant to hold it by one side. And when the Turkish man brazenly puts his hands on the corner of the holy icon, suddenly, a miracle by the Mother of God! His hands became glued to the icon so thoroughly, as if they grew from it. And then the icon lifted itself up in the air with the Turkish man still glued to it, and began hitting itself over the walls of the monastery, until the Turkish man fainted. And the people, seeing this, begun shouting in unison: "Lord, have mercy!" and "Most Holy Birthgiver-of-God, have mercy on us!". And the Turkish merchant fainted that he looked as if he was dead. Then again, the icon came down into the hands of the Christian flock, and the Turk's hands were released, as he came down as if dead. The Christians took him and left him near his merchandise. When late at

---

38 Venance Grumel, 'Le «miracle habituel» de Notre-Dame des Blechernes à Constantinople', *Revue des études byzantines*, 34 (162), (1931), 129–46.
39 Arhimandrit Andronic Popovici, *Istoria Sfintelor Mănăstiri*…, vol. I, p. 125.
40 The Moldavian Prince Gheorghe Ștefan (r. 1653–1658). See Agenția Națională a Arhivelor…, Fond 2119, inventar III, dosar 45, fols 6ᵛ–7.

night, he regained his conscience and feeling ashamed, ran away from the monastery that very night'.[41]

In the description of the miracles performed by the wonder working icon, Andronic actually revealed one of the major causes of pilgrimages and travels of the people from the Principality of Moldavia towards the monastery of Neamț. Describing the fifth miracle he stated that 'because of the many miracles that happened, in many various ways, to people who asked with faith in their hearts and prayed to the icon, the simple people, not understanding why the miracles happened, explained this fact, because 'they bow' namely in this beautiful year, as it is written in *The Chronicles of Moldavia*.[42]

For this reason, a righteous old man, disciple of the Most Righteous Hegumen Paisius, recounted that once upon a time, during the feast day of the monastery, that is the holiday of Ascension of our Lord Jesus Christ, having a discussion with some honest worshipers, who asked the abbot, saying: 'Father, why does the Holy icon not bow any longer?', and the abbot replied 'My sons, I don't know how this thing happened in the past, how the icon 'bowed' before the Lord, and if it is appropriate, for the Mother of our Lord to bow to us, sinners, too, you can judge yourself. And all people know that its holiness that is wonder working. And when the need arises, it performs signs and miracles, for our strengthening and righting, of which, out of many, I will say one too … '.[43]

So, this passage showed beyond any doubts that even a part of the population made pilgrimages to the monastery, the miracles performed by the icon of the Mother of God served as an important catalyst to attract the inhabitants of the Principality of Moldavia to visit this monastic settlement, many wished to be part of the miracle, that it was thought would happen.

Conclusion

My investigation, operated on the data presented by Archimandrite Andronic Popovici, induces me to propose the following outcomes. The monastery of Neamț has become a point of pilgrimage for the inhabitants of the Principality of Moldavia, since the end of the fourteenth century, due to several realities. It was initially visited by people, namely because it was considered the oldest monastic settlement. In addition, the monastery of Neamț was the place where monks were trained, including for other monastic places, thus its fame and reputation as the principal secluded shrine of Moldavia grew. Later, the wonder working icon of the Most Holy and Most Venerated, God-Birther and Immaculate Virgin Mary was given as a gift by John VIII Palaiologos (r. 1425-1448) to Archbishop Iosif I. In such a way the monastery retains the quality to be one of the most important places of attraction for devotes in Moldavia. This enrichment of *sacra* of the country was complemented by the relics of Saint John the

---

41 Agenția Națională a Arhivelor…, Fond 2119, inventar III, dosar 45, 9–10ᵛ.
42 Andronic Popovici refers to one of the editions of 'Letopisețul Țării Moldovei', by Grigore Ureche. The edition and the year cannot be set unfortunately.
43 Agenția Națională a Arhivelor…, Fond 2119, inventar III, dosar 45, 9–10ᵛ.

New. Moreover, it is one of the icons that can be aligned with the relics of Saint John the New of Suceava and Saint Pious Paraskeva. These two saints were designated the protectors of Moldavia, as results of the efforts taken by both the State in the person of the prince and the Church in the person of the archbishop (metropolitan).

Referring to the wonder working icon, it was initially perceived as one of the sacred objects that performed miracles outside the borders of Moldavia. Then, beginning with 1491, the historical acts register a mention, probably, of the first miracles performed locally by the icon of the Mother of God at the monastery of Neamț, that were directly happening on the perimeter of the monastery. Despite the fact that the monastery of Neamț, as the documents show, had in its possession many solemn and holy objects of worship, like the wonder working icon of the Mother of God from the monastery of Secu and the wonder working icon of the Saint Varvara, the related icon, called 'Nemțana' had perpetually been the central piece. It retained its primary place in the worshipping practices of the ordinary people in Moldavia, throughout the medieval and modern times.

I consider this can be explained by several factors. In the first place, I refer to the popularity of the Marian cult among the Christians in Moldavia. Second, the icon was gifted by the emperor John VIII Palaiologos himself, brought from Constantinople, the principal authority centre of Orthodoxy. Third, it needs to be considered that the painter was Germanus I, the Patriarch of Constantinople, as well as this version of icons, painted on both sides were relatively rare in Moldavia. Also, as I have shown, it is necessary to consider the intensity and continuity of miracles performed by this wonder working icon.

This incidence of a saintly figure, authority, divine intervention and place played an important role in increasing of the devotion toward the icon, and as well was 'catalyst' of the journey at the monastery of Neamț, for the pilgrims from Moldavia, and as well for those outside the territory.

Archival Sources

National Agency of Archives of the Republic of Moldova ('Agenția Națională a Arhivelor a Republicii Moldova'), Fond 5.
Agenția Națională a Arhivelor a Republicii Moldova, Fond 2119, inventar III, dosar 72.
Agenția Națională a Arhivelor a Republicii Moldova, Fond 2119, inventar III, dosar 45.
Library of the Romanian Academy ('Biblioteca Academiei Române'), MS 1270, fols 126–35.

References

Arhimandrit Andronic Popovici, *Istoria Sfintelor mănăstiri Neamț și Secu*, vol. I, ed. by Ion Gumenâi (Chișinău: Lexon Prim, 2016).
Arhimandrit Andronic Popovici, *Istoria Sfintelor mănăstiri Neamț și Secu*, vol. III–IV, ed. by Ion Gumenâi (Chișinău: Lexon Prim, 2020).

Elisabeta Negrău, 'Pelerini din Țările Române la Ierusalim. Profiluri sociale și culturale (secolele XVI–XIX)', in *Călători și călătorii. A privi, a descoperi*, vol. I, ed. by Cristina Bogdan, Silvia Marin Barutcieff (București: Editura Universității din București, 2016), pp. 13–38.

Emil Dragnev, 'Sfinții Cefalofori: text și imagine în spațiul creștinătății orientale', in *In honoriem Răzvan Theodorescu*', ed. by Dana Jenei (București: Editura Oscar print, 2019), pp. 109–24.

Florin Grigorescu, *Sfântul Ioan cel Nou de la Suceava în viața credincioșilor* (Suceava: Editura Arhiepiscopiei Sucevei și Rădăuțului, 2003).

Grigore Ureche, *Letopisețul Țării Moldovei*, second edition. Edition carried out, introductory study, index and glossary by Petre. P. Panaintescu (București: Editura de Stat pentru Literatură și Artă, 1958).

Ion Vicovan and Cătălin Adumitroaie, *Cuvioasa Parascheva, sfânta populară a Ortodoxiei, în istoria și în evlavia poporului român* (Iași: Ed. Doxologia, 2011).

Liviu Pilat, 'Pelerinaje și penitenți în Moldova secolelor XIV–XV', in *Spectacolul public între tradiție și modernitate. Sărbători, ceremonialuri, pelerinaje și suplicii*, ed. by Constanța Vintilă-Ghițulescu and Mária Pakucs Willcocks (București: ICR, 2007), pp. 233–48.

Mircea Păcuraru, *Sfinți daco-romani și români* (Iași: Trinitas, 1994).

Nancy Frey, *Pilgrim Stories: On and Off the Road to Santiago* (Berkeley, CA: University of California Press, 1998).

Sorin Iftimi, 'Moaștele Cuvioasei Parascheva și rolul lor în istoria Moldovei', in *Teologia și Viața*, Revista Mitropoliei Moldovei, Iași, XI (LXXVII), 8–12, (2001), 39–50.

Ștefan S. Gorovei, 'Mucenicia Sfântului Ioan cel Nou. Noi puncte de vedere', in *Închinare lui Petre Ș. Năsturel, la 80 de ani*, ed. by Ionel Cândea, Paul Cernovodeanu și Gheorghe Lazăr (Brăila: Editura Istros, 2003), pp. 555–71.

Venance Grumel, 'Le «miracle habituel» de Notre-Dame des Blechernes à Constantinople', *Revue des études byzantines*, 34 (162), (1931), 129–46.

MARIA ALEXANDRA PANTEA

Pilgrimages and Pilgrims in the Arad County as an Expression of the Confessional, Ethnic and Socio-political Realities (1700–1939)

Introduction

The County of Arad, located in the western part of Romania, is an area where several ethnic groups and religious denominations coexist. It is a territory marked by the values of Central European culture and the interference between Orthodoxy and Catholicism.[1]

In this study I aimed to analyze the pilgrimages in Arad area taking into account the ethnic and religious structures, but also the policy pursued by the authorities. In this context, pilgrimages can be considered a mirror of ethnic and religious relations in the area.

There is little research on the pilgrimages organized in this area. This issue has not been addressed in any major scientific paper so far. Some information can be identified in the newspapers and in the memoirs of some intellectuals from the second half of the nineteenth century and the first four decades of the twentieth century. The archives of the Orthodox Archdiocese of Arad offer little information about this issue. More data can be identified at the Roman Catholic Basilica Maria Radna, where there are still offerings from pilgrims who have come here over the centuries. Scientific studies on the history of the Orthodox Church do not mention the pilgrimages of members of this denomination in the area, proof that the Orthodox Church did not consider them as important as the Catholic Church, which used pilgrimages also as a means of spreading Catholicism. In Catholic historiography, there is more information about the pilgrimages to the Maria Radna monastery and the miracles that took place here, attributed to an icon of

---

1 For the history of this region, see *Istoria Transilvaniei*, 3 vols, ed. by Ioan-Aurel Pop and Thomas Nägler (Cluj-Napoca: Academia Română, Centrul de Studii Transilvane, 2016).

Maria Alexandra Pantea • PhD, researcher at the Western University "Vasile Goldiș" in Arad, and Postdoctoral researcher at the University of Bucharest, Romania

Pilgrimage in the Christian Balkan World: The Path to Touch the Sacred and Holy, ed. by Dorina Dragnea, Emmanouil Ger. Varvounis, Evelyn Reuter, Petko Hristov and Susan Sorek (Turnhout, 2023), pp. 145–163.
BREPOLS PUBLISHERS   DOI 10.1484/M.STR-EB.5.132404

the Virgin Mary. Neglecting the subject of pilgrimages in the area in specialized scientific works led me to address this issue and to investigate the coexistence of the two denominations, but also the importance and role of pilgrimages in the area. In writing this study, I used especially the analytical and comparative methods, analyzing the information regarding this subject that I identified in different sources in the context of the epoch.

The evolution of the area has been closely linked to the great events of history. In the medieval documents, Orthodox Romanians are mentioned here, but there was also a spread of Catholicism after these territories became part of the Kingdom of Hungary, starting in the eleventh century. The collapse of the Kingdom of Hungary, following the defeat of Mohacs in 1526, allowed the Ottoman Empire to conquer the region in the mid-sixteenth century. It is a period in which Catholics are persecuted. However, Orthodox believers are more tolerated, Lipova being under the Ottoman rule the seat of an Orthodox Episcopate. At the end of the seventeenth century and the beginning of the eighteenth century, the territory was conquered by the Habsburg Empire, which supported a policy of modernization in parallel with one of Catholicization. One of the reasons behind this Habsburg religious policy was summed up by a Vienna court official, Councilor Borié, as follows: 'The good of the people and the state is better promoted if the people belong to the same religion as the sovereign'.[2] For the Habsburgs, the Church and the state were not 'two totally separate institutions, but intertwined in various forms'. Orthodox monasteries were integrated into new structures and entered 'the political calculus of the imperial rulers'.[3] This religious policy continued to a large extent in the following centuries, despite the political changes that Central Europe went through, and ended as a result of the events of the fall of 1918, when Austria-Hungary collapsed at the end of World War I, and this territory was united with Romania.

In this political and religious context, both Orthodox and Catholic Churches tried to consolidate their positions. Among other measures, they organized important pilgrimages to some specific place of interest. Catholics benefited from the activity carried out by Franciscan monks established at Maria Radna monastery after the signing of the Karlowitz Peace between the Ottomans and the Habsburgs in 1699. The Orthodox community had two important monasteries in the area, at Bezdin and Hodoș-Bodrog, and a bishopric,[4] whose headquarters moved to the Middle Ages from Lipova to Ineu, settling permanently in Arad in 1706.

---

2   Mathias Bernath, *Habsburgii și începuturile formării națiunii române* (Cluj: Editura Dacia, 1994), pp. 164–65.
3   Mihai Săsăujan, *Politica bisericească a Curții din Viena în Transilvania (1740–1761)* (Cluj-Napoca: Presa Universitară Clujeană, 2002), p. 58.
4   About the history of the Orthodox Bishopric of Arad see details in Pavel Vesa, *Episcopia Aradului: istorie, cultură, mentalități, 1701–1918* (Cluj-Napoca: Presa Universitară Clujeană, 2006).

The Beginnings of Pilgrimages in Arad County

The beginnings of pilgrimages in parts of Arad in the modern era are linked to the Maria Radna monastery, which was reorganized after the Habsburg Empire began to control these territories. Pilgrimages have been mentioned in church documents since 1707. At the beginning of the eighteenth century, this area was marked by wars and then by a great plague epidemic, which led people to believe and hope more in pilgrimages. In this context, after the conquest of Banat by the Habsburgs, the monks of Radna supported the organization of pilgrimages by spreading the news about some 'miraculous events'[5] that would have taken place at the monastery. It is the time when 'believers came on endless pilgrimages from far and wide to pray and worship in front of the miraculous icon.'[6] It can be seen that in the eighteenth century, as a result of the measures taken by the authorities of Vienna, Maria Radna monastery developed a lot. It has become the most important landmark of Catholicism in the area. This is the period when the Franciscan monks rebuilt the monastery to turn it into an important pilgrimage center. In 1756 a new church was built here. The works were completed in 1767, when the church was consecrated and a series of events were organized. The events took place between June 6–11, 1767 and were attended by '25 monks, 50 monk-priests, 16 diocesan priests, 2 prebendaries and 12,000 believers of various nationalities. Sermons were given in German, Hungarian, Illyrian, Croatian, Romanian, Bulgarian, Armenian.'[7]

For the Orthodox believers, Lipova became an important center of resistance, where pilgrimages began to be organized after 1744. Their beginnings are related to the actions of the Orthodox monk Visarion Sarai, who gave several sermons to oppose the spread of Catholicism in the area. Following his sermons, near Lipova, 'on a hill near a spring', he erected a cross, 'to which the crowd from all sides gravitated'.[8] The monk's cross became a place of pilgrimage for the Orthodox Romanians in the region of Arad, where serious attempts were made to catholicize by attracting the Orthodox Romanians to Greek Catholicism, a phenomenon that grew in Transylvania[9] and tried

---

5 Timea Lelik and Claudiu Călin, *Maria Radna. Mică monografie istorică și artistică a bazilicii papale și complexului monastic* (Arad: Carmel Print, 2011), p. 40.
6 Timea Lelik and Claudiu Călin, *Maria Radna*, p. 40.
7 Timea Lelik and Claudiu Călin, *Maria Radna*, p. 43.
8 Gheorghe Ciuhandu, *Românii din Câmpia Aradului: de acum două veacuri cu un excurs istoric până la 1752 și însemnări istorice politice ulterioare*, ed. by Constantin Jinga and Remus Feraru (Timișoara: Marineasa, 2005), p. 85.
9 Transylvania is the region located inside the Carpathian arc and belongs today to Romania. In the Middle Ages, it belonged to the Kingdom of Hungary, then it was an autonomous principality under Ottoman suzerainty (1541–1687), and at the end of the seventeenth century it was conquered by the Habsburg Empire. After the reorganization of the Habsburg monarchy as a dualist state under the name of Austria-Hungary, Transylvania was annexed to Hungary. In 1918, it was united with Romania. The population of Transylvania was composed from the beginning of the eighteenth century until 1918 of Romanians, Hungarians, Germans, and other ethnic groups, Romanians representing almost 60 per cent of the total. The name Transylvania is sometimes given, for reasons of convenience of expression, to all the territories west of the Carpathians that were united in 1918 with Romania (Transylvania proper, northeast of Banat, Crișana, and Maramureș).

to expand in Banat.[10] As a result of the events of 1744, a large number of Orthodox Christians came to pray and worship at the cross of the monk Visarion. They attracted the attention of the authorities who took harsh measures to stop the phenomenon in 1745. Those who were still crossing the Mureș River to climb to the monk's cross were to be punished with one hundred whiplashes. If they tried to reach the monk's cross even after that, they were fined twelve florins. Despite these punitive measures, the sermons given in Lipova by the monk Visarion and the way they were received by the Romanian population stopped for a few decades the spread of Catholicism in the area.

In the case of the Orthodox Church, the monastery of Bezdin was also developed. In the eighteenth century, it was rebuilt and had important properties, becoming an important pilgrimage centre for Orthodox people in the area. The patronal feast of the church is 'The Presentation of the Most Holy Mother of God (Theotokos) to the Temple'. Important pilgrimages are here organized on the occasion of the feast of the Assumption, on 28 August according to the Old Calendar. In the nineteenth century, after the separation of the Romanian Orthodox Church from Transylvania from the authority of the Metropolitanate of Sremski Karlovci,[11] Bezdin monastery became the most important Serbian monastery in the area. Occasionally, groups of Romanian Orthodox pilgrims also came to this monastery. According to Hermina Ciorogariu, at the end of the nineteenth century and the beginning of the twentieth century, groups of pilgrims coming on foot from Pecica participated in the feast of the Transfiguration. She also participated several times, being fascinated by the 'solar clock' existing on a wall of the monastery. Once there, the pilgrims were invited to the refectory, being served with fruit and fresh bread.

Another reference point for Orthodoxy in the Arad area is Hodoș-Bodrog monastery. Under the Serbian jurisdiction for a very long period, the monastery returned to the Romanians at the end of the nineteenth century. It became the most important monastic center of the Romanians from Banat and Crișana,[12] numerous pilgrimages being organized there.

---

10   Banat is the region located east of Carpathian Mountains, between the rivers Mureș, Tisa, and Danube. In the Middle Ages, Banat was annexed and ruled by the Kingdom of Hungary from the eleventh century until 1551, when most of it was conquered by the Ottoman Empire. In 1718 Banat was occupied by the Habsburg Empire, which intensely colonized it with a predominantly German Catholic population. Along with the Germans, Romanians (majority), Serbs, Hungarians, and other ethnic groups lived in this region. After 1867, being part of the Kingdom of Hungary within the Dualist Monarchy, Banat was subjected, like Transylvania, to a process of Hungarianization. In 1919, according to the decision of the Paris Peace Conference, the territory of Banat was divided between Romania (66 per cent), Serbia, (32 per cent), and Hungary.
11   For details see Keith Hitchins, *Orthodoxy and Nationality: Andreiu Șaguna and the Rumanians of Transylvania, 1846–1873* (Cambridge, MA: Harvard University Press, 1977).
12   Crișana is a region that belongs to Romania today, but in the Middle Ages it belonged in turn to the Kingdom of Hungary, the Principality of Transylvania, and the Ottoman Empire. In 1686, it was conquered by the Habsburg Empire, after 1867 it belonged to the Hungarian part of Austria-Hungary, and in 1918 united with Romania. It is located on the valleys of the three rivers called Criș: Crișul Alb, Crișul Negru, and Crișul Repede. Its boundaries are to the east the Apuseni Mountains, to the south the Mureș River and to the west the current frontier between Romania and Hungary. The city of Arad is located on the Mureș River, on the border between Banat and Crișana.

Pilgrimage to Maria Radna Monastery, Expression of Ethnic and Confessional Tolerance in the Arad County in the Nineteenth Century

During the nineteenth century, Catholic monks organized important pilgrimages to Maria Radna, the place being famous for the cult of the Virgin Mary and the miracle-working icon existing here. The writer Ioan Slavici, born in 1848 in an Orthodox family in the village of Șiria, near the monastery of Radna, was a good connoisseur of these realities. He wrote that 'worshiping this icon, many sufferers were healed and not a few among those who felt miserable found comfort'.[13] Slavici was also to witness the pilgrimages organized here in the second half of the nineteenth century, 'especially on the Feast of the Assumption, when people gather there from great distances both from Mureș and Banat as well as from the plain and the Criș Rivers, and even from Abrud. Day and night groups of believers passed in front of our house.'[14]

The importance of the pilgrimages organized to Maria Radna and the large number of participants can also be seen from the diary of votive donations concerning the period 1844–1926. Containing about hundred pages, the diary reveals all the offerings brought by the pilgrims. Various objects were donated, such as paintings, icons, cult books, jewellery – earrings, rings, necklaces, hairpins, medals, crosses and many replicas of various parts of the body, but also gold and silver coins – altar pillows, and many other things. Some of these objects can be seen today in the monastery and its museum.[15] Also related to the miraculous healings, spent at the monastery, is the custom of abandoning behind the altar 'crutches, sticks by the sick and the lame, who, being healed by miraculous powers at Radna, no longer needed these objects when they returned home'.[16]

The pilgrimages to Maria Radna monastery were very successful, because the place of worship was located near some important trade routes, which connected Banat and Crișana, but also Transylvania and Hungary. The pilgrimage to Maria Radna also brought some economic benefits to the area. On the occasion of these pilgrimages, an important fair was organized in Lipova on 15 August, which meant that after the liturgy the pilgrims crossed the bridge over Mureș, which connected Radna with Lipova, in order to buy what they needed.

A very interesting fact is that, although Maria Radna monastery is a Catholic place of worship, the miracle-working icon of the Mother of God, that is still found here today, has attracted many Orthodox pilgrims over time. At the end of the nineteenth century, the custom of organizing at least two large pilgrimages to Maria Radna every year was established. The first was on 15 August, when both Orthodox and Catholics celebrate the Assumption of the Blessed Virgin, a very important

---

13 Ioan Slavici, *Lumea prin care am trecut* (București: Minerva, 1978), p. 199.
14 Ioan Slavici, *Lumea*, p. 200.
15 Martin Roos, *Maria – Radna. Ein Wallfahrtsort im Südosten Europas*, II (Regensburg: Schnell & Steiner, 2004), p. 350.
16 Timea Lelik and Claudiu Călin, *Maria Radna*, p. 40.

holiday in the Orthodox world, on which occasion many Orthodox pilgrims arrived here. The second pilgrimage was on 8 September, when the birth of the Mother of God is celebrated in the two Churches, and the number of Catholic pilgrims was much higher.

Major events took place and pilgrimages increased at the end of the nineteenth century. They were the expression of some socio-cultural and political transformations that the Austro-Hungarian society was going through. It was a world that entered the path of modernization but was strongly marked by ethnic and denominational elements, facts supported by both the Catholic and Orthodox churches. Because it was an important means of spreading Catholicism, the Roman Catholic Diocese of Timișoara supported the organization of pilgrimages. In 1892, the Pilgrimage Association of Maria Radna was established in Timișoara, whose statutes were approved by the political authorities in 1909.[17]

At the end of the nineteenth century and the beginning of the twentieth century, many Orthodox Christians arrived at Maria Radna monastery, especially on the occasion of the feast of the Assumption, on which occasion services were performed in several languages, including Romanian, this being done by a Romanian Greek Catholic priest. In some localities in Banat there were important Greek Catholic communities subordinated to the diocese of Lugoj and the Pope of Rome. Founded by the papal bull issued by Pope Pius IX on 26 November 1853, the Greek Catholic diocese of Lugoj supported the process of Catholicization. According to the documents, the diocese supported and encouraged the movement of Greek Catholic believers to the Radna monastery, which meant that at the end of the nineteenth century and the beginning of the twentieth century a significant number of Romanian believers were present at these pilgrimages.

Regarding the presence of Greek Catholic Romanians, but also Orthodox, at the pilgrimages organized at Maria Radna at the end of the nineteenth century, is interesting and important the testimony of the Greek Catholic priest Ioan Boroș from Zăbrani parish. This village is located near Lipova, and at the end of the nineteenth century it was the seat of a Greek Catholic parish that included 16 branches, including Lipova. The priest Ioan Boroș, an important Greek Catholic theologian, was the one who, through his activity for almost two decades, contributed to the consolidation of Greek Catholicism in the area and organized for this purpose pilgrimages to Maria Radna monastery. His notes show that at the end of the nineteenth century he organized a separate pilgrimage from the Catholic Swabians to celebrate the Assumption of the Blessed Virgin and was followed by other Greek Catholic priests in the area. Referring to that pilgrimage, he wrote that he was very pleased, because 'a large number of people from the branches and even Greek Orthodox'[18] participated, and the population moved to the monastery on foot, in 'exemplary order'. Ioan Boroș was the one who greeted the Romanian pilgrims from Banat and 'introduced them in order through Lipova to the Holy Monastery'. On the occasion of the pilgrimages, the priest participated in the Divine Liturgy. During the services he gave two sermons, one on the evening of August 14 in the

---

17 Martin Roos, *Maria – Radna*, I (Regensburg: Schnell & Steiner, 1998), p. 263.
18 Ioan Boroș, *Memorialistică* (Cluj-Napoca: Presa Universitară Clujeană, 2012), p. 137.

chapel and another on August 15 in the open air, the sermons being full of 'religious enthusiasm and conviction'.[19]

For better organization of the pilgrimages at the beginning of the twentieth century, the Greek Catholic Episcopate of Lugoj took some steps among the creation of the 'Mission Reunion',[20] which aimed to maintain spiritual activity for Greek Catholic believers by organizing popular missions. To achieve this goal, the mission sent priests with 'oratorical talent' to speak to the crowd. Among those who led one of these pilgrimages on the occasion of the Feast of the Assumption in 1907 was the young Greek Catholic theologian Nicolae Brânzeu, who accompanied a group of pilgrims. Arriving at Maria Radna monastery, he was deeply moved, because 'more Romanians than Germans had gathered at that feast.'[21] He also writes that a pilgrimage was organized on the occasion of the feast of the Nativity of Mary when more Hungarian Catholics participated.

The massive participation of Romanian Orthodox in Catholic pilgrimages was also possible due to the policy of Catholicization achieved through large Catholic landowners, who urged Romanians to participate and provided transportation. Analyzing the situation of the Orthodox Romanians in these territories at the end of the nineteenth century and the beginning of the twentieth century, we can see that they benefited from some advantages offered by the Roman Catholic Church and those who supported Catholicism in the area, but there was no massive transition of the population from Orthodoxy to Catholicism, a sign that Catholic dogma was not accepted.

Pilgrimages to Hodoş-Bodrog Monastery, an Expression of the Romanian National Spirit at the End of the Nineteenth Century and the Beginning of the Twentieth Century

Orthodox believers participated in large numbers in pilgrimages at Maria Radna monastery, because they did not have a Romanian monastery until 1887. Hodoş-Bodrog was an Orthodox monastery, but it was administered and run by Serbs, and the liturgical language used was the Slavonic one, which was foreign to the Romanians. Until the end of the nineteenth century, the Serbs owned all the Orthodox monasteries in Banat, from where large sums of money went to the treasury of the Orthodox Metropolitanate of Sremski Karlovci. In 1887, after the separation of the Romanian Orthodox Church from Transylvania from the authority of the Metropolitanate of Sremski Karlovci,[22]

---

19   Ioan Boroş, *Memorialistică*, p. 138.
20   Sergiu Soica, *Biserica greco-catolică din Banat în perioada anilor 1920–1948* (Timişoara: Eurostampa, 2012), p. 95.
21   Nicolae Brânzeu, *Memoriile unui preot bătrân*, II-nd edition, ed. by Pia Brânzeu (Timişoara: Marineasa, 2015), p. 359.
22   The hierarchical separation of the Romanian and Serbian Orthodox Churches from the Metropolitan Church of Sremski Karlovci began in 1864. Its implementation lasted several decades, during which time Romanians and Serbs divided the assets of the Orthodox Church. See details in Keith Hitchins, *Orthodoxy and Nationality*.

Cornel Jifcovici, the last Serbian hegumen, was moved to Mesici,[23] and Hodoș-Bodrog monastery became Romanian. The Catholics of Radna did not face these problems, here being a strong Franciscan monastery, involved in a process of Catholicization that manifested itself in several forms and was supported by the political class.

At the end of the nineteenth century, after Hodoș-Bodrog monastery was taken over by the Romanian Orthodox diocese of Arad, the changes took place slowly and, although the service was introduced in Romanian, 'the old customs were still maintained'. These changed only in the last years of the nineteenth century, when the number of Orthodox who reached Maria Radna increased, which impressed negatively the leadership of the Arad Orthodox diocese. The appointment of the theologian Augustin Hamsea as abbot of Hodoș-Bodrog monastery led to a better organization of it and its transformation into an important place of pilgrimage for Orthodox Romanians.

At the beginning of the twentieth century, Hodoș-Bodrog monastery was partially rebuilt and could receive pilgrims, even if it still faced many material and financial problems, as noted by Nicolae Iorga in 1905. Wanting to know the situation of the Romanians in the dualist monarchy, he would also travel to Hodoș-Bodrog monastery. Arriving here, Iorga was impressed by the antiquity of the monastery, stating that it resembles the shape of the oldest churches in Muntenia, built by 'wandering Serbian monks' in the fourteenth century, but also discovered the cells of 'about six unseen monks, mostly elders with no thought of books and a taste for work, and without a special piety'.[24] It is the period when the Orthodox priests became more and more involved in organizing these pilgrimages and it can be seen that more and more groups of pilgrims led by priests arrived at the monastery. According to the press of the time, in 1901 about 12,000 Orthodox believers arrived in Bodrog. This was possible because 'pious and worthy priests led beautiful processions, thus satisfying the desire of the multitude of the people to hear words of consolation in their monastery in their language.'[25] From the beginning of the twentieth century, during the pastorate of Bishop Ioan I. Papp of Arad, the pilgrimages organized to Hodoș-Bodrog monastery 'were perpetuated, on the occasion of the patron saint going to the monastery thousands of believers from the parishes of the diocese of Arad or from the neighbouring ones, especially since the Bishop himself participates in the religious services officiated on the occasion of these manifestations'.[26] In 1907, on the same feast of the Assumption of the Blessed Virgin Mary, about 25,000 believers came there 'from great distances'.[27]

These actions determined the transformation of the monastery into an important pilgrimage point in the area. In 1903, some of the leaders of the Romanians from Banat

---

23 Orthodox monastery located in the southwest of Banat, in present-day Serbia, near the town of Vršac.
24 Nicolae Iorga, *Pagini alese din însemnările de călătorie prin Ardeal și Banat*, 2 vol. (București: Minerva, 1977), II, p. 116.
25 [Anon.] 'La mănăstirea Hodoș-Bodrogului', *Bunul econom*, Orăștie, 1/14 Septembrie 1901, p. 7.
26 Pavel Vesa, *Episcopii Aradului: 1706–2006* (Arad: Gutenberg Univers, 2007), p. 207.
27 Pavel Vesa, *Clerici cărturari arădeni de altădată* (Arad: Gutenberg Univers, 2008), p. 195.

arrived here as pilgrims. In July 1903, when Archpriest Andrei Ghidiu organized a conference,[28] the participants decided to go on a pilgrimage to Hodoş-Bodrog. On this occasion, the theologian Iosif Bădescu gave a speech and showed the importance of pilgrimages, fighting 'from a church and national point of view against pilgrimages to unorthodox monasteries'. It was decided that the pilgrimage should be organized on August 10, 1903. The press also states that the Romanians wanted to organize a 'procession to the Romanian monastery Bodrog, which will end the excursions for us to no avail to Maria Radna'.[29]

Witnessing the events that took place at the beginning of the twentieth century, the teacher Hermina Ciorogariu from Pecica would report that on the occasion of the patron saint, the Assumption of the Blessed Virgin Mary, she participated in the pilgrimage from Bodrog together with a group of Romanian Orthodox and travelled on foot. She also reminds that all the studious youth from the locality, led by the students at the Pedagogical School (Preparandia), 'participate in this pilgrimage'. These manifestations of faith were considered by Hermina Ciorogariu a 'complementary course' because they were attended by representatives of all social categories, which offered young people 'a wider horizon where you met well-mannered people, hardworking peasants, and decent children. I always came away spiritually refreshed'.[30]

Before the outbreak of the First World War, the monastery was an important place of pilgrimage and dissemination of religious propaganda among Romanians. This was possible due to the activity of Augustin Hamsea, who managed to make the monastery 'a sought-after place of worship where thousands of pilgrims came every year to seek spiritual comfort and healing'.[31] By organizing these pilgrimages, the priests were involved in educating and popularizing religious and moral literature among the people. After the achievement of the Great Union of Romanians in 1918, the education of the great masses by the priests manifested itself in the form of defending Orthodoxy, which was considered the ancestral religion.

According to the documents of the time, at the beginning of the twentieth century, but also after the end of the First World War, there were relations between believers and monasteries, marked by organizing pilgrimages on 'the occasion of the patron saint or by charitable institutions that have acquired an increasingly important share in church life'.[32]

---

28 Andrei Ghidiu was archpriest of Oraviţa, then of Caransebeş at the beginning of the twentieth century. He has been involved in many cultural and artistic activities. In 1918 he participated in the Great National Assembly of the Romanians in Alba Iulia, voting for the Union of Transylvania with Romania. See details in Ioan Munteanu, Vasile M. Zaberca, and Mariana Sârbu, *Banatul şi Marea Unire 1918* (Timişoara: Editura Mitropoliei Banatului, 1992), p. 210.
29 [Anon.], 'La mănăstirea Bodrogului', *Biserica şi Şcoala*, Arad, 6/19 Iulie 1903, p. 216.
30 Hermina Ciorogariu, *Caietele Herminei* (Bucureşti: Peter Pan Art, 2010), p. 64.
31 Eugen Arădeanul, Lucian Emandi, and Teodor Bodogae, *Mănăstirea Hodoş Bodrog* (Arad: Editura Episcopiei Aradului, 1980), p. 76.
32 Pavel Vesa, *Episcopii Aradului*, p. 207.

The Integration of Arad in Greater Romania, a New Reality for the Roman Catholic Church

After the Great Union in 1918 and the drawing of new borders, both the Orthodox and the Roman Catholic Church were reorganized, adapting to the new conditions. In the mid-1920s, the two churches were involved in organizing pilgrimages. Considered 'concrete representations of the faith', in the interwar period they became 'the essential concern of the monastery',[33] both for the Orthodox and for the Catholics, but now the way in which the pilgrimages were thought about organized has differentiated, because the emphasis was on the ethnic element and the definition of a confessional ethnic identity.

The Catholic Diocese of Timișoara supported the organization of pilgrimages to Maria Radna. Associations were set up in some wealthy parishes to organize pilgrimages to this monastery, following the model of the association established in Timișoara in 1892. This is the case of associations organized in Lugoj and Jimbolia.[34]

Interesting information on how were organized the pilgrimages to Maria Radna monastery at the beginning of the Interwar Period can be found in the correspondence of the chaplain Augustin Bartoș from Timișoara with the representatives of the Prefecture of Arad. On 23 June 1921, the Roman Catholic chaplain sent a letter to the Prefect of Arad and requested authorization to make a pilgrimage to Maria Radna. The letter briefly presents the situation of Hungarian Roman Catholic believers who want to reach the monastery, a goal that has not been achieved for several years due to political and military unrest. He demands that the pilgrimage be held on August 2 and not on July 26, justifying that only then can the chaplain leave the parish and lead the group of pilgrims. The trip was to be made by train, the departure was set for the morning of 31 July, and the return on 3 August. The Catholic priest assumes responsibility for maintaining order during the pilgrimage, stating that 'pilgrims will be busy with prayer and church singing'. He also mentions that the faithful are preparing for the pilgrimage 'with the greatest joy of the soul' and they are in great need of this pilgrimage, which could not be accomplished in previous years. The priest also asked the prefect that, in case of approval, the leadership of Lipova and Radna districts be announced so that 'pilgrims on their journey should not be upset by anyone, that otherwise the pilgrim believers, instead of praying for the soul, will get their souls damaged and the exercise will be futile'. Following the efforts of the Roman Catholic priest Augustin Bartoș, the Prefect of Arad, Radu Pancu, on 8 July 1921 approved the pilgrimage and proposed that during it a platoon of soldiers be moved to Radna, as well as the gendarmerie in the area, to ensure peace and the smooth running of the event. He recommended that the train carrying pilgrims be a direct or one-stop train.[35]

---

33 Victor Vlăduceanu, *Vechiu monument istorico-religios – Mănăstirea Bodrog* (Timișoara: Victoria, 1939), p. 88.
34 Martin Roos, *Maria – Radna*, I, p. 263.
35 Arad, County Service of the National Archives of Romania ('Arad, Serviciul Județean al Arhivelor Naționale ale României') *Fond Prefectura județului Arad – actele subprefectului*, dos. 27/1921, fol. 3.

As a result of the new realities, in the Interwar Period we can see that, through a stronger involvement of the churches in the organization of pilgrimages, preservation and defence of the confessional identity were also desired. In this context, the Orthodox diocese of Arad took measures to more and more convince Romanians not to go to Maria Radna monastery. Contrarywise, the Catholic Church, which lost its influence in the area as a result of the Union of Transylvania with Romania of 1918–1919, wanted to strengthen its position. But, by carrying out the Agrarian Reform of 1921, both the Catholic and Orthodox Church lost important agricultural areas, leading to a decline in their annual incomes. In this context, emphasis began to be placed on the economic aspect of pilgrimages, which combined with the moral-religious one.

The situation of Maria Radna monastery is described by the historian Nicolae Iorga, who in 1924 arrived in Radna, where he discovered a 'corner of Loreto[36] [...], high and spacious monastery building', but also 'small shops that sell holy objects in all shapes and sizes for all prices'. The historian noted the richness of the Franciscan library, with an 'infinity of well-bound books', but also the former power of the monastery, which in 'residential buildings could house an army', and the surrounding hills, full of vineyards and orchards. Surprised by what he saw, he found that the monastery had reached a difficult situation and received 'from time to time a lot of peasants running for comfort and assurance. Swabians, Hungarians, Romanians, Serbs of all laws come to mind, thinking of the cattle that must be protected from accidents, the harvest that must be guaranteed by hail, along with their own health.'[37]

The Romanian Orthodox Monastery of Hodoș-Bodrog, Place of Pilgrimage and Symbol of Orthodoxy in Interwar Romania

Hodoș-Bodrog monastery was also going through a difficult period at the beginning of the 1920s, a fact largely determined by a too small number of monks residing here, but also by the lack of measures taken by the Arad Bishopric. The situation changed in 1925, after the death of bishop Ioan Ignatie Papp. As early as 1925, the new bishop of Arad, Grigore Comșa, took new measures in order to organize pilgrimages. A circular from July 1925 shows that on the occasion of the feast of the patron saint in Bodrog, 'groups of pilgrims arrive in search of rest and spiritual strengthening at the holy monastery'. It is also stated that the representatives of the diocese will take part in the pilgrimage, contributing to the 'comfort and strengthening of the faithful'. The bishop asked the priests to announce the organization of the pilgrimage and to get involved in organizing groups of believers who were to arrive at the monastery. Where possible, a priest should accompany the group and 'supervise the way believers behave along the way'. The bishop also stated that during his pastorate he wants to strengthen the religious life of the people and for this to happen the feast will have to be better organized of the patron saint of the Holy Bodrog monastery at

---

36 Loreto is an important Catholic pilgrimage center in Italy.
37 Nicolae Iorga, *Pagini alese*, II, p. 219.

the Assumption, when 'groups of pilgrims seek rest and strengthening of the soul'.[38] Examining the documents, we can see that during his pastorate (1925–1935), bishop Grigore Comșa distinguished himself as a defender of Orthodoxy. It is the period when the pilgrimages organized at the Hodoș-Bodrog monastery rose to the 'true revelation of the soul',[39] according to the historian and priest from Arad, Pavel Vesa, and the services held on the occasion of the patron saint were magnificent, often being performed even by the bishop of Arad.

For the reorganization of the monastery, the monk Policarp Morușca was appointed hegumen on 25 November 1925. The new hegumen revived the pilgrimages, which began to be organized within well-established programs. Through his activity, he gave new life to the monastery. He would remember that from 1925 the pilgrimages were reorganized by creating religious missions of three-four days on the occasion of the feast of the Assumption. The best priests in the diocese, who participated with groups of believers, were involved in organizing these pilgrimages.

During the Interwar Period, several pilgrimages were made annually to Hodoș-Bodrog monastery, but the most important one was organized around the 15 August on the occasion of the monastery's patron saint, the Assumption. After the appointment of Policarp Morușca as hegumen of the monastery, great works were carried out to restore and modernize the old place. He is the one who reorganized the pilgrimages and managed to 'create a more appropriate framework for the pilgrims' program, initiating the so-called *Way of the Cross*, which established several prayer and meditation stops in the garden and cemetery of the monastery'. Through these arrangements, the aim was to attract a larger number of believers and transform the monastery into a 'true place of worship'.[40] Policarp Morușca would write that through the measures he took he wanted the monastery to become a place of pilgrimage for high school students, who had to be inspired by a new conception of life and a 'mentality more Christian than the one that dominates public life today'. Policarp Morușca knew well the realities that society was facing and acted in this regard. He believed that the Church should be more involved in educating young people in a national spirit so that they could become 'learned men' who would be 'a good example for people', contributing to their prosperity. The importance of pilgrimages is underlined in several articles in the official publication of Arad Bishopric, *Biserica și Școala*: 'The Holy Hodoș-Bodrog monastery is an old and holy place of pilgrimage of our gentle people, but also our only monastery in Transylvania where, from the past to the more recent time, all the prelates of our holy church have taken the monastic tonsure. Here is the Jerusalem of our Christians in the diocese of Arad, it is *the Pool of Bethesda*, where at the Dormition of the Mother of God our people come to raise to the heavenly throne prayers for their eternal and temporary salvation'.[41]

---

38   Grigorie Gh. Comșa, 'Circulară cătră toți P. O. Părinți protopopi și preoți din eparhia Aradului', *Biserica și Școala*, 2 August 1925, p. 3.
39   Pavel Vesa, *Episcopii Aradului*, p. 208.
40   Eugen Arădeanul, Lucian Emandi, and Teodor Bodogae, *Mănăstirea Hodoș Bodrog*, p. 81.
41   [Anon.], 'Pelerinaj la sf. mănăstire H.-Bodrog', *Biserica și Școala*, 9 August 1925, p. 8.

The reorganization of the pilgrimages led to the arrival at the annual feast in Bodrog of 12,000–14,000 believers in the years 1925–1930. This was the most important pilgrimage, the service being performed by an impressive council of priests, led by the bishop of Arad, who often took the floor showing the importance of the event, which made the pilgrims live solemn moments. The most important point was the *Way of the Cross*, through which a restoration of the way to the Calvary of Jesus Christ was desired.

Pilgrims and Pilgrimages in the Interwar Period, an Expression of the Socio-Political Changes after 1918

In 1926 the pilgrimages were made together with the religious missions and led to the movement of an impressive number of believers to Bodrog monastery. On the occasion of the feast, the activities began on 12 August and there were services, but also religious missions. Priests were asked to come in large numbers to 'refresh their souls at the inexhaustible fountain of living water'. The intellectuals who arrived could be accommodated by some believers in the area, but for this the management of the monastery had to be announced. It was allowed to sell religious books and icons, if they had the blessing of the Holy Synod.[42] Among the thousands of believers who arrived in Bodrog in August 1926 was a group of sixty-eight people from Lupești, led by the priest-teacher Ioan Tomuția. Arriving in Arad, they joined another group of ninety-five believers from Lipova, led by priest Vasile Dăbău. From the accounts of Ioan Tomuția we can see that the pilgrims who arrived in Bodrog were happy and expressed their desire to return annually on the day of the patron saint of the monastery, and the priest was confident that these pilgrimages will make 'sure to stop the great wandering of some of our faithful who, for lack of clarification, stopped at the Catholic monastery in Radna.'[43] The large number of those who arrived in Bodrog on the occasion of the feast of the Assumption of the Blessed Virgin Mary and their needs determined the theologians from Arad to organize several pilgrimages during the most important holidays of the summer. The pilgrimages began at Pentecost and ended on 14 September, when the feast of the Exaltation of the Holy Cross was celebrated. In 1928, the pilgrimages to the Bodrog monastery were no longer made together with the religious missions and were organized in several days, in order to avoid the gathering of a big crowd on 15 August and to turn the feast into a holiday of 'spiritual joy'. During the whole period of pilgrimage, important groups of believers arrived here. The Assumption of the Blessed Virgin, the patron saint of the church, remained the moment of 'general pilgrimage', but religious missions were not organized on this occasion for several days, as in previous years. On the evening of 14 August, a service was held, followed by a church music contest, in which church choirs from

---

42 [Anon.], 'Pelerinajul la Sf. Mănăstire Hodoș-Bodrog. Programul', *Biserica și Școala*, 1 August 1926, p. 2.
43 Ioan Tomuția, 'Impresii de la pelerinajul la Sf-ta M.-re H.-Bodrog', *Biserica și Școala*, 19 Septembrie 1926, p. 5.

all over were able to participate. In the years that followed, the pilgrimages and religious missions for the 'exaltation of the soul, the religious revival, and the moral strengthening of the faithful' were organized between 6 August and 14 September, and each pilgrimage lasted three days.

The changes continued in the following period, being determined by the events facing the society. In 1930, priests were asked to instruct their faithful, because only church songs would be sung according to the 'Orthodox ordinance' and 'foreign loan songs' would be completely removed.[44] In this context, Hodoș-Bodrog monastery played an important role. In 1930, Vasile Goldiș shows that Hodoș-Bodrog monastery is 'a source of consolation for many thousands of faithful pilgrims'.[45]

It is interesting that even in the Interwar Period, a large number of Romanians arrived at the Maria Radna monastery, but now most of them were Greek Catholics. According to the documents, after the Great Union (1918) for the Greek-Catholic diocese of Lugoj 'an important aspect was the regulation of pilgrimages to Radna', where many Greek-Catholic pilgrims from Lugoj and Arad arrived every year. The priest Nicolae Brânzeu, who arrived here in the interwar period and was a diocesan counsellor since 1921, recalls that after the war, during the pilgrimages organized at Maria Radna, many Greek Catholic priests were present. They performed the religious service, collecting beautiful sums of money. As a diocesan counsellor, Nicolae Brânzeu also took care of the 'mission and spiritual leadership of the pilgrimages from Radna'.[46] Pilgrimages were organized on the basis of a well-established program, and services were held only by priests who had been appointed by the Mission Reunion that functioned within the diocese of Lugoj. From the money raised, the priests withheld 'their expenses', while the rest went to the Mission Reunion.

The assertion in Central Europe of an extremist right-wing current,[47] as well as the political rivalry between Romania and Hungary after the unification of Transylvania with Romania in 1918, made the pilgrimages organized by both the Orthodox Church and the Roman Catholic Church give rise to nationalist manifestations. There were some transformations in the ethnic and confessional structure of the pilgrims who arrived at Maria Radna monastery. There is a decrease in the number of Romanians and an increase in the number of Hungarians who came from Hungary as pilgrims for 'soul salvation'. This also led to the emergence of delicate situations and the consideration of the monastery more as a place of propaganda than pilgrimage.

According to the information from the press of the time, the nationalism that was spreading both in Romania and Hungary had an impact on the way in which the pilgrimages were organized. In 1933, an event dedicated to the cult of the Heart of Jesus was organized in Budapest, being considered by a Romanian journalist as

---

44 Arhimandrit Policarp, 'Pelerinajele la sf. Mănăstire H. Bodrog', *Biserica și Școala*, 20 Iulie 1930, p. 2.
45 [Anon.], 'O propunere a d-lui Vasile Goldiș', *Calendar pe anul 1932* (Arad: Editura Tipografiei Diecezane, 1931), p. 74.
46 Nicolae Brânzeu, *Memoriile unui preot bătrân*, p. 359.
47 See details about the rise of the far right in interwar Romania and Hungary in Nicholas M. Nagy-Talavera, *The Green Shirts and the Others: A History of Fascism in Hungary and Romania* (Iași: The Center for Romanian Studies, 2001).

'the expression of Hungarian chauvinism'. A pilgrimage followed to Radna 'under the auspices of the Society of the Cult of the Heart of Jesus, but with revisionist thoughts', according to the same journalist. Greek Catholics, who were Romanians, also took part in the Radna pilgrimage, a fact criticized by the Romanian press of the time.[48] As a result of the existing political situation, in the 1930s an important pilgrimage to Maria Radna was organized between 20 August and 1 September, on which occasion large groups of ethnic Hungarians came and celebrated the feast of St Stephen, a fact considered by the Romanian press as being a gesture of 'shedding the Hungarian irredentist venom', but also a 'defiance of us'. In 1932, during a farewell banquet, 'toasts were held for Greater Hungary', a political diversion of the religious manifestation that displeased Roman Catholic Bishop Augustin Pacha of Timișoara, who 'was present and had to leave the table'.[49]

In 1935, the same bishop was involved in organizing a great pilgrimage to the monastery, which brought more than 73,000 pilgrims, many of them on foot, 'the highest number in the history of Maria Radna'.[50]

In the early 1930s, next to Hodoș-Bodrog monastery, the church in Lipova will stand out as an important centre for the dissemination of Orthodoxy. After the restoration of this church, as a result of the policy pursued by the diocese of Arad, it became a place of pilgrimage. The church was regaining some of its former fame and has been 'reintegrated into its old role as a defender of the ancestral faith.' The transformation of the church in Lipova into a monastery was possible because the place was a symbol of Orthodoxy, and since ancient times the Orthodox Church in Lipova has been visited by pilgrims 'from different places, but a small number, namely our faithful who accompanied pilgrims at the Catholic monastery in Radna, they went to Lipova to confess and commune according to the ancestral law.' This event is part of a series of measures taken by the Orthodox Church that aimed to support 'the ancestral Church' in an area characterized by ethnic and cultural diversity and where in the Interwar Period many neo-Protestant denominations spread. During the Interwar Period, pilgrimages can also be considered a mirror of society. Due to the organization of large pilgrimages by the Roman Catholic Church to Maria Radna monastery and the participation of some Orthodox in them, in 1933 Bishop Grigore Comșa reintroduced the pilgrimages to the Church of the Assumption in Lipova as a 'replica of those organized by Roman Catholics in Radna.' In the years that followed, the church in Lipova became a place of pilgrimage. The priest Ilie Chebeleu from Șoimoș, witness of the events, would write in the parish chronicle: 'Many pilgrims came to the Radna monastery this year, but most of them were attracted by the beautiful church from Lipova where they attended divine services.'[51]

The first pilgrimage, organized in 1932 by the archpriest of Lipova, Fabricius Manuilă,

---

48 [Anon.], 'Informațiuni', *Biserica și Școala*, 9 Iulie 1933, p. 7.
49 C. Mureșan, 'Activitatea iredentistă a Mănăstirei Radna.', *Biserica și Școala*, 26 August 1934, p. 9.
50 *History, Maria Radna, the most significant place of pilgrimage in south-eastern Europe* https://www.mariaradna.com/en/history (accessed on 01.07.2021).
51 Ilie Chebeleu, *Cronica de la Șoimoș* (Timișoara: David Print Press, 2020), p. 226.

was attended by about 2000 believers. In 1933, the church of Lipova was transformed into a monastery, to be a place of pilgrimage where the sons of the Orthodox Church who were 'wandering around the papists from Radna' would be guided.

The transformation of the church into a monastery and the organization of new pilgrimages to Lipova by the Orthodox Church aimed at counteracting the activities organized at the Roman Catholic monastery Maria Radna, where thousands of Orthodox believers arrived. According to information from the press of the time, until 1932 'was ingrained the custom that on the feast of the Assumption of the Blessed Virgin, along with Greek Catholic believers to participate in the Roman Catholic monastery of Maria Radna Greek Orthodox believers also.'[52] In 1933, the number of those who came to Lipova, 'strengthening more and more their ancestral faith' was around 6,000 Orthodox believers from Banat, Crișana, and Transylvania. In 1934, the number of believers was between 6,000–8,000 and they came from the villages on the Mureș Valley and from the Arad Vineyard, but also from 'the greatest distances of Transylvania, Banat, and Crișana'.[53]

The assertion of Lipova as an important ecclesiastical centre diminished the importance of the pilgrimages organized in Bodrog, thousands of pilgrims, led by representatives of the high clergy, reaching Lipova. Here, some politicians of the time also took part in pilgrimages, such as the former minister Sever Bocu, who lived in Lipova. In the following period, pilgrimages were organized in Lipova 'together with religious missions', and the pilgrims arrived here as early as 14 August. In 1937, the priests who were to accompany the groups of believers in Lipova were asked to announce the approximate time of arrival and the number of believers, 'so that they can be housed in the gym of the state mixed gymnasium, at the boarding school of the school of commerce, as well as at the believers in the city.'[54]

At the same time, Bodrog remained the favourite place for many pilgrims from outside the Arad diocese, being an important symbol for the Orthodox world. Victor Vlăduceanu pointed out that the pilgrimages organized in Bodrog during the interwar period reached many pilgrims, so that on the roads near the monastery there were waves of pilgrims coming singing, and 'the great courtyard of the monastery is filled with people'. Here large crowds gathered in prayer, who sometimes had the joy of witnessing miracles, such as the healing of the sick. In August 1933, on the occasion of the feast, pilgrims came here from Caransebeș, Bihor, Abrud, or Câmpeni, but also from the Romanian communities in Hungary, from where 150 believers arrived, led by the priest Sabău Dumitru from Gyula.[55] In 1935, during the two pilgrimages, one on the occasion of the Feast of the Transfiguration on 6 August and the other one on 15 August, on the occasion of the Feast of the Assumption, the monastery was visited by believers from 80 parishes, and 'the priests and the people left satisfied,

---

52 [Anon.], 'Un nou loc de pelerinaj: biserica din Lipova', *Biserica și Școala*, 21–28 August 1932, p. 11.
53 [Anon.], 'Pelerinajele la Biserica ort. română – veche Mănăstire din Lipova – Banat la Adormirea Maicii Domnului în anul 1934', *Biserica și Școala*, 16 Septembrie 1934, p. 4.
54 [Anon.], 'Programa Pelerinajelor la Sfânta Biserici ort. română din Lipova Banat, în zilele de 14 și 15 August', *Biserica și Școala*, 1 August 1937, p. 277.
55 [Anon.], 'Pelerinaj la Sf. Mănăstire a Bodrogului', *Biserica și Școala*, 27 August 1933, p. 3.

for, in addition to satiating their hunger and thirst, they had wherewith to bow their heads.'[56] Among the Arad theologians involved in organizing the pilgrimages at Bodrog in the 1930s was the priest Ilarion Felea, who 'assumes the form of the pilgrimage since then walking with hundreds of believers through the Ceala forest to Bodrog.'[57] In 1937 he went to Bodrog with a hundred pilgrims. Arriving at the monastery, he gave sermons at the first six stops on the *Way of the Cross*. In 1938, together with the priest Florea Codreanu, he published a book of songs for pilgrims entitled *Prayers and Songs for Pilgrims Going to the Holy Monastery*.

The measures taken by the Orthodox Church, but also the concerns regarding the political situation, made that before the outbreak of the Second World War Hodoș-Bodrog monastery was visited by pilgrims from the most remote corners of Banat and Transylvania, but also by Romanians from Hungary and Yugoslavia. According to the press, at the two pilgrimages organized in August 1939 there were pilgrims from the farthest corners of the Diocese of Arad, but their number was smaller, due to 'events of overwhelming importance that the country goes through'.

If at the beginning of the twentieth century the most important pilgrimages were organized at Maria Radna and had a confessional character, in the following decades the situation changed. It happened that in the '30s the pilgrimages organized by Catholics to Maria Radna and by Orthodox to Hodoș-Bodrog exceeded the limit of some traditional religious manifestations, being marked by strong nationalist actions. The takeover by some nationalist elements grew exponentially, especially in the case of the Orthodox Church, which considered that in Greater Romania it is the institution that 'must watch over the happy fulfilment of the destiny of our nation'.[58]

Conclusion

From this research it can be seen that the Arad area is one of ethnic and confessional diversity, a space of interference between Catholicism and Orthodoxy, a reality that has influenced the way in which the pilgrimages were organized here. Important ecclesiastical centres, both Orthodox and Catholic, have been active here over the centuries. The most important monasteries, Maria Radna and Hodoș-Bodrog, are the expression of ethnic and confessional coexistence in the area, even if there were some difficult moments, marked by the rivalry between ethnicities and religious denominations. Pilgrimages organized during this period, initially to Maria Radna, then to several Orthodox places of worship, reflect the mentality of people of those times and are evidence of the transformation and modernization that took place in the late nineteenth and early twentieth century.

---

56 [Anon.], 'Pelerinajele de la Sf. Mănăstire H.-Bodrog din 5–6 și 14–15 august', *Biserica și Școala*, 31 August 1935, p. 2.

57 Ilarion V. Felea, *Opera vieții mele: Ziuar personal* (Arad: Editura Universității "Aurel Vlaicu", 2012), p. 18.

58 [Anon.], 'Pelerinagiile religioase la Sf. Mănăstire Hodoș-Bodrog', *Biserica și Școala*, 27 August 1939, p. 291.

The end of the First World War produced important territorial changes in Central Europe, which had a strong impact on the organization of pilgrimages. In the Interwar Period, they had a much more pronounced political-national connotation, as evidenced by the decrease in the number of Orthodox Romanians who came to Maria Radna and the transformation by the Orthodox Episcopate of Arad of the Church of Lipova into a monastery. In the course of the pilgrimages of the 1930s, one can detect the manifestation of a tension that anticipated the outbreak of a new world conflict.

Archival Sources

Arad, County Service of the National Archives of Romania ('Arad, Serviciul Județean al Arhivelor Naționale ale României'), Fond: Prefectura județului Arad – actele subprefectului.

References

[Anon.],[59] 'La mănăstirea Bodrogului', *Biserica și Școala*, Arad, 6/19 Iulie 1903, p. 216.
[Anon.], 'Pelerinaj la sf. mănăstire H.-Bodrog.', *Biserica și Școala*, 9 August 1925, p. 8.
[Anon.], 'Pelerinajul la Sf. Mănăstire Hodoș-Bodrog. Programul', *Biserica și Școala*, 1 August 1926, p. 2.
[Anon.], 'Un nou loc de pelerinaj: biserica din Lipova', *Biserica și Școala*, 21–28 August 1932, p. 11.
[Anon.], 'Informațiuni', *Biserica și Școala*, 9 Iulie 1933, p. 7.
[Anon.], 'Pelerinaj la Sf. Mănăstire a Bodrogului.', *Biserica și Școala*, 27 August 1933, p. 3.
[Anon.], 'Pelerinajele la Biserica ort. română – veche Mănăstire din Lipova – Banat la Adormirea Maicii Domnului în anul 1934', *Biserica și Școala*, 16 Septembrie 1934, p. 4.
[Anon.], 'Pelerinajele de la Sf. Mănăstire H.-Bodrog din 5–6 și 14–15 august', *Biserica și Școala*, 31 August 1935, p. 2.
[Anon.], 'Programa Pelerinajelor la Sfânta Biserici ort. română din Lipova Banat, în zilele de 14 și 15 August', *Biserica și Școala*, 1 August 1937, p. 277.
[Anon.], 'Pelerinagiile religioase la Sf. Mănăstire Hodoș-Bodrog', *Biserica și Școala*, 27 August 1939, p. 291.
[Anon.] 'La mănăstirea Hodoș-Bodrogului', *Bunul econom*, Orăștie, 1/14 Septembrie 1901, p. 7.
[Anon.], 'O propunere a d-lui Vasile Goldiș', *Calendar pe anul 1932* (Arad: Editura Tipografiei Diecezane, 1931).
Arhimandrit Policarp, 'Pelerinajele la sf. Mănăstire H. Bodrog', *Biserica și Școala*, 20 Iulie 1930, p. 2.
C. Mureșan, 'Activitatea iredentistă a Mănăstirei Radna', *Biserica și Școala*, 26 August 1934, p. 9.
Eugen Arădeanul, Lucian Emandi, and Teodor Bodogae, *Mănăstirea Hodoș Bodrog* (Arad: Editura Episcopiei Aradului, 1980).

---

59 The article has no author or its name cannot be identified.

Gheorghe Ciuhandu, *Românii din Câmpia Aradului: de acum două veacuri cu un excurs istoric până la 1752 și însemnări istorice politice ulterioare*, ed. by Constantin Jinga and Remus Feraru (Timișoara: Marineasa, 2005).

Grigorie Gh. Comșa, 'Circulară cătră toți P. O. Părinți protopopi și preoți din eparhia Aradului', *Biserica și Școala*, 2 August 1925, p. 3.

Hermina Ciorogariu, *Caietele Herminei* (București: Peter Pan Art, 2010).

History, Maria Radna, the most significant place of pilgrimage in south-eastern Europe https://www.mariaradna.com/en/history (accessed on 1.07.2021).

Ilie Chebeleu, *Cronica de la Șoimoș* (Timișoara: David Print Press, 2020).

Ilarion V. Felea, *Opera vieții mele: Ziuar personal* (Arad: Editura Universității "Aurel Vlaicu", 2012).

Ioan Boroș, *Memorialistică* (Cluj-Napoca: Presa Universitară Clujeană, 2012).

Ioan Munteanu, Vasile M. Zaberca, and Mariana Sârbu, *Banatul și Marea Unire 1918* (Timișoara: Editura Mitropoliei Banatului, 1992).

Ioan Slavici, *Lumea prin care am trecut* (București: Minerva, 1978).

Ioan Tomuția, 'Impresii de la pelerinajul la Sf-ta M.-re H.-Bodrog', *Biserica și Școala*, 19 Septembrie 1926, p. 5.

Istoria Transilvaniei, 3 vol., ed. by Ioan-Aurel Pop and Thomas Nägler (Cluj-Napoca: Academia Română, Centrul de Studii Transilvane, 2016)

Keith Hitchins, *Orthodoxy and Nationality: Andreiu Șaguna and the Rumanians of Transylvania, 1846–1873* (Cambridge, MA: Harvard University Press, 1977).

Martin Roos, *Maria – Radna. Ein Wallfahrtsort im Südosten Europas*, 2 vol., I (Regensburg: Schnell & Steiner, 1998), II (Regensburg: Schnell & Steiner, 2004).

Mathias Bernath, *Habsburgii și începuturile formării națiunii române* (Cluj: Editura Dacia, 1994).

Mihai Săsăujan, *Politica bisericească a Curții din Viena în Transilvania (1740–1761)* (Cluj-Napoca: Presa Universitară Clujeană, 2002).

Nicolae Brânzeu, *Memoriile unui preot bătrân*, II-nd edition, ed. by Pia Brânzeu (Timișoara: Marineasa, 2015).

Nicolae Iorga, *Pagini alese din însemnările de călătorie prin Ardeal și Banat*, 2 vol. (București: Minerva, 1977).

Nicholas M. Nagy-Talavera, *The Green Shirts and the Others: A History of Fascism in Hungary and Romania* (Iași: The Center for Romanian Studies, 2001).

Pavel Vesa, *Clerici cărturari arădeni de altădată* (Arad: Gutenberg Univers, 2008).

Pavel Vesa, *Episcopia Aradului: istorie, cultură, mentalități, 1701–1918* (Cluj-Napoca: Presa Universitară Clujeană, 2006).

Pavel Vesa, *Episcopii Aradului: 1706–2006* (Arad: Gutenberg Univers, 2007).

Policarp Moruşca, *Mănăstirea Bodrog* (Arad: Editura Sf. Mănăstiri Bodrog, 1927).

Sergiu Soica, *Biserica greco-catolică din Banat în perioada anilor 1920–1948* (Timișoara: Eurostampa, 2012).

Timea Lelik and Claudiu Călin, *Maria Radna. Mică monografie istorică și artistică a bazilicii papale și complexului monastic* (Arad: Carmel Print, 2011).

Victor Vlăduceanu, *Vechiu monument istorico-religios – Mănăstirea Bodrog* (Timișoara: Victoria, 1939).

MIRELA HROVATIN

The Mother of God of Bistrica Shrine as Croatian National Pilgrimage Center

Introduction

Many researchers agree that pilgrimage sites are very complex places in which religion, history, culture and society intersect and are reflected in the identity of these shrines.[1] Marian shrines have many specificities and they can be observed as changing in their significance through time.[2] Taking all this into consideration, this analysis will focus on the historical and archival data about the shrine of the Mother of God of Bistrica in Marija Bistrica, in order to assess how the shrine became national, how social, religious, historical, economic, and cultural and what other aspects are embedded in it and their roles today when compared to other, mostly Marian shrines in Croatia and Europe. Some of the covered issues are the place of the shrine in Marija Bistrica in the context of the Ottoman rule and Reformation period, incorporation of the old pre-Christian beliefs into the pilgrim's activities and religious piety of pilgrims until today. For the collection of data, I used the methods of interviewing, participant observation and

---

1 Edith Turner and Victor Turner, *Image and Pilgrimage in Christian Culture: Anthropological Perspectives* (New York: CUP, 1978); Ellen Badone, 'Introduction', in *Religious Orthodoxy and Popular Faith in European Society*, ed. by Ellen Badone (Princeton: Princeton University Press, 1990), pp. 3–23; Alan Morinis, 'Introduction', in *Sacred Journeys. The Anthropology of Pilgrimage*, ed. by Alan Morinis (Westport/London: Grenwood Press (1992), pp. 1–28; John Eade and Michael J. Sallnow, 'Introduction', in *Contesting the Sacred: The Anthropology of Christian Pilgrimage*, ed. by John Eade and Michael J. Sallnow (London, New York: Routledge, 1992), pp. 1–29; Simon Coleman and John Eade, 'Introduction', in *Reframing Pilgrimage: Cultures in Motion*, ed. by Simon Coleman and John Eade (London: Routledge, 2004), pp. 1–25; John Eade and Mario Katić, 'Introduction: Crossing the Borders', in *Pilgrimage, Politics and Place-Making in Eastern Europe: Crossing the Borders*, ed. by John Eade and Mario Katić (Farnham: Ashgate, 2014), pp. 1–15; Ian Reader, *Pilgrimage: A Very Short Introduction* (Oxford: Oxford University Press, 2015); *International Perspectives on Pilgrimage Studies: Itineraries, Gaps and Obstacles*, ed. by John Eade and Dionigi Albera (London: Routledge, 2015).
2 Simon Coleman, 'Pilgrimage as Trope for an Anthropology of Christianity', *Current Anthropology* 55 (10), (2014), pp. 281–91.

Mirela Hrovatin • PhD, Assistant Professor at the Croatian Catholic University and Ministry of Culture and Media, Zagreb, Croatia

Pilgrimage in the Christian Balkan World: The Path to Touch the Sacred and Holy, ed. by Dorina Dragnea, Emmanouil Ger. Varvounis, Evelyn Reuter, Petko Hristov and Susan Sorek (Turnhout, 2023), pp. 165–183.
BREPOLS PUBLISHERS   DOI 10.1484/M.STR-EB.5.132405

analysis of archival data from the shrine, including archival and published miracle books. The analysis relies also on my own perceptions as a participant of the culture and religion which have been chosen as appropriate for this work regarding general ethical principles of research of religious themes.

Towards the National Shrine: Historical Aspects

The shrine of the Mother of God of Bistrica in Marija Bistrica is located in the northwestern part of Croatia, not far from the capital city of Zagreb (Fig. 1). Observed on a map, it is approximately half way from the farthest eastern and southern point of the country of Croatia and in northern part of the Western Balkans. Its beginnings are intricately connected to the rule of the Ottoman Empire in these parts of Europe, when after fierce fighting one of the statues of Mary was probably transported to safer areas of northern Croatia, far enough from the battle sites. This is evidenced by the oral story about the shrine leaning on the local toponym of 'Bosna' which is a part of the place of Bedenica Municipality half way from Vinski Vrh where the statue of Mary was first placed, proving that people running from the Ottomans in the fifteenth century came to these parts of Croatia from Bosnia and probably brought the statue of Mary with them[3] as was common in those times.[4] Although this story about the statue cannot be confirmed by historical documents, the facts confirm the movement of population in these areas from various places attacked by the Ottomans,[5] and even several important Croatian Parliament sittings took place in the sixteenth and seventeenth century in nearby town of Krapina because of the imminent danger.[6]

Furthermore, the decline of the important Marian shrine in Remete near Zagreb at the slopes of the Medvednica Mountain must have posed a great problem to the Pauline order who took care of the pilgrimage there. After three attacks by the Ottomans in 1483, 1557 and 1591[7] and finally the 1880 earthquake, the Remete shrine was devastated and lost its ability to attract larger numbers of pilgrims from Zagreb and the surrounding area. Therefore, it is not surprising that the choice of the place for the statue of Mary, brought to Croatia probably by people migrating away from dangerous places in Bosnia and Herzegovina, was based on the intention of keeping it safe during the Ottoman military attacks.

One of the closest adjacent safe places was a chapel on Vinski Vrh hill overlooking the northern part of the Medvednica Mountain with Zagreb being at its south side.

---

3 The former rector of the shrine, L. C., 87 years old, Zagreb, interviewed in 2013.
4 Cf. Marko Dragić, 'Legends and Testimonies about Miraculous Our Lady of Sinj', *Croatica et Slavica Iadertina*, 12 (1), 12 (2016), pp. 153–77.
5 Mirko Valentić, 'Turski ratovi i hrvatska dijaspora u XVI. stoljeću', *Senjski zbornik: prilozi za geografiju, etnologiju, gospodarstvo, povijest i kulturu*, 17 (1), (1990), p. 46.
6 Ratko Vučetić, 'Prostorni razvoj srednjovjekovne Krapine', *Radovi Instituta za povijest umjetnosti*, 24 (2000), p. 17.
7 'Remete', *Karmel.hr*, (s.a.), http://karmel.hr/?page_id=295, (accessed on 5.02.2021).

Fig. 1: The shrine of Mother of God in Marija Bistrica, July 2021. Photograph by Mirela Hrovatin.

After the lost battle in 1545 in Konjščina, the parish priest decided to hide the statue in the church in the valley, which is today the national shrine. The church originates in the fourteenth century and despite the veneration of Mary until the eighteenth century it was consecrated to Saints Apostles Peter and Paul. The statue was revealed as soon as the Ottoman Empire started losing its force, first in 1588 and then in 1684.[8] The second revelation is closely connected to the Pauline Order, as one of its members, the Bishop Martin Borković remembered the veneration of Mary in Bistrica from the beginning of the seventeenth century, which corresponds with the decline of the Remete shrine where he was also a rector. So, it is not excluded that Borković envisioned the new great shrine in this new place after the Remete shrine lost its power. When young, he was probably visiting with his family the old Marian shrine of Volavje and Bistrica[9] and this supports the fact that he knew the Marian pilgrimage sites and needs of believers and the Church for this kind of devotion. In 1731 the shrine was consecrated to Saint Mary of the Snows, and later in 1883 to the Assumption of the Blessed Virgin Mary. Since the statue's last revelation, Mary has been venerated in Marija Bistrica and many pilgrims from various nearby places started to come to the church, co-creating the sacred space of the future national shrine.

---

8 Josip Buturac, *Marija Bistrica: 1209–1993: povijest župe i prošteništa* (Marija Bistrica: Nacionalno svetište Majke Božje Bistričke, 1993), p. 40.
9 Ante Sekulić, 'Biskup Martin Borković (1597–1687)', *Croatica Christiana Periodica*, 9 (15), (1985), p. 67.

Fig. 2: Statue of Mary at the main altar in the shrine of Mother of God in Marija Bistrica, July 2021. Photograph by Mirela Hrovatin.

Several further events augmented the importance and popularity of the newly emerging great shrine. Of importance were the oral stories about the statue being miraculously found[10] which correspond to the efforts by the priests to renew the veneration in this part of Croatia. First, the statue of Mary (Fig. 2) was hidden under the choir of the church in Marija Bistrica. After the evening's service, a strange light was coming from under the choir, and the statue was revealed. It was this story circulating among the pilgrims that motivated the priests to connect the strange light to the statue being hidden in the church, as the priest who hid it did not tell anyone before he died about its exact location.

The second revelation of the statue is connected to the apparition of Mary to the parish priest, first in the church where She pleaded for regaining Her sight and second, in the village, on his way to visit a family, She appeared near his carriage but disappeared when he tried to approach Her. The third and fourth stories are connected to the healing of pilgrims at the new shrine. One tells about regaining the ability to walk by a young girl, and the other about restoration of a woman's sight, clearly connected to the story of the Mary's plea and revelation of the statue. When statistically observed these are two most important pilgrims' motivations for coming to the shrine in Marija Bistrica for many centuries.[11] This new shrine started attracting pilgrims even within a three-day journey which was noted for some other Croatian and European shrines as well during the last several centuries.[12] Some rare cases note longer travel, within five to ten days, but not more than that. Most of pilgrims came from places

---

10 Josip Buturac, *Marija Bistrica: 1209–1993*, p. 46.
11 Mirela Hrovatin, *Kulturnoantropološki pristup zavjetu u izvaninstitucijskoj osobnoj pobožnosti* ('A cultural anthropological approach to vows in non-institutional personal religiosity'), Doctoral thesis (Faculty of Humanities and Social Sciences, University of Zagreb, 2015), p. 257.
12 Cf. William A. Christian, *Person and God in a Spanish Valley* (Princeton: Princeton University Press, 1989), p. 46; Geneviève Herberich-Marx, *Evolution d'une sensibilité religieuse: Témoignages iconographiques et scripturaires de pèlerinages alsaciens* (Strasbourg: Presses universitaires de Strasbourg, 1989), p. 133.

not more than one day away, so with sleeping and coming back it would take them around two-three days all together, which enabled them to get back to their chores on land and tend to their families.[13] Those closer to the shrine would come on major religious holidays or when needed for health and blessings. The name of the place also changed in the eighteenth century from the simple Bistrica, meaning clear water and the crook (small river), to Marija Bistrica meaning that the place has from then been connected to Mary and the Marian shrine there.

The shrine has been developing since the Middle Ages until today following the need of the people both as Catholics venerating Mary in this larger shrine as well as major ethnic affiliation of Croats in the later centuries. The shrine has been constantly extended architecturally and improved aesthetically,[14] and some of the most important events in national and Church history in Croatia have been marked in the shrine. Soon after the beginning of the Croatian Kingdom in the eighth and officially in the tenth century, these central parts of Croatia where the shrine is situated were from the twelfth century ruled also by the Hungarian Empire in the form of a personal union (two countries sharing a mutual king). During the Middle Ages the Croatian nobility tried to regain rule from the Hungarians, and the Church played a huge role in supporting them. However the shrines were still used both by Hungarian as well as Croatian (Slavic) people,[15] and no ethnic affiliation was associated with the shrine at the time. During the fifteenth until the seventeenth centuries, most of the Croatian lands were conquered by the Ottomans, and only these central parts of the once large Croatian Kingdom remained free (so called, *reliquiae reliquiarum* or 'remains of the remains'). It was not until the formation of the national movement in the centuries following the withdrawal of the Ottoman Empire since the end of the sixteenth century that in the Marian shrine Croatian people, including clergy and politically active people, started to support the idea of Croatian statehood. The 1715 donation of a large votive altar by the Croatian Parliament was also an act of confirmation of the shrine as the one visited mostly and massively by Croatian people and their connection to Mary as the 'Queen of Croats' in the oral tradition present until today. In the eighteenth and nineteenth centuries Croatia was within the Austrian-Hungarian Empire, which had been involved in the religious affairs and had a great influence on the processes in the shrine, as explained in the next chapter. The National Movement in the nineteenth century had its reflections in the shrine as some of the priests were supporting political parties, although the Church has always officially advised neutral stand on political matters.[16] The fact that the priests were Croats and descendants of the Croatian nobility contributed to their

---

13 Note that the journey in the previous centuries was made on foot, riding a horse or in a horse carriage.
14 Jasna Turkalj, 'Dr Juraj Žerjavić – »Spiritus agens« izbornoga pokreta i »bune« u Mariji Bistrici 1892. godine?!', *Croatica Christiana Periodica*, 35, 67 (2011), pp. 125–42.
15 Gabor Barna, 'Pilgrimages in Hungary: Ethnological and anthropological approaches', in *International Perspectives on Pilgrimage Studies: Itineraries, Gaps and Obstacles*, ed. by John Eade and Dionigi Albera (London: Routledge, 2015), p. 106.
16 Jasna Turkalj, 'Dr Juraj Žerjavić', p. 128.

feeling for the need to stand for their ethnic and noble identity in opposition to the Austrian-Hungarian rulers and their nobility. This was certainly one of the main reasons for priests' intervening in political matters of the time. The Christian shrines were important identity markers of the European nobility and provided spiritual protection in armed conflicts.[17] All this opposition to the ruling authorities continued throughout the twentieth century until the establishment of the independent state of Croatia in 1991, and the shrine played a huge role in this process.

Introduction of jubilee years since 1750 with the possibility of forgiveness of sin to pilgrims who visit the shrine, make confession, and receive Communion, further motivated the visits to Marija Bistrica. This was strengthened in the twentieth century by receiving the status of the minor basilica by Pope Pius XI in 1923, making the shrine in Marija Bistrica the first such in Croatia. The twentieth century had also several important historical and national events that reflected in the shrine. Two World Wars marked the pilgrims' visits to the shrine, especially as many vowed to visit the shrine if they survived the battles and injuries: 'When he was in World War in 1914 he made a vow to Mother of God of Bistrica, that he will visit Her shrine every year. Indeed, in heavy battles at the front She helped', the testimony noted in 1957.[18]

This military aspect has not only been present in personal prayers, but also in soldiers' coming to the shrine, especially in an organized manner since 1993, to express thankfulness and seek blessing from Mary when going into the battles. It has enhanced the identity of the shrine by fortifying its national significance as well as confirming the role of Mary as protectress of soldiers during war. This military aspect has been present in other European and world Marian shrines, as mentioned. After the war in 1990s for independence of Croatia, the acquittal by the Hague court of Croatian general Ante Gotovina was marked both by a relic of blessed Stepinac and the vow made by the general to Mary which he fulfilled by visiting the shrine in Marija Bistrica.[19] Prayers in the shrine refer also to the 1990s war, not only in Croatia, but also in the neighbouring Bosnia and Herzegovina, proving the broad reach of this Marian shrine: 'Family [surname] gives to the Mother of God of Bistrica two golden coins for happy rescue from war suffering in Sarajevo', the testimony noted in 1996.[20]

---

17 Cf. Szabolcs Serfőző, 'Pilgrimages of Emperor Leopold I in Central Europe', *Radovi Instituta za povijest umjetnosti*, 41 (2017), p. 61.

18 *Knjiga uslišanja, milosti, zagovora i čudesa Bl. Dj. Marije Majke Božje Bistričke* ('The Book of Answered Prayers, Graces, Vows and Miracles Granted by the Blessed Virgin Our Lady of Marija Bistrica'), 2012, Hrvatsko nacionalno svetište Majke Božje Bistričke, https://www.svetiste-mbb.hr/stranica/zapisi-uslisanja-milosti-zagovori-i-cudesa (accessed on 20.11.2020).

19 Marijana Belaj and Mirela Hrovatin, 'Cultural Practices in Sacralisation of Place: Vows in the Shrine of Our Lady of Marija Bistrica', in *Sacralization of Landscape and Sacred Places. Proceedings of the 3rd International Scientific Conference of Mediaeval Archaeology of the Institute of Archaeology*, ed. by Juraj Belaj et al. (Zagreb: Institut za arheologiju, 2018), pp. 343–51; *Gotovina s obitelji u M. Bistrici: Zahvalio je Majci Božjoj na slobodi* [Gotovina with His Family in M. Bistrica: He Thanked the Mother of God for His Freedom], Večernji list, 18 November 2012, https://m.vecernji.hr/vijesti/gotovina-s-obitelji-u-m-bistrici-zahvalio-je-majci-bozjoj-na-slobodi-476654/komentari?page=4 (accessed on 8.03.2021).

20 *Knjiga uslišanja, milosti, zagovora i čudesa Bl. Dj. Marije Majke Božje Bistričke*, https://www.svetiste-mbb.hr/stranica/zapisi-uslisanja-milosti-zagovori-i-cudesa (accessed on 20.11.2020).

With the Communist rule starting right after the World War II, the service of blessed Aloysius Stepinac, then the cardinal, was marked by the opposition to the oppressing regime. For several decades pilgrims were under surveillance by the state police, and no fights took place. Already in 1935 during the 250th anniversary of the finding of the statue and during its coronation, some of the Serbs in Belgrade, then the center of the Kingdom of Yugoslavia, criticized the overall display of symbols of ethnicity by Croats,[21] including the national flag and the royal crown. The crown was a copy of the alleged crown of the first Croatian rulers from the early Middle Ages and it was made of gold donated by nobility and citizens. The blessing of the crowns for Mary and baby Jesus, whom she holds in her arms, and the sermon was led by the charismatic archbishop-coadjutor blessed Stepinac, and the archbishop of Zagreb Antun Bauer who pronounced the Mother of God of Bistrica as the Queen of Croatians. In 1938 there was an unsuccessful attempt to steal the crowns, so later only on special occasions are the two crowns used.

Blessed Stepinac governed the shrine in Bistrica as archbishop since the 1930s, so he envisioned the future development of the national shrine. One of his projects was the Path of the Cross on the nearby hill, which was built much later, at the end of the century, but which has become an integral part of the shrine's imagery for pilgrims from the last two decades of the twentieth century until today (Fig. 3). Besides visiting and praying to the statue of Mary, the majority of pilgrims in these recent decades included as obligatory also going through the Path of the Cross which ends with the statue of Jesus Christ lying down after crucifixion (Fig. 4). Through insights by participant observation, I have seen that many pilgrims today touch this statue with less and less of those touching the altar with the statue of Mary in the shrine what was usual in the past. This shows the shift from veneration of Mary towards focusing more on Jesus, as the Catholic Church has been advising believers after the second Vatican Council.

During World War II and until Croatia became an independent state, the shrine was very important for keeping national and religious identity. One of the most important persons at that time was the mentioned Cardinal Aloysius Stepinac who marked the shrine both during his life and after his death. He was prosecuted at court in the former state of Yugoslavia for having cooperated with the former regime of Independent State of Croatia, a state which lasted for a short time during the World War II and was connected to the Axis powers.[22] There are indications that he was poisoned; he died when he was sixty two. His importance for open expression of national and religious identity was confirmed in 1998 when he was beatified by Pope John Paul II who said: 'Blessed Aloysius Stepinac in this way represents Croatia that

---

21 Mario Jareb, 'Blagoslov hrvatske zastave u Mariji Bistrici 3. 11. 1935. kao ogledalo odnosa jugoslavenskih vlasti i Katoličke Crkve prema hrvatskim nacionalnim simbolima u drugoj polovici tridesetih godina 20. stoljeća', *Milosti puna: glasilo Svetišta Majke Božje Bistričke*, 16, 46 (2010), p. 38.
22 For more details on the proccess and the historical context see Esther Gitman, *Alojzije Stepinac – Pillar of human rights* (Zagreb: Krscanska sadasnjost, 2019).

Fig. 3: Pilgrims on the thirteenth station of the Path of the Cross in Marija Bistrica. The first pilgrimage of the Croatian Catholic University, July 2021. Photograph by Mirela Hrovatin.

Fig. 4: Pilgrims leave gifts (in money) near the statue of Jesus Christ at the fourteenth station of the Path of the Cross in Marija Bistrica, July 2021. Photograph by Mirela Hrovatin.

wishes to forgive and reconcile, purifying its memory of hatred and winning over evil by good'.[23]

On internet pages of the shrine and other sources it is emphasized how the beatification of Stepinac was the greatest event in the history of the shrine, with more than half a million pilgrims and Church and state authorities welcoming the Pope and participating in the event.[24] In this way not only the shrine's importance was confirmed, but also the national and religious identity of the majority of Croats now living in a new independent state as well as respect of other people and the need to live peacefully with others. As I was present at the event, it really was very important to so many whose identity is based on being both Catholic and Croat, seeing it as inseparable. It was mixed together with the feeling of being repressed in the former Yugoslavia, as one interviewee illustrates:

> My family was hidden believers. In the evening they would pray, but not openly, because people should not have known that we are Croats, because dad was a military officer and it shouldn't be openly shown.[25]

Stepinac was the symbol of all those aspects for people during this event. The year 1998 for beatification was not accidental, as it was the time after the 1991–1995 Homeland War in which many Croats and people of other ethnicities died or were displaced, so this was the period of peaceful reintegration of multiethnic areas in Croatia.[26] Going a step back, the proclamation of the shrine as national by the bishops on the feast of the Assumption of Blessed Virgin Mary in 1971 during the VI International Mariological and XIII International Marian Congress held there was a significant step forward in the awakening of the sense of the need for national independence which was behind the Croatian Spring movement[27] that 'opposed unitarism' in the former state of Yugoslavia and wanted to 'reform economic, cultural and political life in cultural institutions' in Croatia.[28] The feast being one of the most important Catholic Marian celebrations with around 200,000 people, mostly Croats, coming to the shrine from Croatia as well as different parts of the world, the believers gladly accepted the decision. Their presence formed one of the most numerous gatherings of Croats Catholics in Marija Bistrica until then and confirmed the need for a shrine that would be connected to their ethnical identity, which proves the idea that such 'religious institutions keep national unity'.[29] Around ten years after, the National Eucharist Congress in 1984,

---

23 Vedran Klaužer and Damir Galoić, *Papa putnik - bistrički hodočasnik 1998–2018* (Marija Bistrica: Ogranak Matice hrvatske u Mariji Bistrici, 2018), p. 66.
24 Vedran Klaužer and Damir Galoić, *Papa putnik - bistrički hodočasnik 1998–2018*, p. 66.
25 Croatian Catholic from Zagreb, N. K., b. around 1950s, Zagreb, interviewed in 2012.
26 Antun Šundalić, 'A model of peaceful reintegration and the possibility to live together', *Društvena istraživanja: časopis za opća društvena pitanja*, 6 (2–3), (28–32), (1997), p. 222.
27 Domagoj Sremić, 'Društvene i teološke odrednice Rimokatoličke crkve u Hrvatskoj u jeku društveno-političkih previranja 1971. godine', *Cris*, XVI (1), (2014), p. 65.
28 'Ancient Shrine at Vinski Vrh', *Hrvatsko nacionalno Svetište Majke Božje Bistričke*, (s.a.), https://www.svetiste-mbb.hr/jezik/detaljno/en/ancient-shrine-at-vinski-vrh-1499-1545 (accessed on 3.03.2021).
29 John Eade and Mario Katić, 'Introduction: Crossing the Borders', in *Pilgrimage, Politics and Place-Making in Eastern Europe: Crossing the Borders*, ed. by John Eade and Mario Katić (Farnham: Ashgate, 2014), p. 11.

celebrating the finding of the miraculous statue, repeated the festive atmosphere with around 400,000 pilgrims and the significance of the national shrine. The holiday of Mary of God of Bistrica was also established then. All the greater events at the shrine resulted also in the improvement of infrastructure (including nearby roads) and the architectural expansion of the shrine and surrounding area. Some other processes at the shrine of Marija Bistrica through the centuries, including the sacralization of space, have been already described in a previous research.[30]

The Bistrica Shrine as a European Pilgrimage Site

In past centuries, as I have mentioned, it was mostly three days travel that a pilgrim in Europe would take to visit some of the bigger shrines in the wider area, and many of the stories in the book written by the shrine's chaplain Berke mentioned this duration for coming to the shrine. With all the shrine's stories and pilgrims' testimonies, together with special events organized by the Catholic Church to sustain the shrine as one of the most important in the northern part of what is today Croatia, the popularity of the shrine spread also to Croatia's neighboring countries such as Slovenia, Bosnia and Herzegovina, Hungary and some others. This information is given in some of the notes in the shrine's books of miracles as the places of pilgrims' residence are mentioned[31] and in historical data.[32] Pilgrims from these countries sought the same as the pilgrims from Croatia, mostly health for themselves or their family members, annual blessings and similar. So, the motivation was primarily religious and pilgrims wanted to be close to Mary they believed She was in a way present in the shrine, especially in the statue at the main altar as the miraculous stories inscribed this meaning into it. They would pray at the shrine, leave gifts, flowers, candles and personal objects such as jewelry, crutches, embroidery and wedding dresses, circumambulate the altar, pay for the holy mass, go to confession, take with them blessed (holy) water and various blessed objects as souvenirs and for further spiritual protection at home. Certain number of pilgrims would leave a note expressing their gratitude and describing their wishes, resolved situations, prayers and so on. In this sense, the practices of pilgrims at the shrine in Marija Bistrica were the same as in other major shrines in this part of Europe, such as Máriagyűd in Hungary and Olovo in Bosnia and Herzegovina. A somewhat newer shrine in Brezje and other places in Slovenia were not at first Marian, so the catchment area of the rather significant shrine in Marija Bistrica in previous centuries was extending beyond Croatian lands, from Slovenia and Bosnia

---

30 Cf. Marijana Belaj and Mirela Hrovatin, 'Cultural Practices in Sacralisation of Place', pp. 349–50.
31 *Knjiga uslišanja, milosti, zagovora i čudesa Bl. Dj. Marije Majke Božje Bistričke* https://www.svetiste-mbb.hr/stranica/zapisi-uslisanja-milosti-zagovori-i-cudesa (accessed on 20.11.2020).
32 Petar Berke, *Kinč osebujni slavnoga Orsaga Horvatckoga to jest: Čudnovita pripečenja i osebujne Milošče, kotere pri čudnovitom kipu Marije Bistričke više vre let se skazuju, s kratkum od kipa ovoga hištorijum, i hasnovitem navukom, pobožnem putnikom marijanskem na vekše njihovo razveselenje, po nevrednom negda mesta ovoga kapelanu Petru Berke na pervo postavlene*, written in 1775, reprinted edition, ed. by Alojz Jembrih (Marija Bistrica: National Shrine of Mother of God of Bistrica, 1995), p. 153.

and Herzegovina all the way to Hungary and Styria (today part of Austria). For many Slovenians in the centuries before the nineteenth century and even until the middle of the twentieth century, a visit to the shrine was an expression of piety, as the archival data shows. It is not to be forgotten that the services and other activities in the shrine were held in Croatian, one of the Slavic languages easily understood by the pilgrims coming from today's neighboring countries, especially those living near today's borders with Croatia.

As this part of Croatia was ruled by the Austrian-Hungarian Empire, the rulers Maria Theresa and her son Joseph II started to influence Church matters in the eighteenth century. At first, many traditional pilgrimages disappeared because of the bans imposed by those rulers but soon after this, it was allowed to retain usual festivities, and this strengthened the Catholic identity of pilgrims from many parts of Croatia and nearby neighbouring countries. The visits from other people besides Croatians were probably the reason why the Austrian Empress Maria Theresa in 1775 allowed the processions and pilgrimage for longer than one day's duration to Marija Bistrica on the bequest of the Bishop Galjuf who explained it in his letter to the court written in 1774:

> Because this place is sacred to the peoples in the same measure as Mariazell is to the Austrians, the Styrians and neighbouring Hungarians. And we see that it brings similar fruits of mercy and spiritual comfort so it is publicly known that sometimes come there also Orthodox Greeks attracted by the wide known sacredness of the shrine.[33]

Within this context, by publishing his book for pilgrims in the same century, Berke as the shrine's chaplain kept Catholic identity of pilgrims and shrine alive.[34] He clearly emphasizes throughout his book the need to pray to Mary and stay faithful to Catholicism, noting that Mary of Bistrica is 'the helper of our kingdom', as noted in previous oral stories such as the one from 1724.[35] In other European shrines there have probably been such dichotomies present, as some examples show: 'Her mother was Protestant, but she nevertheless went to thank the Virgin for having protected her daughter in the accident, and left one ex-voto in the shrine [in Thierenbach, France]'.[36]

Besides ethnic aspects, religious affiliation has been perpetually confirmed by the various religious activities connected to the shrine in Marija Bistrica. The issue of choosing Christianity over Islam was a major one for the preservation not only of one belief system, but also of a specific way of life and culture in this part of Europe during the times of the Ottoman Empire. The Ottomans brought with them a very different set of social, ethical, moral and cultural values, and over time people started accepting it as part of their everyday functionality, especially when certain economic

---

33 Petar Berke, *Kinč osebujni slavnoga Orsaga Horvatckoga to jest'*, p. 92.
34 cf. Alojz Jembrih in Petar Berke, *Kinč osebujni slavnoga Orsaga Horvatckoga to jest'*, pp. 90–92.
35 Petar Berke, *Kinč osebujni slavnoga Orsaga Horvatckoga to jest'*, pp. 139–40.
36 Geneviève Herberich-Marx, *Evolution d'une sensibilité religieuse: Témoignages iconographiques et scripturaires de pèlerinages alsaciens* (Strasbourg: Presses universitaires de Strasbourg, 1989), p. 88.

benefits would come for those who peacefully choose Islam over Christianity.[37] As the Empire moved towards the northern part of the Western Balkans, the rectors of the shrine in Marija Bistrica started using pilgrims' stories to convince people to stay faithful to their old religion, that of Christianity. Berke brings several examples, and one is cited here:

> […] one soldier was imprisoned in Istanbul … and his superior started persuading him to receive Islam […] but he started praying to God and asked Mary of Bistrica for help. She freed him miraculously after the prayer. He later came to Bistrica and confirmed this under oath. The testimony noted in 1723.[38]

As Croatian ethnicity was closely connected to Christianity since the arrival of the Croats in this part of Europe, the shrine has been important in shaping the idea of belonging to the Croatian Kingdom, as already mentioned. Croatian autonomy was partly lost during the centuries due to more powerful empires, such as Venetian, Austrian-Hungarian and Ottoman, however, it was still remembered as glorious by the Croatian people, especially the nobility. So when Berke was writing his book about the shrine, he did not forget to mention over and over again the importance of Mary as the protectress of the majority of Croatian people living in these areas as well as the memory of 'famous Kingdom of Croatia'. This motif appears in the introductory part as well as in the miracle stories. He also used the motif of going back to Christianity/ Catholicism of several people who already accepted Islam, but after imprisonment they pleaded to Mary and realized that the 'true religion' which brings them help is Christianity. 'As the historian Erik Fügedi noticed, it was exactly that captivity that was considered more devastating for the soul than the body, because it often implied the possibility of accepting Islam, because accepting Islam was the only way out of the captivity'.[39] So, it was common to pray to Mary for help in the battle:

> On more occasions good and pious soldiers of the famous kingdom of Croatia have known defense and help from Mary of Bistrica, especially in the time of the last battle against Turks […] residents of the Zrinski town and fortress wanted to sell it to the enemy, but some pious heroes would not surrender it, instead they started persuading that they all plead Mary of Bistrica for protection and help […]. The testimony noted in 1738.[40]

Although the danger from the Ottoman attacks subsided in the sixteenth century, it was then that Catholicism in the Western Balkans was challenged further, this time by the Reformation. The movement took root in Slovenia and neighboring European countries to the north of Croatia, however resistance was fiercer in Croatia. There were several reasons, for this among which was the close connection of the Croatian

---

37 Dijana Pinjuh, 'Conversions to Islam in Bosnia and Herzegovina, and the Connections between Converts and their Christian families, from the Ottoman Conquest to the End of the Seventeenth Century', *Povijesni prilozi*, (37, 55), (2018), p. 210.
38 Petar Berke, *'Kinč osebujni slavnoga Orsaga Horvatckoga to jest'*, pp. 138–39.
39 Andrić Stanko, *Miracles of Saint John Capistran* (Osijek: Matica hrvatska Osijek, 1999), p. 216.
40 Petar Berke, *Kinč osebujni slavnoga Orsaga Horvatckoga to jest'*, pp. 167–68.

Catholic Church to the Vatican as well as to believers. As the Empress allowed pilgrimage in the Marija Bistrica shrine in the eighteenth century, the veneration of Mary continued and was encouraged by the Church authorities. In this way, the people kept their old traditions and were less prone to new religious influences. As a Pauline, the Bishop Borković was an overt opponent of Protestantism, and probably because of that he greatly influenced the need to restore the Marian pilgrimage in this part of Croatia. The Pauline Order has its headquarters in Poland and is also connected to the most important Marian shrine of the country, Jasna Góra in Częstochowa.[41] The Máriavölgy shrine in Slovakia, once part of Hungary, is also connected to Pauline Order,[42] so further research might reveal more clearly these connections. It is not without significance that the Austrian emperor Joseph II banned the Pauline Order as Paulines were influencing Croatian national culture and education, and probably those of other European peoples.[43] Through Marian devotion, the main danger of Protestantism taking root in Croatia was averted, similarly to Hungarian cases of Marian shrines and the Counter-Reformation movement.[44]

As was the case with many European Catholic shrines, it was after the II Vatican Council that the shrine started to develop new contacts for and with pilgrims of a new era, and today it welcomes various national and international pilgrims from around the world, but mostly Croats and the diaspora.

Old Pre-Christian Beliefs and the Bistrica Shrine

As many other Catholic shrines in Europe and the world, the shrine in Marija Bistrica had to deal for many centuries with old, pagan or pre-Christian beliefs which pilgrims brought with them to the shrine. Instead of forbidding certain activities and even beliefs of pilgrims, the shrine used it in the construction of its significance for many believers. One example is the notion of a votive prayer, a vow which included a promise of pilgrimage or gift if the plea is fulfilled and which has been practiced for centuries by pilgrims although the Church considered it unnecessary because the shrine provided holy masses, blessings, confession and similar officially accepted services for pilgrims.[45] However, due to oral transmission of effective practices within family and local community circles, it has been impossible to forbid such practices,

---

41 Cf. Anna Niedźwiedź, 'Competing Sacred Places: Making and Remaking of National Shrines in Contemporary Poland', in *Pilgrimage, Politics and Place-Making in Eastern Europe: Crossing the Borders*, ed. by John Eade and Mario Katić (Farnham, Burlington: Ashgate 2014), p. 86.
42 Cf. Gabor Barna, 'Pilgrimages in Hungary: Ethnological and anthropological approaches', in *International Perspectives on Pilgrimage Studies: Itineraries, Gaps and Obstacles*, ed. by John Eade and Dionigi Albera (London: Routledge, 2015), p. 102.
43 Kristijan Herceg, 'Obrazovanje pavlina u Hrvatskoj', *Spectrum: ogledi i prinosi studenata teologije*, (1-4), (2009), p. 36.
44 Gabor Barna, 'Pilgrimages in Hungary' , p. 96.
45 Cf. Mirela Hrovatin, 'Negotiating with the Sacred Other: The Ancient Mechanisms of the Personal Vow Practice', *International journal of religious tourism and pilgrimage*, 8 (1), (2020), pp. 11–23.

including circumambulation of the altar, touching the altar, leaving notes on the walls and papers at the shrine, and so on, which continue till the present day.

Besides the symbolic and realistically inexplicable details in the stories about the finding of the lost statue and a disappearing unknown lady which established the shrine as the place of Mary's presence, similar to many other sacred places, the shrine started to use pilgrims' pleas as part of its reality. Pilgrims could come to the altar and say their prayers in the previous centuries, they could tell their prayers to the priests and clergy at the shrine or leave a note in the prayer book or in a letter they would place near the statue. All those prayers and supplications would be brought to the altar by the priests during Holy Mass, that is, directed to Mary, and through her to Jesus and God.

Berke in his book for pilgrims mentioned these prayers which contain many different stories about supernatural beings, witches, demons in form of animals attacking pilgrims either at home or even on their way to the shrine, and similar, so called, supernatural occurrences. All these stories are taken as valid and the troubles caused by these creatures, for which it was presumed that belong to the devil, are solved after the prayer is directed towards Mary, and specifically Mary of God of Bistrica:

> Michael, the parish priest in Stupnik, told about this miraculous event [...] One evening as he was going home, an unclean spirit on a horse came towards him, and after this one another, and after them a lot more, and in various ways they started scaring him, and then they wanted to instruct him that the hell pit is opened for him, and that he must go into it with them without any other choice. They grabbed him and started to drag him with them. As he was scared, he thought about Mother of Bistrica, and when he called her to help with great assurance, he noticed near him Jesus with Mary in the image of the statue of Bistrica and saint Michael Archangel, and those hellish riders were gone in a moment [...]. The testimony noted in 1702.[46]

Not going into further details of the religious and cultural symbolism of horsemen and the analogy of the priest's name Michael with the Archangel's, it is obvious how in previous centuries such stories were considered relevant and important in connection to Christianity which successfully resolved all the tribulations and problems people had. These stories have various other moral-didactic goals, as well as some other roles which focus on the shrine itself.[47] To strengthen the importance and power of the shrine in Marija Bistrica, some stories even mention efforts of visiting another, smaller or closer Marian pilgrimage site, but those efforts fail, and pilgrims need to go to Marija Bistrica in the end to resolve their problem:

> She was several years obsessed with an unclean spirit [...] and visited many sacred places and searched for help [...] But all in vain, until she finally with firm hope and humble heart took refuge in the merciful Mary of Bistrica. When

---

46 Petar Berke, 'Kinč osebujni slavnoga Orsaga Horvatckoga to jest', pp. 114–15.
47 Cf. Gabor Barna, 'Pilgrimages in Hungary', p. 103.

she quickly did it, the enemy of her soul was forced to leave her. And afterwards she came here to express thankfulness and bring a gift herself. The testimony noted in 1690.[48]

One of the reasons for taking those beliefs seriously and trying to help pilgrims was that most of the shrine's rectors were Croatians and usually also born in the place near the shrine or area in this part of Croatia having a similar cultural background to most pilgrims coming to the shrine. All this contributed to the affirmation of Croatian ethnic identity, as this was the cultural capital of Croatians as Slavic people who accepted Christianity. Slowly, people were giving up their old beliefs and practices, and started replacing them with officially proscribed rituals, such as paying for the Holy Mass, praying for overall wellbeing and similar. It is also not surprising that Orthodox Christians, both Croats and Serbs, because of belonging to similar Slavic culture as Croatian Catholics, would come to the shrine in hope of getting help from the sacred other, which they believed was present at the shrine on the basis of many pilgrims' testimonies. This practice continued until today, as this example shows: 'An Orthodox mother from Zagreb prays the Mother of God of Bistrica for the health of her son [name], to get well', the testimony noted in 1998.[49]

Today the shrine in Marija Bistrica has a well-established annual schedule of pilgrimages and official services, and it still gathers a large number of Croatians from Croatia and those who emigrated to other parts of the world, in total around 800 000 pilgrims per year. In recent years, it has been partly replaced in its religious significance for pilgrims by the shrine in Medjugorje as the data from interviews and archives shows. However, as the other shrine is in Bosnia and Herzegovina, Marija Bistrica still holds its national importance. So, Medjugorje is more of an international shrine rather than one reflecting Croatian identity, as many people from different countries and of different ethnical, religious and cultural backgrounds go there on pilgrimage and feel it as their spiritual place.[50]

Many pilgrims mention this newer shrine of Medjugorje in the notes that they leave in Marija Bistrica. Visits of pilgrims to both these shrines are common, and they are combined with visits to the Marian shrines in the places of the origin or living, such as the shrine in Sinj, Trsat, Aljmaš in Croatia, and Olovo, Podmilačje and some other in Bosnia and Herzegovina. Visits to the major European shrines are also very important to pilgrims from Croatia, usually as an important one-time life event and spiritual renewal or transformation. Recent decades see also many trips to the Holy Land as more people can afford to go and this is what overshadows any Marian or saint shrine according to pilgrims' testimonies. Slovenian visitations to Marija Bistrica are much rarer in recent decades, and visits from Bosnia and Herzegovina

---

48 Petar Berke, *Kinč osebujni slavnoga Orsaga Horvatckoga to jest'*, pp. 102–03.
49 *Knjiga uslišanja, milosti, zagovora i čudesa Bl. Dj. Marije Majke Božje Bistričke* https://www.svetiste-mbb.hr/stranica/zapisi-uslisanja-milosti-zagovori-i-cudesa (accessed on 20.11.2020).
50 Marijana Belaj, *Milijuni na putu. Antropologija hodočašća i sveto tlo Međugorja* (Zagreb: Jesenski i Turk, 2013), p. 78–91.

are more common as many people since the 1990s war moved to Croatia and then back to Bosnia and Herzegovina, or emigrated further to Austria, Germany and other European countries. So, the shrine today mostly accommodates Croatians from all over the world. Usually when visiting Marija Bistrica, those pilgrims also visit the main cathedral of Saint Stephen in Zagreb where the remains of The Blessed Aloysius Stepinac are displayed, expressing in this way their ethnical identity and praying for the ease of hardships of emigration. The data shows that another important shrine visited also by pilgrims originating from Bosnia and Herzegovina is the Basilica of The Sacred Heart of Jesus where the remains of the Bosnian-Herzegovinian Blessed Ivan Merz are displayed.

Conclusion

The shrine in Marija Bistrica has many characteristics of a national shrine that can be compared to national shrines in Europe and world. The shrine played a huge role in maintaining Christianity in this part of Europe during the Ottoman Empire rule and later in inhibiting the spread of the Reformation. This was done through various activities by the priests governing the shrine. During the Ottoman rule they continually highlighted the role of the Christian faith for spiritual benefits of a person praying to Mary or coming to the shrine. During the Reformation period, they asked for permission from the Austrian-Hungarian rulers to continue with pilgrimage on the basis of the international character of the shrine, and in this way secured the continuation of Catholic tradition in the areas connected to the Mother of God of Bistrica shrine. During the last two centuries several large historical events took place at the shrine, so the shrine has become a place where the national and religious identity of Catholic Croats has been clearly affirmed and reaffirmed. The fact that most priests governing the shrine have been Croats and belonged to the same culture as the majority of pilgrims, only augmented the role of the shrine in constructing the ethnic and cultural identity of Croatian pilgrims, to make it become a national shrine.

Through the centuries, pilgrims have been inscribing their own meanings and experiences into the shrine in Marija Bistrica, and besides ethnic and cultural aspects of their specific identity, it was very important for pilgrims' religiosity. The Catholic Church has been continually reinforcing the significance of the shrine for pilgrims, first through accepting oral stories about Mary's apparition and miraculous healings, and later through taking in the experience pilgrims have had at the shrine or while praying to Mary of Bistrica, including the pre-Christian Slavic beliefs that pilgrims incorporated into their notion of Christian faith. For the majority of people in the northwestern and central part of Croatia, the shrine in Marija Bistrica is still felt as home, and familiar place than other shrines in Europe. The shrine of the Mother of God of Bistrica in Marija Bistrica shaped a part of European identity in the area surrounding the shrine and even beyond, which confirms its significance as one of the larger shrines in the Western Balkans.

References

Alan Morinis, 'Introduction', in *Sacred Journeys. The Anthropology of Pilgrimage*, ed. by Alan Morinis (Westport/London: Grenwood Press, 1992), pp. 1–28.

Alojz Jembrih, 'Pogovor uz pretisak', in *Kinč osebujni slavnoga Orsaga Horvatckoga to jest: Čudnovita pripečenja i osebujne Milošče, kotere pri čudnovitom kipu Marije Bistričke više vre let se skazuju, s kratkum od kipa ovoga hištorijum, i hasnovitem navukom, pobožnem putnikom marijanskem na vekše njihovo razveselenje, po nevrednom negda mesta ovoga kapelanu Petru Berke na pervo postavlene*, published first in 1775, reprinted edition, ed. by Alojz Jembrih (Marija Bistrica: National Shrine of Mother of God of Bistrica, 1995), pp. 19–105.

Anna Niedźwiedź, 'Competing Sacred Places: Making and Remaking of National Shrines in Contemporary Poland', in *Pilgrimage, Politics and Place-Making in Eastern Europe: Crossing the Borders*, ed. by John Eade and Mario Katić (Farnham, Burlington: Ashgate, 2014), pp. 79–99.

Andrić Stanko, *Miracles of Saint John Capistran* (Osijek: Matica hrvatska Osijek, 1999).

Ante Sekulić, 'Biskup Martin Borković (1597–1687)', *Croatica Christiana Periodica*, 9 (15), (1985), 65–88.

Antun Šundalić, 'A model of peaceful reintegration and the possibility to live together', *Društvena istraživanja: časopis za opća društvena pitanja*, 6 (2–3), 28–29 (1997), 217–33.

Dijana Pinjuh, 'Conversions to Islam in Bosnia and Herzegovina, and the Connections between Converts and their Christian families, from the Ottoman Conquest to the End of the Seventeenth Century', *Povijesni prilozi*, 37 (55), (2018), 205–28.

Domagoj Sremić, 'Društvene i teološke odrednice Rimokatoličke crkve u Hrvatskoj u jeku društveno-političkih previranja 1971. godine', *Cris*, XVI (1), (2014), 65–76.

Edith Turner and Victor Turner, *Image and Pilgrimage in Christian Culture: Anthropological Perspectives* (New York: CUP, 1978).

Ellen Badone, 'Introduction', in *Religious Orthodoxy and Popular Faith in European Society*, ed. by Ellen Badone (Princeton: Princeton University Press, 1990), pp. 3–23.

Esther Gitman, *Alojzije Stepinac - Pillar of human rights* (Zagreb: Kršćanska sadašnjost, 2019).

Gabor Barna, 'Pilgrimages in Hungary: Ethnological and anthropological approaches', in *International Perspectives on Pilgrimage Studies: Itineraries, Gaps and Obstacles*, ed. by John Eade and Dionigi Albera (London: Routledge, 2015), pp. 95–113.

Geneviève Herberich-Marx, *Evolution d'une sensibilité religieuse: Témoignages iconographiques et scripturaires de pèlerinages alsaciens* (Strasbourg: Presses Universitaires de Strasbourg, 1989).

Ian Reader, *Pilgrimage: A Very Short Introduction* (Oxford: Oxford University Press, 2015).

Jasna Turkalj, 'Dr Juraj Žerjavić – »Spiritus agens« izbornoga pokreta i »bune« u Mariji Bistrici 1892. godine?!', *Croatica Christiana Periodica*, 35 (67), (2011), 125–42.

John Eade and Michael J. Sallnow, 'Introduction', in *Contesting the Sacred: The Anthropology of Christian Pilgrimage*, ed. by John Eade and Michael J. Sallnow (London, New York: Routledge, 1992), pp. 1–29.

John Eade and Mario Katić, 'Introduction: Crossing the Borders', in *Pilgrimage, Politics and Place-Making in Eastern Europe: Crossing the Borders*, ed. by John Eade and Mario Katić (Farnham: Ashgate, 2014), pp. 1–15.

Josip Buturac, *Marija Bistrica: 1209–1993: povijest župe i prošteništa* (Marija Bistrica: Nacionalno svetište Majke Božje Bistričke, 1993).

Kristijan Herceg, 'Obrazovanje pavlina u Hrvatskoj', *Spectrum: ogledi i prinosi studenata teologije*, (1-4), (2009), 30–36.

Marijana Belaj, *Milijuni na putu. Antropologija hodočašća i sveto tlo Međugorja* (Zagreb: Jesenski i Turk, 2013).

Marijana Belaj and Mirela Hrovatin, 'Cultural Practices in Sacralisation of Place: Vows in the Shrine of Our Lady of Marija Bistrica', in *Sacralization of Landscape and Sacred Places. Proceedings of the 3rd International Scientific Conference of Mediaeval Archaeology of the Institute of Archaeology*, ed. by Juraj Belaj et al. (Zagreb: Institut za arheologiju, 2018), pp. 343–51.

Mario Jareb, 'Blagoslov hrvatske zastave u Mariji Bistrici 3. 11. 1935. kao ogledalo odnosa jugoslavenskih vlasti i Katoličke Crkve prema hrvatskim nacionalnim simbolima u drugoj polovici tridesetih godina 20. stoljeća', *Milosti puna: glasilo Svetišta Majke Božje Bistričke*, 16, 46 (2010), 31–42.

Marko Dragić, 'Legends and Testimonies about Miraculous Our Lady of Sinj', *Croatica et Slavica Iadertina*, 12 (1), 12 (2016), 153–77.

Mirela Hrovatin, *Kulturnoantropološki pristup zavjetu u izvaninstitucijskoj osobnoj pobožnosti* ('A cultural anthropological approach to vows in non-institutional personal religiosity'), Doctoral thesis (Zagreb: Faculty of Humanities and Social Sciences, University of Zagreb, 2015).

Mirela Hrovatin, 'Negotiating with the Sacred Other: The Ancient Mechanisms of the Personal Vow Practice', *International journal of religious tourism and pilgrimage*, 8 (1), (2020), 11–23.

Mirko Valentić, 'Turski ratovi i hrvatska dijaspora u XVI. stoljeću', *Senjski zbornik: prilozi za geografiju, etnologiju, gospodarstvo, povijest i kulturu*, 17 (1), (1990), 45–60.

Petar Berke, *Kinč osebujni slavnoga Orsaga Horvatckoga to jest: Čudnovita pripečenja i osebujne Miloščc, kotere pri čudnovitom kipu Marije Bistričke više vre let se skazuju, s kratkum od kipa ovoga hištorijum, i hasnovitem navukom, pobožnem putnikom marijanskem na vekše njihovo razveselenje, po nevrednom negda mesta ovoga kapelanu Petru Berke na pervo postavlene*, published first in 1775, reprinted edition, ed. by Alojz Jembrih (Marija Bistrica: National Shrine of Mother of God of Bistrica, 1995).

Ratko Vučetić, 'Prostorni razvoj srednjovjekovne Krapine', *Radovi Instituta za povijest umjetnosti*, 24 (2000), 7–22.

Simon Coleman, 'Pilgrimage as Trope for an Anthropology of Christianity', *Current Anthropology* 55 (10), (2014), 281–91.

Simon Coleman and John Eade, 'Introduction', in *Reframing Pilgrimage: Cultures in Motion*, ed. by Simon Coleman and John Eade (London: Routledge, 2004), pp. 1–25.

Szabolcs Serfőző, 'Pilgrimages of Emperor Leopold I in Central Europe', *Radovi Instituta za povijest umjetnosti*, 41 (2017), 59–66.

Vedran Klaužer and Damir Galoić, *Papa putnik - bistrički hodočasnik 1998–2018* (Marija Bistrica: Ogranak Matice hrvatske u Mariji Bistrici, 2018).

William A. Christian, *Person and God in a Spanish Valley* (Princeton: Princeton University Press, 1989).

Online Sources

'Ancient Shrine at Vinski Vrh', *Hrvatsko nacionalno Svetište Majke Božje Bistričke*, https://www.svetiste-mbb.hr/jezik/detaljno/en/ancient-shrine-at-vinski-vrh-1499-1545 (accessed on 3.03.2021).

'Gotovina s obitelji u M. Bistrici: Zahvalio je Majci Božjoj na slobodi', Večernji list, 18 November 2012, https://m.vecernji.hr/vijesti/gotovina-s-obitelji-u-m-bistrici-zahvalio-je-majci-bozjoj-na-slobodi-476654/komentari?page=4 (accessed on 8.03.2021)

'Hrvatsko proljeće', *Proleksis enciklopedija online*, https://proleksis.lzmk.hr/27229/ (accessed on 10. 12.2020).

Marija Bistrica, *Hrvatska enciklopedija, mrežno izdanje*, Leksikografski zavod Miroslav Krleža, https://www.enciklopedija.hr/natuknica.aspx?id=38913 (accessed on 22.03.2021)

'Remete', *Karmel.hr*, http://karmel.hr/?page_id=295 (accessed on 5.02.2021)

'Knjiga uslišanja, milosti, zagovora i čudesa Bl. Dj. Marije Majke Božje Bistričke' ('The Book of Answered Prayers, Graces, Vows and Miracles Granted by the Blessed Virgin Our Lady of Marija Bistrica'), 2012, *Hrvatsko nacionalno svetište Majke Božje Bistričke*, https://www.svetiste-mbb.hr/stranica/zapisi-uslisanja-milosti-zagovori-i-cudesa (accessed on 20.11.2020).

CONSTANTIN NECULA

Pilgrimage in the Romanian Orthodox Church

Aspects of the Pedagogy of Faith

Introductory Note

The mystery of pilgrimage can be analyzed from different and distinct perspectives such as spiritual, social or psychological. In the last few years, scholars have approached the Christian phenomenon of pilgrimage in relationship to social pedagogy. It has been considered a prevailing influence contributing to a new culture of life and profile of the community in places that host pilgrims. Moreover, it determines the contents of giving away one community's faith, which finds itself in a dynamic journey of finding God. Therefore, I should assert that pilgrimage has a fundamental pedagogical character shaped from the very beginning. Preserving this pedagogical feature, the pilgrimage in the Romanian Orthodox space has some particularities due to the specific profile of the country shaped by its history.

The purpose of my research study is to identify the essential characteristics of pilgrimage here, for they place it at the core of the cultural life of the Church and of the people in Romania and refine its anthropological dimension. In this paper, I aim to present the pilgrimage phenomena in Romania from both the pedagogy of faith and the social pedagogy perspectives, which were strongly connected during the communist period, when pilgrimage was characterized by a particular dynamic related to its role in educating people on the authentic history of Romania.

Social pedagogy perspective is related to the importance of the pilgrimage phenomenon in different eras and geographies. In Romania it is the expression of how the monasteries become great transformers of the catechetical and pastoral structure that was needed to face ideological control, especially under dictatorships of different orientations. Romania like the other countries in Balkan Peninsula was under societal pressure, which generated the restoration of pastoral theology and therefore, led to changes including the social communication of the Revealed Truth.

When analyzing pilgrimage, the researcher is conditioned to go beyond phenomenology – places, data, and miracles. In other words, the roots of the pilgrimage pedagogy mystics should be identified. The concept refers to God's pedagogical plan

---

Constantin Necula • PhD, Dr Habil., Tenured Professor at the Lucian Blaga University, Sibiu, Romania

Pilgrimage in the Christian Balkan World: The Path to Touch the Sacred and Holy, ed. by Dorina Dragnea, Emmanouil Ger. Varvounis, Evelyn Reuter, Petko Hristov and Susan Sorek (Turnhout, 2023), pp. 185–199.
BREPOLS ❧ PUBLISHERS   DOI 10.1484/M.STR-EB.5.132406

of revealing Himself to people along history and people's response to it. In other words, it is connected with God's pilgrimage to the world and people's journey to fulfil the innate yearning to find the Truth. Therefore, it relates both to revelation and conversion phenomena. I mention here only three paradigmatic cases to illustrate the concept. First, God, Himself, is a pilgrim to the world, besides people, and He comes with all His power of empathy and love. He walked with the prophets in the Old Testament era, then revealed Himself in Jesus Christ, who entered the world as fully God and fully man. Jesus promised to extend his journey, accompanying his disciples 'to the very end of the age' (Matthew 28:16–20). Second, the case of the Pentecost are paradigmatic. Pilgrims far across the Diaspora, from Parthia to Rome filled Jerusalem (Acts 2:8–11) coming for the festival of Shavuot, which was a pilgrimage festival. After Peter's first public sermon, three thousand people repented and were 'baptized in the name of Jesus Christ for the forgiveness of sin' (Acts 2:37–42). At that moment, with the power of the Spirit the Church was born. Certainly, many of those pilgrims went back home across the Roman world, carrying the new faith and the good news of the Gospel. Thirdly, Saint Paul's case is also a paradigm. Paul journeys as Saul the persecutor to find Jesus's body but on his way he met Jesus alive and converted to the new faith, becoming Paul the pilgrim on the Christian faith way.

Definition, Context, and the Scripture Pattern

I use a dictionary of theologians' and sociologists' common preoccupations to define the term 'pilgrimage' from the Orthodox Theology perspective. However, because there is not such a great oeuvre of common points of view, I will use the *Dictionary of Patristic Theology*[1] that is the most popular work of the missionary ethos of the Orthodox Church. According to it, the term 'pilgrimage' derives from the Latin term 'peregrinatio', which means to travel abroad. Christians used it with the meaning of a journey made to pray at a holy place. It is linked to the prayer of the heart or 'Jesus Prayer' ('Lord Jesus Christ, son of God, have mercy of me, the sinner') practised at the great saints and martyrs' tombs. That was an old funeral ritual developed by Christians, particularly in the liturgical way.[2]

Pilgrimage theology seems to have been assumed as a cultural genesis long before the moment of Pentecost, which marked the beginning of the Church as a divine-human institution. The Wise Men's journey, the shepherds' visit to Baby Jesus, and the Holy Family's flight into Egypt are considered in the pilgrimage theology artifacts of the phenomena connected to pilgrimage. Actually, the worship of the Wise Men is related to the old custom of searching and finding those people who can change human history. The shepherds' journey reminds us of the simplicity of the true worshipers in spirit and truth. The path to Egypt is directly connected to

---

1 John Anthony McGuckin, *Dicționar de Teologie Patristică*, trans. by Dragoș Dâscă and Alin-Bogdan Mihăilescu (Iași: Doxologia, 2014), p. 375.
2 John Anthony McGuckin, *Dicționar de Teologie Patristică*, p. 375.

the chosen people escaping over the Red Sea. Moreover, it is a journey of avoiding death. All these journeys[3] were linked to the fulfillment of the prophecies of the coming of the Messiah. Thus, pilgrimage has at its core a strong eschatological vein.

The Christians' Holy Places have become over time landmarks of pilgrimages. One of them is Mount Tabor, the place of the Transfiguration of Christ. The development of understanding this place as a pilgrimage site and the spiritual pedagogy that it generates can be traced to the homiletical culture developed in the Mount Tabor account.[4]

We should remember that long before these 'fragments of pilgrimage', the Lord himself was a Pilgrim paying attention to the Law. His journeys were in close relationship with the Jewish feasts celebrated at the Temple of Jerusalem, which was the core of the Jewish community ritual culture. What Jesus' earthly pilgrimage brought to the worship was the careful observation of its spiritual content. Moreover, He enabled polycentric worship. The Apostles continued the custom, for they often came back to Jerusalem on the traditional feasts, especially for Pentecost. However, the new core of these returning pilgrimages was Jesus' Tomb instead of the Temple. The Holy Tomb would be the centre of worship even after AD 135, when Hadrian built two temples on Golgotha and the Holy Sepulcher (a Temple of Aphrodite and Jupiter), defiling the sacred place. Both temples would be destroyed.[5]

Historical Patterns of Pilgrimage in Romania and the History of the Patterns

Looking back on the history of pilgrimages in the Romanian Orthodox Church, I note some patterns of pilgrimage, some of them very specific to the Romanian Space.

It is were was recorded a delay in the Romanian Orthodox Church concerning the pilgrimages to the Holy Tomb. An increasing number of pilgrims were registered only after 1921.[6] This does not mean that eminent personalities of Romanian history had not journeyed – sometimes alone but seldom in groups – to Jerusalem, Constantinople, or Alexandria. Very often they went to Mount Athos, which was a pilgrimage centre closer than those of the Near East. Some pilgrims (e.g. Nicodemus of Tismana, Paisius

---

3   Adalbert G. Hamman, *La vita quotidiana dei primi cristiani* (Italia: Biblioteca Universale Rizzoli, 1993), pp. 42–66. Additional information of the period of martyrdom in the volume of Daniele Rops, *La Chiesa degli Apostoli e dei Martiri*, vol. I. (Torino-Roma: Marietti, 1957), pp. 347–435.
4   Dom Michel Coune and Moine de Saint-André-lez-Bruges, *Bucuria Schimbării la Față după Părinții Răsăriteni*, trans. by Eugen-Adrian Truța, ed. by Dom Michel Coune (Alba-Iulia: Reîntregirea, 2017), p. 275.
5   See the analysis proposed by Dario Garribba and Marco Vitelli, *Le città del cristianesimo antico. La Galilea e Gerusalemme* (Trapani: Il Pozzo di Giacobbe, 2019), p. 219.
6   One of the works presenting these pilgrimages, is authored by Fr. Iosif Trifa's, *Pe urmele Mântuitorului. Însemnări din călătoria la Ierusalim* (Sibiu: Oastea Domnului, 1927), (2nd edition, 1928). Olga Greceanu, one of the prominent intellectual women of the Church, authored a representative work, *Pe urmele Pașilor Tăi, Iisuse…* (București: Idaco, 2008).

Velichkovsky, Vasile of Poiana Mărului, and Gheorghe of Cernica and Căldărușani)[7] who went to the Theotokos' Holy Mountain for their spiritual progress, came back and became founders of monastic places.

Considering the history of pilgrimage in the Early Church in the Romanian space, I note two moments considered to be historical patterns of pilgrimage in Romania. *The Martyrdom of Saints Epictetus and Astion of Halmyris* is the first one. They suffered martyrdom in the years 298–303 or perhaps even earlier, during the reign of Diocletian. Epictetus was a priest and Astion his disciple. They received the crown of martyrdom on July 8, 290, according to the so-called *Martyrologium Hieronymianum*. When retelling the story of their martyrdom, one of the well-known historians of the Romanian Orthodox Church, Reverend Mircea Păcurariu,[8] perceives the strong connection among martyrdom, pilgrimage and conversion. Astion's parents pilgrimed to Halmyris in Scythia accompanied by three imperial young servants, to support their child, who was suffering persecution and torture. However, they arrived too late, only on the third day after the burial and found a tense but favourable atmosphere created around the holy martyrs' death. It was the most auspicious moment for their conversion to Christianity. Vigilantus (who is supposed to be the author of the account of Astion's martyrdom), preached to them for a week about Jesus Christ's new teaching to whom, their son and the 60-year-old priest Epictetus had given their lives. After he announced to them the Word of God, a priest named Bonosus, who had been hidden from the cruel persecutions, prayed a lot for them and made them catechumens. Forty days later, Bishop Evanghelicus, who was probably from the city of Tomis,[9] baptized them. He stayed with them for eight days, and then went to a city nearby.[10] The two new Christians, Alexander and Marcelina, went back to their homeland and took the righteous Vigilantius and the honest priest Bonosus with them. They shared all their wealth with the poor, as it is appropriate for God's chosen people.[11]

Mihail Diaconescu,[12] mentions that the Act of the Martyrdom of Saints Epictetus and Astion was first translated in the eighteenth century by Hierodeacon Ștefan Dascălul,

---

7   Serafim Joantă, *Roumanie. Tradition et culture hesychastes* (Paris: Coll. Spiritualité orientale, 1987). The Romanian edition was published in 1994.
8   Mircea Păcurariu, *Sfinți daco-romani și români* (Iași: Trinitas, 2000), pp. 42–43. See also the translation of the *Act of the Martyr* at Nestor Vornicescu, 'Pătimirea Martirilor Epictet și Astion (de la cumpăna secolelor III–IV)', trans. by David Popescu, in *Una din primele scrieri ale literaturii române străvechi* (Craiova: Editura Mitropoliei Craiovei, 1990), pp. 67–109.
9   Flavio Placida, *L'epoca d'oro della catechesi. L'insegnamento e la prassi dei Padri della Chiesa* (Italia: Urbaniana University Press, 2020), p. 239.
10 Mircea Păcurariu, *Sfinți daco-romani și români…*, pp. 42–43. See also the translation of the *Act of the Martyr* …, pp. 67–109.
11 Constantin Necula, 'Exigențele convertirii oglindite în Actele Martirice - izvor primar', in *Ale Tale dintru ale Tale. Liturghie - Pastorație - Mărturisire. Prinos de cinstire adus IPS Dr Laurențiu Streza la împlinirea vârstei de 60 de ani*, ed. by Dorin Oancea, Constantin Necula, Ștefan Toma, and Cristian Vaida (Sibiu: Andreiana, 2008), pp. 677–720.
12 Mihail Diaconescu, 'Actul Martiric al Sfinților Epictet și Astion de la Halmyris' in *Istoria Literaturii Dacoromane*, ed. by Mihail Diaconescu (București: Alcor Edimpex, 1999), pp. 434–43.

who used a Russian version. This Romanian translation was made in the context of the renewal of hesychastic monastic life initiated by Saint Paisius Velichkovsky. Mihail Diaconescu also mentions that later on, Metropolitan Veniamin Costache (1768–1846) published it in 1814 at the monastery of Neamț, in the volume *Viețile Sfinților din luna iulie* ('The Life of the Saints in July').

The volume was published three times at Căldărușani, Bucharest, and Chișinău. Apart from the original, the oldest edition may be found in the volume *Vitae Patrum*.[13]

We discussed this Act of Martyr for several reasons. First, it is a historical document[14] witnessing the first pilgrimage to the tomb of a saint recorded in the territory of Romania. Second, Astion's mother should be seen as one of the confessing women of the Early Church, who used to go on a pilgrimage like Paula, Melania the Elder, Melania the Younger, Egeria.[15] Finally, Astion's family members' true conversion, their involvement in the catechetical process and in building the first 'missionary cell', prove them active Christians.

The consequences of the martyrdom depicted here are paradigmatic for the fruits of the pilgrimage. Therefore, comparing the journey of Astion's family to the holy place of his death, with the pilgrimage practice today, both the goal and the pedagogical role of the pilgrimage become obvious. Every year millions of people leave the comfort of their homes and spend their savings enduring hardships to reach holy sites. The analysis of different forms of pilgrimage[16] show that the purpose of the pilgrimage is not the beauty of the buildings there, but the knowledge of faith. The main goal of Christian pilgrimage is to foster the understanding of the faith through catechesis and therefore to reinforce and strengthen the life in Christ. Moreover, it is the pedagogy of The Holy Spirit that works in the core of pilgrims' hearts. Therefore, the pilgrimage at the holy places is also an inner journey to fulfill the innate yearning to find the Truth.

We can identify here the main characteristics of the pilgrimage that are still valid today, e.g., the death of a loved one, looking for inner silence, conversion, family pilgrimage, and community involvement in the pilgrimage effort.

Almost all the features can be found in the two pilgrimages in the Romanian space, namely the pilgrimages to the relics of Saint Paraskeva of the Balkans (Iași)[17] and Saint Demetrius the New, also known as Demetrius Basarabov[18] (Bucharest). Apart from these two "classical", pilgrimages, we remembered that the most important pilgrimages

---

13   Herbert Rosweyde, *Vitae Patrum* (Belgium: Antwerpen, 1615).
14   The acts of martyrdoms are historical documents, hagiographical tex, because they are copies made by Christians, of judges reports issued by Romans authorities. See *Actele martirice* ('The Acts of the Christian Martyrs') trans. by Ioan I. Rămureanu (București: Editura Institutului Biblic și de Misiune al Bisericii Ortodoxe Române, 1997), p. 12.
15   Francesca Allegri, *Donne e Pellegrine dall'Antichità al Medioevo* (Milano: Jaca Book, 2012), pp. 3–12.
16   Ahmad Nooruddeen and Jahangeer Khan, 'The Phenomenon of Pilgrimage in World Religions', in *The Review of Religions*, August 2020, https://www.reviewofreligions.org/23807/pilgrimage-in-world-religions/ (accessed on 14.06.2022).
17   Ioachim Băcăuanul, *Cultul Sfintei Parascheva în Ortodoxie – Cercetare hagiografico- liturgică* (Roma: Filocalia, 2013).
18   *Sfântul Dimitrie Izvorâtorul de Mir și Sfântul Dimitrie Basarabov* (București: Meteor, 2015).

of the Orthodox Christians in Romania are linked to monasteries whose main feast day is the Dormition of the Theotokos (Nicula and Tismana monasteries). For centuries, the tomb of Saint Joseph the Younger of Partoș, Metropolitan of Timișoara, was a milestone for an almost continuous pilgrimage. The same phenomenon is registered today in the cases of Fathers Arsenie Boca (Prislop) and Iustin Pârvu (Petru-Vodă).

Saint John Cassian's works, *Așezămintele Mănăstirești* ('Monastic Settlements') and *Convorbiri Duhovnicești* ('Spiritual Conversations') are the second key-texts that I discuss here. They are authoritative texts of Christian culture and can help us understand the pilgrimage pedagogy. Saint John Cassian's good friend, Saint Germanus of Dobrogea, accompanied him on a spiritual journey looking for a life model. Here, for example, is a text that reflects this perspective:

> When I was in the desert of Scete, where the most excellent monastic fathers are and where all perfection flourishes, in company with the holy father Germanus (who had since the earliest days and commencement of our spiritual service been my closest companion both in the Coenobium and in the desert, so that to show the harmony of our friendship and aims, everybody would say that a single heart and soul existed in our two bodies), I sought out Abbot Moses, who was eminent amid those splendid flowers, not only in practical but also in contemplative excellence, in my anxiety to be grounded by his instruction: and together we implored him to give us a discourse for our edification…[19]

This kind of pilgrimage would be identifiable at every stage of Church life in the Romanian territory. Metropolitan Antonie Plămădeală offered us a history of this phenomenon in two of his works, *Teachers of Romanian Thought and Feeling*[20] and *Tradition and Freedom in Romanian Spirituality*.[21] His study of Saint Germanus fostered a new assessment of the two saints' pilgrimage, emphasising they were the first reporters of the heart prayer practice in the monastic space explored by them.

Therefore, there are two steady pilgrimage patterns in the history of the Romanian Orthodox Church.[22] On the one hand, it is the ascetic, toilsome pilgrimage, when the pilgrim reaches a spiritual place, looking for the inward silence. On the other hand, the person goes on a quiet pilgrimage, looking for a pattern of spiritual life and asking how to achieve the Christian calling.[23]

---

19 St John Cassian, *First Conference of Abbot Moses*, chapter 1, https://www.newadvent.org/fathers/350801.htm (accessed on 14.07.2021).
20 Antonie Plămădeală, *Dascăli de cuget și simțire românească* (București: Editura Institutului Biblic și de Misiune a Bisericii Ortodoxe Române, 1981), p. 547.
21 Antonie Plămădeală, *Tradiție și libertate în spiritualitatea românească*, 410; 1st edition (Sibiu, 1983), 2nd edition (București, 1995); 3rd edition (București, 2010).
22 See Valentin-Lucian Beloiu, *Pelerinaj spre Rai – Turismul religios în Sfântul Munte* (București: Evanghelismos, 2020); Kyriacos C. Markides, *Darurile deșertului. Calea uitată a spiritualității creștine*, trans. by Anca Irina Ionescu (București: Herald, 2021).
23 Ioanichie Bălan, *Pateric Românesc. Cuprinde viața și cuvintele unor Sfinți și Cuvioși Părinți ce s-au nevoit în mănăstirile românești (Secolele IV–XX)* (Galați: Editura Arhiepiscopiei Tomisului și Dunării de Jos, 1990), p. 704.

Another pattern. An intermediary pilgrimage pattern links to the annual journey of the Orthodox Christians belonging 'The Army of the Lord'. It starts on Saturday vesper in the Metropolitan Cathedral of Sibiu and continues to Pentecost Sunday when the pious pilgrims cross the main traffic arteries of Sibiu. Then, they participate in the Divine Liturgy at Fr. Joseph Trifa's tomb, the founder of the movement. The youth assemblies of the Lord's Army,[24] which take place every year (excepting 2020 and 2021), are other pilgrimage events. Organized on the Sunday of Thomas, they are missionary and pastoral events for the laity, regularly attended by about 1,500 and 5,000 people.

Pilgrimage Behaviour and Religious Tourism: Between Devotion and Indifference

Recently, the world has begun to deny the pilgrimage. In Romania, especially after 2000, the mass media constantly tends to judge the two major yearly pilgrimages, namely the pilgrimages to Saint Paraskeva of the Balkans (Iași) and Saint Demetrius Basarabov (Bucharest). Annually, excepting last year, Romania's largest religious pilgrimage brings about two million faithful to Iași, without counting the people who come to pray at the relics of Saint Paraskeva all over the year. In this context, mass media launched negative campaigns full of clichés that easily manipulates especially uninformed people.

The second-largest pilgrimage in Romania, which takes place in Bucharest, is less mocked than the pilgrimage to Iași. However, the pilgrimage to Șumuleu Ciuc, paradigmatic for the Catholic pilgrimages organized in Eastern Europe, gathered Hungarian-speaking Roman Catholic believers and is supported by a press campaign. Comparing Romanian mass media attitudes towards the pilgrimage to Saint Paraskeva (Iași) and Șumuleu Ciuc, we denounce its preconceived ideas on pilgrimage. It treats with disrespect the value of the pilgrimage for believers, trying to denigrate one to the detriment of another, depending on the confession. Regardless of how worrying the situation may be, and how malicious mass media intentions are, we should understand that the Christian-Orthodox pilgrimages message in Romania is the manifestation of both a people seeking God and of God who has always been a Pilgrim that looks to His people.

Pilgrimages forbidden and cancelled by the communist government of the country have been restarted immediately after the Revolution of 1989. One example is the pilgrimage to Maglavit. In the 1930s and 1940s, one of the most interesting mass cultures of pilgrimage appeared in Maglavit. The specificity of the Maglavit pilgrimage is that the cult of the main character, the visionary Petrache Lupu, was not authenticated by the synod's decisions but only by people's piety towards him. The place of Petrache Lupu's supernatural vision, who was a young shepherd, became

---

24 For further information relating to the subject, see the magazines of the Association *Oastea Domnului*, *Iisus Biruitorul* and *Timotheos* (Sibiu).

one of the largest pilgrimage sites and gathered a huge crowd. People went there to attend the Divine Liturgy and were filled with the simple, popular shepherd's sermons. Petrache was sent to prison during the communist period so the pilgrimage site of Maglavit was erased from the pilgrimage map. After 1990, a monastery was built to restore the spirituality of the place, followed by a series of on-site research. Contemporary people, who do not know the story of the Maglavit pilgrimage doubt its authenticity. Authentic or not, it proved to be the manifestation of the spiritual thirst of a devastated people economically disoriented and socially wounded by the First World War.

In the Christian conscience of the people, only one place in Romania would enjoy such a reception, the place in the Olt meadow, from Ionești, which is marked today also by a monastery. The 'Holy Trinity' monastery, also known as the 'Fearful Judgment' monastery, is located in the commune of Buzoești in Argeș, Ionești village. It was built between 1999 and 2019 in the place of a former monastic settlement that dated from Michael the Brave's time (1558-d. 1601). According to local tradition, the place is full of spirituality. The story of the miracles from Ionești begins in 1997, with the dream of an elderly person from the Ionești. He told the locals how the Mother of God appeared to him in a dream three times, asking him to build a settlement to worship and rest, by the Ionești fountain. The man spread the word in the village and, with the contribution of the faithful, erected a crucifix on the place indicated by the Mother of God in a dream. According to locals, three crosses appeared in the sky during the consecration service of the crucifix. The story of the miracles from Ionești spread quickly among the faithful and brought, over time, many pilgrims of different confessions convinced of the miraculous virtues of the place.[25]

The pilgrimage had some distinguishing characteristics in Romania during the communist period that should be more carefully investigated. All sorts of trips organized for the working people by the National Tourism Office (ONT) or even the Youth Tourism Office (BTT) often hid important spiritual destinations in our country. However, besides the socialist culture of the industrial sites, people often discovered the real culture preserved in the monasteries.

The workers used to visit the monasteries in Bukovina (North of Moldavia), which remain until today the foremost pilgrimage sites.[26] They were built during the fifteenth and sixteenth centuries, starting with the reign of Alexandru cel Bun (Voivode Alexander the Good, r. 1400-1432) or even earlier. The residence of the medieval state of Moldavia from Dragoș Vodă's reign to the fourteenth century was Baia, first documented in 1300. It was a city that linked the great trade routes of Europe.

---

25 Sorin Preda, 'Noi miracole creștine la Ionești', in *Formula AS*, No. 1385 (27.09.2019–2003.10.2019), http://arhiva.formula-as.ro/1999/362/societate-37/noi-miracole-crestine-la-ionesti-574 (accessed on 7.08.2021).

26 *Sfânta Mănăstire Putna*, ed. by Iacov Putneanul (Mănăstirea Putna: Centrul de Cercetare și Documentare 'Ștefan cel Mare' al Sfintei Mănăstiri Putna, 2010), p. 57.

The other milestone of the Romanian Orthodox pilgrimage is represented up to today by the monasteries of the Archdiocese of Râmnic (Vâlcea County).[27] The third is the historical welcoming land of Maramureș, where tourist flow is exceedingly high. Many tourists also visit places of worship. Moreover, Romanian Orthodox monasteries of Gorj County such as the monasteries of Tismana[28] and Polovragi are important spiritual and cultural sites as well. Besides the beautiful churches of the fourteenth and fifteenth centuries, pilgrims can visit Constantin Brâncuși's magnificent sculptural ensemble in Târgu Jiu (the residence town of the Gorj County).

We have to admit that most of the pilgrimages naturally coincided with the feast days of the churches, which were transformed on fair days when commercial aspects prevail. The phenomenon of the great fair (e.g. Tismana, Bistrița, Horezu, and Polovragi fair) was re-instated between 1930 and 1989, especially in the southern and south-western regions of Romania. Today, the commercial aspect is much reduced compared to that time and covered by moments of personal history stored in people's memories. The collective memory registered vivid remembrances, such as the joint trip and dinner, the participation in the liturgical celebration, seldom in the Divine Liturgy. At the end of a pilgrimage, people used to return home carrying books, incense, crosses, and icons. Moreover, they were relating to others their experiences of the place, accommodation, trip, and facilities.

Patriarch Justinian of Romania wisely used the pilgrimage opportunity for the pastoral mission by establishing in the 1950 and 1955 training courses to prepare guides for monasteries and monastic museums. Therefore, the monasteries became not only welcoming pilgrimage places, but also sources of unadulterated national history and exceptional historical discourses, untouched by the ideological communist virus. We should mention that Putna monastery had a famous guides team, whose patriotic diatribe against communism were listened to even by the atheists. The pilgrimage was promoted by carefully edited and printed materials, which really mattered in the editorial profile of the time.[29]

In the period between 1970 and 1989, nothing was more valuable than an album of the visited monasteries. Students' compositions were no longer censured. Besides, the parents were no longer investigated to clarify their children's purpose to have visited the monastery. Therefore, we can assert that the family group or parish pilgrimage increased the Christian content value of the pilgrims' lives. Moreover, the pilgrimage had in the Christian Orthodox community a particular shape. It was organized for a group of pilgrims who are most often accompanied by a clergyman. It also has intermediate stages.

In Transylvania, on 15 August, important pilgrimages are organized to the monasteries of Nicula and Moisei. There were special journeys attended by the pilgrim communities,

---

27 *Cetățile Credinței – mănăstiri și schituri din Arhiepiscopia Râmnicului* (Baia Mare: Proema, 2010), p. 287.
28 See the story of the Romanian Orthodox monasteries of Gorj County, which are strong centers of pilgrimages in the volume: *Oltenia de lângă Cer* (Craiova: Editura Mitropoliei Olteniei, 2006).
29 It should be mentioned, for the beauty of its writing and images, the classical work of Valeriu Anania, *Cerurile Oltului. Școliile Arhimandritului Bartolomeu la imaginile fotografice ale lui Dumitru F. Dumitru* (Episcopia Râmnicului și Argeșului, 1990), p. 335. It was ready to be published since 1989.

who walked tens of kilometres, singing particular songs, carrying icons and religious flags (the Roman labarum), fasting, and praying in the churches they encountered en route. This pattern of pilgrimage was transferred somewhat from the spirituality of the pilgrimage carried out in the Greek-Catholic communities in the Interwar Period, when Orthodox believers used to journey together with the Greek Catholics.

Most of the pilgrimages in Romania have even today an ecumenical dimension. People's devotion often goes beyond denomination and religion and is manifested especially in areas with multi-denominational populations. People of different faith or religion used to participate in the pilgrimages of other denominations and visit various landmarks of their faith. In this sense, it is worth mentioning the feasts or visits at the Teothokos icons of Lipova (in a Franciscan complex) and Cacica. Moreover, the visits of two Popes, John Paul II and Francis became occasions of joint pilgrimage and accountability to Christian unity. In different cities like Buhuși, the Christian community welcomes the Jewish one, which journeys to show during a feast appreciation of the founder Rabin. The pilgrimage to the tomb of protomartyrs Zoticos, Attalos, Kamasis, and Filippos in Niculițel (Tulcea County) is important also for the Muslim community. In short, places, communities, and regions acquire new meanings due to pilgrimages.

Post-1989 pilgrimage reveals new places of Christian testimony, namely the communist prisons. Excepting the penitentiary of Râmnicul Sărat, 80 per cent of the penitentiaries are still functional and marked through memorials (the largest are in Sighetul Marmației and Aiud) the places of great human dramas, in which thousands of souls were committed to the Gospel. This type of pilgrimage goes beyond confession and develops a particular ritual including remembrance of the dead, readings from testimonies, and visits to museum collections. Most of the participants in pilgrimages are youngsters and young adults.[30]

The Pilgrim's Words or the Pilgrim's Spiritual Dictionary

Is there a specific pilgrimage vocabulary? Undoubtedly! On one hand, it widely depends on both the religious and the local discourse adaptability to the pilgrim's needs, who come from far away. On the other hand, we do not know why pilgrim tend to adapt his vocabulary to the local one, seeking to convert his communication to that specific of the area. Perhaps, because he wants to respond to the hospitality with friendship.

Pilgrims on the road aim in general at spiritual achievement. The priests who organize a pilgrimage aim at community cohesion. Therefore, pilgrimage becomes an exercise of pastoral practice. Pilgrims constitute homogeneous groups, even if only during the pilgrimage. Moreover, a common memory language is developed, and a responsible priest can foster it through post-pilgrimage activities, which preserve the enriched memory linked to other spiritual experiences.

---

30 See Mirel Bănică, *Nevoia de miracol. Fenomenul pelerinajelor în România contemporană* (Iași: Polirom, 2014).

An interesting aspect of the pilgrimage is the folklore connected with it. Songs or high anecdotal texts, sermons and media presentations, on-scene reports or even real apologetic literature on pilgrimage, published books or simple informing catechesis are part of the folk culture.[31] The tradition is often recorded in the folk discourse: 'The guardian angel counts every pilgrim's step to the monastery'. Undoubtedly, the analysis of the supporting text (hymns, prayers, and sermons) reveals the simplicity and the harmony between the language of the popular theological culture and the theological language expressing the Romanian pastoral thinking on pilgrimage.[32]

What about the pilgrim's profile? My direct observation of the pilgrims indicates that the group is characteristic of the entire population. Their age, always a subject of dispute with the representatives of the anticlerical current, indicates that not only seniors attend the pilgrimage. It is important to note that one of the strongest Christian youth associations in Romania is the Romanian Orthodox Christian Students Association (ASCOR) of Iași. The great number and force of the volunteers prove the presence of youths integrated into the general mission of the Church.

Statistical data on the young volunteers (e.g. at the International Meeting of Orthodox Youth)[33] expressed the youths' need for conscious and coordinated involvement in the mission and pastoral of the Church. Fortunately, the youth have formed a strong core to support the Christian communities to overcome different events (e.g. organizing Easter or funeral service of Archbishop Pimen of Suceava and Rădăuți)[34] during the pandemic.

A Map of the Pilgrimages in the Orthodox Romania?

It is possible to produce a map. However, it should encompass all regions of the country reflecting the intra-parish pilgrimages of the Epiphany feast or Palm Sunday, which were restored in the liturgical tradition of Romanian Orthodoxy.

I have reiterated in my study a series of benchmarks on pilgrimage, which, after all, is a liturgical act. In addition, the unprecedented development of this phenomenon, which was fostered by the foundation of a specialized agency of the Church – Basilica Travel, should be mentioned.

---

31 *Sfântul Dimitrie cel Nou, ocrotitorul Bucureștilor. Cuvinte către pelerini, studii și mărturii contemporane* (București: 'Cuvântul Vieții', 2021), p. 464.
32 Constantin Necula, 'Pedagogia teologică a pelerinajului creștin (un posibil punct de vedere ortodox)', *Review of Ecumenical Studies*, 1 (2009), pp. 21–30.
33 Constantin Necula, 'Pelerin cu tinerii' in *Participant's guide. Unity. Faith. Nation / Ghidul Participantului. Unitate. Credință. Neam, ITO 2018* (Sibiu: Mitropolia Transilvaniei, Arhiepiscopia Sibiului, 2018), p. 25. See also Constantin Necula, 'Tineretul ortodox, între colectiv și comuniune' in *Lumina Educației*, 4 Martie, 26 (2017), pp. 1, 2, http://ziarullumina.ro/tineretul-ortodox-intre-colectiv-si-comuniune-120437.html (accessed on 11.06.2021).
34 Arhiepiscoia Sucevei și Rădăuțului, *In Memoriam. Un an de la strămutarea la cele veșnice a Înaltpreasfințitului Părinte Pimen* (Suceava: Crimca, 2021).

Today, as might be expected, many pilgrims practice 'cultural tourism' for it is in vogue all over the world. However, we find out that a great number of people journey to the classical pilgrimage sites (e.g. The Holy Land, Petra, Egypt, Mount Athos, Constantinople, the Churches of the Apocalypse in Turkey, the Rila in Bulgaria, Kyiv Pecherska Lavra in Ukraine, and several in Russia) and discover a series of Western European sites like Bari (Saint Nicholas), Padua (Saint Luke), Milan (Saint Ambrose), Rome, and Ravenna.

Is this a redistribution of interest in pilgrimage? Undoubtedly, yes. With the development of the Romanian diaspora in the last twenty years, the pilgrimage map has been extended. Who could imagine, forty years ago, that people could travel to Israel without too much effort or NEPSIS conferences of the Romanian young adults in the West would take place in Marseille (in memory of Saint John Cassian) or at Saint Albert Abbey in England?

Interesting literature, e.g., the 'Akathist' hymns and the saints' lives accounts have developed simultaneously with the pilgrimage phenomenon. We should remember those pilgrims' efforts, who brought into Romania information about the history and ascetic life of Saint John the Russian, Saint David of Evia, Saint Ephrem the Younger, or Saint Nectarios. Moreover, the pilgrims who visited the monastery of Ormylia in Greece came with valuable information about Father Emilianos from the monastery of Simonopetra. Therefore, we notice a change in values and a dynamic iconology necessary to strengthen the internal forgotten ecumenism of Orthodoxy, mandatory for the inner unity of the orthodox confession. Pilgrimages, according to the immediate pastoral principles, 'import' saints, discover customs and traditions linked with their lives, and let epiphany take place in the mystery of experiencing God in these spiritual journeys.

Conclusion

Related both to revelation and conversion phenomena, the Christian pilgrimage ('peregrination') is an inner journey to fulfill the innate yearning to find the Truth. It determines the contents of one community's faith, during a dynamic journey knowledge of God and led to changes including the social communication of the Revealed Truth.

Approached by the scholars in relationship to social pedagogy in the last years, the Christian phenomenon of pilgrimage is considered to have strongly contributed to a new culture of life and profile of the community in places that host pilgrims. Hence, its anthropological dimension and fundamental pedagogical character.

In the Romanian space, the Christian pilgrimage preserves this strong pedagogical character and has some particularities due to the specific profile of the country shaped along with its history. Analysing the *Act of Saints Epictetus and Astion of Halmyris* that relates the first pilgrimage to the tomb of a saint recorded in the territory of Romania, as well as a fragment of *Saint John Cassian's works*, we identified the main characteristics of the pilgrimage still valid today, e.g., the death of a loved one, looking for inner silence, conversion, family pilgrimage, and community involvement in the pilgrimage effort. Besides the two steady pilgrimage patterns in the history of the

Romanian Orthodox Church, namely the ascetic, toilsome one, when the pilgrim is looking for the inward silence, and the quiet pilgrimage, when the pilgrim is looking for a pattern of spiritual life to achieve the Christian calling, we find in the Romanian Orthodox Church history an intermediary form of pilgrimage attended by the pious people of the Lord's Army and connected to the Pentecost and its founder tomb. It is the educational-formative pilgrimage that generated journeys not only to the spiritual sites but also to people whose charisma determined a considerable 'spiritual migration'.

During the communist period, the pilgrimage phenomena in Romania was characterized by a particular dynamic related to its role in educating people on the authentic history of Romania and Christian faith. The Patriarch Justinian wisely used the pilgrimage opportunity for the pastoral mission by preparing guides for monasteries and monastic museums. Therefore, the monasteries became not only welcoming pilgrimage places, but also sources of unadulterated national history untouched by the ideological communist virus.

Pilgrimages forbidden by the communist government have been restarted immediately after the Revolution of 1989. Most of the pilgrimages in Romania have even today an ecumenical dimension. People's devotion often goes beyond denomination and religion and is manifested especially in areas with multi-denominational populations. The development of the Romanian diaspora in the last twenty years, extended the pilgrimage map and many pilgrims practice cultural tourism. However, the statistical data on the young volunteers (e.g. at the International Meeting of Orthodox Youth)[35] expressed the youths' need to get involved in the mission and pastoral of the Church, manifested also through pilgrimage.

Besides numbers, researches, and expository works, pilgrimage transforms people. It converts and influences cultural profiles, including the economic ones. Nevertheless, the greatest role of the pilgrimage is the fundamental change in human living, an experience of those who attend such an event. The strong reality around it motivates the people around.

References

Actele martirice, introductory study, translation, notes and comments by Ioan I. Rămureanu (București: Editura Institutului Biblic și de Misiune al Bisericii Ortodoxe Române, 1997)

Adalbert G. Hamman, *La vita quotidiana dei primi cristiani* (Italia: Biblioteca Universale Rizzoli, 1993).

Ahmad Nooruddeen and Jahangeer Khan, 'The Phenomenon of Pilgrimage in World Religions', in *The Review of Religions*, August 2020, https://www.reviewofreligions.org/23807/pilgrimage-in-world-religions/ (accessed on 14.06.2022)

---

35 Constantin Necula, 'Pelerin cu tinerii', p. 25. See also Constantin Necula, 'Tineretul ortodox, între colectiv și comuniune', pp. 1, 2.

Antonie Plămădeală, *Dascăli de cuget și simțire românească* (București: Editura Institutului Biblic și de Misiune a Bisericii Ortodoxe Române, 1981).

Antonie Plămădeală, *Tradiție și libertate în spiritualitatea românească*. 1st edition (Sibiu, 1983); 2nd edition (București, 1995); 3rd edition (București, 2010).

Antonie Plămădeală, 'Sfântul Gherman din Dacia Pontică, un străroman ignorant', *Mitropolia Ardealului* (MA), Year XXXIV, No 5 (1989), 3–19.

Arhiepiscopia Sucevei și Rădăuților, *In Memoriam. Un an de la strămutarea la cele veșnice a Înaltpreasfințitului Părinte Pimen* (Suceava: Editura Crimca, 2021).

Cetățile Credinței – mănăstiri și schituri din Arhiepiscopia Râmnicului, ed. by Emilian Lovișteanu (Baia Mare: Proema, 2010).

Constantin Necula, 'Exigențele convertirii oglindite în Actele Martirice - izvor primar', in *Ale Tale dintru ale Tale. Liturghie - Pastorație - Mărturisire. Prinos de cinstire adus IPS Dr Laurențiu Streza la împlinirea vârstei de 60 de ani*, ed. by Dorin Oancea, Constantin Necula, Ștefan Toma, and Cristian Vaida(Sibiu: Andreiana, 2008), pp. 677–720.

Constantin Necula, 'Pedagogia teologică a pelerinajului creștin (un posibil punct de vedere ortodox)' *Review of Ecumenical Studies*, 1 (2009), 21–30.

Constantin Necula, 'Tineretul ortodox, între colectiv și comuniune', *Lumina Educației*, 4 Martie (2017), 1, 2. http://ziarullumina.ro/tineretul-ortodox-intre-colectiv-si-comuniune-120437.html (accessed on 11.06.2021).

Constantin Necula 'Pelerin cu tinerii', Participant's guide. Unity. Faith. Nation / *Ghidul Participantului. Unitate. Credință. Neam, ITO 2018* (Sibiu: Mitropolia Transilvaniei, Arhiepiscopia Sibiului, 2018), p. 25.

Daniel Rops, *La Chiesa degli Apostoli e dei Martiri*, vol. I (Torino-Roma: Marietti, 1957).

Dom Michel Coune and Moine de Saint-André-lez-Bruges, *Bucuria Schimbării la Față după Părinții Răsăriteni*, translated by Eugen-Adrian Truța, ed. by Dom Michel Coune (Alba-Iulia: Reîntregirea, 2017).

Emilian Popescu, 'Saints Épictète et Astion, martyrs à Halmyris', in *Christianitas dacoromana*, ed. by Emilian Popescu (București: Editura Academiei Române, 1994), pp. 92–99.

Flavio Placida, *L'epoca d'oro della catechesi. L'insegnamento e la prassi dei Padri della Chiesa* (Italia: Urbaniana University Press, 2020).

Francesca Allegri, *Donne e Pellegrine dall'Antichità al Medioevo* (Milano: Jaca Book, 2012)

Hippolyte Delehaye, 'Les Martyrs Epictète et Astion' in *Bulletin de la Section Historique*, *sous la direction de N. Iorga*, Tome XIV (1928), 1–5.

Herbert Rosweyde, *Vitae Patrum* (Belgium: Antwerpen, 1615).

Ioachim Băcăuanul, *Cultul Sfintei Parascheva în Ortodoxie – Cercetare hagiografico- liturgică* (Roma: Filocalia, 2013).

Ioanichie Bălan, *Pateric Românesc. Cuprinde viața și cuvintele unor Sfinți și Cuvioși Părinți ce s-au nevoit în mănăstirile românești (Secolele IV–XX)* (Galați: Editura Arhiepiscopiei Tomisului și Dunării de Jos, 1990).

Iosif Fr. Trifa, *Pe urmele Mântuitorului. Însemnări din călătoria la Ierusalim* (Sibiu: Oastea Domnului, 1927).

John Anthony McGuckin, *Dicționar de Teologie Patristică*, trans. by Dragoș Dâscă and Alin-Bogdan Mihăilescu (Iași: Doxologia, 2014).

Kyriacos C. Markides, *Darurile deșertului. Calea uitată a spiritualității creștine*, trans. by Anca Irina Ionescu (București: Herald, 2021).

Le città del cristianesimo antico. La Galilea e Gerusalemme, ed. by Dario Garribba and Marco Vitelli (Trapani: Il Pozzo di Giacobbe, 2019).

Mihail Diaconescu, 'Actul Martiric al Sfinților Epictet și Astion de la Halmyris', in *Istoria Literaturii Dacoromane*, ed. by Mihail Diaconescu (București: Alcor Edimpex, 1999), pp. 434–43.

Mircea Ielciu, *Har și libertate în viziunea Sfântului Ioan Casian* (Pitești: Paralela 45, 2002).

Mirel Bănică, *Nevoia de miracol. Fenomenul pelerinajelor în România contemporană* (Iași: Polirom, 2014).

Mircea Păcurariu, *Sfinți daco-romani și români* (Iași: Trinitas, 2000).

Nestor Vornicescu, 'Pătimirea Martirilor Epictet și Astion (de la cumpăna secolelor III–IV)', trans. by David Popescu, in Nestor Vornicescu, *Una din primele scrieri ale literaturii române străvechi* (Craiova: Editura Mitropoliei Olteniei, 1990), pp. 67–109.

Olga Greceanu, *Pe urmele Pașilor Tăi, Iisuse* (București: Idaco, 2008).

Oltenia de lângă Cer (Craiova: Editura Mitropoliei Olteniei, 2006).

Sfânta Mănăstire Putna, ed. by Iacov Putneanul (Mănăstirea Putna: Centrul de Cercetare și Documentare 'Ștefan cel Mare' al Sfintei Mănăstiri Putna, 2010).

Sfântul Dimitrie Izvorâtorul de Mir și Sfântul Dimitrie Basarabov (București: Meteor, 2015).

Sfântul Dimitrie cel Nou, ocrotitorul Bucureștilor. Cuvinte către pelerini, studii și mărturii contemporane (București: 'Cuvântul Vieții', 2021).

Sfântul Ioan Casian, *Scrieri alese – Așezămintele Mănăstirești și Convorbiri Duhovnicești*, trans. by Vasile Cojocaru and David Popescu (București: Editura Institutului Biblic și de misiune a Bisericii Ortodoxe Române, 1990).

Serafim Joantă, *Roumanie. Tradition et culture hesychastes* (Bégrolles: Abbaye de Bellefontaine, 1987).

Sorin Preda, 'Noi miracole creștine la Ionești', in *Formula AS*, No. 1385 (27.09.2019–2003.10.2019). Retrieved from http://arhiva.formula-as.ro/1999/362/societate-37/noi-miracole-crestine-la-ionesti-574 (accessed on 7.08.2021).

St John Cassian, *First Conference of Abbot Moses*, chapter 1. Retrieved from https://www.newadvent.org/fathers/350801.htm (accessed on 14.07.2021).

Valentin-Lucian Beloiu, *Pelerinaj spre Rai - Turismul religios în Sfântul Munte* (București: Evanghelismos, 2020).

Valeriu Anania, *Cerurile Oltului. Școliile Arhimandritului Bartolomeu la imaginile fotografice ale lui Dumitru F. Dumitru* (Episcopia Râmnicului și Argeșului, 1990).

EMMANOUIL GER. VARVOUNIS

Pilgrimage Rituals and Places in Modern Greece

Introduction: Methodology and Questions to be Addressed

In the present article we give the essence, the character and the aims involved in pilgrimages in Greece today. The central question for scholars is whether Christian pilgrimage in contemporary Greece possesses features that link it to the religious and cultural identity of the Greeks themselves. The article compares the central Orthodox Christian rituals tied to pilgrimage and to the most important places to which pilgrimages are made, that is, Jerusalem, the monasteries of the Holy Mountain, at Meteora and on Patmos and rituals associated with saints of our own age with basic Christian pilgrimage as conducted by other peoples.

As for the methodology, to answer these questions, we use material from the fieldwork of the author and of others and from material on the Internet. We also make use of the literature, Greek and non-Greek, and draw comparisons with similar examples, while also examining the forms of ritual involved from a historical perspective. We also used the historical and social method of Folklore, i. e the examination of phenomena in their historical perspective, but also in their modern social functionality. We approach matters from a perspective of religious folklore and ethnology, while making reference to various historical issues. We also look at the way in which old ritual practices associated with pilgrimages survive today and at the changes and adaptations that they have undergone.

Pilgrimage in Greece: Historic Roots and Contemporary Practices

In Greece today, the phenomenon of popular pilgrimage tourism is in full flood. Parishes, associations and even tourist agencies proper organize trips and pilgrimages to monasteries and other pilgrimage sites of Orthodoxy. The habit is growing and spreading, so becoming one of the chief expressions of contemporary Greek popular religious

> **Emmanouil Ger. Varvounis** • Professor of Folklore at the Department of History and Ethnology and Director of the Laboratory of Folklore and Social Anthropology of the Democritus University of Thrace, Greece

Pilgrimage in the Christian Balkan World: The Path to Touch the Sacred and Holy, ed. by Dorina Dragnea, Emmanouil Ger. Varvounis, Evelyn Reuter, Petko Hristov and Susan Sorek (Turnhout, 2023), pp. 201–220.
BREPOLS ❧ PUBLISHERS   DOI 10.1484/M.STR-EB.5.132407

sensibility and activity. Similar phenomena are moreover to be observed among other peoples, since today the old habit of religious pilgrimage has acquired new dimensions and a modern content, with a result that we usually term 'pilgrimage tourism'.

In particular, we look in this piece at pilgrimage folk art, that is, at the objects offered pilgrims at the pilgrimage centres of Greece as part of pilgrimage rituals. This we do, since one of the basic principles that inform the mentality of the pilgrim is the desire to bring back something from the holy spot, the church, the monastery or the pilgrimage site that he or she has visited, in order to commemorate the visit. This is the foundation for a large part of the tourist industry concerned with 'pilgrimage' or 'religious tourism', which, as we have said, is constantly expanding in Greece today.

In the light of all this, the main insight to which one is led is that in Greece today the meaning of the sanctity of journeys of pilgrimage has either diminished or at least altered in the minds of the pilgrims themselves and that new conditions have led to gradual, but genuine secularization of pilgrimages and the rituals that surround them.

In Greek traditional culture, the concept and practice of pilgrimage is directly associated with the Holy Land. Indeed, for such pilgrimages the term *hatziliki* is used, which derives from the Arabic *hadjdj*, referring to the Muslim pilgrimage to Mecca.[1] Thus pilgrims to the Holy Land are *hatzides*,[2] a term that is frequently combined with the surname of the individual and forms the first compound element in many Greek surnames,[3] so indicating that some ancestor or ancestors of the person bearing such a name made the pilgrimage to the Holy Sepulchre.

The Muslims of Greece and neighbouring areas in the Middle East, however, also carry out their obligation to make their own pilgrimage and they do so scrupulously and meticulously. Their actions mean that the tradition of pilgrimage remains alive to the present day in the Balkans and in the Middle East.[4]

Descriptions that have survived show that in the past Christians from central Greek lands, from the Balkans and from Asia Minor travelled regularly and in groups to make the pilgrimage to Palestine, so as to receive the longed-for title of 'pilgrim'.[5] They left in groups in a festival atmosphere from their homeland in autumn and reached the Holy Land, where they celebrated Christmas itself and the other festivals of the twelve days of Christmas. They remained there during Lent, Easter and the post-Easter period, to return to their homelands, laden with amulets, gifts and souvenirs of their pilgrimage.[6] In their villages they were welcomed back with

---

1 See Bernard Lewis, 'Hadjdj', in *The Encyclopaedia of Islam*, ed. by Bernard Lewis et al., 3rd ed. (Leiden-London: Brill and Luzac & Co., 1986), III, pp. 31–38.
2 René Tresse, Le Pelegrinage syrien aux villes saintes de l' Islam (Paris: Impr. de Chaumette, 1937), pp. 12–13.
3 Μανώλης Γ. Βαρβούνης, *Λαϊκή λατρεία και θρησκευτική συμπεριφορά των κατοίκων της Σάμου* (Αθήνα: Πνευματικό Ίδρυμα Σάμου Ν. Δημητρίου, 1992), pp. 145–47.
4 Δημήτριος Πετρόπουλος, Ερμόλαος Ανδρεάδης, *Η θρησκευτική ζωή στην περιφέρεια Ακσεράι-Γκέλβερι* (Αθήνα: Κέντρο Μικρασιατικών Σπουδών, 1971), pp. 113–17.
5 See Henri Ellenberrger, 'Releve des Pelegrinages du Depertement de la Vienne', *Nouvelle Revue des Traditions Populaires*, 2 (4), (1950), pp. 331–35.
6 Βασιλική Χρυσανθοπούλου, 'Οι χατζήδαινες της Πέρθης', *Λαογραφία*, 33 (1985), pp. 129–54.

great festivity and official receptions, a sign of the new and prominent position they would then occupy in their communities.[7]

As bibliography points out, the pilgrimage is an important factor in the formation of religious folklore at a supra-national level,[8] since it brings together various peoples, who are certainly bearers of many various religious folk traditions. Thus the habit of a making sacred migratory journey contributes to the formation of a community of the faithful[9] who all share the same credo and embrace the basic principles of faith. Indeed, even on pilgrimages today one can see the survival of medieval habits of worship and pilgrimage practices,[10] something that reveals the continuity of outlook and concepts down the ages.

Modern Greek Pilgrimage Rituals

In Greek folk culture today, the habit of making sacred journeys continues in the form of trips undertaken for the purpose of pilgrimage, frequently organized by parishes and metropolitan sees, although they are also undertaken by associations concerned with religious and spiritual matters. Pilgrimages are certainly a subject for city-based folklore research and one that has so far not been looked at in any systematic fashion, despite the importance pilgrimages have for the study of Greek popular religious behaviour today. One hopes that this present brief study will make a small contribution to the matter, although it will certainly not exhaust the subject. The material for the study derives from fieldwork in various parishes of Attica, Greece, during the period 2004–2007, which involved interviews based on specialized questionnaires as is often the case with the relevant non-Greek literature on contemporary pilgrimage.[11]

One should note at the outset that technology-driven changes in the method and conditions of travel for pilgrims have changed the nature and frequency of pilgrimages. The faithful are now in a position to make more than one pilgrimage a

---

7 Ξενοφών Κ. Άκογλου, *Από τη ζωή του Πόντου. Λαογραφικά Κοτυώρων* (Αθήνα: Τυπογραφείο Γ. Π. Ξένου, 1939), pp. 218–22.
8 Vítězslav Štajnochr, *Die wundertätige Maria. Mariendarstellungen aus europäischen Wallfahrtsorten. Aus der Sammlung der Ethnographischen Abteilung des Nationalmuseums in Prag* (Sandl: Wallfahrtsmuseum Neukirchen b. Hl. Blut, 1995), pp. 65–66.
9 Philip V. Bohlman, 'Pilgrimage, Politics, and the Musical Remapping of the New Europe', *Ethnomusicology*, 40 (3), (1996), 409–10; Alfons Brügger, *Wallfahrtskapelle St Wolfgang im Uechtland* (Lindenberg, Wilhelm Fink Verlag, 1996), p. 28.
10 Raymond Oursel, 'Cluny und der Jakobsweg', in *Santiago de Compostela. Pilgerwege*, ed. by Paolo Caucci von Saucken, trans. by Marcus Würmli (Augsburg: Weltbild, 1995), pp. 120–21; Jan van Herwaarden, 'Der mittelalterliche Jakobskult in der Niederlanden', in *Santiago de Compostela, Pilgerwege*, ed. by Paolo Caucci von Saucken, trans. by Marcus Würmli (Augsburg: Weltbild, 1995), pp. 338–40.
11 The research protocols of the primary material have been submitted to the 'Folklore Archive' of the Department of History and Ethnology of the Democritus University of Thrace (Komotini).

year, to destinations both far and near.[12] The change from sacred migratory journey to pilgrimage excursion has influenced the frequency with which such trips are made and promoted a growing tendency towards secularization, which is very obvious in trips made by pilgrims of all kinds.[13] Pilgrimages today combine religion and devotion with entertainment and the pilgrimage can be easily repeated in successive visits, which in the past were impossible, because of the conditions and dangers then involved in distant journeys.

Associations, local sees and above all parishes are the bodies who organise such pilgrimages. During the course of the year, they usually run one large trip to a major pilgrimage centre abroad, alongside many smaller trips, a day or two days in length, to places of pilgrimage in Greece, that is, to monasteries and churches. This is also the pattern outside Greece, too, followed by various religious and ecclesiastical organizations and groups.[14] This combination of pilgrimages large and small and ancient and modern means that the faithful are in a position to form a fuller and more complete view of the state of religion today, so that they are able both to bond more closely with the religion of their fathers[15] and with the tradition that every faith creates and conveys over time to those who embrace it.[16] Thus, it is no coincidence that established pilgrimages and the processes that they involve pass into folk narratives and tales,[17] that is, into vernacular literature of various peoples.

As part of this, monasteries of lesser religious importance become prominent as objects of pilgrimage, as do objects of pilgrimage that combine the natural environment, various facilities and combinations of travel and excursion, so becoming part of pilgrimages today. Thus a day trip or afternoon walk is usually combined with more than one monastery or visits to various sites of pilgrimage in the same area, to add weight and fullness to the programme. This phenomenon is also to be observed among non-Greeks, too, such as the Hungarians[18] and the Croats,[19] since it is this that determines the aims of pilgrimage trips organized in the way we have outlined above. The concentration upon minor, even unimportant pilgrimage destinations certainly

---

12 Reinhard Haller, *Einmal im Leben auf den Heiligen Berg. Bayerische Wallfahrten nach Böhmen* (Grafenau: Morsak, 1995), pp. 160–61.
13 Claudine Fabre-Vassas, 'Paraschiva-Vendredi: la sainte des femmes, des travaux, des jours', *Terrain*, 24 (1995), pp. 62–64.
14 Liselotte Blumauer-Montenave, *Gäste des Wallfahrtsortes Mariazell. Eine Dokumentation* (Wien: Wiener Katholische Akademie, 1996), pp. 201–02.
15 Ingo Gabor, 'Die Wallfahrtskapelle zum Hl. Blut in Schwenningen', *Württembergisch-Franken*, 80 (1996), pp. 172–73.
16 Roland Gröber, 'Maria Hilf, ein deutsches Wallfahrtsbild in Südtirol', *Der Schlern*. 70 (5), (1996), 259–73.
17 Robert Plötz, 'Jakobspilger', in *Enzyklopädie des Märchens*, ed. by Rolf Wilhelm Brednich et al. (Berlin: Walter de Gruyter, 1993), VII, pp. 459–67.
18 Gábor Barna, 'Mariazell und Ungarn. Die Verehrung der Magna Domina Hungarorum', in *Schatz und Schicksal. Steirische Landesausstellung*, ed. by Helmut Eberhart and Heidelinde Fell (Graz: Kulturreferar der Steiermarkischen Landsregierung, 1996), pp. 281–94.
19 Stefan Raimann, *Das Wallfahrtswesen der burgenländischen Kroaten. Dargestellt am Beispiel der Wallfahrtsorte Mariazell, Loretto und Eisenstadt-Oberberg* (Grosspetersdorf: Benua, 1996), pp. 91–94.

adds to the content of the sacred migratory journey,[20] while also contributing to its distancing from the thrilling religious experience that informs pilgrimages to the sacred sites of every religion, which, in reference to Christianity, means the Holy Land and the Holy Sepulchre.[21]

The whole question is also tied to the increasing religious honour paid to recent saints and martyrs in the world of contemporary Greek popular religion. Places of pilgrimages such as those of Saints Raphael, Irini and Nikolaos on Lesbos or of Saint Ephraim at Nea Makri in Attica attract an increasing proportion of such trips by pilgrims. Werner has noted that the degree to which individuals turn to new pilgrimage sites depends upon how far such persons subscribe to folk traditions of wonderworking.[22] Indeed, the more the miracles reported in connection with a particular place of pilgrimage, the greater the number of visitors seeking the miraculous intervention of divine grace. The academic literature has certainly noted the direct link between such wonderworking tradition and numbers of visits or visitors. The expectation that there will be some miraculous intervention in daily life is the basic reason why this type of pilgrimage trip exists today.[23] Also, the study of the matter comes to the conclusion that the deepest motivations of participants in pilgrimages were always such, since for such persons the liturgical honour paid to a saint,[24] to an icon or to holy relics is directly related to the thaumaturgical traditions that surround them. Where such traditions are absent, there is no established and continuous folk worship.[25]

Pilgrimages today are mainly organized by tourist agencies, to which the church authorities concerned entrust the organization of practical details.[26] This has a direct impact upon the substance and structure of the pilgrimage and is something that distinguishes older pilgrimages from those of today.[27] The true difference lies in the fact that journeys of pilgrimage are organized more as trips and excursions, which tends to lessen the devotional spirit and the concept of religious dedication that

---

20 Dominik Wunderlin, 'Zeugen zugerischer Wallfahrtsfrömmigkeit', *Zuger Neujahrsblatt*, 4 (1996), pp. 44–51.
21 Stefan Wollmann, 'Wallfahrten in der Oberlausitz', *Oberlausitzer Hausbuch*, 7 (1995–1996), pp. 120–23.
22 Paul Werner, 'Der altbayerische Herrgott St Leonhard in Inchenhofen', *Charivari*, 22 (10), (1996), pp. 107–11.
23 Paul Mai, 'Die Entwicklung der Hedwigswallfahrten in Deutschland nach 1945', in *Das Bild der heiligen Hedwig in Mittelalter und Neuzeit*, ed. by Eckhard Grunewald and Nikolaus Gussone (München: Oldenbourg Wissenschaftsverlag 1996), p. 252.
24 Bernhard A. Reismann, 'Der Mittelpunkt aller Herrlichkeit auf Erden. Mariazell und die Zeller Wallfahrt in Reisebeschreibungen des 19. Jahrhunderts', in *Schatz und Schicksal. Steirische Landesausstellung*, ed. by Helmut Eberhart and Heidelinde Fell (Graz: Kulturreferar der Steiermärkischen Landsregierung, 1996), p. 215.
25 Károly Kerenyi, *La Madonna ungherese di Verdasio. Paesaggi dello spirito e paesaggio del' anima*, trans. by Anna Ruchat (Locarno: Armando Dadò, 1995), p. 43.
26 Paul Post, 'The Modern Pilgrim. A Study of Contemporary Pilgrims' Accounts', *Ethnologia Europaea*, 24 (1), (1994), pp. 85–100.
27 György Orosz, 'Pilger, singende Wandlerbettler im altrussischen Staat', *Acta Ethnographica Hungarica*, 39 (3–4), (1994), p. 389.

existed in the past.[28] For example, pilgrims stay less and less in group accommodation that pilgrimage centres usually offer, as is the case at the monastery of Aghios Rafael on Mytilene, at the monastery in Sinai or at the monastery of the *Megalohari* on Tinos. Instead, they prefer the facilities offered by hotels, accommodation in which is included in the price of the trip. The constant focus on the part of the pilgrim on the substance of the sacred sojourn that he or she has embarked upon is diminished and an element of entertainment is introduced, which tends to increase material comforts, while diminishing the spiritual aspect of the pilgrimage.[29]

Between Tradition and Modernity, Sanctity and Secularization

The scholarly literature has registered the occurrence of this development in pilgrimages amongst other peoples, too. Also, in the relationship between devotion and entertainment that is now being upended it is easy to discern the transformation from tradition to modernity and from sanctity to secularization,[30] which is similar to what can be observed in general in the folk religion of Europe.[31] Seen like this, changes in the innermost substance of pilgrimages that we have considered above have a general importance for the study of contemporary folk religion and religious sentiment, in that pilgrimages tend to become divorced from mysticism, so turning more towards externally-oriented social events and activities. We have here the phenomena of secularization, which are to be seen more and more in the manifestations of folk religion among various populations.[32] We are living in a period of transition, in which various changes are transforming old patterns into new forms of collectivity in folk religion.

Nevertheless, the degree to which there is participation and acceptance of these new tendencies varies from people to people. For Greeks, who maintain a close daily relationship with Orthodoxy, tradition and the Church, this innermost mystical relationship of man to the divine has not been fully done away with, something that many scholars have noted among other peoples. In urban parishes, where one naturally expects that there will be differences in regard to greater modernization in accord with the general urban conditions in which parish work is carried out, research shows that the central aim of those who take part in such pilgrimages is the pilgrimage itself, that is, their aim is to acquire religious and spiritual experiences, rather than

---

28 Manuel C. Díaz y Díaz, 'Die Liber Sancti Jacobi', in *Santiago de Compostela*, ed. by von Saucken, p. 44.
29 Emanuela Renzetti, *Un cammino di devozione. Il pellegrinaggio a Sabiona del 1994* (San Martin de Tor: Istitut Ladin Micurà de Rü 1995), pp. 25–27.
30 Ludwig Baumann, 'Das Gnadenbild von Weissregen', in *Der Regen. Kultur und Natur am Fluss*, ed. by Bärbel Kleindorfer-Marx (Amberg: Buch & Kunstverlag Oberpfalz, 1996), p. 106.
31 Robert Böck, 'Die Wallfahrt zu Unserer Lieben Frau in der Aich bei Oberbernbach (Landkreis Aichach-Friedberg)', *Bayerisches Jahrbuch für Volkskunde*, 12 (1996), pp. 171–72.
32 Sabine Ragaller, *Die Holzkirchener Kerzenwallfahrt nach Bogenberg* (Holzkirchen: Pfarrgemeinderat Holzkirchen, 1995), pp. 139–41.

merely enjoy the entertainment and the trip. Thus Greek Orthodox Christians in Greece take part in pilgrimages primarily to enjoy the blessings offered by the places that they visit and the sacred objects for which they undertake the pilgrimage, rather than to become acquainted with the place itself or to acquire new experiences in general, as is the case with some peoples of Europe.[33]

Pilgrimage and Greek Religious Tourism: Rituals and Religious Folk Art

We need now to examine the relationship between pilgrimages and so-called 'religious tourism', which is currently growing continuously, both in Greece and abroad.[34] The concept of 'religious tourism' includes the reality of these organized pilgrimage trips and is not negative, in that it does mean that the worldly aspect of the activity during the trip is stressed over the religious devotion involved.[35] Setting the balance between internal, spiritual processes and external, worldly activities, between the fun one has on a trip and religious ritual, depends on both organizer and participant. In fact, what the term 'religious tourism' really indicates is the need to handle matters in the face of something that is constantly growing, that is, the appearance of pilgrimages that for various reasons have remained obscure or have been an entirely local matter and the systematic attempt to maintain the purely religious nature of such journeys.[36] If we see things from this point of view, it becomes legitimate to talk about 'religious tourism', if we bear in mind the various conditions that we have already mentioned that have led to the development of pilgrimages that retain the spiritual and ritual character that always characterized Orthodox pilgrimages as they developed over time. Indeed, I think it might be better to use the phrase 'pilgrimage tourism', in that it is the particular conditions pertaining to pilgrimages, rather than general religious needs that define the nature of this phenomenon.

Contemporary religious folk art that rests upon the existence of religious tourism is directly connected with pilgrimages. One of the most basic principles that informs the psychology of the pilgrim is the desire to take some souvenir from the place of pilgrimage – church or monastery or some other place of pilgrimage that one has visited – so as to hold close to oneself the blessing derived from the place of pilgrimage

---

33 Romana Gabriel, 'Viele Wege führen nach Mariazell. Aspekte zum Thema "Wallfahrt heute"', in *Schatz und Schicksal. Steirische Landesausstellung*, ed. by Helmut Eberhart and Heidelinde Fell (Graz: Kulturreferar der Steiermarkischen Landsregierung, 1996), pp. 273–80.
34 Ottavia Niccoli, 'Madonne di montagna. Note su apparizioni e santuari nelle vali alpine', in *Cultura d'élite e cultura popolare nell'arco alpino fra Cinque e Seicento*, ed. by Ottavio Besomi and Carlo Caruso (Basel – Berlin: Birkhäuser, 1995), pp. 95–119.
35 Reinhard Haller, 'Wallfahrten auf dem Goldenen Steig und seinen Zubringern', in *Kulturregion Goldener Steig. Aufsätze zur Ausstellung*, ed. by Peter Becher, Sigrid Canz, and Jozo Džambo (München: Adalbert Stifter Verein 1995), pp. 80–89.
36 Johann Hirnsperger, 'Die Erhebung der Wallfahrtskirche Maria Plain zur Basilica Minor. Kirchenrechtliche Erwägungen', *Mitteilungen der Gesellschaft für Salzburger Landeskunde*, 135 (1995), p. 160.

and to extend infinitely in one's imagination the psychological stimulation and religious experiences that the pilgrim has experienced and felt during the pilgrimage.[37] This is, besides, the foundation of a large part of the tourist industry connected with an increasingly developing pilgrimage tourism or religious tourism, with the blessing and collaboration of all the great religions and, in the case of Greece, of the Church.

This is hardly something recent. Museums throughout the world hold collections of objects of Christian art[38] – to restrict ourselves just to Christian and in particular to Orthodox pilgrimage tourism – that were manufactured with this psychological need of the faithful pilgrim expressly in mind. Naturally, this phenomenon is present today, when various reasons decree that man return once more to the transcendent and to the beyond, with the result that pilgrimage sites receive enormous numbers of visitors. As is to be expected, these souvenirs possess a form comprehensible and acceptable to the individuals at whom they are directed.[39] That is to say, in terms of shape and expression they fall within the category of folk art and therefore represent types of contemporary religious folk art, all closely linked to the nature of pilgrimages, as we shall see.

If one examines these objects of religious art, one sees the outlook and concepts that lead to their creation and use. Here the truth of the assertion by Classie[40] that the study of objects is the first step to examining human thought and actions, is borne out, particularly when such thought and action are revealed in a cultural context known as 'tradition'. In any case, the experiential relationship of the common man to his environment leads him to form a system of thought that rests on the material objects in his environment. This system he himself has formulated on the basis of its utility and ideology, so that he can make both real and symbolic use of these objects.[41] Culture expressed through materiality, in the view of Classie, constitutes the projection of one's feelings and sentiments onto the external world. Thus the common man participates and is diffused in this folk culture, matters to which the theory of 'empathy' ('Einfühlung') speaks most convincingly.[42]

---

37 See Βασίλειος Δεληγιάννης, 'Το χατζηλίκι στα Κουβούκλια της Προύσσης', Μικρασιατικά Χρονικά, 2 (1939), pp. 418–19; Ξενοφών Κ. Άκογλου, Από τη ζωή του Πόντου. Λαογραφικά Κοτυώρων (Αθήνα: Τυπογραφείο Γ. Π. Ξένου, 1939), pp. 218–22; Δημήτρης Λουκόπουλος, Δημήτριος Πετρόπουλος, Η λαϊκή λατρεία των Φαράσων (Αθήνα: Μουσικό Λαογραφικό Αρχείο – Κέντρο Μικρασιατικών Σπουδών, 1949), pp. 56–57.

38 See Robin Cormack, *Writing in Gold. Byzantine Society and its Icons* (New York: Oxford University Press, 1985), pp. 50–94.

39 Πετρόπουλος and Ανδρεάδης, Η θρησκευτική ζωή, p. 116; Χρυσανθοπούλου, 'Οι χατζήδαινες της Πέρθης', pp. 148–49; Ιωάννης Μ. Χατζηφώτης, Ο λαϊκός πολιτισμός του Καστελλορίζου (Αθήνα: Σύνδεσμος των Απανταχού Καστελλοριζίων «Ο Άγιος Κωνσταντίνος», 1982), p. 111; Edward David Hunt, *Holy Land Pilgrimage in the Later Roman Empire AD 312–460* (Oxford: Oxford University Press, 1982), pp. 128–54.

40 Henry Glassie, *Material Culture* (Bloomington and Indianapolis: Indiana University Press, 1999), p. 41.

41 Αλέκος Ε. Φλωράκης, 'Η εθνογραφική τεχνολογία. Όψεις θεωρίας και εφαρμογής', Εθνολογία, 6–7 (1998–1999), p. 32.

42 Henry Glassie, *Material Culture*, p. 41; Σταυρός Σταυρίδης, Η συμβολική σχέση με το χώρο. Πώς οι κοινωνικές αξίες διαμορφώνουν και ερμηνεύουν το χώρο (Αθήνα: Κάλβος, 1990), p. 70.

As a part of material folk culture, religious folk art has been, and is, the object of numerous theories and schools. Barbara Kirshenblatt-Gimblett,[43] for example, has attempted to define the beginning and end of the particular importance of an object and its comprehension by the people. This is a fruitful line of thought, whose concepts, terms and conclusions can certainly be used, at least partially, in the examination of contemporary forms of popular religious art in Greece. If one accepts this view, that objects interpret, objectify and make experience material, one grasps more easily the older, but still extremely observant, assertion made by Papadopoulos that the study of material culture is, in the end, simply a new way of understanding and interpreting historical phenomena and the phenomena of culture in general, in all its complex totality.[44]

In any case, one need to examine whatever factors are involved in these distinctions and how they function in society and how they are expressed through the structures and conditions of everyday life. In this respect, the view of Bogatyrev is more timely than ever, that the significance and social use of objects are unbreakably linked to each other[45] and that the message of every object is bound up with how, where, when and by whom it is used. The basic theoretical question, to which we will attempt to offer an answer, is whether this relationship also works in reverse, too.

Perhaps, then, we have cases in which objects already charged, as it were, with various religious meanings and ideological orientations are then re-used in contemporary religious folk art, with the aim of making emotional reference to the past that is the common possession of those who are members of the same religion and the same national and cultural community. Perhaps we have in pilgrimage tourism and in the forms of folk art that accompany it a deep-rooted ideological charge that fills these objects, which exactly for this reason are employed to give meaning once more to the true dimensions of the world. This charge imposes on the relationship of subjective and objective dimensions an old and now strengthened, or modified, meaning, rather than extracting or deriving a new meaning from this relationship.

Blessing Objects and 'Memorial Places'

Let us now consider the material we examine here. The objects to which we are referring are usually defined as 'objects of piety' and area sold as 'blessings', in small shops located in the area of the pilgrimage site, which means that any profit goes to the monastery or pilgrimage site. They are also sold by private persons outside the sacred area, particularly so in large monastic centres. It is to this environment that the shops in the monastery courtyards and areas in front of courtyards in monasteries

---

43 Barbara Kirshenblatt-Gimblett, 'Objects of Ethnography', in *Exhibiting Cultures. The Poetics and Politics of Museum Display*, ed. by Ivan Karp and Steven D. Lavine (Washington: Smithsonian Institution Press, 1991), p. 388.
44 Στέλιος Αγ. Παπαδόπουλος, 'Υλικός πολιτισμός', *Εθνολογία*, 3 (1994), p. 216.
45 Peter Bogatyrev, *The Function of Folk Costume in Moravian Slovakia*, trans. by Richard G. Crum (Paris: Mouton, 1971), p. 15.

in Meteora, in Uranoupolis or in Daphne, where the faithful enter Mount Athos. However, the institution of selling alone distinguishes these from the older monastic practice of the 'blessing', since these 'blessings' are offered free, while objects of contemporary ecclesiastical folk art are merchandise that is traded and is subject to the rules of the market-place.

One category of these items of merchandise consists of print material of various types. It includes biographies of wise spiritual fathers, tales of miracles and visitor guides, books offering spiritual help and publications recording the impressions of previous visitors. There are also books and leaflets of folk poetry or at least poetry in folk style, the product of today's printed folk poetry, whose content is religious and highly emotive. Then we have objects of religious symbolism that have a particular charge and meaning for the faithful, for example, icons, produced from materials of various cost, that reproduce the chief icon or the main thaumaturgical icons of the monastery in question, for whose sake the whole pilgrimage is made. Here it is literally true that the icon is the signifying centre point of the church[46] and its significance extends throughout all the symbolic and ritual procedure involved in the arrival of the pilgrim, who wishes to take with him or her, a souvenir of their journey of pilgrimage.[47] They prefer copies, symbolically strengthened with supernatural power, of the icon for whose sake they have made their journey.

These icons, whether of paper or stuck on wood, in frames that display elementary wood carving or religious symbols and generally in a variety of forms, are sanctified because they symbolically compress space, time and the supernatural that hovers over them, or so the faithful believe. They are paintings, photographs or silk-screen printings, decorated with silver or glazed, either life size or in miniature, in the form of a triptych, diptych or amulet. This latter may be a badge or button, plastic-covered icon or an amulet for the car, fitted with magnets on their reverse. In any case, however, these copies, irrespective of their worth or materials, function as memory places (*lieux de mémoire*),[48] in that they bear an ideological, symbolic and metaphysical load. This is immediately comprehensible and automatically recalls for the faithful who see it or buy it memories and emotional reactions.

The use of these items gives a new meaning to other familiar objects that do not in themselves necessarily have any religious meaning. I mean amulets for individuals and amulets or decoration for cars. These unite old forms with new uses and make up a sizeable slice of objects of contemporary religious folk art, that is, items connected with spiritual tourism. Triangular amulets, containing the Cross and scriptural quotations are certainly part of Greek religious art. The entry of the automobile into our daily

---

46 *Wallfahrt und Bilderkult. Gesammelte Schriften*, ed. by Hans Dünninger and Wolfgang Brückner (Würzburg: Echter, 1995), pp. 474–75.
47 Walter Lutz, 'Die staatliche und kirchliche Untersuchung einer gesetzeswidrigen Wallfahrt von Limburg zur Beselicher Kapelle am 14. September 1845', *Archiv für mittelrheinische Kirchengeschichte*, 46 (1994), p. 155.
48 Angelika Petitini, 'Leonhardsverehrung und Wallfahrt in Inchenhofen', *Augsburger Volkslundliche Nachrichten*, 2 (1), (1995), pp. 15–26.

lives has also led to the creation of many ornaments intended as decoration.[49] Such decorations are products of contemporary religious art, since the town-dweller has transferred to this popular current means of transport decorative patterns and views and concepts linked to older and certainly more traditional means of transport. Cars are adorned as much with the aim of decorating them as with the goal of protecting them from the evil eye, so that the vehicle and its passengers enjoy supernatural protection from various lurking dangers.

Knitted crosses with beads to keep the evil eye at bay, metal crosses, small icons, either self-adhesive or equipped with magnets are examples of these items that decorate cars. The central icon or the main object of devotion of the monastery or pilgrimage site in question takes pride of place on the item, so that the faithful believe that divine blessing and supernatural power emanating from the object is transmitted to them and to the car. The icon undergoes a reductive process, widespread in popular religious art, from being a common and commercial object to one that is unique and non-commercial.[50] The common amulet often displays a wonder-working icon, gains especial power through its reference to the icon, acquires uniqueness and becomes symbolically charged and ties the faithful closer to the particular pilgrimage. This ritual relationship becomes truly personalized and is projected forward through time by means of this piece of religious folk art.

This tendency to extend the sacred into daily life and the ecclesiastical into the secular, to extend the imagined representation of religious experiences and experiences associated with pilgrimages into mundane daily life is necessary for the faithful, who wish like this to extend the religious performances that they have witnessed that offer psychological relief. Such a tendency is to be seen chiefly in rosaries, a fundamental and popular form of contemporary religious folk art.[51] Having once been a tool for measuring the passing of time in prayer, rosaries have now become amulets. They are purchased and passed in the sign of the Cross above sacred relics and wonderworking icons.[52] Having undergone this process, they are considered to have acquired some of the supernatural power of such unique religious objects and have in their turn transferred it to the individual who possesses the object.

Today's rosaries have the form of a bracelet, although they may sometimes be decorated with precious beads or beads in the form of the protective eye, which, as folk religious belief has it, offer protection from the evil eye. Multi-coloured and gaudy, they are a classic case of old wine in new skins. They are particularly charged objects, which are now acquiring new significance and new use, adapting their old

---

49 Arturo Soria y Puig, 'Der Jakobsweg und die Jakobswege in Spanien', in *Santiago de Compostela*, ed. by von Saucken, p. 204.
50 Roberto Morozzo della Rocca, 'Piazza San Pietro', in *I luoghi della memoria. Simboli e miti dell'Italia unita*, ed. by Mario Isnenghi (Roma: Laterza, 1996), pp. 513–14.
51 Franca Romano, 'La Madonna Pellegrina. Apparizione della Madonna della Pace a Capri, 1984', *La Ricerca Folklorica*, 33 (1996), p. 130.
52 Bernhard Samitsch and Michaela Steinböck, 'Letzter Ausweg Maria. Die Mariazeller Votivbilder im kulturhistorischen Vergleit', in *Schatz und Schicksal. Steirische Landesausstellung*, ed. by Helmut Eberhart and Heidelinde Fell (Graz: Kulturreferar der Steiermarkischen Landsregierung, 1996), p. 224.

symbolic load to the contemporary societal norms and to the particular needs of today's pilgrims. Rosaries are now produced for children and teenagers, blue and pink for boys and girls respectively, in a clear attempt at the extreme secularization of what was once strictly sacred.

The same is to be observed when new materials, such as plastic, are used to manufacture objects such as flasks for holy water or oil from the lamps of wonderworking icons. Such flasks are decorated with Christian symbols or depictions of holy scenes. Plastic, which has had a powerful impact on the world of Greek folk culture, here meets popular religious art and leads it forward to new forms and shapes, which are indeed also a worthy object of Modern Greek folklore.

This contemporary religious folk art is directly tied to pilgrimage tourism, which is continually growing, since it is a product purchased by mass pilgrims. This art is a form of the extension of the blessing offered the pilgrim, a material point of memory and recall of religious emotions and experiences, a souvenir,[53] as it were, in the truest sense of the world. Thus, such objects are purchased with rapidity and manufactured with corresponding speed. Here an image, since it is already charged with symbolism and adorned with some of the supernatural power possessed by the original, is purchased by pilgrims. As Glassie realized,[54] the interpretation imposed by the consumer overshadows the meaning assigned to the original by its creator, since communication and consumption are closely linked and are always determined by any changes in the social context. The context in which the object is located and how it will be used influence its social meaning. In this case, however, the object in question is already symbolically charged, thanks to its lengthy liturgical use. It radiates such meanings out to possible purchasers, so that its symbolic charge defines to a significant degree the interpretative context that consists of the social factors in which it is placed, comprehended and interpreted.

Symbols and Symbolisms: Holy Decoration in Pilgrimage Religious Art

As for symbols, in the reproduction of old traditional symbolisms and ways of expression, the religious symbols and depictions of the central religious symbol or object of worship in the monastery or place of pilgrimage in question naturally dominate. Objects of religious folk art depict the wonder-working icon of the monastery or church, the saint or display a photograph of the reliquary with the holy relics most representative of each pilgrimage site. This is a sort of declaration of identity, which defines the point whence the supernatural power emanates and defines its origin and the connection to the pilgrimage of every such object.

---

53   Horst Schweigert, 'Die Gnadenstatue und das "Schatzkammerbild" von Mariazell', in *Schatz und Schicksal. Steirische Landesausstellung*, ed. by Helmut Eberhart and Heidelinde Fell (Graz: Kulturreferar der Steiermarkischen Landsregierung, 1996), pp. 89–105.
54   Henry Glassie, *Material Culture*, p. 57.

Here the view that there is a direct link between the utility and decorative worth of objects and products of religious folk art is clearly true.[55] These objects are used symbolically and ritually, in family worship and religious behaviour. In fact, however, seen even from this standpoint, they are objects of utility that bridge the gap between the material and spiritual life of the common man. That they convey these particular meanings is apparent from the way in which they retain the shapes and forms of the past, these being in folk thought firmly tied to religious practices, as is the case with rosaries and amulets. In the case of new types of objects, such as amulets for cars, small self-adhesive icons and so on, it also arises from the use of symbols and images that are permanently loaded with similar symbolic significance.

Icons and objects possessing particular supernatural power and religious ideological signification are reused in the creation of religious art, so as to endow the item of religious folk art in question with a special place. As Calvet observes, the icon is functioning here as a 'guide for the memory' or as 'a prompting towards speech',[56] since the visual aspect is truly to be considered a memory place. The use of images that are well-known and charged with ritual significance in various types of contemporary religious folk art redefines relations between object and individual, which, in the final analysis, in the view of Glassie,[57] define absolutely the meaning of objects in the material culture of the common people. The amulet becomes unique, and the adorning of the car becomes an effective precautionary measure,[58] since in folk thought, a well-known thaumaturgical image transmits something of its wonderworking nature to the work of art, thereby allowing the individual who possesses it to enjoy divine protection and to convey the memory of emotional moments during the pilgrimage to his future daily life.

In the second case, perhaps the most interesting, these images informed with religious messages are intentionally used to invest objects with new meanings. No new meaning here evolves here from the relationship between the subjective and objective aspects of the objects. Instead, through the form or image old religious ideological patterns return and are expressed through objects that are new in terms of forms and functionality. Thus, the classic understanding regarding the relationship and balance between the meaning and the social use of objects is inverted and a peculiar type of process is introduced that is directly linked to the reuse and handling of tradition.

In fact, what we have here is a type of folklorism that, as one often finds, is the generative cause behind many phenomena in contemporary folklore. This occurs when old forms of expression employed in folk art and traditional religious life have now acquired new meanings and are being used in commercial ways. The new forms thus created require the ideological support offered by old symbols, as

---

55 Walter Stipperger, 'Oberes Ennstal. Wallfahrten im Schatten der Josefinischen Zeit', *Da schau her*, 17 (4), (1996), pp. 19–20.
56 Louis-Jean Calvet, *Η προφορική παράδοση*, trans. by Marilena Karyolemou (Αθήνα: Καρδαμίτσας, 1995), p. 91.
57 Henry Glassie, *Material Culture*, p. 59.
58 Volker Knierim, 'Auto, Fremde Tod. Automobile und Reisen in zeitgenössischen deutschsprachigen Sensationserzählungen', *Fabula*, 26 (1985), pp. 230–44.

they do not otherwise attract the interest of the common man, who can recognize and interpret these old symbols and forms. He regards the use of these symbols as completely natural and unexceptional in a conservative system of ideologies and practices, outlook and behaviour, which is what traditional religious sensibility and behaviour is, in all its numerous expressions.[59] Besides, the processes that lead to the shaping of contemporary pilgrimages are similar, in that they have evolved into a new and autonomous phenomenon, deserving of investigation, in contemporary religious folklore.

Similar forms and standardized patterns of decoration are also to be found on objects destined for the graves of loved ones and for cemeteries. These, too, are to be considered objects of religious folk art and are frequently sold in the souvenir shops in monasteries and places of pilgrimage that we have mentioned. Such items of mass artistic folk activity include lamps, frames for photographs, censers, icons for grave candle holders and items of decoration, in plaster or brass, of a funereal nature. Such objects are accompanied by the memory of the deceased and form what Vovelle has termed 'material indices'[60] that pertain to the end of life. That they are decorated with religious symbols is due to the fact that the deceased is now in 'another world', in a sphere beyond tangible human reality and in direct contact with the divine and the beyond. Thus, the deceased is now an active part of the current religious and spiritual world of a traditional community.

The mass production and decoration of these items tends to increase their consumption, which is ever increasing.[61] This means, in the view of Hallam and Hockey[62] that popular notions of the sacred have absorbed new concepts pertaining to the transitory and the temporary.[63] This is the basic reason why one finds in contemporary religious folk art decorative subjects, rendered in wood or metal, that were already current in early Christian times, there executed in marble or stone. This new use of such motifs, in addition to its interesting ideological roots, leads to equally interesting artistic achievements that give a new impulse and new form to the products of religious folk art.

Dem. Loukatos, in his treatment of the impact of tourism on traditional life in Greece, in 1978 wrote about 'archéo-folklore touristique' in Greece,[64] considering it one of the forms of contemporary folklore of the time. Today, in view of what we observe and note above, we may perhaps talk about a peculiar 'Christiano-folklore' that

---

59 Johannes Lang, 'Zur höheren Ehre Unserer Lieben Frau. Volksfrömmigkeit, Wallfahrtswesen und das siebenhundertjährige Jubiläum des Gnadenbildes auf der Gmain im Jahre 1776', *Salzburg Archiv*, 22 (1996), pp. 187–90.
60 Michel Vovelle, *Ο θάνατος και η Δύση από το 1300 ως τις μέρες μας*, 2 τόμοι (Αθήνα: Νεφέλη, 2000), I, pp. 38–39; Ευριδίκη Αντζουλάτου-Ρετζίλα, *Μνήμης τεκμήρια* (Αθήνα: Παπαζήσης, 2004), p. 41.
61 Ευριδίκη Αντζουλάτου-Ρετζίλα, *Μνήμης τεκμήρια*, p. 39.
62 Elizabeth Hallam and Jenny Hockey, *Death, Memory and Material Culture* (Oxford and New York: Berg 2001), pp. 4, 18.
63 Hallam and Hockey, *Death, Memory*, pp. 4, 18.
64 Demetrios S. Loukatos, 'L'archéo-folklore touristique en Gréce', *Lares*, 44 (1978), 99–106; Idem, 'Folklore and Tourism in Greece', *International Folklore Review*, 2 (1982), pp. 65–69.

has a touristic aspect to it, too. It is particularly oriented towards today's burgeoning pilgrimage tourism. It involves the main form of expression in contemporary religious folk art. This is developing and perhaps in future may transmute into something else, thereby determining the path of the path of folk art, whose progressiveness is living and real.

Conclusion

If, in the light of everything that we have explored above, if one looks in overall terms at today's pilgrimage trips as organized in Greece and in many places abroad,[65] one sees truly that they are the natural continuation and development of older sacred sojourns, now adapted to today's cultural, social and material conditions. Changes in the means of transport, the ways in which pilgrimages are conducted and in travel conditions, along with the much greater ability to take part and the much smaller effort and fatigue involved therein, has meant that the age of the pilgrims now falls into different groups and that all have a much greater chance of taking part more frequently and even repeated the sacred sojourn at regular intervals.[66] Furthermore, the handing over of the organization of these journeys to travel agents means that the details of the trips differ from those known from earlier pilgrimage tradition and established for centuries. Thus there is a tendency towards the evolution in contemporary society of new, modern traditions informing pilgrimage.

The unavoidable question, however, after all this, is whether and how far the sacred nature of the pilgrimage lessens or changes in the mind of the pilgrim. That is, have the new conditions described above led to a gradual, but real secularization of pilgrimages? We have already looked above at some of the views on this question, where the trends in the literature on the subject are clear. Some scholars tend to see a secularization,[67] while others see a sequence of natural developments that do not, however, affect the basic essence of the pilgrimage and the feelings of sanctity in the minds of the participants.[68] Clearly, the conclusions that any study draws depend on the particular case and the people and the population sample involved.

---

65 Michael Haren, 'Lough Derg, the Continent of Europe and the Recesses of the Mind', *Donegal Annual* 46 (1994), pp. 107–14.
66 Constanta Cristescu, 'Pilgrimage and Pilgrimage Song in Transylvania', *East European Meetings in Ethnomusicology*, 1 (1994), pp. 30–43.
67 Bertrand Schlund, 'Pèlerinage des hommes et jeunes gens de Mulhouse et environs à Thierenbach', *Annuaire Historique de la Ville de Mulhouse*, 5 (1993), p. 133; Paul Mai, 'Klöster im Bistum Regensburg und ihre "Hauswallfahrten"', in *Wallfahrten im Bistum Regensburg: zur Tausendjahrfeier des Todes des Hl. Bischofs Wolfgang*, ed. by Georg Schwaiger and Paul Mai (Regensburg: Verlag des Vereins für Regensburger Bistumsgeschichte, 1994), p. 74; Humbert Moser, *Andacht und Sinnbild. Marianische Andachtsbilder steirischer Wallfahrtsorte* (Graz: Verlag für Sammler, 1994), pp. 43, 76, 104.
68 Sylvie Maurer, 'L' unique voie de la purification. Notre-Dame de Neubois', *Revue des Sciences Sociales de la France de l' Est*, 21 (1994), 98–103. Birgitta Klemenz, 'Das Wallfahrtsmuseum Inchenhofen. Die Verehrung des heiligen Leonhard', *Amperland*, 30 (1994), pp. 221–26.

In Greek folk culture today, if we draw our conclusions from what we have examined here, matters are clear. The idea that the pilgrimage is sacred remains non-negotiable in the mind of the pilgrim and in the practices of devotion that the pilgrim follows. This is obvious from the importance that assigned to objects of contemporary religious folk art that we have discussed. The purchase and acquisition of these objects is a vital component in the rituals of the pilgrim's journey. Naturally, feelings of sanctity and how far they outweigh, or do not outweigh, any feelings of worldliness, depends on the goal of the individual and the aim of the pilgrimage. Such feelings of sanctity are clearly less intense on day-long or half-day pilgrimages made to small monasteries or other pilgrimage sites in the locality and obviously much greater and indeed predominate, if the pilgrimage is to be made to some notable site of Orthodoxy or of Christianity in general, such as the Holy Land, Sinai, Mount Athos, Meteora or Patmos.

Clerics form the link between today's pilgrimage journeys and the old, predominant feeling of sanctity. It is they who usually lead the groups of pilgrims as heads of their parishes, as the spiritual leaders of associations and organizations or as metropolitan bishops, who are the organizers behind every trip. With their speeches and addresses and with the religious acts over which they preside during the journey (such as the singing of psalms on the bus) and at the destination (conducting communion or vespers, supplications and blessings at the pilgrimage site), they help maintain the religious character of the whole enterprise. This, in the end, is what distinguishes the pilgrimage from a simple trip. The latter is organized by a travel agent on its own, while the former is organized with the help of a travel agency, but under the spiritual supervision and guidance of a religious or ecclesiastical body. In the case of simple trip, it is clearly merely a trip. In the case of the pilgrimage, we have today's version of a holy sojourn or journey of pilgrimage, with all the spiritual and ritual elements that we have mentioned and that indeed constitute the difference between these two types of journey to the Holy Land or to important centres of worship.

Seen thus, journeys of pilgrimage, as yet one more expression of the modernity of Greek folk culture, are a basic and substantial ingredient of contemporary folk religious sensibility and of the traditional religious behaviour of the common people. They thus deserve to be studied not only from the point of view of sociology or pastoral psychology. They also deserved to be examined from the point of view of such disciplines as religious folklore.

References

Αλέκος Ε. Φλωράκης, 'Η εθνογραφική τεχνολογία. Όψεις θεωρίας και εφαρμογής', *Εθνολογία*, 6–7 (1998–1999), 31–59.

Alfons Brügger, *Wallfahrtskapelle St Wolfgang im Uechtland* (Lindenberg, Wilhelm Fink Verlag, 1996).

Angelika Petitini, 'Leonhardsverehrung und Wallfahrt in Inchenhofen', *Augsburger Volkslundliche Nachrichten*, 2 (1), (1995), 15–26.

Arturo Soria y Puig, 'Der Jakobsweg und die Jakobswege in Spanien', in *Santiago de Compostela. Pilgerwege*, ed. by Paolo Caucci von Saucken, trans. by Marcus Würmli (Augsburg: Weltbild, 1995), pp. 195–232.
Barbara Kirshenblatt-Gimblett, 'Objects of Ethnography', in *Exhibiting Cultures. The Poetics and Politics of Museum Display*, ed. by Ivan Karp and Steven D. Lavine (Washington: Smithsonian Institution Press, 1991), pp. 386–443.
Bernard Lewis, 'Ḥadjdj', in *The Encyclopaedia of Islam*, ed. by B. Lewis et al., 3rd ed. (Leiden-London: Brill and Luzac & Co., 1986), III, pp. 31–38.
Bernhard A. Reismann, 'Der Mittelpunkt aller Herrlichkeit auf Erden. Mariazell und die Zeller Wallfahrt in Reisebeschreibungen des 19. Jahrhunderts', *Schatz und Schicksal. Steirische Landesausstellung*, ed. by Helmut Eberhart and Heidelinde Fell (Graz: Kulturreferar der Steiermarkischen Landsregierung, 1996), pp. 209–19.
Bernhard Samitsch and Michaela Steinböck, 'Letzter Ausweg Maria. Die Mariazeller Votivbilder im kulturhistorischen Vergleit', in *Schatz und Schicksal. Steirische Landesausstellung*, ed. by Helmut Eberhart and Heidelinde Fell (Graz: Kulturreferar der Steiermarkischen Landsregierung, 1996), pp. 219–39.
Bertrand Schlund, 'Pèlerinage des hommes et jeunes gens de Mulhouse et environs à Thierenbach', *Annuaire Historique de la Ville de Mulhouse*, 5 (1993), 129–52.
Birgitta Klemenz, 'Das Wallfahrtsmuseum Inchenhofen. Die Verehrung des heiligen Leonhard', *Amperland*, 30 (1994), 221–26.
Claudine Fabre-Vassas, 'Paraschiva-Vendredi: la sainte des femmes, des travaux, des jours', *Terrain*, 24 (1995), 57–74.
Constanta Cristescu, 'Pilgrimage and Pilgrimage Song in Transylvania', *East European Meetings in Ethnomusicology*, 1 (1994), 30–43.
Demetrios S. Loukatos, 'L'archéo-folklore touristique en Gréce', *Lares*, 44 (1978), 99–106.
Demetrios S. Loukatos, 'Folklore and Tourism in Greece', *International Folklore Review*, 2 (1982), 65–69.
Δημήτρης Λουκόπουλος, Δημήτριος Πετρόπουλος, *Η λαϊκή λατρεία των Φαράσων* (Αθήνα: Μουσικό Λαογραφικό Αρχείο – Κέντρο Μικρασιατικών Σπουδών, 1949).
Δημήτριος Πετρόπουλος, Ερμόλαος Ανδρεάδης, *Η θρησκευτική ζωή στην περιφέρεια Ακσεράι-Γκέλβερι* (Athens: Κέντρο Μικρασιατικών Σπουδών, 1971)
Dominik Wunderlin, 'Zeugen zugerischer Wallfahrtsfrömmigkeit', *Zuger Neujahrsblatt*, 4 (1996), 44–51.
Edward David Hunt, *Holy Land Pilgrimage in the Later Roman Empire AD 312–460* (Oxford: Oxford University Press, 1982).
Emanuela Renzetti, *Un cammino di devozione. Il pellegrinaggio a Sabiona del 1994* (San Martin de Tor: Istitut Ladin Micurà de Rü 1995), pp. 25–27.
Elizabeth Hallam, Jenny Hockey, *Death, Memory and Material Culture* (Oxford and New York: Berg 2001).
Ευριδίκη Αντζουλάτου-Ρετζίλα, *Μνήμης τεκμήρια* (Αθήνα: Παπαζήσης, 2004).
Franca Romano, 'La Madonna Pellegrina. Apparizione della Madonna della Pace a Capri, 1984', *La Ricerca Folklorica*, 33 (1996), 125–49.
Gábor Barna, 'Mariazell und Ungarn. Die Verehrung der Magna Domina Hungarorum', in *Schatz und Schicksal. Steirische Landesausstellung*, ed. by Helmut Eberhart and

Heidelinde Fell (Graz: Kulturreferar der Steiermarkischen Landsregierung, 1996), pp. 281–94.

György Orosz, 'Pilger, singende Wandlerbettler im altrussischen Staat', *Acta Ethnographica Hungarica*, 39 (3–4), (1994), 381–93.

Henri Ellenberrger, 'Releve des Pelegrinages du Depertement de la Vienne', *Nouvelle Revue des Traditions Populaires*, 2 (4), (1950), 331–57.

Henry Glassie, *Material Culture* (Bloomington and Indianapolis: Indiana University Press, 1999).

Horst Schweigert, 'Die Gnadenstatue und das "Schatzkammerbild" von Mariazell', in *Schatz und Schicksal. Steirische Landesausstellung*, ed. by Helmut Eberhart and Heidelinde Fell (Graz: Kulturreferar der Steiermarkischen Landsregierung, 1996), pp. 89–105.

Humbert Moser, *Andacht und Sinnbild. Marianische Andachtsbilder steirischer Wallfahrtsorte* (Graz: Verlag für Sammler, 1994).

Ιωάννης Μ. Χατζηφώτης, *Ο λαϊκός πολιτισμός του Καστελλορίζου* (Αθήνα: Σύνδεσμος των Απανταχού Καστελλοριζίων «Ο Άγιος Κωνσταντίνος», 1982).

Ingo Gabor, 'Die Wallfahrtskapelle zum Hl. Blut in Schwenningen', *Württembergisch-Franken*, 80 (1996), 151–74.

Jan van Herwaarden, 'Der mittelalterliche Jakobskult in der Niederlanden', in *Santiago de Compostela. Pilgerwege*, ed. by Paolo Caucci von Saucken, trans. by Marcus Würmli (Augsburg: Weltbild, 1995), pp. 333–48.

Johann Hirnsperger, 'Die Erhebung der Wallfahrtskirche Maria Plain zur Basilica Minor. Kirchenrechtliche Erwägungen', *Mitteilungen der Gesellschaft für Salzburger Landeskunde*, 135 (1995), 159–88.

Johannes Lang, 'Zur höheren Ehre Unserer Lieben Frau. Volksfrömmigkeit, Wallfahrtswesen und das siebenhundertjährige Jubiläum des Gnadenbildes auf der Gmain im Jahre 1776', *Salzburg Archiv*, 22 (1996), 173–92.

Károly Kerenyi, *La Madonna ungherese di Verdasio. Paesaggi dello spirito e paesaggio del' anima*, trans. by Anna Ruchat (Locarno: *Armando* Dadò, 1995).

Liselotte Blumauer-Montenave, *Gäste des Wallfahrtsortes Mariazell. Eine Dokumentation* (Wien: Wiener Katholische Akademie, 1996).

Louis-Jean Calvet, *Η προφορική παράδοση*, trans. by Marilena Karyolemou (Athens: Καρδαμίτσας, 1995)

Ludwig Baumann, 'Das Gnadenbild von Weissregen', in *Der Regen. Kultur und Natur am Fluss*, ed. by Bärbel Kleindorfer-Marx (Amberg: Buch & Kunstverlag Oberpfalz, 1996), pp. 105–12.

Μανώλης Γ. Βαρβούνης, *Λαϊκή λατρεία και θρησκευτική συμπεριφορά των κατοίκων της Σάμου* (Αθήνα: Πνευματικό Ίδρυμα Σάμου Ν. Δημητρίου, 1992).

Manuel C. Díaz y Díaz, 'Die Liber Sancti Jacobi', in *Santiago de Compostela. Pilgerwege*, ed. by Paolo Caucci von Saucken, trans. by Marcus Würmli (Augsburg: Weltbild, 1995), pp. 39–56.

Michael Haren, 'Lough Derg, the Continent of Europe and the Recesses of the Mind', *Donegal Annual* 46 (1994), 107–14.

Michel Vovelle, *Ο θάνατος και η Δύση από το 1300 ως τις μέρες μας*, 2 τόμοι (Αθήνα: Νεφέλη, 2000).

Ottavia Niccoli, 'Madonne di montagna. Note su apparizioni e santuari nelle vali alpine', in *Cultura d'élite e cultura popolare nell'arco alpino fra Cinque e Seicento*, ed. by Ottavio Besomi and Carlo Caruso (Basel – Berlin: Birkhäuser, 1995), pp. 95–119.

Paul Mai, 'Klöster im Bistum Regensburg und ihre "Hauswallfahrten"', in *Wallfahrten im Bistum Regensburg: zur Tausendjahrfeier des Todes des Hl. Bischofs Wolfgang*, ed. by Georg Schwaiger and Paul Mai (Regensburg: Verlag des Vereins für Regensburger Bistumsgeschichte, 1994), pp. 58–83.

Paul Mai, 'Die Entwicklung der Hedwigswallfahrten in Deutschland nach 1945', in *Das Bild der heiligen Hedwig in Mittelalter und Neuzeit*, ed. by Eckhard Grunewald and Nikolaus Gussone (München: Oldenbourg Wissenschaftsverlag 1996), pp. 247–57.

Paul Post, 'The Modern Pilgrim. A Study of Contemporary Pilgrims' Accounts', *Ethnologia Europaea*, 24 (1), (1994), 85–100.

Paul Werner, 'Der altbayerische Herrgott St Leonhard in Inchenhofen', *Charivari*, 22 (10), (1996), 107–11.

Peter Bogatyrev, *The Function of Folk Costume in Moravian Slovakia*, trans. by Richard G. Crum (Paris: Mouton, 1971).

Philip V. Bohlman, 'Pilgrimage, Politics, and the Musical Remapping of the New Europe', *Ethnomusicology*, 40 (3), (1996), 375–412.

Raymond Oursel, 'Cluny und der Jakobsweg', in *Santiago de Compostela. Pilgerwege*, ed. by Paolo Caucci von Saucken, trans. by Marcus Würmli (Augsburg: Weltbild, 1995), pp. 115–48.

Reinhard Haller, *Einmal im Leben auf den Heiligen Berg. Bayerische Wallfahrten nach Böhmen* (Grafenau: Morsak, 1995).

Reinhard Haller, 'Wallfahrten auf dem Goldenen Steig und seinen Zubringern', in *Kulturregion Goldener Steig. Aufsätze zur Ausstellung*, ed. by Peter Becher, Sigrid Canz, and Jozo Džambo (München: Adalbert Stifter Verein 1995), pp. 80–112.

René Tresse, *Le Pelegrinage syrien aux villes saintes de l'Islam* (Paris: Impr. de Chaumette, 1937).

Robert Böck, 'Die Wallfahrt zu Unserer Lieben Frau in der Aich bei Oberbernbach (Landkreis Aichach-Friedberg)', *Bayerisches Jahrbuch für Volkskunde*, 12 (1996), 169–84.

Roberto Morozzo della Rocca, 'Piazza San Pietro', in *I luoghi della memoria. Simboli e miti dell'Italia unita*, ed. by Mario Isnenghi (Roma: Laterza, 1996), pp. 512–23.

Robin Cormack, *Writing in Gold. Byzantine Society and its Icons* (New York: Oxford University Press, 1985).

Robert Plötz, 'Jakobspilger', in *Enzyklopädie des Märchens*, ed. by Rolf Wilhelm Brednich and et al. (Berlin: Walter de Gruyter, 1993), VII, pp. 459–67.

Roland Gröber, 'Maria Hilf, ein deutsches Wallfahrtsbild in Südtirol', *Der Schlern*. 70 (5), (1996), 259–73.

Romana Gabriel, 'Viele Wege führen nach Mariazell. Aspekte zum Thema "Wallfahrt heute"', in *Schatz und Schicksal. Steirische Landesausstellung*, ed. by Helmut Eberhart and Heidelinde Fell (Graz: Kulturreferar der Steiermarkischen Landsregierung, 1996), pp. 273–80.

Sabine Ragaller, *Die Holzkirchener Kerzenwallfahrt nach Bogenberg* (Holzkirchen: Pfarrgemeinderat Holzkirchen, 1995).

Σταυρός Σταυρίδης, *Η συμβολική σχέση με το χώρο. Πώς οι κοινωνικές αξίες διαμορφώνουν και ερμηνεύουν το χώρο* (Αθήνα: Κάλβος, 1990).

Sylvie Maurer, 'L' unique voie de la purification. Notre-Dame de Neubois', *Revue des Sciences Sociales de la France de l'Est*, 21 (1994), 98–103.

Stefan Raimann, *Das Wallfahrtswesen der burgenländischen Kroaten. Dargestellt am Beispiel der Wallfahrtsorte Mariazell, Loretto und Eisenstadt-Oberberg* (Grosspetersdorf: Benua, 1996).

Stefan Wollmann, 'Wallfahrten in der Oberlausitz', *Oberlausitzer Hausbuch*, 7 (1995–1996), 120–23.

Στέλιος Αγ. Παπαδόπουλος, 'Υλικός πολιτισμός', *Εθνολογία*, 3 (1994), 215–27.

Βασιλική Χρυσανθοπούλου, 'Οι χατζήδαινες της Πέρθης', *Λαογραφία*, 33 (1985), 129–54.

Βασίλειος Δεληγιάννης, 'Το χατζηλίκι στα Κουβούκλια της Προύσσης', *Μικρασιατικά Χρονικά*, 2 (1939), 400–20.

Vítězslav Štajnochr, *Die wundertätige Maria. Mariendarstellungen aus europäischen Wallfahrtsorten. Aus der Sammlung der Ethnographischen Abteilung des Nationalmuseums in Prag* (Sandl: Wallfahrtsmuseum Neukirchen b. Hl. Blut, 1995).

Volker Knierim, 'Auto, Fremde Tod. Automobile und Reisen in zeitgenössischen deutschsprachigen Sensationserzählungen', *Fabula*, 26 (1985), 230–44.

Walter Lutz, 'Die staatliche und kirchliche Untersuchung einer gesetzeswidrigen Wallfahrt von Limburg zur Beselicher Kapelle am 14. September 1845', *Archiv für mittelrheinische Kirchengeschichte*, 46 (1994), 141–62.

Walter Stipperger, 'Oberes Ennstal. Wallfahrten im Schatten der Josefinischen Zeit', *Da schau her*, 17 (4), (1996), 19–20.

Wallfahrt und Bilderkult. Gesammelte Schriften, ed. by Hans Dünninger and Wolfgang Brückner (Würzburg: Echter, 1995).

Ξενοφών Κ. Άκογλου, *Από τη ζωή του Πόντου. Λαογραφικά Κοτυώρων* (Αθήνα: Τυπογραφείο Γ. Π. Ξένου, 1939).

DORINA DRAGNEA

The Pilgrimage Practice in Moldova as a Medium for Displaying of the Official and Vernacular Religiosity

Introduction

The phenomenon of pilgrimage became, after the fall of communism, one of the revived forms of collective manifestation of religiosity by Orthodox Christians in the Republic of Moldova. At the beginning of the 1990s, a process of re-sacralization took place, and after their destruction by the Soviet regime, monasteries were re-converted from a profane place into a sacred site under the auspices of the Church, parishioners, as well as the government. In the same context, officially, according to surveys, the indices of religiosity seem to have risen during the last decades. A study elaborated in 2016,[1] informs that 94 per cent of citizens of Moldova said they believed in God, over 90 per cent of respondents declared they used prayer as a direct spiritual communication with God, and 36 per cent of citizens had been on at least one pilgrimage in their lifetime. These data show a re-birth of the religious conscience freely manifested publicly, without fear, and can be as well explained by the fact that this is the first result of the social duty and involvement of the Church, after the fall of a regime with an atheist ideology. In the view of some researchers, this situation is explained by the fact 'Orthodoxy as a whole has been engaged in the reconstruction – if not invention – of a post-Soviet Moldovan national tradition, which has been mainly founded on religion. This religious tradition is a rediscovery made by a young clergy, partly still in the course of institutionalization, and by believers who had for decades only a private religiosity, confined to domestic rituals and few festivities'.[2]

---

1 Ovidiu Voicu, Jenifer Cash, and Victoria Cojocariu, *Biserică și Stat în Republica Moldova*. Fundația Soros Moldova. Centrul pentru Inovare Publică (Chișinău: Bons Offices, 2017), pp. 11–12, 15.
2 Davide N. Carnevale, 'A Context-Grounded Approach to Religious Freedom: The Case of Orthodoxy in the Moldovan Republic', *Religions*, 10 (5), 2019, p. 327.

> **Dorina Dragnea** • PhD, Head of the Applied Research and Promotion Sector, Immaterial Heritage and Traditional Culture Department, National Institute of Heritage, Bucharest, Romania

Pilgrimage in the Christian Balkan World: The Path to Touch the Sacred and Holy, ed. by Dorina Dragnea, Emmanouil Ger. Varvounis, Evelyn Reuter, Petko Hristov and Susan Sorek (Turnhout, 2023), pp. 221–238.
BREPOLS 🕮 PUBLISHERS   DOI 10.1484/M.STR-EB.5.132408

Additionally, during the last three decades, it is witnessing a modernized and resized ritual and ceremonial form of pilgrimage. The religious traditional practices, which lurked in a drowsy state, have now erupted in response to unmet spiritual needs. Recent confessions about divine interventions shared by believers, positive feelings experienced in sacred places, and advice for going to worship shrines for help have all been assimilated by the collective mind. Therefore, certain shrines became pilgrimage destinations, thus catalyzing this phenomenon.

Analyzing pilgrimage in Moldova, Church-state and Church-parishioners relations are revealed. The modalities of facing and mitigating the socio-economical crisis by the community, using faith, and the cross features of the Balkan Orthodox tradition and Slavic-Russian Orthodoxy in ritual forms of the pilgrimage performance is observed. This devotional act and expression of the collective piety record and narrate a history of mentalities, such as the shared images and beliefs, and the intensity of the religious feeling, the instruments, and forms by which the local community adapts to the new value contexts.

My investigation is argued as well by the fact that the phenomenon of pilgrimage has been insufficiently examined by scholars in the Republic of Moldova. In research on religious life and the church, this theme is mentioned in passing, in the background of other thematic lines. There are few scientific studies, of which it is significant to mention the research of Romeo Cemârtan.[3] The researcher, conducting open discussions with pilgrims at various monasteries in Moldova, stresses a concurrent manifestation 'the secularization of the pilgrimage becomes an unfortunate reality, but on the other hand, at the opposite pole of this phenomenon we encounter diverse forms of religious fanaticism',[4] that need further analisys. Also, articles with historical perspectives, and informative and cathehetic purposes[5] were published by various authors, clerics or theologians. Some historical evidence can be identified, such as the charismatic pilgrimage constructed around Hieromonk Inochentie, the leader of the Inochentism,[6] a local religious movement within Orthodoxy at the beginning of the twentieth century. The processions with the miracle-working icon of the Mother of

---

3   Romeo Cemârtan 'Destinațiile religioase ale pelerinilor din Republica Moldova', *Buletin Științific. Revistă de Etnografie, Științele Naturii și Muzeologie. Fascicula Etnografie*, 17 (30), (2012), 101–08.
4   Romeo Cemârtan, 'Patrimoniul cultural și semnificația pelerinajului contemporan', *Buletin Științific. Revistă de Etnografie, Științele Naturii și Muzeologie. Fascicula Etnografie*, 15 (28), (2011), p. 127.
5   Maxim Melinti, 'Influența Sfântului Munte Athos asupra vieții spirituale și culturale a Moldovei', *Tyragetia: Istorie. Muzeologie*, 1 (16), No. 2, (2007), 143–48; Paul Mihail, 'La Muntele Athos (din cartea 'Jurnalul călătoriei de studii în sud-estul Europei')', *Luminătorul*, 5 (26), (1996), 43–56; Octavian Moșin, 'Pelerinajul – înnoire și îmbogățire a vieții spirituale', *Altarul Credinței*, 13 (2003) p. 8; Octavian Moșin, 'Râvnind sfințenia: Schimb de moaște între Moldova și Dobrogea', *Altarul Credinței*, 9 (2005). p. 6; Vadim Cheibaș, 'Sfântul Munte Athos – lăcașul Maicii Domnului', *Altarul Credinței*, 30 iunie, 10 (2001), 4–5, etc.
6   See more at, Nicolae Popovschi, *Mișcarea de la Balta sau inochentismul în Basarabia. Contribuții la istoria vieții religioase a Românilor din Basarabia* (Chișinău, Moldova: Tipografia Eparhiala – "Cartea Româneasca", 1926); James A. Kapaló, *Inochentism and Orthodox Christianity. Religious Dissent in the Russian and Romanian Borderlands* (London and New York: Routledge, 2019); Dorina Onica, 'The Inochentism: Faith, Ritual Practices, and Sacred Spaces. New Data and Approaches', *Hiperboreea*, 7 (2), (2020), 203–31.

God from the monastery of Hârbovăț, performed during the interwar period, should also be taken into account for pointing out the historically recent evidences about the relationship with holiness and the Church. Thus, I notice the contemporary pilgrimage practice preserves features secured by tradition, such as historically accumulated peculiarities in the context of the religious, socio-economical, and political reality of society and the interventions, adaptations of the local community to the specifics of the modern challenges, as well as ways of understanding and practicing religion.

Focusing on the statements made above, the key question of the research is in which way the official religion prescriptions and the local expressions of vernacular religiosity are intertwining during the pilgrimage, simultaneously revealing its performance features in a post-socialist society.

The chapter will discuss the factors and needs that motivate people to go on pilgrimage. The beliefs, ritualized behaviors, gestures, formulas, ritual and ceremonial practices, and divine intervention narratives will be stated and portrayed at each stage of the spiritual journey. As a result, it will be depicted the pilgrimage as a tolerant medium for displaying of the syncretism between official canonic forms of acting and folk customs, oriented to fulfil the assorted needs of the believers.

Field research is the main method used, that was sequentially carried out at various monasteries and sacred places, during 2011–2012, 2014, 2019, and interviews were also recorded in 2020–2021 too. For drawing an integrative screen of the pilgrimage performance in Moldova, I have chosen the pilgrimage practices to the monasteries of Hârbovăț, Țipova, Saharna, and Hâncu, convents of Călărășeuca and Cușelăuca for analyzing, which are known more or less for two reasons. The practices enacted there are conforming to the canonical rules, revealing in such a way the role of the Church in the pastoral care of the faithful. And on the other hand, there are practices, of a popular or syncretic nature, which have provoked controversies, debates. In both cases, numerous pilgrims were constantly attracted. For achieving the goal and for the in-depth understanding of this fusion of realities, the interviews and open discussions with the pilgrims; visits to monasteries as a pilgrim and as a researcher; the direct and participatory observation; the historical synthesis method and description; a critical and reflexive analysis were applied.

The data collected in the course of ethnographic fieldwork are approached and theoretically outlined on the basis of two perspectives. It is crucial and deserves analysis 'the human behaviour through using 'pilgrimage' as a case-study rather than focussing on the institution itself as a firmly bounded category of action',[7] situating my analysis, in such a way, on a phenomenological approach. The beliefs, local forms of understanding and the devotion acts towards *sacra* and holy express interesting expressions for following the interdependence between the orthodoxy and orthopraxy.[8] Also, my discourse is drawn for analyzing and comprehending the

---

7 Simon Coleman, 'Do You Believe in Pilgrimage? Communitas, Contestation and Beyond', *Anthropological Theory*, 2 (3), (2002), p. 363.
8 Chris Hann and Hermann Goltz, 'Introduction: The Other Christianity?', *Eastern Christians in Anthropological Perspective*, ed. by Chris Hann and Hermann Goltz (Berkley, Los Angeles, London: University of California Press, 2010), pp. 1–29.

religion as it is lived during the pilgrimage keeping in mind the Marion Bowman's dimensions interference of official religion, folk religion and individual religion.[9]

The Structure and Process of the Archetypal Journey

The negative experiences of the 90s, like economic crisis, socio-political instability, and unemployment caused the increase in the transnational migration tendencies. The conjunction of these circumstances affected every family and individual, who was put in the situation of searching solutions, and alternatives to face the new challenges and realities for them. The most intimate traumas began to be of the families, in which one of the partners has chosen to go abroad for work. As a consequence, since the 2000s, many divided families and children raised by their grandparents were noticed.

Therefore, during my fieldwork, I recorded many confessions of the people, who assert that several times, were advised for going on pilgrimage to the monastery in seeking help. This decision has occurred as a result of repetitive attempts of finding the rational cause, answers, and solutions to their problems. At the moment when they could not understand the concrete cause of their distresses, they have considered them to have been caused by sorceries and charms, or by committing grave sins. Consequently, I have noticed that the pilgrimage performed for thanksgiving, devotion to the Divinity, is visibly blurred by the one performed to ask for, implore and find healing. This is an indicator and screen of the real daily life of society.

Respectively, there are social problems (the difficulty of finding a job in the country or going abroad), which the folk belief is that they are caused by *legarea drumului* ('the tying of the road'), there are personal sentimental problems (preventing divorces, obstacles to get married), the last one referred to as *legarea cununiilor* ('the tying of weddings') and health problems (cancer, persons with disabilities, infertility) called *boli grele* ('heavy diseases'). As Victor Turner said, 'religious beliefs and practices are something more than grotesque reflections or expressions of economic, political, and social relanshionships; rather are they coming to be seen as decisive keys to the understanding of how people think and feel about those relanshioships, and about the natural and social environments in which they operate'.[10]

The chosen liturgical periods for doing pilgrimage are during the four fasting periods of the religious year, especialy during the Lent; at *hram* ('the feast of the patron saint') of the monastery, the signifiant religious calendar feasts of the year (Christmas, Epiphany, Annunciation, Easter, the Descent of the Holy Spirit, the Dormition of the Mother of God, the Elevation of the Holy Cross) and the bringing of relics and miracle-working icons in some shrines. Pilgrims believe that the holiness and miraculous power of the worship place on these days are

---

9 Marion Bowman, 'Phenomenology, Fieldwork and Folk Religion', in *Religion: Empirical Studies*, ed. by Steven Sutcliffe (Aldershot: Ashgate, 2004), pp. 3–18.
10 Victor Turner, *The Ritual Process. Structure and Anti-Structure* (Ithaca, New York: Cornell Paperbacks, Cornell University Press, 1977), p. 6.

amplified by the Liturgy of the Hours officiated by high-rank clergy, the presence of the devotion artifacts, and as well by the attendance of monks known for their humble life.

During the pilgrimage path, the succession of processional moments, such as the listening of Akathists, the singing of apocryphal songs and religious hymns in chorus by the pilgrims, the sharing of various stories about the sacred shrine, the individual or collective prayer constructs and expresses 'the spirituality of the road',[11] a ritual identity and the common faith in help. If the pilgrim travels alone, he encounters a meditative and interrogative trance with himself.

The stage of getting closer consists of enacting consecutive ritual behaviors. Pilgrims usually enter the church and make the sign of the cross, worship, and kiss the icons as a devotion testimony. As weel, in popular lore, it is believed that as many icons are kissed as sins are forgiven. The devoted lighting candles in front of the icon of the Mother of God or of Jesus Christ, of the saint whose name he/she bears, or of the saint who is the protector of their home and family.

Pilgrims also write on separate papers the names of the family members to be read during the Liturgy, *la vii* ('at the living ones') and *la adormiți* ('at the dead ones'). Usually, at the priest's advice, the pilgrims note their name or of the person who needs help on a separate paper, to be read at 40 Proskomedia, 40 Liturgies or Akatists. Most of the believers bring offerings (oil, flour, *colaci*,[12] other food products, and money) that they give to the monastery, as well various cakes, or candies that they offer as alms to those present at the Liturgy. During the Divine Liturgy ritual, the pilgrims become part of both the collective and the individual devotion, synchronously manifested. The pilgrim reads holy paragraphs; he recites in a whisper or utters in his mind his own prayer, either for thanksgiving, forgiveness or for help. This silent prayer is most often accompanied by specific liturgical gestures as kneeling, or *mătanii*,[13] which externalize it and strengthen its function and finality. The created atmosphere shows that as Heather J. Coleman stated 'the liturgy is not just about words, but about gestures, images, sounds, tastes, and scents that, together with the words, express the truths of the faith. This embodiment extends beyond ritual to the material world'.[14] A few hours of physical sacrifice, in which the position of staying up alternates with doing repetitive kneelings is a form of penance, humility, self-control, fueled by the desire to receive the Divine blessing, good thoughts, and atonement, to rehabilitate himself towards the Divinity. The climax of the pilgrimage is approached by receiving Holy Communion. This point of culmination is complemented by the worship and set of performed practices at the shrine and its sacred agents, which constitute its

---

11 Raymond Oursel, *Pélerins du Moyen age. Les hommes, les chemins, les sanctuaires* (Paris: Fayard, 1978), p. 49.
12 It is a bread braided ring-shaped, which is used in the Balkans as well as in Eastern Europe as a ritual and ceremonial bread.
13 Reverence made by believers from the staying-up position to the ground.
14 Heather J. Coleman, 'Introduction: Faith and Story in Imperial Russia', in *Orthodox Christianity in Imperial Russia. A Source Book on Lived Religion*, ed. by Heather J. Coleman (USA: Indiana University Press, 2014), p. 11.

core or satellites. The related spiritual enactments are believed by the community to be effective, respected, and sometimes judged, especially by young people.

Prayer Pilgrimage for Healing and for Roots Cleaning

The people go on pilgrimage for praying individually or collectively, in unique sites, which they believe to be impregnated with a sacred presence, healing power, and in such a way they feel that they are experiencing closeness to God. These sites may be isolated monasteries or even poorer, not necessarily very visited, because pilgrims believe that faith and the need for help are not displayed publicly, it is an intimate state. I recorded several ritual scenes of the prayer act, which emphasizes not only the faith but also the hope of the individual, as well as a rich substratum of reminiscences of pre-Christian beliefs and popular habits, combined with practices of sympathetic magic, all born from despondency. An original insight of the individual experienced faith is provided by the confessions of a middle-aged woman, who prefer for dual strategies. She as a supplicant in a healing by proxy[15] is taking into account and is following the canonical advice of the spiritual priest, as well as she is performing personal acts, considering them to be efficient.

> When my daughter was a teenager, she didn't have menstruation. She was hospitalized, doctors said she was healthy. At that moment, an old woman told me someone in my family had committed grave sins. Then, I talked to my mother; she admitted that being a midwife she aided a woman to have an abortion. I had abortions too. Therefore, it was a sin of generations that needed to be atoned for. I went to the monastery in Țipova. The priest advised me, my mother, and my daughter, to keep all four fasting seasons of the year, on Wednesdays and Fridays, to pray a lot, and to receive the Holy Communion. In addition, I wrote our names to be read by the priest during the 40 Liturgies of Preparation. The priest told me my daughter should baptize a child, become a godmother, and give alms to other kids. I, as a mother, every night prayed to the Holy Trinity to forgive my sins, in the cave church in Țipova, because I knew it was a place with great powers.[16]

In the same line, I mention of a category of believers comes to the Horodiște (Țipova) monastery to pray for deceased relatives. They call them 'prayers for cleansing the roots'. These are prayers for forgiveness and cleansing from ancestral sins. Even if the *parastas* (from Greek: *parástasis*) is performed by the priest conforming to canonical rules, the people have included their practices, such as the bringing of alms, not in the usual form of *koliva*[17] sweetened with sugar, but *colivă vie* ('living koliva'). It is prepared from sprouted wheat and decorated only with dried fruits, namely from

---

15 Thomas J. Csordas, *The Sacred Self - a Cultural Phenomenology of Charismatic Healing* (Berkeley, Los Angeles, London: University of California Press, 1997), p. 33.
16 A. L., 48 years old, female, Horodiște, interviewed in 2019.
17 It is a ritual dish based on boiled and sweetened wheat that is used for commemoration of the dead.

the harvests of the earth. After the group prayer, they give people as alms small parts of the koliva, as the tradition is. In this sense the ritual plays a social role, calling for solidarity, cohesion, emphaty.

Pilgrims go to the monasteries to have soul conversations with the spiritual father, a monk, or a nun, and to receive advice and solutions to the problems and difficult situations they face. The imperative solution to all the problems, which were identified from the discussions with the pilgrims, is writing the name to be uttering during the 40 Liturgies. During this time, the believer's behavior and actions must resonate with the prayer read in the church for him, so the individual must fast, confess, and receive the Holy Communion. The central principle of this healing period is the idea that 'ten priests can pray for you, but if you do not do this individually; it will be in vain, nothing will help you'.

Perpetual pilgrims offer a substantial source of information. They are bearers and providers of stories and cases, which they share with beginners, as they mentor and persuade, burdened people who are seeking healing. In this way, the beliefs and customs as 'religious conviction emerges on the human plane',[18] and through custom, they gain credibility.

> A good friend of mine was unable to have kids for six years. I went together with her to the monastery, and a sister (nun) opened the Psalter[19] for her [I never did that. It's a sin.] Then, the nun advised her to give six *hulubași*[20] as alms to six children, to fast, and to pray. Then, she got pregnant.[21]

> A friend who had breast cancer, constantly went to the monastery for attending the Liturgy, fasted and read the Akathist of Saint Luke the Blessed Surgeon, she prayed at the miracle worker icon of Mother of God *Pantanassa*. As long as she did this, her situation improved. Then, she went abroad; consequently she could not come to the monastery and soon died. The prayer helps a lot.[22]

A particular case is that people go to the monastery asking for healing prayers for a person possessed by demons,[23] practice which from the mid 2000s until relatively recently; being collectively performed became a phenomenon. Even if it was contested, judged, and blamed, exorcism became a spectacle sought on by hundreds of believers

---

18 Clifford Geertz, *The Interpretation of Cultures. Selected Essays* (New York: Basic Books, Inc., Publishers, 1973), p. 113.
19 In the second half of the 2000s, the archimandrite of one monastery (whose names I will not give, in order to cover his identity) in central part of the country, used to open the Psalter for the parishioners. Hundreds of pilgrims went to the monastery every week for this, to find out what is the cause of their problems and to receive advice, solutions to them. In a short time, these visits for help became a phenomenon. People built around this spiritual father a high authority, even if he was performing a controversial divination practice. However, the pilgrims were considering that in this way the church is getting closer to the people, to their needs.
20 This is a type of bread, made from two strands of dough, having the shape of a dove. It is offered as alms, especially to kids.
21 L. P., 61 years old, female, psychologist, Chișinău, interviewed in 2021.
22 A. Z., 53 years old, female, teacher, Rezina, interviewed in 2020.
23 See more in this matter at Jill Dubisch, *In a Different Place. Pilgrimage, Gender and Politics at a Greek Island Shrine* (Princeton, N.J.: Princeton University Press, 1995).

weekly. It can be considered a type of spiritual healing pilgrimage with a mystical nature. Every Thursday in the evening, pilgrims from everywhere and of all ages traveled to the north of the country, to the monastery of Saharna, where at midnight, a group of priests read the *Moliftele* (from Old Church Slavonic: *molitva*) of Saint Basil the Great and performed the Sacrament of the Holy Anointing. During the divine service, each individual kept a lighted candle in his hand, concentrating on the formulas uttered by the priests but also on the names of all who attended the ritual, including their own. During the prayer, there was an amalgam of hilarious sounds, groans, faints, wriggling bodies on the ground, and violent reactions were produced by the possessed. These intense behaviors and mythical ecstasies were viewed by all the others with pity, fear, bewilderment, wonder, as well with amazement, especially by young people, who go there having rather a desire for curiosity. Then, after the ritual, the people sat in a few rows, and each passed to be checked with *copia* (Slavonic: *Kopié*)[24] if they were unbewitched. In fact, in this ritual scenario, the spear, an instrument of sacred vessels, used for cutting the prosphora during the Liturgy of Preparation, is manipulated as a scanning tool for the devils of the bodies of mentally unstable sinners.

The constant attendance of hundreds of people proves they are searching for something magical, which can transform their lives overnight. In fact, we cannot speak of a pure religiosity based on canonical rules and church teachings, but one intertwined with forms of individual religiousness, giving an essence of mysticism to religious rituals, credibility to various practices of occultism, and to customs and popular beliefs that still remain active in the collective mind, especially of the lower and middle social strata. Thus, the religious feeling and the chosen healing methods that are infused by reminiscences of folklore continue to be vivid, among individuals coming here, from rural as well as from urban areas. In reaction to this phenomenon, in 2016, the Synod of the Orthodox Church of Moldova condemned the practice of exorcisms, noting they are representations of a 'sickly mysticism, after which the people outside of the Church is attracted, and which some priests dare to use it. These ordinances took root especially in certain monastic settlements and gathered many desperate, confused, and sick people [...] Many pilgrims and parishioners who witness such exorcism scenes are not only disturbed but downright frightened... '.[25] Thus the institution of the Church constantly is monitoring and sometimes negotiating the behavior of parishioners and pilgrims in order to avoid deviations from official religious practices.

The Local Miracle-Working Icon of the Mother of God from the Monastery of Hârbovăț

This icon of the Mother of God, called *Gârbovița*, is honored with great devotional consistency and embraces thousands of pilgrims around her, especially on 21 October, when it is celebrated. Miracles of this icon have been recorded since 1816, and worship

---

24 In Romanian folklore, *copia* is also known as *săgeată* ('arrow') because of its shape (i.e. spear).
25 Sinodul Bisericii Ortodoxe din Moldova. Proces – verbal nr. 002 din 11.02.2016.

practices increased after it remained intact during consecutive arson attacks and demolitions of the monastery.

In regard to the tradition of processions with the icon and pilgrimages, there are various historical source documents. In the second half of the nineteenth century and at the beginning of the twentieth century, itineraries were established through all the parishes, where the icon was to be taken for worship. For example, on 30 September 1919, in addition to an itinerary that had already become known, a series of rules were published that were to be observed when the icon would arrive in the city of Chișinau: 'all the clergy of the Orthodox churches, in gilded robes and in parish processions will come to the cathedral… The group of each church will have in front the best and most beautiful churchly flags, worn by people dressed in costumes, which the churches have for this purpose. The Ministry of Bessarabia together with the Group of Divisions displayed on the streets of the city an appeal to the population to participate at the meeting of the holy icon, to hoist the flags, and to keep the shops closed'.[26] The tradition of bringing the icon for worship to various villages is preserved until the contemporary day.

The pilgrim, who stands in the queue to worship the icon, has a tense body, keeps his eyes closed, raises his face to the sky or on the contrary lowers it, feeling unworthy, he engages in deep prayer or monologue, which grows with intensity the closer he gets to the icon, experiencing 'the divine as an emotional or physiological state rather than a human-like conversation partner'.[27] Arriving in front of the icon, the pilgrims touch it with the new clothes and towels for giving to their family members. By ritually touching it, they believe the items receive the blessing and the healing power, thus demonstrating the belief in contagious magic. In this case, the association between miracle-working icons and divinity transcends the materiality in the religious imagination, and the fact that because the pilgrim managed to touch it, he receives from this the satisfaction and an induced certainty that he is impregnated by a part of the sanctity of the icon, and he feels with a fulfilled soul. Sometimes the collective perception is wrongly configured, because the source of power is not the object of worship, but the belief in the saintly figure that is imagined on this item. In such a situation is justifiable the assertion of Durheim that 'the man who has obeyed his God, and who for this reason thinks he has his God with him, approaches the world with confidence and a sense of heightened energy'.[28] Also, the crawling passing under the icon became a ritual gesture made with the thought and conviction 'to regain your health', even you are elderly you should put effort on this, for feeling your sacrifice – a pilgrim explains. The faith of people in the power of the miracle-working icon cured them of mental ailments, dental disease, paralysis, heart disease, foot disease – healing miracles that continue to happen today.

---

26 *Luminătorul: Jurnal bisericesc*, an. 12, nr. 17–18, (1919), pp. 7–8.
27 Paul Froese and Jones Rory, 'The Sociology of Prayer: Dimensions and Mechanisms', *Social Sciences*, 10 (2021), p. 26.
28 Emile Durkheim, *The Elementary Forms of Religious Life*, trans. by Karen E. Fields (New York: The Pree Press, 1995), p. 211.

The Relics of Local Saints

Blessed Agafia (Maranciuc) (b. 1819–d. 1873) was canonized in 2016, by the decision of the Synod of the Orthodox Church of Moldova,[29] and the entirety of her relics are kept at the convent of Cuşelăuca (founded in 1786). Her hagiography[30] presents the story which explains that her bodily infirmity has become a blessing and healing for the pilgrims with the same disease who worship her relics and tomb. Being very young, Agafia embarked on her own pilgrimage to Pecherskaya Lavra in Kyiv, as her parents did not take her with them. On the way, at night, she fell into a well, fracturing both legs, thus remaining paralyzed. According to apocryphal sources, she lived in this well for three years, when she was found by a shepherd. After this moment, brought to the home of her parents, who considered her dead, Agafia, due to the gift of clairvoyance and the power to heal, had an impact on the religiosity of the locals. Later, she came to the convent, respecting the request of the Mother of God that was shown to her in a dream. Several local narratives tell of healings during her life, when she spiritually guided the locals, also after her death. Most healings are of paralysis and muteness; additionally, pilgrims come to pray to maintain their families united, to heal loved ones who suffer from alcohol and drug addiction, and smoking.

Even if the pilgrims worship the relics, which are inside the convent, many of them visit the tomb of the saint, which is inside the cemetery. Therefore, the pilgrims perform a re-transfer of energy sources, returning to the initial place of worship. The healing process consists of performing certain bodily gestures which, depending on the pilgrim's problem, must be repeated several times, in the belief that this persistence would ensure his healing. The pilgrim when arrived at the Blessed Agafia's tomb says the prayer Our Father, makes the cross sign, kisses the icon, and prays for what he/she wants. Then, he rolls over the grave three times. Some people roll six or nine times. The pilgrims take soil from the grave and carry it with them, as they believe it protects them. They touch their face with this soil or put it on places where they feel pain or illness. An elderly woman says 'I heard about many healings at the tomb of Saint Agafia. I saw a paralyzed woman. Her husband brought her to pray there, after being for three times there, she returned home on her feet'. The majority of pilgrims believe in these healings, confirming with their own experience, others contest and consider these divine interventions as myths.

An important place of pilgrimage is the relics of *The Blessed Macarie of Saharna* (b. 1888–d. 1969), especially on 26 May, when it is celebrated. His hagiography[31] says that as a child he turned his attention to faith, pilgrimages and in adolescence, he wanted to become a monk. He became hegumen and clergyman of the monastery of Saharna during a period of time when he began healing possessed people through

---

29 Procesul verbal nr. 003 din 26.05.2016 al şedinţei lucrărilor Sinodului Bisericii Ortodoxe din Moldova.
30 'Sfântă din Basarabia: Viaţa şi minunile Sfintei Fericite Agafia de la Cuşelăuca', *Altarul Credinţei*, https://altarulcredintei.md/sfanta-din-basarabia-viata-si-minunile-sfintei-fericite-agafia-de-la-cuselauca/ (accessed on 28.03.2021).
31 Viaţa Cuviosului Macarie, https://manastirea-saharna.md/viata-cuviosului-macarie/ (accessed on 28.03.2021).

prayers, so pilgrims constantly came to him for help. After forced departures to various monasteries in the '50s, he returned to the monastery of Saharna, which in 1964 was transformed into a psychiatric hospital by the Soviet authorities, so the pious Macarie would live for few years in an underground hut in his native village Buciuşca, neighboring the monastery of Saharna. After being exhumed, he was canonized on 21 December 1995, and the bones were taken to the monastery, officially becoming worshiped. His tomb in the village cemetery had become a worship place long before, immediately after his death.

Per usual, the pilgrim is waiting in the queue leading to the relics, often crowded and compact. He is subjected to a psychological and emotional test – the patience of waiting; and of a physical one – standing up. This sacrifice is rewarded by the ecstatic emotion experienced when he approaches the sacred, the holiness that can bring him healing. Pilgrims go worshipping to be cured of skin ailments and mental illnesses. The testimonies record that the people were healed by the saint's apparitions, by the anointing with oil taken from the candle near to the relics, or they worshiped and prayed to his relics.

Sacred Topography: Seclusion and Climbing the Path to the Salvation

Victor Turner claims 'all sites of pilgrimage are believed to be places where miracles once happened, still happen, and may happen again'[32] and this peculiarity in Moldova alongside the religious shrines is revealed by the holy rocks (cliff), caves-hermitages, stones, that gain their reputation of being sacred topography, found within the territory of monasteries and enveloped by various folklore expressions. Also, doing frequent research works in the pilgrimage destinations, group pilgrimages or individual religious visitations, discussing with the people I met at the respective sites, I noticed that almost always these spaces are perceived as therapeutic landscapes.[33]

I will give some examples in this context. For instance, according to the results of archaeological excavations, local history researches, the alphabetical and numerological inscriptions on the walls of the cells, the monastery of Horodişte (Ţipova), dug into the rocky banks of the Dniester River in twelfth – thirteenth centuries, was an astronomical observatory, a solar temple in the pre-Christian period, and a significant Orthodox spiritual center in the Medieval Period.[34] In addition, the monastery was dependent on the monastery of Zograf on Mount Athos,[35] and the monks led a

---

32　Victor Turner and Edith Turner, *Image and Pilgrimage*, p. 6.
33　Wilbert M. Gesler, *Healing Places* (Oxford: Rowman and Littlefield Publishers, Inc., 2003), p. 17.
34　Romeo Cemârtan, Complexul Muzeal Mănăstirea Rupestră Medievală Horodişte', *Buletin Ştiinţific. Revistă de Etnografie, Ştiinţele Naturii şi Muzeologie. Fascicola Etnografie şi Muzeologie*, 25 (38), (2016), pp. 166–76.
35　Sergius Ciocanu, 'Mănăstirea Horodişte de lângă satul Ţipova. Consideraţiuni privind devenirea ei istorică', *Buletin Ştiinţific. Revistă de Etnografie, Ştiinţele Naturii şi Muzeologie. Fascicola Etnografie şi Muzeologie*, 3 (16), (2005), p. 34–35.

hesychast life specific to the Holy Mountain. Over time, this domesticated landscape[36] not only technical but also sacralized, with proven energetic and therapeutic powers has attracted many pilgrims for praying and religious tourists looking for esoteric and paranormal practices,[37] and for making vigils in the cave church and the rock cells. This situation is also appropriate to the fact that many natural monuments (rocks, caves once inhabited by ascetics and hermits) are associated with various legends, and narratives[38] that tell about their power, mysterious events that happened there.

During my ethnographic fieldwork several narratives were recorded showing that pilgrims go to monasteries to legitimate for themselves the sacredness of the place and to express 'the nostalgia for paradise',[39] that they are continuously searching for. At Țipova, where the monks' cells were, there is a rock corridor, where it is believed that an act of synergy between the request, the will, and the prayer of the sinner, and the grace of the Lord offered to him is taking place. People who come there have to fast in advance, meditate, become aware of their sin or that of their relatives, and have deep confidence in the energetic power and holiness of the place. A local story, narrated in the 2000s for attracting the pilgrims, relates that this passage adjusts its entrance space depending on the sins of the individual who wants to go through it. Thus, those with great sins will not be able to pass or will remain blocked, being necessary for the presence of a priest, and the individual to confess them.

The best time of the day for praying in this cell is the sunrise. Before crawling through the passage carved in stone, the pilgrim makes three great acts of reverence, thanking the Creator for everything. When he arrives at the cell, where the first ray of sunshine at the spring equinox enters here, people pray for health.

> A woman came to this rock-cell, and while she was reading the Akathist of Saint Nectarios[40] she was holding white clay in her hand. That's how she loaded it with healing energy. Later, at home, the woman prepared a solution from a spoon of this white clay and a glass of water. And drank it. She thus was cured of bowel cancer.[41]

The effectiveness of such an effort is justified by the interference of three agents: the healing power of the place; the prescribed time (at sunrise) is beneficial for prayer; and the liminal place – a cave in a rocky area, hard to reach.

---

36 John Eade, 'The invention of sacred places and rituals: Comparative study of pilgrimage', *Religions*, 11(12), (2020), p. 649, doi:10.3390/rel11120649.
37 Romeo Cemârtan, 'Destinațiile religioase ale pelerinilor din Republica Moldova', *Buletin Științific. Revistă de Etnografie, Științele Naturii și Muzeologie. Fascicola Etnografie și Muzeologie*, 17 (30), (2012), p. 104.
38 Ludmila Iftodi and Ion Grițcu, *Mănăstirea Țipova* (Chișinău, 2007).
39 Mircea Eliade, *Tratat de istorie a religiilor*, the 5th edn, preface by Georges Dumézil, trans. by Mariana Noica (București: Humanitas, 2013), pp. 388–89.
40 Here is referring to Nectarios of Aegina (b. 1846–d. 1920), which is venerated in Eastern Christian Orthodoxy and celebrated at 9 of November. The believers in their prayers addressed to the saint are asking for healing, especially of cancer diseases.
41 L. L., 51 years old, female, teacher, Horodiște, interviewed in 2021.

Fig. 1: Icons placed on the floor and pieces of paper with wishes written on them. Inside of *the Cave of Vavila* from the monastery of Saharna, 2015. Photograph by Dorina Dragnea.

Another important place for pilgrim's journey is the Cell-Cave[42] of Vavila from the monastery of Saharna (established in 1776). This cell, which belonged to the pious Bartholomew, and was a cave church in the twelfth – fifteenth centuries, is considered to be a hidden, calm and peaceful place. The pilgrims used to put in its walls and cracks small pieces of paper written on them with their wishes or requests, believing in their coming true (Fig. 1). According to other testimonies, in the past, pilgrims collected sand from this cell, which they took with them and scattered around their houses, considering it brought peace to the family. In this cell, prayers and vows are also made, as a seal sign for this, a small icon is placed down next to the wall and a candle is lit.

An interconnection example of the 'apparitional pilgrimage' manifestation with an evidence of a divine consecrated topos is associated with the Grimidon Rock-cliff, at the top of which is a stone with the Mother of God's footprint. Mircea Eliade stated that 'the stones always derive their cult value from the divine presence that transfigured them...'[43] and in our case, this visible evidence of the Mother of God's trace on earth has appeared when She showed herself to the first hegumen of the monastery, Bartholomew, after he kept a period of 40 days of fasting and prayer. She indicated to him the place to build the future monastery (Holy Trinity Church). The local tradition is that every pilgrim who arrives at the monastery climbs to the top of the rock, where a small chapel houses the footprint of the Mother of God. Once

---

42   Such a cave of desires also exists at the Țipova monastery, where pilgrims leave coins and their wishes written on papers.
43   Mircea Eliade, *Tratat de istorie a religiilor*, pp. 245–46.

there, the pilgrims light a candle, make the sign of the cross, worship, pray, and some of them request something in particular. People go up there to find solutions to the problems that grind them, to feel a spiritual relaxation. People overcome the impotence of the body; they 'bring their bodies' [44] to obtain peace of mind. In these moments, the pilgrim expresses a search for himself and of the meditative state, for his interior spiritual life – as many pilgrims assert.

The Healing Springs and the Epiphany of the Water

The faith in the power of the water is proven by the content of a rich practice of folk devotion, ritual baths, and emersions as part of a symbolic rite of passage performed by pilgrims. The pro-eminent impact of concentration and aggregation of pilgrims towards healing springs is fueled by the eternal desire of people to attach themselves to the miraculous and the belief in the power of this thaumaturgic, the vital need for healing, believing in a superior and unearthly force that sanctifies the resources of the earth, proving the indigenous traces of the geopiety.[45]

At the convent of Hâncu (founded in 1678) on the Eve of the Epiphany (18 January, Julian calendar) the waters are sanctified, according to the Eastern Orthodox Christian tradition. The invention consists in the fact that the Liturgy of obtaining *aghiasma* ('holy water') is performed at midnight. Pilgrims gather from the country and abroad to attend it. Being organized in processions they carry *prapuri* ('churchly flags'), icons in their hands, and accompany the priests to the Holy Water Spring on the territory of the convent. After the service, men dressed in white, even children, take a ritual bath in the pool arranged near the spring. Bathing in the water at this time is an act of courage because according to popular belief and calendar it is considered the coldest day of the year. In fact, a ritual exchange takes place; the people try and offer the resistance of their body in exchange for gaining the forgiveness of their sins and spiritual renewal. In such a way the body becomes ritualized because it 'is invested with a 'sense' of ritual' [46] and enters into a ritual process. The pilgrims stated, 'like this, our ancestors have proceeded, we maintain the tradition. After bathing, it's like starting a new life. You feel warm even if it's freezing outside'. At the monastery of Saharna, a similar water sanctification service is held as well, where pilgrims from the northern part of the country gather. This tradition of celebrating the liturgy at night is debated by pilgrims, considering it is organized for attracting people, to generate a spectacular atmosphere. In such a way the variety of events, actions executed in the places of worship indeed respond to the demands and desires of the crowd, so a tacit compromise accepted by both sides is made.

---

44 Michael Winkelman and Jill Dubisch, 'Introduction. The Anthropology of Pilgrimage', in *Pilgrimage and Healing*, ed. by Jill Dubisch and Michael Winkelman (Tucson: The University of Arizona Press, 2005), XXIV.
45 John Kirtland Wright, *Human Nature in Geography*, Fourteen Papers, 1925–1965 (Cambridge: Harvard University Press, 1966), p. 251–52.
46 Catherine Bell, *Ritual Theory, Ritual Practice* (Oxford: University Press, 2009), p. 98.

Additionally, the pilgrims go to the Healing Spring from the last monastery, thoroughly believing in its power and energy. The custom combines the religious ritual, a sincere faith, the psychological aspects, and the people's aura. Before the ritual bath, the pilgrim utters the formula 'Heal my mental and physical ailments with your life-giving source,| Cleanse me, my Lord, to me,| Your sinner servant (name),| From all diseases, temptations, and misfortunes.| In the name of the Father, the Son, and of the Holy Ghost,| Amen'. Then he enters the pool, makes the sign of the cross, immerses, and kisses the wooden cross placed in front of the pool. This act with a thaumaturgical purpose, is performed three times. After the ritual bath, the pilgrim utters 'Thank you, Lord,| For your source of life,| For cleansing the soul and body of your sinful servant (name) from all evil|'.[47] Consequently, he who immerses himself in the waters is like to be renewed from 'old identities and lives'.[48]

There are several apparitional legends and confessions about the healing water springs from the convent of Călărășeuca, located in the north part of the country, recorded more thoroughly since the nineteenth century. According to one, re-shared by pilgrims, when the monastery was lived by monks, during an Easter Liturgy, an angel with seven candles in his hand appeared. He placed one candle in front of the church, where the first spring sprang; he put three candles in the forest, where three other springs sprang up; the angel put the last three in the forest near the monastery, where the other three springs burst. Analysing an interview of the nun Amfilochia from this convent, I noticed the recalling of the holy feminine occurrences[49] at these springs as generator of healing and several testimonies about other divine healing interventions: 'people drink water, bring it home and add it to the bath, believing it heals. A miracle happened to a four-year-old girl who was blind. She came to the convent with her mother. While the mother washed her face with spring water, the little girl told her she saw a woman wearing a blue dress nearby. Her mother didn't believe her. They went home and in a few days, the little girl regained her eyesight. Paralyzed, deaf-mute, blind, people with foot diseases were healed. In this place the miracles are occured by the providence of God'.[50]

In the defile from the monastery of Horodiște (Țipova), some believers, considered to be part of the New Age cults, go at sunrise, under the highest waterfall, because it is where it is thought the living water is. They sit under the current of water and perform energy charging rituals. Previous to these rituals, they fast, and during the last three days, consume only water. While they stand under the waterfall, they take a plant of greater celandine (*Chelidonium majus*), twist it between their fingers and say 'May the God cleanse us, heal us', then they swallow it with nine swallows of water.

---

47 The formula is written on the wall of the building where the pool is located, at the entrance.
48 Veronica Strang, *The Meaning of Water* (Oxford: Berg Publishers, 2006), p. 92.
49 Gary R. Varner, *Sacred Wells: A Study in the History, Meaning, and Mythology of Holy Wells and Waters* (New York: Algora, 2009), pp. 145–50.
50 Cuvintele Credinței. Mănăstirea Călărășeuca, https://www.youtube.com/watch?v=pdSqW7N5oNI (accessed on 23.02. 2021).

The Holy Apotropaic Guards of the Return to the Mundan Life

After passing through the sacred threshold and expressing in gestural, sensory, and verbal form the praise brought to the Divinity, or calling upon his intervention through intense prayers, the pilgrim gradually leaves the capsule of the pilgrimage and returns to the world, to mundane reality. And, to keep in touch with the feeling of safety experienced before, pilgrims always buy ritual objects, which they believe will act as safeguards. There are several categories of items, but the most original are the following. There are very small pillows, which contain pieces of priestly garments, incense, and sometimes pieces of relics. This amulet as a protective symbol is attached to the coat, to remain unseen. Wooden rosaries with the image of the 12 Apostles on them are boutht and worn to protect from evil eyes and maleficent forces. In some monasteries, sanctified protective belts of the 'Mother of God' are sold, which are a purple, red or black cloth ribbon, on which a prayer is written. The former pilgrim girds himself with it, and always wears it. Every pilgrim buys bottles with sanctified water, boxes of incense, myrrh, wax, and oil candles, to use in domestic ritual practices. The offer of the monasteries is more and more oriented towards trade, having the religious tourists as a focus group as well. Colourful beaded bracelets, wood or plastic crosses for worn on the chest, icons, and souvenirs are selling. Eco-food products and health products prepared at the monastery are increasingly appreciated, considering that they are more efficient because the raw material was obtained with prayer and using eco methods.

Conclusion

As outcomes of the research, double edge performances are noticed. Pilgrimage in Moldova represents a form of churchly revival, a rehabilitation of the spiritual life of the local community after a long atheistic period, lasted until 1990. It is as well a medium to discover the sorrows of the people and their endeavour for passing over the socio-economic changes at the beginning of the twenty-first century.

During the procession the pilgrims intensely meditate on their worries and descend with thoughts into the depths of their souls; they try performing every ritual gesture prescribed by church canons and as well of those with folk character, putting in both case their last hope in God's help. The visiting by the pilgrim or even the religious tourist of the caves and the cells carved in stone, once inhabited in hesychasm by hermits or monks, and the spending of an introspective period there; sprinkling with holy water and immersion in the water of healing springs; worship of miracle-working icons and relics; the going to holy altars to pray and read prayers for particular problems and situations; all these ritual behaviours performed in sacred places, during a self-chosen time or a liturgical one, build the pilgrimage path from Moldova.

The faith, motivations, gestures, and beliefs expressed during pilgrimage, recorded as well by testimonies, combine more antinomies like the vivid behaviour of religious bigotry and the beginning of a slightly secularization process. Distinct syncretic elements of the fusion of official Christian Orthodox teachings and pre-Christian reminiscences that have their roots in local history, folk culture and mentality are noticed. The desire for miracles and the contestation of this holy magic remain to be a concurrent attitude. Leisure visitations at the shrines for some and a tense state of prayer for others, displays the particular way of individuals for understanding the holiness, and for taking the necessary peace from the sacred site.

References

Catherine Bell, *Ritual Theory, Ritual Practice* (Oxford: University Press, 2009).
Chris Hann and Hermann Goltz, 'Introduction: The Other Christianity?', *Eastern Christians in Anthropological Perspective*, ed. by Chris Hann and Hermann Goltz (Berkley, Los Angeles, London: University of California Press, 2010), pp. 1–29.
Clifford Geertz, *The Interpretation of Cultures. Selected Essays* (New York: Basic Books, Inc., Publishers, 1973).
Davide N. Carnevale, 'A Context-Grounded Approach to Religious Freedom: The Case of Orthodoxy in the Moldovan Republic', *Religions*, 10 (5), 2019, 314–32.
Emile Durkheim, *The Elementary Forms of Religious Life*, trans. by Karen E. Fields (New York: The Pree Press, 1995).
Gary R. Varner, *Sacred Wells: A Study in the History, Meaning, and Mythology of Holy Wells and Waters* (New York: Algora, 2009).
Heather J. Coleman, 'Introduction: Faith and Story in Imperial Russia', in *Orthodox Christianity in Imperial Russia. A Source Book on Lived Religion*, ed. by Heather J. Coleman (USA: Indiana University Press, 2014), pp. 1–21.
Jill Dubisch, *In a Different Place. Pilgrimage, Gender and Politics at a Greek Island Shrine* (Princeton, N. J.: Princeton University Press, 1995).
John Eade, 'The Invention of Sacred Places and Rituals: Comparative Study of Pilgrimage', *Religions*, 11 (12), (2020), 2–12, doi: 10.3390/rel11120649
John Kirtland Wright, *Human Nature in Geography*, Fourteen Papers, 1925–1965 (Cambridge: Harvard University Press, 1966).
Leighanne Higgins and Kathy Hamilton, 'Therapeutic Servicescapes and Market-Mediated Performances of Emotional Suffering', *Journal of Consumer Research* 45 (2019), 1230–53.
Ludmila Iftodi and Ion Grițcu, *Mănăstirea Țipova* (Chișinău, 2007).
Luminătorul: Jurnal bisericesc, an. 12, nr. 17–18 (1919), 7–8.
Marion Bowman, 'Phenomenology, Fieldwork and Folk Religion', in *Religion: Empirical Studies*, ed. by Steven Sutcliffe (Aldershot: Ashgate, 2004), pp. 3–18.
Michael Winkelman and Jill Dubisch, 'Introduction. The Anthropology of Pilgrimage', in *Pilgrimage and Healing*, ed. by Jill Dubisch and Michael Winkelman (Tucson: The University of Arizona Press, 2005), X–XXXVI.
Mircea Eliade, *Tratat de istorie a religiilor*, the V-th edn, preface by de Georges Dumézil, trans. by Mariana Noica (București: Humanitas, 2013).

Ovidiu Voicu, Jenifer Cash, and Victoria Cojocariu, *Biserică și Stat în Republica Moldova*. Fundația Soros Moldova. Centrul pentru Inovare Publică (Chișinău: Bons Offices, 2017).

Paul Froese and Jones Rory, 'The Sociology of Prayer: Dimensions and Mechanisms', *Social Sciences*, 10 (2021), 15–33.

Raymond Oursel, *Pélerins du Moyen age. Les hommes, les chemins, les sanctuaires* (Paris: Fayard, 1978).

Romeo Cemârtan, 'Patrimoniul cultural și semnificația pelerinajului contemporan', *Buletin Științific. Revistă de Etnografie, Științele Naturii și Muzeologie. Fascicula Etnografie*, 15 (28), (2011), 121–30.

Romeo Cemârtan 'Destinațiile religioase ale pelerinilor din Republica Moldova', *Buletin Științific. Revistă de Etnografie, Științele Naturii și Muzeologie. Fascicula Etnografie*, 17 (30), (2012), 101–08.

Romeo Cemârtan, 'Complexul Muzeal Mănăstirea Rupestră Medievală Horodiște', *Buletin Științific. Revistă de Etnografie, Științele Naturii și Muzeologie. Fascicola Etnografie și Muzeologie*, 25 (38), (2016), 166–76.

Sergius Ciocanu, 'Mănăstirea Horodiște de lângă satul Țipova. Considerațiuni privind devenirea ei istorică', *Buletin Științific. Revistă de Etnografie, Științele Naturii și Muzeologie. Fascicola Etnografie și Muzeologie*, 3 (16), (2005), 24–38.

Simon Coleman, 'Do You Believe in Pilgrimage? Communitas, Contestation and Beyond', *Anthropological Theory*, 2 (3), (2002), 355–68.

Thomas J. Csordas, *The Sacred Self - a Cultural Phenomenology of Charismatic Healing* (Berkeley, Los Angeles, London: University of California Press, 1997).

Veronica Strang, *The Meaning of Water* (Oxford: Berg Publishers, 2006).

Victor Turner and Edith Turner, *Image and Pilgrimage in Christian Culture. Anthropological Perspectives* (New York: Columbia University Press, 1978).

Victor Turner, *The Ritual Process. Structure and Anti-Structure* (Ithaca, New York: Cornell Paperbacks, Cornell University Press, 1977).

Wilbert M. Gesler, *Healing Places* (Oxford: Rowman and Littlefield Publishers, Inc., 2003).

BILJANA ANĐELKOVIĆ

From a Local Sanctuary to the 'Ostrog of Djerdap'

The Role of Monasticism in Creating the Most Visited Pilgrimage Destination in Serbia[1]

In the last few decades, the practice of pilgrimage in Serbia has gained a large number of devotees. The collapse of communism, the creation of a nation-state and numerous social crises are the three most commonly cited reasons for the increased interest in religion, but they do not exhaust all of the complexities of this issue. Seeking answers to this question on an individual level reveals several basic reasons why people visit monasteries: meetings with clergy, getting to know the national history, the belief that monasteries are the only sources of spirituality, etc. However, the largest number of devotees come to monasteries because of the belief that they can find healing in monasteries, or, that they can protect themselves from diseases there. The most visited monasteries of the Serbian Orthodox Church (SOC), not only in recent times but also throughout history, are monasteries that possess a miraculous relic that is believed to bring healing.

The Tumane monastery is currently the most visited monastery of the SOC, with an annual number of visitors ranging from a few hundred thousand to a million.[2] There is not a media outlet in Serbia that hasn't published a story about the monastery or hosted one of the monks with the intention of presenting the 'miracle' taking place in Golubac municipality to the public. My interest in Tumane began some years before the monastery became famous. Between 2012 and 2014, when I was conducting

---

[1] This paper is the result of work at the Institute of Ethnography SASA funded by the Ministry of Education, Science and Technological Development of RS, based on the contract on realization and funding of scientific research at the SRO in 2021, number: 451–03-9/2021–2014/200173. from 05.02.2021.

[2] The data on the number of visitors was stated by the hegumen of the monastery in an interview for the daily newspaper *ALO* on 14 March 2021, https://www.alo.rs/vesti/drustvo/posle-jakih-i-dirljivih-reci-igumana-dimitrija-svi-vernici-ce-se-uputiti-u-manastir-tumane/394809/vest (accessed on 4.04.2021).

Biljana Anđelković • PhD, Research Associate at the Institute of Ethnography of the Serbian Academy of Sciences and Arts, Serbia

Pilgrimage in the Christian Balkan World: The Path to Touch the Sacred and Holy, ed. by Dorina Dragnea, Emmanouil Ger. Varvounis, Evelyn Reuter, Petko Hristov and Susan Sorek (Turnhout, 2023), pp. 239–255.
BREPOLS ❧ PUBLISHERS   DOI 10.1484/M.STR-EB.5.132409

research on folk traditions about SOC monasteries, believed to have been built by Miloš Obilić, Tumane was inhabited by a sisterhood led by Hegumenia Serafima.[3] At that time, the monastery was occasionally visited by locals, as well as pilgrims who would visit sporadically, as part of a pilgrimage to the other monasteries in this area. There was not much information online nor in the media, the monastery had no profiles on social media, and not much historical data was available. The website of the local tourist organization listed sparse information about the monastery, and travel agencies and organizers of pilgrimages seldom offered a visit to Tumane. Changes became more visible when the sisterhood was replaced by a young monastic fraternity led by Hegumen Dimitrije in 2014. As the sudden fame of this monastery coincides with the arrival of the fraternity, the chapter analyzes their role in the creation of the public perception of the monastery. As this is a monastery that has, by some accounts, been active since the Middle Ages, and had never had the importance or 'fame' it has today, one must assume that, over the last few years, something that goes beyond *spiritual magnetism* occurred.[4] This probably has something to do with the promotion of the monastery among local church communities and parishes, among the SOC faithful, and subsequently in the media. In that regard, I will begin with Ian Reader's claim that 'whatever magnetism a pilgrimage site or route might have, in the eyes of potential pilgrims, may not be constant but may be highly contingent on how places are publicized, represented and imaged in the public domain and on how successful other potentially competing pilgrimages may be projected and portrayed by the interest groups surrounding them'.[5] Starting from this standpoint, in this chapter I will present, interpret and analyze the role of the fraternity in the promotion of the monastery, as well as their contribution to redefining the image of the monastery among the pilgrims. The main questions I want to answer in this chapter are: What specific actions of monasticism have contributed to the promotion of monasteries, what type of narrative contributed the most to that, and how open were the media in Serbia to monasticism and the promotion of monasteries? The research data was collected between 2016 and 2020. I have visited Tumane during major religious events in 2017, 2018 and 2020, in order to notice a change primarily in the number of pilgrims and visitors and to establish a link between media promotion of the monastery and a sharp increase in the number of visitors. During each visit to the monastery, I conducted fifteen interviews with the pilgrims to determine *when*, from *whom* and *what* they had heard about the monastery before arriving. I also recorded the visual transformation the monastery underwent in this period. Since the arrival of the fraternity to Tumane, I have followed their activities at the monastery itself, their guest appearances at other parishes, collected their public narratives, analyzed their TV appearances, and spoken with organizers of pilgrimage voyages.

---

3 Miloš Obilić is a legendary character from the Middle Ages mentioned in many epic songs in which he is represented as a hero who killed the Turkish sultan Murat at the Battle of Kosovo in 1389.
4 James Preston, 'Spiritual Magnetism: An Organizing Principle for the Study of Pilgrimage', in *Sacred Journeys. The Anthropology of Pilgrimage*, ed. by Alan Morinis (London: Greenwood Press, 1992), p. 33.
5 Ian Reader, *Pilgrimage in the Marketplace* (New York: Routledge, 2014), p. 39.

Tumane: Location, History, and Folklore

The Tumane monastery is located in the vicinity of Djerdap (the Djerdap gorge), which represents the natural border between Serbia and Romania. In this part of Serbia there was once a large number of hermitages and hermit-monks who engaged in asceticism there. Some of these ascetics are revered saints of the Serbian Orthodox Church today. Saint Zosim Sinait, who had lived close to the contemporary Tumane monastery, is one of them. The cult of this saint, who lived in the fourteenth century, was widespread among the local population who had revered him for centuries, but it had not spread further until recently. There is no reliable data on the original construction and the founder of the monastery. The first mention of a monastery in the village of Tuman is in a Ottoman defter (tax registry) from the sixteenth century, at the time of Murad III (d. 1595).[6] The monastery had been torn down, burned and destroyed many times over its history. The contemporary church was built and consecrated in 1924. The lack of historical data is supplemented by folk oral tradition that states that the Tumane monastery was built by Miloš Obilić, a mythical folk hero, who is believed to have accomplished one of the most important heroic feats in Serbian history: killing the Ottoman Sultan Murad I, during the Battle of Kosovo in 1389. According to folk narrative, Miloš Obilić's castle was situated on the territory of the village Dvorište, not far from the monastery. One on occasion, Miloš went hunting, and accidentally wounded the hermit Zosim at the nearby hermitage. Wanting to help the hermit, Miloš put him on his horse and took him home. However, on their way back, in the place where the contemporary church is, Zosim said *tu mani i pusti me da umrem* ('put me down here and let me die'). As penance for the accident, Miloš Obilić founded the monastery in the spot where the monk died.[7] Before the church was finished, Miloš received a summons from the Serbian prince Lazar that read *tu mani zadužbinu* ('leave your legacy church') and go to the Battle of Kosovo. According to legend, Miloš died in battle, and the church was finished by the locals.

'Renewal': The Development of the Monastery after the Arrival of the Fraternity

An important change and a new chapter in the life of Tumane monastery began with the arrival of the monastic fraternity in October of 2014. One of the youngest fraternity of the SOC began renovating the monastery soon after their arrival. On the state of the monastery at that time the hegumen wrote recently: 'The entire monastery complex was in a bad state [...] Even at first glance, it was clear that we were in for a long and

---

[6] Olga Zirojević, *Crkve i manastiri na područja Pećke patrijaršije do 1683 godine* (Beograd: Istorijski institut i Narodna knjiga, 1984), p. 197; Srećko Petrović, 'Prilog raspravi o nazivu manastira Tuman', *Zbornik Matice srpske za društvene nauke*, 166 (2018), p. 272.

[7] The folk tradition was recorded during the nineteenth century by Јоаким Вујић, *Іоакіма Вуича Славено-Сербскаго Списателя Путешествіе по Сербіи: во кратцѣ собственномъ рукомъ нѣгъ овомъ списано у Крагоевцу у Сербіи* (Будим: Печатано у Славено. Сербской и восточны прочи языка печатни Кралевскога Всеучилища Пештанскаго, 1828).

arduous renovation process'.[8] Even though the monastery was in far better repair than can be gleaned from the hegumen's words, the renovations drew a lot of attention from locals of the neighbouring villages. The curiosity and the desire of the faithful to follow the events at the monastery resulted in more visitors. The work on fixing up the monastery over the last five years encompassed the renovation of the living quarters, the churchyard, the church itself, as well as the building of a *gostoprimnica* (the restaurant),[9] the forming of a petting zoo for children, the renovation of the hermitage of Saint Zosim (wherein Saint Zosim lived and prayed, the hermitage is located one kilometre from the monastery).[10] For the first time the space outside the cave where the ascetic lived has been fixed up, and a building that long stood in disrepair was renovated. Once, this hermitage was a cult place for the locals who brought and left gifts: bouquets of flowers, coins, towels, some food, and drink, even cigarettes as there is a folk belief that the dead can smoke a cigarette or consume alcohol that has been spilled on the ground.[11] The hermitage was desecrated a number of times because of these gifts. Thieves would take the gifts or the money, and sometimes they left rubbish behind or relieved themselves. A summer house was built in the churchyard where a liturgy is held in the open, the economy of the monastery was developed (the cultivation of trout, beekeeping, etc.), and a complete infrastructure was built (a parking lot, a road leading from the monastery to the hermitage, and the riverbed was escarped). Where once there was only a church and the living quarters, now there is a large monastery complex. Nearby there is also a natural spring believed to have healing powers, so the monks repaired the access way to the spring as well.

    The material changes in the monastery correspond to changes in other activities of the fraternity. Simultaneously with the construction and infrastructural works in the monastery, the monks also performed other activities that may have significantly contributed to the monastery being familiar outside the local framework. One of the first and most important was the spread of the cults of the Tumane saints. This was accomplished in a number of ways: by visiting parishes across Serbia, posting on the monastery website or social networks, guest appearances on television, the writing of books and brochures. These activities provided the 'audience' with basic information about the monastery, but also about the 'miracles' that occur there after

---

8 See Ušli smo u hram, otkrili mošti, a crkvom se raširio miomiris! Ovo je priča o manastiru u kome bolesni ozdrave, a zdravi odu sa utehom i mirom, https://www.alo.rs/vesti/drustvo/manastir-tumane-iguman-dimitrije-ispovest/353723/vest (accessed on 25.03.2021).

9 *Gostoprimnica* was built across the road from the monastery, where the monastery mill used to be located. It is along the local road, and faithful, travelers and pilgrims can stop by and order food and drink. The *gostoprimnica* doesn't have prices; the guests leave a contribution for the renovation of the monastery if they wish. This concept relies on the orthodox hospitality which was characteristic of SOC monasteries at the time of their founding in the Middle Ages. The food served here is mostly produced at the monastery (cheese, kajmak, wine, rakija, homemade juice, homemade pies and cakes made according to old monastery recipes, and trout from the monastery fish pond).

10 Vladan Petrović and Ninoslav Golubović, 'The Hermitage of Saint Zosim near the Monastery Tuman (Golubac)', in *Cult Places to the Border*, ed. by Dragoljub B. Đorđević, Dragan Todorović, and Dejan Krstić (Niš: JUNIR, 2014), p. 177.

11 Vladan Petrović and Ninoslav Golubović, 'The Hermitage of Saint Zosim', p. 179.

praying to the saints. The choice of 'miracles', or rather, the narratives about miracles is not surprising, considering the appearance of miracles in churches and monasteries of the SOC has been used since the 1990s to legitimize cult places around which ritual traditions were constructed in order to integrate the (local/ethnic/national) community.[12] Even though miracles always entailed a certain public aspect and had an important role in mobilizing the faithful,[13] the use of new technologies and the media elevated the promotion of miracles to a whole new level. Whereas the use of new technologies and social networks was not a very widespread practice in the monasteries of the Serbian Orthodox Church in that time, it was easier for the monks to impose themselves in relation to other monasteries.

Also important for the promotion of the monastery were the books about it, written by hegumen Dimitrije. The existence of monographs and brochures about monasteries is nothing new and many SOC monasteries have them. They are sold in monastery gift shops and serve to give visitors information about the founder of the monastery, relics held there and the frescoes. However, the fraternity of Tumane introduced an original idea: they hold public promotions of all their books, so a large number of people are informed about each new publication. Also, the sale of their books goes outside the confines of the church – their books – and especially the latest one *Manastir Tumane: čudo ljubavi Božje* ('Tumane monastery: a miracle of God's love'), are not only sold at the monastery and online, but also at kiosks and supermarkets. This shows that the monks are conducting missionary work using all available means in order to reach the wider public and attract more pilgrims to the monastery. On the other hand, the fact that the book is available for purchase outside the monastery indicates that Tumane went beyond the usual framework and ways of public recognition of monasteries by entering the market using well thought out and implemented marketing tools, thereby positioning itself as an element of general cultural heritage as well as part of everyday life, approachable and available to people with different needs and interests. In this way, magnetism, as a form of passive and mystical attraction was practically lost, replaced by active introduction, information, and persuasion. Thus, the fraternity diminishes the possibility of the monastery's identity being constructed by others, faithful or laypeople, simultaneously, to a certain extent, indulging the tastes of the audience.

Promotion of Miracles: Spreading the Cults of the Tumane Saints

The public production of miracles and the promotion of saints always serve to attract the faithful, while attracting a large number of visitors is good for the monasterie's

---

12 Lidija Radulović, '(Hiper) produkcija čuda i čudesnih dela: značenja narodnih i crkvenih interpretacija i njihov značaj za proces desekularizacije u Srbiji', *Etnoantropološki problemi* 7 (2012), p. 912.
13 Lidija Radulović, '(Hiper) produkcija čuda', p. 912.

economy. The production of miracles at Tumane began not a full week after the arrival of the fraternity to the monastery, when the grave of monk Jakov (Arsović) who was buried at the monastery cemetery in 1946 was opened. When the grave was opened, the relics were found intact, with nails, skin, and hair. The relics were transferred to a reliquary which was then taken into the monastery, where they are displayed as one of the most important monastery holy relics. This was the first in a slew of 'miracles' that occurred at the monastery and was the cause for Hegumen Dimitrije to appear as a guest speaker at parishes throughout Serbia over the next few months, and introduce SOC faithful to this strange and mostly unknown monastic figure of the twentieth century, as well as to spread the word of the Tumane monastery. It is interesting that the promotion of the monastery began with this event, as Jakov was not ordained at Tumane, he happened to die at the nearby village Rabrovo, and was buried at the monastery graveyard according to his wishes. Monk Jakov was ordained at Žiča monastery in the 1930s by Bishop Nikolaj Velimirović (1881-1956), who is considered 'one of the best educated people of his time' and one of the 'most important church dignitaries after Saint Sava'.[14] Jakov (Arsović) had a very atypical life journey for a monk. He was ordained in the inter bellum period and was one of the most well educated Serbs of his time: he had obtained two doctorates – one from the Sorbonne and one from the University of Montpellier in France. He had worked at the embassy of the Kingdom of Yugoslavia until the 1930s, when he decided to become a monk. The life of this monk was also atypical as he had chosen an extreme form of asceticism (by twentieth century standards), at least for the SOC, which entailed avoiding communication with other people, rarely sleeping, not eating at the refectory with the other monks and only eating food scraps he found, being scarcely clothed and going barefoot. He was a great missionary; he edited and published a number of Orthodox magazines. For giving out religious texts and praying during WWII, he was arrested and beaten by the German soldiers several times, and after the war he was persecuted by the new communist government. The last time he was beaten by the police was on a train in 1946, just a few days before he died. It is assumed that he died from his injuries. For his perseverance in missionary work in spite of police persecution, he is represented as the personification of resistance to the communist regime that had committed great injustices against the priesthood and monastics of the SOC after World War II. Even though the life of Jakov was presented as an interesting example of Serbian monasticism of the twentieth century, and his relics as 'miraculous relics', this did not attract many faithful or pilgrims to Tumane. What had influenced the influx of faithful and pilgrims to a much larger extent were the narratives the monks recorded about the miracles of Saint Zosim

14 Jovan Byford, *Denial and Repression of Antisemitism: Post-communist Remembrance of the Serbian Bishop Nikolaj Velimirovic* (Central European University Press, 2008). The cult of bishop Nikolaj Velimirović began to develop while he was still alive, because certain church authorities dubbed him 'the thirteenth apostle', 'the Chrysostom of our days' (meaning John Chrysostom), 'a pillar of spirituality', and the elevation of his character and work peaked in 2003, when he was canonized as a saint of the SOC.

Sinait. At one guest appearance in 2016, when talking about Saint Zosim and his miracles the hegumen stated:

> We begin with your temple [...] in order to establish his cult among Orthodox Serbs, as we often go on pilgrimages to different places, outside our country, and often forget those saints and sacred relics that are here, close to us, and that are not only worthy of our attention but quite obviously places where the blessing of God is present. Tumane monastery is a place like that.[15]

Even then it was obvious that, by emphasizing the miracles and miraculous healings in their appearances the monks wanted to draw a parallel to Ostrog monastery, situated in Montenegro, the monastery that was the most visited SOC monastery at the time. In order to emphasize the effect of his words the hegumen told an anecdote he claimed to have heard from the local villagers who had visited Ostrog:

> Down at Ostrog, the monks chastised them. It is alright for you to come here once, but you shouldn't come again. At home you have a great sacred place and a great saint. And he told me: Father, if they hadn't told us [about Tumane] we would've had no idea. [...] Because of all of this and all the lovely miracles we witness every day there, the people somehow recognized this wonderful thread of Saint Zosim and dubbed his monastery 'the Ostrog of Djerdap', comparing Saint Zosim to Saint Vasilije who is, among our people, synonymous with a miracle worker saint.[16]

The mention of Tumane as 'the Ostrog of Djerdap' became more frequent, and just the mention in this context caused much attention and a desire among the faithful to visit Tumane. Comparing Tumane monastery with Ostrog monastery turned out to be a great strategy for recognizing Tumane as an important pilgrimage destination and resulted in an influx of a great number of visitors. Constructing the identity of Tumane as 'the Ostrog of Djerdap' and connecting this monastery with Ostrog in narratives and presentations by the Tumane monastic fraternity, enabled even those less informed to understand that this is a 'healing' monastery. This short syntagm ('the Ostrog of Djerdap'), which contains two territorial denotations (Djerdap and Ostrog), the second of which has a strong and clearly defined symbolic meaning, represents an attempt to, with few words and using a widely understood and accepted cultural code, step out into the public arena with a 'label' that denotes appropriate classification. Connecting a little known monastery with the arguably best known and most visited 'healing' monastery of the SOC that contains one of the most revered relics of the SOC (the relics of Vasilije of Ostrog), arises from the need to represent Tumane to the general public through comparison with something that has a clear and well-acknowledged meaning – 'the holiest place'. The faithful are thus not only given information but are also provided with 'emotion', that in turn calls

---

15 The spiritual gathering where the hegumen spoke was held at the Hram Vaznesenja Gospodnjeg in Žarkovo (Belgrade), in December 2016.
16 Ibid.

for appropriate 'action'. On the other hand, this also serves to give an interesting redistribution of power among holy places. In this way, further respect is given to the monastery that represents the 'role model', the hierarchy among monasteries is further emphasized and supported, but the possibility of 'competition', with the role model as well as other monasteries is also heralded. This is a specific kind of struggle for the faithful, but also an alternative to the distant and expensive Ostrog. It is also a way of strengthening local and regional identity, the narrowing of religious space which serves to point out that the local or regional community can offer the faithful everything they need. This pompous entrance into the public sphere and attempt at gaining 'high monastic status', through association with Ostrog monastery, is, thus, not a static and unilinear strategy for popularizing the monastery, but also, potentially a move toward decentralizing the system of monasteries of the SOC, and redefining their hierarchy, by showing that propaganda can influence the ideas of the faithful, and thus, their movement and choice in the matter of pilgrimage destinations. A monastery can be elevated, but it can also, if there is an interest for it, be easily replaced. Of course, in practice, the church as an institution is not the only factor influencing this process and often cannot channel the behaviour of the faithful as it might want. However, there is no doubt that it is still a very important factor.

'Gathering' and 'Chaos' as Indicators of the Importance of a Sacred Place

The *sabor* ('gatherings') or ('mass gatherings') of the faithful, also called *sabranje* are traditionally organized by all SOC monasteries at important religious holidays. *Sabor* gatherings are a very old practice, with roots in the Middle Ages when monasteries were important administrative church centres and centres of spiritual and social life. In the vicinity of some monasteries, cities, villages and markets developed for centuries, which made them important for the feudal economy.[17] *Sabor* retained their importance during the Ottoman Period in Serbia, as Serbs had the right to gather at monastery churches at the time of the monastery *slava*. It had an important social role in Serbian traditional culture, as relatives from distant places met; people met spouses and traded.[18] Also, it had an important role in the meeting of Serbs from distant parts of the country in the late nineteenth and early twentieth century, which contributed to the 'feeling of unity' of ethnic Serbs.[19] Every SOC monastery celebrates one or more of these gatherings. Annually, the greatest number of the faithful congregates at the monasteries for these events. For this reason, these gatherings can be, and often are, taken as the measure of attendance of a certain monastery, or rather, as a measure of

---

17 Radmila Radić, 'Monasticism in Serbia in the Modern Period: Development, Influence, Importance', in *Monasticism in Eastern Europe and the Former Soviet Republics*, ed. by Ines Angeli Murzaku (New York: Routledge, 2016), p. 191-92.
18 Vladimir Karić, *Srbija: opis zemlje, naroda i države* (Beograd – Novi Sad: Kultura – Pravoslavna reč, 1997 [1887]).
19 Tihomir Đorđević, *Makedonija* (Pančevo: Izdavačka knjižara "Napredak", 1920), p. 159.

importance of the holy place and the respect given to it by the faithful and pilgrims. Before the arrival of the monastic fraternity, Tumane monastery was most visited on the holiday *Cveti* and at the time of the monastery *slava*: *Sabor Svetog arhangela Gavrila*, most of the pilgrims came from the neighbouring villages, meaning that the pilgrimages were local.[20]

After the arrival of the fraternity to the monastery the number of holidays celebrated saw a significant increase. Today, the monastery celebrates the holidays: Prepodobni Zosim i Jakov Tumanski ('Venerable Zosim and Jakov of Tumane'), Obretenje moštiju prepodobnog Jakova Tumanskog ('Discovery/finding of the relics of Saint Jakov of Tumane'), Sveti Nektarije Eginski ('Saint Nectarios of Aegina') – a piece of his relics was received some years ago, Vidovdan, as well as different jubilees (the monastery celebrated 80 years since the discovery of the relics of Saint Zosim, and 70 years since the death of Saint Jakov in August 2016, in 2019 the monastery celebrated 630 years of existence, during 2020 the relics were put into new reliquaries and 100 years since the death of Saint Nectarios of Aegina were celebrated, etc.). These celebrations are a way for the fraternity to keep the dynamic of their relationship to the public high, always finding a new reason for mass gatherings of the faithful at the monastery.

One of the most important *sabor* gatherings at the monastery, and the event that greatly contributed to the fame of the monastery and the interest of the media and pilgrimage travel agencies was held in May 2017. This event entailed the redressing of the relics of Saint Zosim, Jakov (Arsović) was canonized as a Saint of the SOC, and the renovated hermitage of Saint Zosim was consecrated. During the event, the monastery was visited by almost 15,000 people, which was an exceptionally large number for an, as of yet, unknown monastery.[21] The event was attended by bishops of the SOC, employees of the government office for relations with religious groups, businessmen, the local population, and pilgrims. Almost all travel agencies that organize pilgrim voyages in Serbia brought at least one bus full of pilgrims, and kilometres long rows of cars and busses attested to the great number of people who wanted to witness the event. Frequent guest appearances by Hegumen Dimitrije at spiritual gatherings and roundtables, in religious radio and television programs that preceded

---

20 *Slava* is a Serbian Orthodox Christian tradition of the ritual glorification of one's family's patron saint. In addition to Christmas and Easter, it is the most important family ceremony that venerates a family's patron saint. The *slava* is also celebrated by monasteries because monastery churches usually have the name of the saint to whom the church is dedicated and whose day is celebrated in the church calendar.

21 During religious holiday celebrations or important jubilees monasteries are often attended by a few hundred up to a few thousand people. The exceptions are some monasteries such as Ostrog, Đunis and some others that are visited by 10,000–20,0000 pilgrims during celebrations. The number of pilgrims usually isn't bigger than this, but in the past there have been examples of 100,000 to 200,000 people attending important jubilees such as the celebration of 600 years of Studenica monastery. See Vjekoslav Perica, *Balkan Idols: Religion and Nationalism in Yugoslav States* (New York: Oxford University Press, 2002). These were extremely large gatherings of the faithful which were possible at a specific moment of Serbian history, when the awakening of Serbian national identity occurred and a large number of people went to monasteries, among other things, to affirm their ethnic and national identity.

the event, as well as activity on social networks were of great importance in informing the faithful about the event.[22] As he is aware that, for many of the faithful, an individual trip to the monastery is neither simple nor cheap, the hegumen sometimes pointed them toward organizers of pilgrim voyages who would 'gather a group and visit the monastery', which made organizing easier for interested pilgrims. The recognition of the importance of establishing cooperation between the organizers of pilgrim voyages and the monastic fraternity certainly helped the promotion of the monastery and its saints. In Serbia it is common practice for the organizers of pilgrim voyages to give out information about future tours after each trip, so the annunciation of the pilgrimage to Tumane and the redressing of the relics of Saint Zosim in May 2017 lasted a couple of months. The redressing of the relics was heralded as something 'the faithful should not miss'.[23] In this way, it was suggested that this event will become important both for the monastery and the SOC, but also for the 'story' they will later be able to 'tell their descendants'.

It was expected that this gathering will be specific in a lot of ways, as the redressing of relics is not done often within the SOC, and the canonization of a saint is, in itself, an important event.[24] For many of the faithful, the most important motive for attendance was the redressing of the relics of Saint Zosim. I assume that, at that time, neither the pilgrims nor the organizers of the pilgrim voyages expected that the redressing of the relics will become common practice: on the initiative of the fraternity, redressing is now done annually. It is uncertain whether the monks themselves knew how large of an influence their guest appearances at

---

22   At a number of spiritual gatherings I attended in parish churches in Belgrade a few months before the *sabor* in 2017, I spoke to the gathered faithful, and many of them hadn't heard about the monastery. I met a small number of those who had visited it, but it turned out they were originally from that part of Serbia. For the audience, the miracles that accompanied the renovation of the monastery were a confirmation of 'God's activity in that place' and 'the force of God that appeared in our time'. Aside from the miracles that accompanied the renovation, the monks spoke about the miraculous healing that happened to those who prayed to Saint Zosim. They mostly chose examples of serious diseases such as cancer, leukemia, sepsis, tumors as well as sterility in married couples which was cured after praying at the relics Saint Zosim. These narratives greatly influenced the rise in interest for the monastery as well as the spread of the cult of Saint Zosim. Some of these stories were published in a small book right before the sabor gathering in May 2017, and distributed free with one of the most circulated daily newspapers in the country ('Alo'), about a week before the gathering. More than a 100 thousand copies of the book were distributed. Even though it is impossible to determine the full effect the book and other texts about Tumane had on the number of pilgrims in 2017, it can certainly be concluded that it introduced a great number of readers to Saint Zosim, as I had seen many people on public busses reading the book. During his guest appearances the hegumen invited the faithful to 'come to the monastery to bow to the holy place and the saints of Tumane'.
23   One of the guides I had travelled to other monasteries with a month before, heralded the gathering at Tumane as 'historically important' and said that we should attend the 'prayer events' that day so we could later 'tell our grandchildren that we were part of the event'.
24   Some of the more frequent redressing of relics are the redressing of the relics of Saint Vasilije of Ostrog that takes place every 7 years, and the redressing of bishop Nikolaj that takes place every 10 years. The relics of other saints are redressed a lot less often. For example, in 2010 the relics of Saint Stefan of Piper were transferred to a new reliquary, they were redressed after 300 years, and the reliquary is replaced every 100 years.

various venues would have. Judging by the look of the *sabor* gathering in May 2017, one could conclude that the number of pilgrims overcame the expectations of the fraternity. It was obvious that the monastics planned ahead and put great effort into the organization of the event. Parking space for pilgrim busses was organized, traffic police regulated the traffic, and tour guides were given programs with a timetable in order to prepare the faithful and possibly instruct them on how to behave. However, the number of vehicles and pilgrims even in the early morning was so great that it became obvious that it would be hard to keep order in such a great mass of people. All around the monastery it was 'chaos'. The timetable and program were disrupted, and no one knew what was happening inside the church: whether the liturgy had started, whether it had ended, whether the relics had been redressed, etc. In the huge crowd, a number of people waiting to bow to the relics fainted due to exhaustion, hunger, heat and lack of oxygen. People were shoving each other, wanting to get into the church as soon as possible and bow to the relics of Saint Jakov of Tumane and the miraculous icon of the Mother of God of Kursk. Because of this, a pilgrim woman standing in front of me began to cry, commenting that the situation is not 'very Christian'. One organizer who had brought two busses with about 150 pilgrims that day said she would never bring pilgrim groups to Tumane during big holidays again.[25] The situation I observed was the opposite of the feeling of calm, comfort and the feeling of *sabornost* ('togetherness').[26] Moreover, the pilgrims were angry, fought amongst themselves, shoved each other, and the atmosphere was tense and uncomfortable. It was also chaos outside the renovated hermitage, where it was planned for the relics of Saint Zosim to be brought in a lity procession. The pilgrims who had visited the hermitage as a cult place before wanted to go into it, which was forbidden. They did not understand that the basic idea of the fraternity was to have the reliquary taken into the renovated hermitage first, or it hadn't mattered to them as they were used to seeing it empty. The pilgrims who were there for the first time also did not know what the 'custom' was and how they should behave. The invention of new traditions and the introduction of new holidays and *sabor* meetings is part of the process of constructing the new identity of a monastery and inevitably lead to mismanagement and confusion amongst all the actors. Many of the actors feel confused and somewhat fearful because of the lack of knowledge and, to a degree, misunderstanding of the process as a whole and the intentions of other actors in the process. We can assume that new things are introduced with a certain intent, that there are a number of ideas or concepts which go through a certain 'procedure' of acceptance, which is marked by different ways of adapting to the capabilities and

---

25 The comment of this organizer is important, especially keeping in mind that next year she brought a group that was almost double in size. This example shows how much the interest in visiting Tumane grew in about a year, and the extent to which the organizers are, despite personal attitudes, dependent on the economic gain provided by such events. It shouldn't be forgotten that most organizers promote future pilgrimages during the bus rides, meaning that, during mass events they advertise to a huge number of pilgrims.
26 The concept of 'sabornost' is in many ways similar to the concept of *communitas* suggested by Victor Turner (1969).

requirements of the SOC and the monastery itself. Also, the introduction of new things shows the extent to which the fraternity really understood the needs of the pilgrims or the faithful, the extent to which it managed to bring the monastery closer to them, or rather the extent to which the faithful managed to understand and bring themselves closer to the 'ideas' of the fraternity. Collision or discrepancy between what was thought up on an institutional level on the one hand, and what is put into effect on the individual level on the other, is solved by mutual understanding, communication and changing dispositions. The fraternity of Tumane monastery seems to display great flexibility, anticipating events in advance and fining solutions in a timely manner. However, in many cases, the events they put into motion exceed them, both conceptually and organizationally.

After this *sabor* gathering the interest in visiting the monastery skyrocketed. Even though I had recorded many comments of dissatisfied pilgrims that day, many of whom were revolted by the huge crowd, and because they had not managed to get a piece of Saint Zosim's vestment,[27] the coming days and weeks proved my assumption that the pilgrimage to Tumane had not met the faithful's expectations wrong. The pilgrims who had been there that day spoke delightedly of their experience. All the negative impressions were erased from their stories. No one mentioned that many of the faithful did not get to bow to the relic of Saint Zosim, nor get a piece of the vestment, neither there was a huge crowd. Moreover, those who did mention the crowd emphasized it in a positive manner, because the huge number of people was 'proof that it's a very holy place'. Those who had not been there felt like they missed out on something great and important, and wanted to go on a pilgrimage to Tumane. The huge interest of the faithful had gotten this monastery onto the itinerary of pilgrimage agencies more often than in previous years.

After this *sabor* gathering, the organization of the events remained more or less the same, except that the number of people was greater every time. Aside from Ostrog monastery, Tumane became the only monastery on regular offer at tourist agencies in almost all cities in Serbia. 'The phenomenon of Tumane' and 'the number of miracles at Tumane' were topics often discussed in the media. The hegumen and the monks were often in the public eye through guest appearances in different local and regional programs – informative, news, entertainment and religious. A number of reports dealt with biographies, their personal stories and roads that led them to the monastery. This was an efficient way (maybe without conscious forethought) to bring them closer to the faithful and the pilgrims. Even the pilgrims who came to the monastery for the first time had the feeling that they knew the monks, which contributed to their feeling of closeness to the fraternity. In their relationship with the pilgrims the monks are very open and friendly. They used their presence in the public eye to get closer to the faithful and lessen the

---

27 After the redressing of the relics of Saint Zosim, the old vestment was cut into pieces and given out to the faithful. It turned out that there weren't enough pieces for all the gathered visitors, which was a clear sign that the number of pilgrims exceeded the expectations of the monastic fraternity. Official pilgrim agencies got a piece of cloth which they gave out to the pilgrims, while others were left out.

distance that is usually present between monks and laypeople. In this context, two of the monks, with the blessing of the hegumen, continued to nurture the love of rock'n'roll and heavy metal they had before being ordained. Their repertoire contains songs by Iron Maiden, Metallica, Deep Purple and others. Their acoustic cover of Iron Maiden's 'Wasting Love' had over 70,000 views on YouTube in three days. Even though there has been some critique by conservative faithful and representatives of the church because of the music they play, many found it 'very cute'. This is not the only reason the fraternity received criticism. Part of the public and the church critiques the fraternity for over commercializing the monastery, but the fact remains that the fraternity really managed to attract the faithful and create a sense of camaraderie among them. Even though in the first few years it was not like that, nowadays the pilgrims who go to the *sabor* gatherings are much more patient, careful and used to crowds. It is also apparent that there is a certain order and that the pilgrims know how to behave better than they did in the first years after the arrival of the fraternity. The fraternity introduced the practice of reading out prayers every hour which is one of the main reasons the faithful come to the monastery. Also, they gave the impression of a team at the service of people who come to the monastery. Pilgrims who visit the monastery, even those not familiar with the rules or those who are not religious, feel 'love and acceptance' from the fraternity. Not only does the monastic fraternity accept all people who come to the monastery, regardless of ethnic or religious belonging, the faithful and others who hear about the miraculous healings at the monastery but cannot come themselves, call on the phone and ask about reading out prayer, and the monks oblige them. Even though many monasteries of the SOC are visited by members of other confessions, this is not public data. The monks of Tumane however openly speak about how members of all peoples and faiths are welcome at the monastery if they approach the saints with faith.

In a recent interview the hegumen spoke about the critics of Tumane: 'You can never please the malicious and the envious, whoever they might be. And if they do not like the mission and concept of Tumane, let them make better where they are. We are here to support them'.[28] The hegumen of the monastery is aware of the road that needed to be taken in order to create a sacred place like Tumane. Regardless of the critique aimed at the monastics, the number of people who come to Tumane and show gratitude to the fraternity is a clear indicator that people find what they need at Tumane monastery. The fraternity offers the pilgrims what they expect and what they visit monasteries of the SOC for in the first place: hospitality, holy relics, a piece of national mythology, history, miraculous healings, and beautiful natural surroundings connected to tourist centers such as Golubac and Srebrno Jezero.

---

28 See Posle jakih i dirljivih reči igumana Dimitrija, svi vernici će se uputiti u manastir Tumane!, https://www.alo.rs/vesti/drustvo/posle-jakih-i-dirljivih-reci-igumana-dimitrija-svi-vernici-ce-se-uputiti-u-manastir-tumane/394809/vest?fbclid=IwAR2huFjkIAa17cg6Sm3VIvCsBtJSxpN2EPugyAqGBNvYrJ6ij2E9G-Pct5g (accessed on 29.03.2021).

Tumanci: A World of Dedicated Faithful

Through their openness to pilgrims of varying levels of religious knowledge and education, the fraternity try to attract the faithful with different narratives and symbolism, adapting to the needs of the pilgrims. One of the more important narratives is that Tumane monastery is a sacred place 'renovated by the people' and that 'belongs to the people'.[29] Hegumen Dimitrije once said: 'I have always said that this monastery belongs to all those who love it and pray to God within it. People of different faiths come, and all are welcome because all are God's children. The Orthodox are here in the wholeness of liturgic community, this should be emphasized. Others come to pray. There are many examples of the saints helping people of other faiths. The kind of faith and the kind of heart one brings determines the kind of gift they receive'.[30] It is a very specific discourse because it redefines the very concept of a monastery, which is, by definition 'the home of monks', a place where they go in order to separate themselves from the 'world' and diminish their contacts with society at large. The fraternity of Tumane monastery continually sends the message that they want to attract that 'world', that they are 'here for the people', thus displaying a modern version of monasticism entirely open and appealing to the faithful. Because the fraternity is not numerous enough to cover the organizational needs of receiving a large number of pilgrims, the monks had to enlist the help of the faithful. In this was they created a circle of people who help the monastery with different segments of preparation for large events. This group of people the monks named *Tumanci* (the people close to the Tumane monastery). Over time, this name came to refer to all those who directly or indirectly contribute to the development of the monastery or to the increase in the numbers of faithful who come to the monastery. Regarding this community, one of the monks, father Petar said:

> What I noticed, this phenomenon so to speak, is that Tumane monastery is not only comprised of the fraternity, but that there are people all over Serbia and elsewhere who feel like they are *Tumanci*. That is what they call themselves. There are always welcome. They participate in the life of this monastery, come here often, help, they have their role [...] The fraternity of Tumane is expanding and becoming a big family, a church community that goes beyond the fraternity itself.[31]

The formation of an informal community of faithful and the monastic fraternity, recognized by both the faithful and the monks contributed to the creation of a very specific image of the monastery among pilgrims. Moreover, it led to a redefining of the concept and primary function of the monastery because the pilgrims came to accept the idea that 'the monastery lives only when we visit it' and that 'when you visit Tumane monastery you experience the wholeness of monastic life which is open to

---

29 See Posle jakih i dirljivih reči igumana Dimitrija..., (accessed on 29.03.2021).
30 See Posle jakih i dirljivih reči igumana Dimitrija..., (accessed on 29.03.2021).
31 See Sampanjac sa Jasminom Anom 349 Manastir Tumane, https://www.youtube.com/watch?v=mWRib4qrWS0 (accessed on 2.09.2020).

people. Therefore, it is not only for the monks, but for everyone', as one devotee said. The monastic fraternity created an atmosphere that is open to anyone visiting the monastery for whatever reason – healing, thankfulness for answered prayers, curiosity, spiritual searching, or the desire to spend a nice weekend at the monastic holdings. In the meantime, the fraternity uses the opportunity to attract people to attend the liturgy and Holy Communion. This monastery displays a certain 'trend' within the SOC: that the measure of strength of a monastery should be the number of people who visit it. Throughout history, the strength of the SOC monasteries was determined by the number of holy people staying at the monastery, or by the size of the brotherhood or sisterhood living there. The building of a large number of monasteries by the SOC in postsocialism caused a lesser number of monks/nuns at the monasteries themselves, because the extant monastics were distributed to the new monasteries. Thanks to religious tourism and mass pilgrimages, as well as the creation of representative holy places, the not so little issue of the lack of monastics in the SOC is obscured.

Conclusion

The transformation of Tumane from a small, unknown monastery to the most visited pilgrimage site of the SOC occurred so fast and unexpectedly that it was impossible not to wonder which factors contributed to it. In this chapter, I focused on one of the most important - on the promotion of Tumane monastery by the monastic fraternity, who are positioned the monastery on the map of pilgrimage tourism as the biggest healing shrines of the SOC. However, it is clear that the monastic fraternity, without the help of other actors, could not have completely independently influenced this transformation. The organizers of spiritual tribunes and pilgrimages, representatives of local and state institutions, local villagers, salesmen of local produce and others also contributed. The media support the monastery received was far greater than the support given to any other monastery, including those who were also known for miraculous healing. The fact that various individuals and institutions, including the SOC leadership, supported the efforts of the monastic fraternity in commercializing the sanctuary by promoting miracles shows a high degree of tolerance for tendance a magical relationship to relics, which is still widespread among Orthodox believers. A large number of believers, as research shows, continue to go on pilgrimages to meet practical needs (such as healing, for example), while others expect to strengthen their national identity by visiting SOC monasteries.

The Tumane monastery was suitable because it was able to adapt its identity formula to the current demands of the market. Based on the anthropological analysis, it can be concluded that the monastic fraternity has almost complete control over the narratives about the monastery, as well as over their distribution. All the stories and all the practices that are carried out in the monastery, including the new ones (such as redressing of the relics, a lity procession to the hermitage, etc.) began after their arrival. Also, they began to spread the cult of Tuman saints, which was necessary in order to draw the attention of the religious and the general public to the monastery. The fraternity has shown the ability to mobilize a huge number of believers, which is the largest capital of the Tumane monastery and can be extremely important in achieving different social and political goals. The success of the fraternity lies in the fact that some of the biggest SOC shrines are located in other countries (Hilandar on Mount Athos, Ostrog in Montenegro…), while many SOC monasteries are in Kosovo and Metohija where most Serbs can hardly come. It is obvious that, for several reasons, the part of the public in Serbia that is in favor of the SOC had the need for a new object of identification, gathering and worship. In such circumstances, the monastic fraternity, with great effort and commitment, created the 'the Ostrog of Djerdap' outside Montenegro and the endowment of Miloš Obilic, i.e. 'Kosovo shrine outside Kosovo'. Thanks to timely observation and recognition of that need, the monastic fraternity adequately responded to it, thoughtfully uniting different discourses and practices based on them.

References

Ian Reader, *Pilgrimage in the Marketplace* (New York: Routledge, 2014).

James Preston, 'Spiritual Magnetism: An Organizing Principle for the Study of Pilgrimage', in *Sacred Journeys. The Anthropology of Pilgrimage*, ed. by Alan Morinis (Westport, Conecticut - London: Greenwood Press, 1992), pp. 31- 46.

Jovan Byford, *Denial and Repression of Antisemitism: Post-communist Remembrance of the Serbian Bishop Nikolaj Velimirovic* (Central European University Press, 2008).

Јоаким Вујић, *Іоакіма Вуича Славено-Сербскаѓо Списаѫеля Путешествіе по Сербіи: во кратцѣ собственномъ рукомъ нѣѓ овомъ списано у Краѓоевцу у Сербїи* (Будим: Печатано у Славено. Сербской и восточны прочи языка печатни Кралевскоѓа Всеучилища Пештанскаѓо, 1828).

Lidija Radulović, '(Hiper)produkcija čuda i čudesnih dela: značenja narodnih i crkvenih interpretacija i njihov značaj za proces desekularizacije u Srbiji', *Etnoantropološki problemi* 7(2012), 919–33.

Olga Zirojević, *Crkve i manastiri na područja Pećke patrijaršije do 1683 godine* (Beograd: Istorijski institut i Narodna knjiga, 1984).

Radmila Radić, 'Monasticism in Serbia in the Modern Period: Development, Influence, Importance', in *Monasticism in Eastern Europe and the Former Soviet Republics*, ed. by Ines Angeli Murzaku (New York: Routledge, 2016), pp. 190 - 217.

Srećko Petrović, 'Prilog raspravi o nazivu manastira Tuman', *Zbornik Matice srpske za društvene nauke*, 166 (2018), 263 - 280.

Tihomir Đorđević, *Makedonija* (Pančevo: Izdavačka knjižara "Napredak", 1920).

Victor Turner, *The Ritual Processs: Structure and Anti-Structure* (Ithaca-New York: Cornell Paperbacks - Cornell University Press, 1969).

Vjekoslav Perica, *Balkan Idols: Religion and Nationalism in Yugoslav States* (New York: Oxford University Press, 2002).

Vladan Petrović and Ninoslav Golubović, 'The Hermitage of Saint Zosim Sinait near the Monastary Tuman (Golubac)', in *Cult Places to the Border*, ed. by Dragoljub B. Đorđević, Dragan Todorović, and Dejan Krstić (Niš: JUNIR, 2014), pp. 173 - 86.

Vladimir Karić, *Srbija: opis zemlje, naroda i države* (Beograd – Novi Sad: Kultura – Pravoslavna reč, 1997 [1887]).

Online sources

Posle jakih i dirljivih reči igumana Dimitrija, svi vernici će se uputiti u manastir Tumane!, https://www.alo.rs/vesti/drustvo/posle-jakih-i-dirljivih-reci-igumana-dimitrija-svi-vernici-ce-se-uputiti-u-manastir-tumane/394809/vest?fbclid=IwAR2huFjkIAa17cg6Sm3VIvCsBtJSxpN2EPugyAqGBNvYrJ6ij2E9G-Pct5g (accessed on 29.03.2021).

Sampanjac sa Jasminom Anom 349 Manastir Tumane, https://www.youtube.com/watch?v=mWRib4qrWS0 (accessed on 2.09.2020).

Ušli smo u hram, otkrili mošti, a crkvom se raširio miomiris! Ovo je priča o manastiru u kome bolesni ozdrave, a zdravi odu sa utehom i mirom, https://www.alo.rs/vesti/drustvo/manastir-tumane-iguman-dimitrije-ispovest/353723/vest (accessed on 25.03.2021).

VASSILIKI CHRYSSANTHOPOULOU

Revitalizing Identity through Pilgrimage to an Aegean Island

Memory, Ritual Practice and Communal Belonging at the Annual Celebration of Saint Panteleimon's Feast in Saria, Greece

An Identity-constructing Pilgrimage Employing a Distinct Vernacular Idiom

This paper explores the annual pilgrimage to the church of Saint Panteleimon on Saria, a depopulated Aegean Island, and its effects on the maintenance and transmission of social values, religious beliefs and cosmological ideas, and especially on the revitalization and negotiation of communal identity among pilgrims. It draws its inspiration and its ethnographic material from my participation in this pilgrimage on 26 and 27 July 2009.

Saria is a small island north of the larger island of Karpathos in the southeastern Aegean. The inhabitants of the village of Olymbos, lying in the north of Karpathos, made their living from agriculture and animal husbandry during the nineteenth and the twentieth century up to the 1970s in Saria, when economic changes and migration caused its depopulation. Since then, *Sariátes*[1] and other Olymbitans have returned there annually to celebrate the feast of Saint Panteleimon, on 26 July (vespers) and on 27 July (the Saint's memory).

There are several aspects to this pilgrimage deserving of analysis, some of which we explore here. First this is a pilgrimage occurring on a depopulated island. The pilgrims go there both to venerate Saint Panteleimon on his feast and to recall life on the island and their ancestors, who lived there, which they do by celebrating together, sharing collective memories, and reflecting on and thus revitalizing their identity. This local, identity-constructing pilgrimage is an example of a type of pilgrimage, in which once inhabited, but now deserted ancestral places are visited. These pilgrimages occur at various religious sites in Greece, and possibly in other areas of the Balkans.

---

1 People, whose families were settled on Saria in the past.

Vassiliki Chryssanthopoulou • Associate Professor in Folklore Studies at the Department of Philology, National and Kapodistrian University of Athens, Greece

Pilgrimage in the Christian Balkan World: The Path to Touch the Sacred and Holy, ed. by Dorina Dragnea, Emmanouil Ger. Varvounis, Evelyn Reuter, Petko Hristov and Susan Sorek (Turnhout, 2023), pp. 257–278.
BREPOLS PUBLISHERS   DOI 10.1484/M.STR-EB.5.132410

Such annual pilgrimages also function as *antamómata* or 'reunions', since they bring together individuals who are connected with sacred places through a shared sense of origin, past and belonging, symbolically expressed by the sacred site (church or monastery) to which the pilgrimage is made. Participation is easier than it might be, because of the time of year when these festive celebrations (*paniyíria*) and/or pilgrimages (*proskynímata*) to saints' shrines take place, namely during the summer months, when people can take their holidays. Such pilgrimages provide the opportunity for pilgrims to express, negotiate and restructure their religious and social identities.[2]

And so, we look here at the vernacular ritual practice of the *glendi* pursued by the pilgrims. This is a communal celebration involving traditional music and the singing of *mantinádes* or improvised rhyming couplets extemporized by the singers in the church courtyard during the communal meals held on the eve and on the day of the saint's feast after the church services.[3] Such vernacular ritual practices, which

---

[2] On feasts and festivals in Greece, see Ευάγγελος Αυδίκος, Εορταί και πανηγύρεις. Σύνορα, λαϊκά δρώμενα και τελετές (Θεσσαλονίκη: Επίκεντρο, 2017). On religious festivals and their rituals, see Μανόλης Γ. Βαρβούνης, Θεμελιώδεις έννοιες και μορφές της ελληνικής θρησκευτικής λαογραφίας (Αθήνα: Στρατηγικές εκδόσεις Ι. Φλώρος, 2013), pp. 346–50. Pontian Greeks' pilgrimages to the monastery of the All Holy One of Soumelá (*Panayia Soumelá*) in their historical homeland in Turkey, as part of 'tourism of nostalgia', have been researched in Μυροφόρα Ευσταθιάδου, Ταξιδεύοντας στον Πόντο. Τουρισμός της νοσταλγίας (Αθήνα: Μένανδρος, 2018). On the importance of summer festivals and pilgrimages in Greece, see, among others, Δημήτριος Σ. Λουκάτος, Τα καλοκαιρινά (Αθήνα: Εκδόσεις Φιλιππότη, Λαογραφία-Παράδοση 3, 1981), p. 100. On Castellorizian Greek-Australians' pilgrimages to the Holy Land as a rite of passage in the mid-1980s, see Βασιλική Χρυσανθοπούλου, 'Οι Χατζήδαινες της Πέρθης', Λαογραφία, 33 (1982–1984), 130–54. Jill Dubisch investigated the popular pilgrimage to the church of the All Holy One (*Panayía*) of the Annunciation on the Aegean island of Tinos by focusing on the idea of the journey for the pilgrims and for the researcher; see Jill Dubisch, *In a Different Place. Pilgrimage, Gender, and Politics at a Greek Island Shrine* (Princeton, New Jersey: Princeton University Press, 1995).

[3] 'Glendi' is a term used to signify communal or group celebrations involving eating, drinking, music and dance throughout Greece. 'Glendia' (plural of 'glendi') have evolved over the years to include new cultural and material elements that symbolize the social and economic transformations of particular communities. The *glendi* on the island of Karpathos ('karpathiko glendi'), however, and especially its more traditional version as practised by Olymbitans ('olymbitiko glendi'), presents distinctive features revolving round the communal discourse expressed by improvised oral composition and singing. These *glendia* have been studied extensively by folklorists and anthropologists in their various dimensions and have been included in the Greek National Inventory of Intangible Cultural Heritage of the Hellenic Ministry of Culture and Sports (see http://ayla.culture.gr > karpathiko-glenti-2019; http://ayla.culture.gr > olympitiko-glenti). On the Karpathian and the Olymbitan *glendi* see, among others, Anna Caraveli, 'The Symbolic Village: Community Born in Performance', *Journal of American Folklore*, 98 (1985), 259–86. Pavlos Kavouras, 'Glendi and Xenitia: The Poetics of Exile in Rural Greece (Olymbos, Karpathos)' (unpublished doctoral thesis, New School for Social Research, Ann Arbor, Michigan, U.M.I., 1990). Μαρία Γ. Ανδρουλάκη, 'Το γλέντι στην Όλυμπο Καρπάθου, Τεχνικές Συλλογικής Έκφρασης και Επικοινωνίας', in *Κάρπαθος & Λαογραφία, Δ΄ Διεθνές Συνέδριο Καρπαθιακής Λαογραφίας [Κάρπαθος, 8–12 Μαΐου 2013]*, ed. by Μηνάς Αλ. Αλεξιάδης and Πόπη Κ. Ξανθάκου (Αθήνα: Ινστιτούτο Λαϊκού Πολιτισμού Τμήματος Φιλολογίας, Ε.Κ.Π.Α. – Καρπαθιακός Οργανισμός Πολιτισμού, Άθλησης, Παιδείας Δήμου Καρπάθου, 2016), pp. 178–91. Βασιλική Χρυσανθοπούλου, 'Ο τόπος της πατρίδας στο λόγο και στις εθιμικές τελετουργίες των Καρπαθίων της Καμπέρρας Αυστραλίας', in *Κάρπαθος & Λαογραφία, Γ΄ Διεθνές Συνέδριο Καρπαθιακής Λαογραφίας [Κάρπαθος, 21–26 Μαρτίου 2006]*, ed. by Μηνάς Αλ. Αλεξιάδης (Αθήνα: Πνευματικό Κέντρο Δήμου Καρπάθου & Νομαρχιακή Αυτοδιοίκηση Δωδεκανήσου – Επαρχείο Καρπάθου, 2008), pp. 1027–74.

powerfully symbolize such pilgrimages, are often discernible in local or regional pilgrimages that attract members of certain cultural groupings, as is the case with the pilgrimage examined here.[4]

As various scholars of religion and folklore point out, the concept of 'vernacular religion' looks at religion as experienced, understood and practiced by people themselves in their individual and collective diversity.[5] This concept takes us beyond rigid dichotomies of 'official' and 'folk' religion, in that it pays attention 'to the process of religious belief, the verbal, behavioural, and material expressions of religious belief, and the ultimate object of religious belief.'[6] Such a concept allows one to examine individual and collective manifestations of faith, belief, and ritual with greater freedom in the context of pilgrimages and other religious events. This analytical tool is especially suitable in the case of groups with a long or even ancient religious tradition, in which several generations of worshippers have contributed to shaping a system of communal belief and ritual practice founded on their particular historical and environmental circumstances.[7] Here we attempt to demonstrate the ways in which community discourse expressed through this vernacular ritual idiom revolves round the saint and his church and reveals him, his church and his pilgrimage to be key symbols of Olymbitan identity.

Research Methodology

The largest part of the ethnographic information presented and analyzed in this paper derives from my participation in, and recording of, the pilgrimage to Saint Panteleimon

---

4 On the difficulty of trying to develop general models of pilgrimage and on pilgrimage 'as a highly complex and multifaceted phenomenon', see Dubisch, *In a Different Place*, p. 44.
5 On vernacular religion in relation to the concept of genres in folklore studies, namely of written, performative and oral genres, as it is applied to the study of religious faith and practice, see *Vernacular Religion in Everyday Life: Expressions of Belief*, ed. by Marion Bowman and Ülo Valk (New York & London: Routledge, 2012).
6 Leonard Primiano, 'Vernacular Religion and the Search for Method in Religious Folklife', *Western Folklore* 54 (1), (1995), p. 44, in Marion Bowman, 'Vernacular Religion, Contemporary Spirituality and Emergent Identities. Lessons from Lauri Honko', *Approaching Religion*, 4 (1), (May 2014), 101–13.
7 On the issue of continuity in the study of religious ritual in Greek tradition see selectively Margaret Alexiou, *The Ritual Lament in Greek Tradition* (Greek Studies: Interdisciplinary Approaches, Washington, D.C.: Rowman and Littlefield, 2002); Charles Stewart, *Demons and the Devil: Moral Imagination in Modern Greek Culture* (Princeton Modern Greek Studies, Princeton, New Jersey: Princeton University Press, 1992); Laurie Kain Hart, *Time, Religion, and Social Experience in Rural Greece* (Lanham, Maryland: Rowman & Littlefield Publishers, Inc., 1992); Ελένη Ψυχογιού, *'Μαυρηγή' και Ελένη. Τελετουργίες θανάτου και αναγέννησης* (Αθήνα: Δημοσιεύματα του Κέντρου Ερεύνης της Ελληνικής Λαογραφίας 24, Ακαδημία Αθηνών, 2008); Marilena Papachristophorou, *Myth, Representation, and Identity. An Ethnography of Memory in Lipsi, Greece* (London: Palgrave Macmillan, 2013); David Sutton, 'Ritual, Continuity and Change: Greek Reflections', *History and Anthropology*, 15 (2), (2004), 91–105; Βασιλική Χρυσανθοπούλου, 'Από τη λαϊκή λατρεία στην τελετουργία και τη θρησκευτική συμπεριφορά: Η "μεταβαλλόμενη συνέχεια" των λαογραφικών προσεγγίσεων', in *Λαογραφία και Ανθρωπολογία. Μια συμβολή στον διάλογο*, ed. by Βασίλης Νιτσιάκος and Παρασκευάς Ποτηρόπουλος (Αθήνα: εκδόσεις Ι. Σιδέρης, 2018), pp. 263–319.

on 26 and 27 July 2009. I undertook this pilgrimage with my husband, a diaspora Olymbitan from Australia, thus experiencing the event as a person associated with the pilgrims by way of affinity and friendship, while also being a participant observer and acting as an ethnographer. I had visited Saria two years earlier, during the summer of 2007, with Anastasia Avdellí, an elderly woman who had been the last inhabitant of the island before settling in Diafáni, the port of Olymbos, to spend the last years of her life in greater security and comfort. Anastasia had been a *vóskitsa*, a shepherdess, throughout her life on Saria. I saw the deserted houses (*metohóspita*) of the families that had made their living from the farming of crops, olive and almond trees, and from the herding of sheep, goats and some cows, for many decades. Together we visited the many 'monasteries', as Olymbitans call the churches or chapels belonging to various families, to light the oil lamps and cast incense around the icons.

My 2007 research visit to the island in the company of a knowledgeable local inhabitant provided me with useful insights regarding the landscape, the history, and especially, the memories and feelings that many Olymbitans share about Saria, once an important source of wealth for their community. However, my knowledge of Karpathian, and more specifically, of Olymbitan culture, derives from a long-term, deep, and multi-sited research engagement with Olymbitans and other Karpathians, both on the island of Karpathos and in the diaspora communities of Rhodes, Athens/Piraeus, and Australia.[8] This research experience has provided me with an understanding of the importance for Olymbitans of the *glendi*, the traditional singing of spontaneous rhyming distichs or *mantinádes*, accompanied by music played on the local instruments, *lyra* and lute, and followed by dancing, which takes place during the ritual events of the annual and of the life cycles and even on informal occasions.

The structure of the pilgrimage has generally remained unchanged over many decades and the same applies to the structure of the *glendi*. However, the thematic units (*themata*) developed through the singing of *mantinádes* during the various *glendia* differ according to the historical and social circumstances of each pilgrimage. That is, they vary according to the people who make up the group of singers, the audience, and the events, recent and present, that the group has experienced.[9] In this sense, each pilgrimage to Saria is unique, its particular character being expressed through its *glendi*. As Victor and Edith Turner put it, 'while it may be useful to apply to pilgrimage systems the concept of the organism-environment fields in space-time, it must not be forgotten that each pilgrimage has its own entelechy, its own immanent force

---

8 On multi-sited ethnographic research, a method increasingly employed in the study of contemporary mobile, transnational and diasporic individuals and communities, see George Marcus, 'Ethnography in/of the World System: The Emergence of Multi-sited Ethnography', *Annual Review of Anthropology*, 24 (1995), 95–117, whereby the researcher follows and studies the movements of people, products and ideas globally. See also Arjun Appadurai, *Modernity at Large. Cultural Dimensions of Globalization* (Public Worlds, vol. 1, Minneapolis, London: University of Minnesota Press, 1996).

9 Pavlos Kavouras has proposed the 'inter-performative examination' of the *glendia*, namely the comparison between past, present and future *glendia*, to show their similar structure and their diversified themes and dynamics, according to the historical circumstances (Παύλος Κάβουρας, 'Αυτοσχέδιο διαλογικό τραγούδι και γλεντικός συμβολισμός στην Όλυμπο Καρπάθου', *Εθνολογία*, 2 (1993), p. 192.

controlling and directing development.'[10] I focus on the pilgrimage of 26–27 July 2009, since my personal and contextual experience sharpened my interpretation of this event. Moreover, the main focus of this pilgrimage *glendi* concerned the implementation of a vow to Saint Panteleimon, a topic strictly relevant to the understanding of this pilgrimage, and central to pilgrimages, in general.

Saint Panteleimon of Saria: The Background to the Pilgrimage

Written and oral sources show that the monastery of Saint Panteleimon was created in the 1700s by three or four monks, who had gone to Saria from Crete, probably to escape invaders. They sheltered in the area known as 'Kalo(g)erokamáres', meaning 'Monks' caves', where they lived temporarily before moving to an elevated and thus safer place, where they built a church, a large house (*koúfi*), a cell, a cistern, a threshing floor, and a second house with sleeping facilities, storage and a hearth.[11] This is where the monastery stands to this day, although it was renovated and enlarged in 1947, its church acquired a new dome in 1975, and a pier and concrete steps leading to the church from the harbour were created in 1992 to facilitate access. Most of the recent improvements were implemented through donations by Olymbitans from Saria living in the diaspora, a pattern which continues to the present, as we will see below. The monks devoted themselves to agricultural and pastoral tasks and the monastery prospered during the 1800s, when it acquired considerable property both on Saria and in Olymbos and Diafáni, where its monks and benefactors came from. The descendants of these families, *Sariátes*, as they are called by other Olymbitans, are passionately committed to maintaining the church and its pilgrimage and constitute the nucleus and the driving force of its organization, as will become clear below. The Church Committee of Diafáni, aided by other Olymbitans with a connection to Saria in the past, is the organizing force behind the annual pilgrimage to Saint Panteleimon.[12]

During the nineteenth century and for the first half of the twentieth century, Saria was an important area, where Olymbitans procured their living. In addition to those permanently settled there, several families possessed land and animals on the island and undertook regular trips there to sow and harvest their crops, ferrying donkeys, cows, and mules back and forth to carry out these agricultural tasks and bring to

---

10 Victor Turner and Edith Turner, *Image and Pilgrimage in Christian Culture. Anthropological Perspectives* (New York: Columbia University Press, 1978), p. 25.
11 The skulls of these monks, buried in a vaulted grave close to the western part of the monastery, can be seen by people visiting the site.
12 For detailed information on the history of the monastery of Saint Panteleimon, see Fr. Minas Ernias' account published in Γιώργος Η. Ζωγραφίδης, Άλα πούππα να πάμε στη Σαρία (Διαφάνι Καρπάθου, 2008), pp. 112–19. The inhabitants of Diafáni, the harbour of Olymbos, a separate village *c.* 10 km. east of Olymbos, are also Olymbitans by ancestry, as also were the inhabitants of Saria. Olymbos was created on the slope of the homonymous mountain, nowadays known as 'Prophet Elias', during the seventh–ninth centuries A.D (=anno Domini), by the ancient inhabitants of the settlements of Vrykoús, in the north of Karpathos, and of Saria, for protection against pirates.

Olymbos farming and pastoral products.[13] The difficulties involved in transporting farm animals on heavily laden boats through the Stenó strait between Saria and Karpathos are depicted in 'rowing' or 'Sariátika' songs, sung by the rowers to keep the rhythm of the oars and encourage themselves in this difficult job.[14] This way of transport, the *antíirma*, lasted till the 1960s. It now symbolizes Olymbitan values and their collective myth, namely persistence, hard work in tough conditions, the pursuit of self-sufficiency and the strength of character Olymbitans acquired because of this way of life.

Saint Panteleimon's church has always been the centre of Olymbitan pilgrimage. My elderly informants remembered lively feasts in the 1960s at 'Ai Pandelémona' or 'Ai Pandelémo', as they refer to the saint and his church. On the eve of the feast of the Saint, 26 July 2009, my husband and I joined other Olymbitan pilgrims at Diafáni to sail on a passenger boat to Saria.[15] After an hour's journey on a choppy sea, we disembarked at the harbour of Me(g)a Gialó and started climbing the steps to the monastery at the top of the hill, together with men and women carrying clothes and food, an ascending walk of about twenty minutes.

Vespers (*esperinós*) started. Papa-Minás, that is, Fr. Minás of the parish of Diafáni, had arrived earlier. He had accompanied the miraculous icon of Saint Panteleimon, covered from top to bottom on its stand with votives offered by the faithful, proof of people's powerful belief in this selfless healing saint.[16] The monastery icon is kept in the main church of Diafáni, where it has been transferred together with other valuable heirlooms and sacred objects for safety reasons. Thus Saint Panteleimon's icon also journeys to its original home on Saria every year together with the Olymbitan pilgrims, to bless the island and the pilgrims, before returning to its current home in Diafáni. Thus, the icon and the saint have also accompanied the migration of the community from Saria, and like these Olymbitan migrants, the icon and the saint undertake this annual pilgrimage to their original abode.

This was a communal feast. The chanters (*psaltes*) were Olymbitans, who also participated in singing at the *glendi* after the communal meal of the eve. Men and

---

13 On the close economic relationship between Olymbos and Saria see Ευδοκία Ολυμπίτου, 'Ένα οδοιπορικό στη Σαρία της Καρπάθου: Ο χώρος και οι άνθρωποι', in *Κάρπαθος και Λαογραφία. Β΄ Διεθνές Συνέδριο Καρπαθιακής Λαογραφίας (Κάρπαθος, 26–29 Σεπτεμβρίου 2001)*, ed. by Μηνάς Αλ. Αλεξιάδης (Αθήνα: Πνευματικό Κέντρο Δήμου Καρπάθου, Νομαρχιακή Αυτοδιοίκηση Δωδεκανήσου – Επαρχείο Καρπάθου, 2003), pp. 511–27.
14 See Μανόλης Μακρής, 'Τα 'Σαριάτικα' κωπηλατικά τραγούδια', Η΄ Πολιτιστικό Συμπόσιο της Στέγης Γραμμάτων και Τεχνών Δωδεκανήσου (Κάρπαθος 1993), *Δωδεκανησιακά Χρονικά*, 16 (1998), 265–84.
15 A few non-Olymbitans also attended the pilgrimage, including some academics from Crete who came by speedboat and a schoolteacher serving at the primary school of Olymbos during that period.
16 On icons in Greek Orthodox worship, see Margaret E. Kenna, 'Icons in Theory and Practice: An Orthodox Christian Example', *History of Religions*, 24 (4) (May 1985), 345–68. On Olymbitan women's vows to the saints in the form of multi-coloured covers or *skepes* for their icons, see Βασιλική Χρυσανθοπούλου, 'Ενδύοντας τις εικόνες: Συμβολικές και κοινωνικές διαστάσεις στα γυναικεία τάματα ("σκέπες") της βόρειας Καρπάθου', in *Κάρπαθος & Λαογραφία, Δ΄ Διεθνές Συνέδριο Καρπαθιακής Λαογραφίας [Κάρπαθος, 8–12 Μαΐου 2013]*, ed. by Μηνάς Αλ. Αλεξιάδης and Πόπη Κ. Ξανθάκου (Σειρά Αυτοτελών Εκδόσεων, Αρ. 9, Αθήνα: Ινστιτούτο Λαϊκού Πολιτισμού Τμήματος Φιλολογίας, Ε.Κ.Π.Α. – Καρπαθιακός Οργανισμός Πολιτισμού, Άθλησης, Παιδείας Δήμου Καρπάθου, 2016), pp. 1029–55.

women cooked and served, while women brought to church large, round loaves of bread (*prósforo, panofóri*), which they had made and put in baskets beautifully decorated with basil, to be blessed and distributed to the pilgrims by the priest. The pilgrims clearly view commensality and communal singing and dancing, which take place after the religious service, as a continuation of the sacred event itself.

On the following day, after the church service, the blessing and distributing of the bread by the priest (*artoklasía*) and the blessing of each pilgrim with holy oil, we were treated to honey puffs (*loukoumádes*) and sweet drinks by the church committee; we shared a meal, and left the church, our trip back now occupying our thoughts. There was no *glendi*, although the singers sat at their table with the priest and sang various *apolytikia*, i.e. hymns to saints whose churches stand in the surrounding area.

Fig. 1: Saint Panteleimon's icon laden with votive offerings (*támata*). Photograph by Vassiliki Chryssanthopoulou, 2009.

The structure of this particular pilgrimage saint's feast does not seem to have changed for many decades, and is similar to other local festivals, such as the better-known one of 'Saint John the Beheaded' (*tou Ai-Yianni tou apokefalistí*).[17] It is celebrated on 29 August in a subterranean chapel at Vrykoús, in the northwest of Karpathos, an area where an ancient settlement had existed till about seventh century AD. Since the chapel of Saint John can be seen from that of Saint Panteleimon, a well-known *mantináda* presents the two healing saints communicating in the following way:

Saint Panteleimon looks at Saint John
And together they decide to visit the sick.

---

17 Georgios S. Amargianakis, a musician-folklorist at the Hellenic Folklore Research Centre of the Academy of Athens, described a similar, yet richer and more extensive procedure in his fieldwork report of the July 1970 pilgrimage to Saint Panteleimon. A fully-fledged *glendi* took place on 27 July, which continued inside the boat taking the pilgrims back to Diafáni, and then at the Diafáni café (*kafenío*). Amargianakis stresses the emphasis placed on community feeling and the transmission of skills manifested by experienced *lyra* and lute players, who endeavoured to share their instruments with the younger members of the group, encouraging them to demonstrate their own skills and talent (Γεώργιος Σ. Αμαργιανάκης, 'Εντυπώσεις από μια μουσικο-λαογραφική αποστολή στην Κάρπαθο το 1970', in *Κάρπαθος και Λαογραφία. Πρακτικά Α΄ Συνεδρίου Καρπαθιακής Λαογραφίας (Κάρπαθος, 26–27 Μαρτίου 1994)*, ed. by Μηνάς Αλ. Αλεξιάδης (Αθήνα: Έκδοση Επαρχείου Καρπάθου, 1998–2001), p. 66. See also Ζωγραφίδης, *Άλα πούππα*, referring to the history of the monastery of Saint Panteleimon and containing a section dealing with the *glendia* held during the 1962 and the 1996–2000 pilgrimages (pp. 159–232). For a description of the 2018 pilgrimage *glendi* at Saint Panteleimon see Γιώργος Η. Ζωγραφίδης, *Τυπικό και δεοντολογία των παραδοσιακών διασκεδάσεων στην Όλυμπο Καρπάθου* (Ρόδος: Έκδοση Αδελφότητας Ολυμπιτών Ρόδου "Η Βρυκούς", 2020), pp. 234–48.

The *Glendi*: Communal Singing and Its Thematic Units

After Vespers on the eve of the feast of Saint Panteleimon, we all sat round the tables laid out in the church courtyard and dinner was served. The men who were to sing (*glendistés*) were sitting at a separate table with the priest at its head. When people finished eating, the characteristic sound of forks being tapped on plates was heard, a traditional way of applauding in communal ritual meals in Karpathos and a sign that the *glendi* was about to start. The Olymbitan *glendi* follows a specific immutable order (*taxi*). On occasions such as religious feasts, the priest starts by singing the saint's characteristic hymn or *apolytikion* and various *troparia* and hymns relating to the saint celebrated or to other saints or to the specific period of the ecclesiastical year. The priest's singing is followed by the singing of *syrmatiká*, i.e. narrative songs, sung by well-respected community singers, *meraklídes*, whose presence is required, if the *glendi* is to progress successfully. In addition to composing significant *mantinádes*, these leading singers endeavour to enhance intra-communal bonds by encouraging other singers, especially younger ones, to participate in the poetic dialogue. The *syrmatiká* are sung *a capella*, until the time for the *mantinádes* to start, which are always accompanied by the *lyra*.

In the chaos of preparations before setting off, the pilgrims had forgotten to bring the *lyra*. There was a sigh of relief when we realized that a *lyra* had arrived from Diafáni, so that the *glendi* could continue. Without a *lyra*, a *glendi* cannot take place, since it is the playing of the *lyra* that encourages singers to compose *mantinádes* and create a sung dialogue. The *lyra* player (*lyristís*), normally a member of the community, usually knows the particular tune (*skopós*) that each singer likes and plays it, to encourage or help him extemporize his verses. The arrival of the *lyra* with some Olymbitans from Diafáni, who, despite not being told, had realized that it was missing, since no communication by phone from Saria was possible, was greeted enthusiastically as a 'miracle' attributed to the saint. Michalis Karanikolas, descended from a family of the area, who had not played for many years, kept the *glendi* going, by playing for many hours during the eve of Saint Panteleimon's feast day. The following *mantinades* mention the miraculous arrival of the *lyra*:

> Tonight, I was disappointed, I am telling you the truth,
> When we gathered here, and I did not see a lyra.
> Your grace made them aware, and they brought the lyra
> Therefore, I pray to You to give them health.
>
> *(by Nikos Karanikolas)*[18]

---

18 Karpathians consider *mantinádes*, or rhyming couplets, to be personal creations. Each *mantináda* is a unique and inalienable creation by a particular composer pertaining to a specific context, not to be sung or recited again either by the same or by another person. Thus, their composers are mentioned by name in this paper, following generally accepted practice. They follow the traditional, 15-syllable iambic metre of Greek folk composition and use certain stereotypical expressions known to the community, which facilitate composition (see also Walter J. Ong, *Orality and Literacy. The Technologizing of the Word* (London and New York: Routledge, Taylor & Francis Group, 2002 [first

The main *glendi* of the July 2009 pilgrimage took place on the eve of the saint's feast. Each verse of the rhyming couplet was first uttered by its composer, then repeated in chorus by the entire group or at least some of its members, thus expressing group support for the singer, while also giving him time to formulate the next verse. The singers progress through a series of thematic units (*themata* or topics) concerned with the participants and their circumstances, allowing all those who wish to contribute to each *thema* to sing their *mantinades*, before proceeding to the next topic. In what follows I deal with several thematic units of this particular *glendi*, as they relate to the main question of this paper, namely to the expression, discussion, and revitalization of the pilgrims' religious, social and cultural identity.

Saint Panteleimon as Sacred Symbol for the Community of Pilgrims

The *glendi*, as well as the pilgrimage as a whole, is primarily an expression of the pilgrims' belief in the power of their saint, Saint Panteleimon, and manifests their collective desire to honour this 'lonely saint' in his home on Saria. Saint Panteleimon is popular throughout Greece and is worshipped as a selfless saint concerned with healing. His name in Greek translates as 'the one who bestows charity on all, the all-merciful one'. He is believed to heal wounds and alleviate pain of all kinds. 'Healer of those suffering' (*Giatré ton poneménon*) is a common invocation to Saint Panteleimon in *mantinádes* from Karpathos and other islands. This belief is based on the story of his life, according to which he practiced medicine in Bithynia during the late third century and suffered martyrdom in 305 for his belief in Christ. There are several major churches and chapels dedicated to the saint throughout Greece, as well as the famous monastery of Saint Panteleimon, belonging to the Russian Orthodox Church, in the monastic community of Mount Athos. The Saint, known as 'Saint Pantaleon' by his original name, is also honoured in the Catholic and Anglican religious traditions.

The first *thema* of the *glendi*, therefore, consisted of several *mantinádes* referring to the Saint, his healing powers, and Olymbitans' desire to be with him on his feast. However, the singers referred to the Saint throughout the *glendi*. They linked their experiences, feelings, as well as their plans, to Saint Panteleimon, who thus appears to function as a 'summarizing' or sacred symbol in Olymbitan culture.

In her seminal paper, Sherry Ortner defines key symbols as public symbols which play a central role either in terms of the priority of their meanings in relation to other meanings of the system in which they exist, or in terms of their organizational role in relation to this system.[19] Ortner terms the first type of key symbols as 'summarizing'. They are 'primarily objects of attention and cultural respect; they synthesize or 'collapse'

---

edition, 1982]). It is almost impossible to translate these *mantinádes* from Greek to another language, since they are in poetic form, characterized by metre and rhyme; I have made every effort to render their meaning, at least, as accurately as possible.

19 Sherry B. Ortner, 'On Key Symbols', *American Anthropologist* 75 (5), (1973), 1338–46.

complex experience and relate the respondent to the grounds of the system as a whole. They include most importantly sacred symbols in the traditional sense.' She calls the second type 'elaborating symbols', which order or 'sort out' experience either by providing cultural 'orientations' or by ordering action, i.e. by providing cultural 'strategies'. Elaborating symbols either include 'root metaphors', or 'key scenarios' of action.[20] In the verses quoted below, Saint Panteleimon appears as a summarizing or sacred symbol, condensing the meaning of 'high level values, ideas, cognitive assertions, etc.' for the pilgrims. Saint Panteleimon is not simply a potent symbol of the local Orthodox tradition and faith; he also sums up the past of Saria and of the entire Olymbitan way of life and values; indeed, he represents their charter of being for Olymbitan pilgrims.

We give some *mantinádes* on the *thema* of the saint:

> The Saint is dynamic. He takes care of everything,
> Every year in his feast, he fills us with joy.
> Most of our fellow villagers always plan ahead,
> When the Saint celebrates his feast, to be with him.
>
> *(by Michalis Hirakis)*

Life Abroad (*Xenitiá*) and Return to the Homeland for Diaspora Olymbitans

Xenitiá or 'life away from the homeland' was the second topic discussed through *mantinádes* at the *glendi*. It constitutes a pervasive experience and condition for all Olymbitans, since most of them, instead of living in Olymbos, live either in other parts of Greece (such as Athens, Piraeus, and Rhodes) or abroad (mainly in the U.S.A., Canada, Australia, or Belgium). The pilgrimage to Saint Panteleimon is particularly connected with this aspect of Olymbitan experience, since large-scale migration from Olymbos was responsible for the depopulation of Saria and the changes in its cultural landscape. Saint Panteleimon's church symbolizes the old Olymbitan presence on the island. The pilgrimage now symbolizes resistance to the negative effects of migration upon Olymbos, the homeland, and a way for Olymbitans symbolically to reclaim their old lands, past life, and identity.

The *thema* of *xenitiá* is triggered by the presence at the *glendia* of Olymbitans who have returned from abroad.[21] In the pilgrimage analyzed here, the participation of several diaspora Olymbitans was celebrated in verse and attributed to the saint, whose care and blessing was said to have enabled them to join the pilgrimage. Saint Panteleimon himself, whose icon travels to his church on Saria every year, is presented as experiencing the pain of loneliness, in a way similar to that of diaspora Olymbitans. The *thema* of *xenitiá* was also inspired by the participation of a diaspora

---

20 Ortner, 'On Key Symbols', p. 1344.
21 See selectively, Kavouras, *Glendi and Xenitia*. Μαρία Γ. Ανδρουλάκη, 'Να πούμε για την Παναγιά σήμερο στην Αυλή της, Ξενιτεμένοι ήρθασι και Φίλοι στη Γιορτή της …: Δεκαπενταύγουστος στην Όλυμπο Καρπάθου', *Τύπος της Κυριακής*, 13 Αύγουστος 2000, pp. 12–14.

Olymbitan, Nikos M. Anastasiadis, who had spent most of his life in Australia and had returned to Greece recently. Since Anastasiadis was a recognized *meraklís*, or good singer, in the Olymbitan community, his *thema* provoked a rich exchange of improvised *mantinádes*. His return was presented as a 'gift' from the Saint, which Anastasiadis, an architect, had to 'return' by drawing up plans for the church's new belltower (*kampanarió*), to be built through a donation from another diaspora Olymbitan, Manolis Vassilarakis – a topic developed in the next *thema*. Several *mantinádes* of this thematic unit refer to the feelings of retrospective nostalgia expressed by these diaspora Olymbitans, for their youthful years before migration. Here are some characteristic *mantinádes*:

[on the loneliness felt by the Saint and by Olymbitans abroad]

All day and night long alone, in this lonely land,
You wait for us to come, whether the sea is calm or rough.

(by Nikos M. Anastasiadis)

He is not alone, Niko, there are people following him,
And he goes and heals whoever is in pain.

(by Nikos Karanikolas)

You were not alone, Niko. The Saint was helping you,
And your thought was always committed to return.

(by Antonis Vassilarakis)

The Saint has been proved to be a healer.
And all those living abroad return to be at his feast.

(by Michalis Hirakis)

[on life abroad, nostalgia and thanks to the Saint]

I turn my mind back to nineteen fifty-three.
And I remember the moment when I left Saria.

(by Nikos M. Anastasiadis)

They took away our youth, although we were strong,
Canada took mine, and Australia took yours.

(by Antonis Vassilarakis)

Since I like the company, and the lyra plays mildly and sweetly,
I have thrown away all the problems of the past.

(by Nikos M. Anastasiadis)

Saint, we have all been awaiting his return.
Please send your grace to protect him.

(by Antonis Vassilarakis)

[on the plans concerning Saint Panteleimon's belltower to be implemented by N. A.]

Eh, now that you have come, Niko, many projects will happen.
Make us the plans for the Saint.
The projects will continue, if we have health,
And we will have the Saint as a jewel on Saria.[22]

(by Antonis Vassilarakis)

I have drawn the lines and have filled the paper,
And all your plans will be fulfilled.[23]

(by Nikos M. Anastasiadis)

A Vow to the Saint as Inter-generational Debt: The *Thema* of the Belltower

Most of the *mantinádes* of the previous thematic unit were composed by people whose families had earned their living on Saria in the past. Antonis Vassilarakis, a member of the Diafáni church committee, who tried to persuade Nikos Anastasiadis to create the plans for the new belltower of Saint Panteleimon's church, belonged to such a family and had been active in the organization of the saint's pilgrimage for years. In this *thema*, the group of singers elaborate on the issue of the new belltower as a vow to the saint by an Olymbitan from Saria, no longer alive, now to be carried out by his son as a debt to the saint transcending generations and involving the entire community. The deceased Olymbitan donor, Yiannis Vassilarakis, who had lived in Canada and had been an important benefactor of Saint Panteleimon in his lifetime, was Antonis' brother. His son, Manolis Vassilarakis, solemnly and eagerly promised to meet the expenses involved in the rebuilding of the church's belltower and so fulfil his father's vow to the saint.

The *mantinádes* sung during this thematic unit refer to values of communal cooperation and to the prestige to be accrued by serving the saint and the community. They praise individuals and families who have contributed to the maintenance of the pilgrimage site and invoke the saint's blessing on its future benefactors. They formulate a communal strategy towards preserving and embellishing Saint Panteleimon's church, thus ensuring the continuation of the annual pilgrimage and feast and, through it, the continuation of the Olymbitan presence on Saria. The words *praxi* ('action') and *erga* ('works, projects') are employed in these *mantinádes*. This supports the view that both the *glendi* and Saint Panteleimon, in whose honour it takes place, constitute 'elaborating

---

22 The project mentioned here concerns the creation of the plans for the building of Saint Panteleimon's belltower, developed extensively in the following thematic unit.

23 N. A. uses the past tense in this *mantináda*. Having made a promise to prepare the plans for Saint Panteleimon's belltower, he is bound by it. Thus, his part of the project may be considered to have already been implemented.

symbols', in Sherry Ortner's sense of the term discussed earlier. They contribute to the ordering of conceptual experience (what Pepper calls 'root metaphors') and to the ordering of action (cultural strategies which include 'key scenarios' necessary for their implementation).[24] The two key symbols, the celebrated saint and the *glendi* taking place in his honour and veneration, are inextricably bound to each other, and together they inform the distinctive vernacular character of the pilgrimage.

The 'vow' (*tama*, in Greek) to the saint, in its multifaceted manifestations by various pilgrims, who contribute different kinds of goods or services to enable the realization of the pilgrimage, was the central topic of the communal singing on 26 July 2009. The main idea of this *thema* centred on the firm belief that an ancestor's vow should be fulfilled by his living descendant. The entire group of singers exchanged *mantinades* which developed a communal strategy to enable the implementation of this vow. These *mantinades* demonstrated that the vow to the saint transcended time and space and even the lifespan of the person who made it, and so made clear that it was to be fulfilled, both as an individual and a communal project. They illustrated how the vow binds the pilgrims to Saint Panteleimon, to Saria and to the Olymbitan community, identity, and culture.

The word *tama* describes both the action of making an offering to a saint and the offer itself and may relate either to a promise or to giving thanks for the fulfilment of a prayer.[25] The pilgrimage itself to Saint Panteleimon of Saria constitutes a 'tama' for several pilgrims. Marcel Mauss examined exchanges between men and divinity as part of his classic theory of the gift. In Mauss' view, a gift or vow to a saint awaits its appropriate return.[26] 'The saints are God, but a familiar, closer, more accessible kind of God, so that a person may even ... strike "agreements" with them.'[27] However, exchanges between human and sacred persons are asymmetrical since the sacred person is superior by definition and his/her return follows a different pattern. As Juliet du Boulay notes when quoting her Greek informants' words,

> A vow is a vow, and you must carry it out even if you don't get what you want. [...] Any element of calculation is unfitting to the relations between the believer and the heavenly world, and loyalty to the vow and faith in the saint should take the place of an insistence on the strict reciprocity of a commercial bargain. [...] The vow, like the simple gift, is ideally not so much a conditional demand for

---

24 Stephen Pepper, *World Hypotheses* (Berkeley and Los Angeles: University of California Press, 1942), in Ortner, 'On Key Symbols', p. 1344.
25 On vows and votive offerings, see selectively Νικόλαος Γ. Πολίτης, 'Αναθήματα κατ' ευχήν', *Λαογραφία*, 2 (1910–1911), pp. 125–30. Ευρυδίκη Αντζουλάτου-Ρετσίλα, 'Το ελληνικό τάμα στο πέρασμα των αιώνων', in her book, *Πολιτιστικά και Μουσειολογικά Σύμμεικτα* (Αθήνα: Εκδόσεις Παπαζήση, 2005), pp. 21–29. Sophia Handaka, 'Anthropological Reflections on Greek Orthodox Votive Offerings (Tamata), with Reference to the Mikes Paidousis Collection' (D. Phil. Thesis, University of Oxford, 2005). On women's vows in northern Karpathos, see Χρυσανθοπούλου, 'Ενδύοντας τις εικόνες'.
26 Marcel Mauss, 'Essai sur le don. Forme et raison de l' échange dans les sociétés archaiques', *Année Sociologique*, I (1923–1924), 30–186.
27 For an interpretation of gifts and vows to the saints as of primarily economic nature, see Μηνάς Αλ. Αλεξιάδης, 'Do ut des', *"Δωδώνη", Επιστημονική Επετηρίς του Τμήματος Ιστορίας και Αρχαιολογίας της Φιλοσοφικής Σχολής του Πανεπιστημίου Ιωαννίνων*, 16 (1), (1987), p. 259.

patronage as a way of keeping the relationship open, thus permitting the saint's power to operate when the time is ripe.[28]

Vows to Saint Panteleimon, his church and his pilgrimage are certainly intended to keep his blessing flowing to the individual pilgrims and to the entire community, in the sense described above. The rhyming couplets composed in the saint's honour during the pilgrimage celebration present individual vows and gifts to the saint as symbolically relating to the entire community.[29] However, by virtue of addressing the entire community, these vows or gifts also bestow prestige on the people who offer them.

[a vow to the saint as intergenerational debt]

I have my father's advice together with his blessing,
To look after the Saint, as that was his vow to him.

(by Manolis Vassilarakis)

Eh, now that you have committed yourself, I am worried no longer.
We will soon see the projects which need to be done for the Saint.

(by Antonis Vassilarakis)

So, then, prepare the plans for me to create a belltower.
To please the souls, wherever they may be.

(by Manolis Vassilarakis, addressing Nikos M. Anastasiadis)

I am contributing paper and ink,
And you should take care so that the project may happen quickly.

(by Nikos M. Anastasiadis)

[communal collaboration for the church project with the saint's help]

Many people have helped, others will help, too.
Put in your own touch from Anastasiadis' kin group.

(by Nikos Karanikolas)

Come to its installation, too, to supervise it.
Make sure that you will follow the rules of our tradition, Niko.

(by Minas Balaskas)

I have been trying for eleven years now, I am committed to my vow.
And I see the church bell hanging loose.

(by Manolis Vassilarakis)

---

28 Juliet du Boulay, *Cosmos, Life, and Liturgy in a Greek Orthodox Village* (Limni, Evia, Greece: Denise Harvey (Publisher), 2009), pp. 321–23.
29 A similar interpretation of gifts to gods and sacred persons is analyzed in Maurice Godelier, *L' énigme du don* (Paris: Librairie Arthème Fayard, 1996).

Fig. 2: The church of Saint Panteleimon at Saria, which had no belltower at the time. Photograph by Marita and Horst Hundemer, 2010.

> The Saint has power and will perform this task.
> Only be patient till next summer.
>
> *(by Manolis Orfanos)*
>
> Inside the big, concrete-ridden city
> I will make enviable plans for you.[30]
>
> *(by Nikos M. Anastasiadis)*
>
> Every time the church bell rings, may it add years to your life
> And may the Saint's blessing on you, Niko, be eternal.
>
> *(by Nikos Karanikolas)*
>
> [praise to the church's benefactors]
>
> In my father's memory is all that I will do.
> For he was very devoted to our Saint.
> I hold on to my vow, and do turn it into action.[31]
> I promise that I will be faithful to my word.
>
> *(by Manolis Vassilarakis)*
>
> Manoli, don't be sad, the vow will happen,
> And may the Saint help you, by giving health to you.
>
> *(by Antonis Vassilarakis)*

---

30 The singer refers to Athens, where he lived after returning from Australia.
31 The phrase in Greek is 'kámeté to praxi'.

> You are like your father who was a leader,
> You will have the Saint's favour upon yourself.
>
> *(by Nikos Karanikolas)*
>
> My father contributed a lot, and may people recognize it,
> And may they allow me to implement my vow.
>
> *(by Manolis Vassilarakis)*
>
> We all recognize it, I will say it aloud again.
> I will utter it loudly, for others to know, too.[32]
>
> *(by Nikos Karanikolas)*
>
> They were not only donors, they were leaders, too.
> The projects which have taken place progressed comfortably.
>
> *(by Michalis Hirakis)*
>
> Mina, Michali, Niko, try your very best.
> May the Saint protect your children and grandchildren.
>
> *(by Minas Agapios)*

Music, Memory, Space and Time: The Playing of the *Lyra* Awakens Old Saria

The following *thema* was a poetic dialogue between the (male) singers and a woman, Kalliope Hiraki, on the loss of people and the old Olymbitan way of life.[33] It gave a reflexive and metaphysical tone to the *glendi*, which was further developed in the last thematic unit. This unit expresses the Olymbitan pilgrims' views regarding space and time and focuses on music as a way to link past and present, to recreate collective memories and revitalize communal identity.

Space is essential for the recreation of memories. Halbwachs suggests that we need to focus on the space that our imagination or our thoughts can recreate at every moment, so that one or another category of memories may reappear.[34] In this last thematic unit of the pilgrims' *glendi*, the music of the *lyra* brings back memories of the past, reanimates and symbolically 'tames' again the landscape of

---

32 This *mantináda* by Karanikolas, a member of an influential family from Saria, has special value as testimony to the benefactions bestowed by Yiannis Vassilarakis and his family to Saint Panteleimon, thus contributing to their prestige in the Olymbitan community.
33 This *thema* illustrates how emotions are given gendered expression during the *glendi*. Despite the great theoretical and ethnographic interest involved, lack of space unfortunately does not allow us to take the matter further here. I hope to deal with the subject elsewhere.
34 Maurice Halbwachs, *Η συλλογική μνήμη*, edited and with preface by Anna Mantoglou (Athens: Παπαζήσης, 2013), pp. 167–68.

Saria, which has become a wilderness through the lack of human presence on the island. The playing of the *lyra* by a local inhabitant, who had learnt how to play it on the island itself as a youth, is believed to soothe and invite both the souls of its old inhabitants and the inanimate landscape itself to rejoice and participate in this awakening of old Saria. The cosmological unit created by the singers' imagination and memory and expressed through singing and the playing of the *lyra*, transcends the boundaries of time and space, to unite past, present, and future, thus recreating the communities of Saria and Olympos in their eternal, imagined dimensions. Here are some of these *mantinádes*:

[on the lyra player and the music of the lyra]

The lyra has got tired and has become untuned,
But as it plays the tunes, it goes back to the old times.

(by Kalliope Hiraki)

The lyra is fine, you are the ones who misunderstand.
I think that you are looking for a pretext to go to sleep.

(by Manolis Vassilarakis)

He learnt to play the lyra here, and he wishes to continue.
He does not want to forget his childhood years.

(by Minas Karanikolas, for his brother, Michalis, the lyra player)

[on the lyra awakening the souls of dead Sariátes, the mountains, and the pilgrims' memories]

If it is possible for the souls of those departed to hear, Michali,
Tonight our entire Saria will be rejoicing.

(by Nikos Karanikolas)

If it is possible for the souls departed to feel, Michali,
I believe they will have started a glendi to honour our Saint.

(by Manolis Vassilarakis)

The mountains will take pride in the lyra's playing tonight,
As they will recognize an old acquaintance.

(by Minas Agapios)

If it were possible for the mountains to feel, then rivers would start to flow,
Because of the endless weeping that happened on them.

(by Manolis Vassilarakis)

The memories went many years back,
And tonight, you will awaken them with your lyra.

(by Minas Karanikolas)

Fig. 3: The group of singers including Kalliope at the glendi of the feast of Saint Panteleimon on Saria, 26.07.2009. Photograph by Vassiliki Chryssanthopoulou.

> I remember all these mountains full of people.
> Now they rejoice only one day a year.
>
> *(by Nikos Karanikolas)*
>
> The shepherds have gone, the sheepfolds are destroyed,
> They have gone away, and they have not come back again.
> Many people left this place never to return to it.
> They were buried far away in foreign lands (xenitiá).
>
> *(by Minas Karanikolas)*

As Scheer notes, 'practices not only generate emotions, but [...] emotions themselves can be viewed as a practical engagement with the world.'[35] The feelings of pain and loss that the Olymbitan pilgrims express through shared memories that they cast in poetic form to the accompaniment of the *lyra* are better understood as historically grounded and embodied 'emotional practices'. As the *mantinádes* quoted above illustrate, Olymbitan pilgrims have a clear sense of linear reality and of the historicity of their experience. They sing of the changes that time has brought in their own lives, and in the way of life and the landscape of Olymbos and Saria in general. The message expressed is clear: Return to the past is impossible. The structures and symbols of the old farming and pastoral ways of life, have disappeared irreversibly. The only

---

35 Monique Scheer, 'Are Emotions a Kind of Practice (and Is That What Makes Them Have a History)? A Bourdieuian Approach to Understanding Emotion', *History and Theory*, 51 (May 2012), p. 210.

Fig. 4: The church of Saint Panteleimon in 2015 with its newly built belltower, the fulfilment of the vow taken at the glendi of the 2009 pilgrimage. Photograph by Marita and Horst Hundemer.

thing for these Olymbitan pilgrims to do is to move on, with resilience and hope, and with a strong sense of a shared past, an attitude that soothes the feelings of pain brought about by loss and death.

Conclusions

Our analysis of the pilgrimage to Saint Panteleimon of Saria illustrates ethnographically and attempts to interpret anthropologically the case of diaspora pilgrimages to once inhabited and now deserted ancestral places, a phenomenon widespread in Greece and in other parts of the world.

A pilgrimage is a social and cultural phenomenon which, in addition to being a channel for the expression of faith and religious feelings, also allows for the articulation, reaffirmation, and negotiation of social distinctions of individuality within collectiveness. This is the case with the pilgrimage to Saint Panteleimon, in which different identities and roles are vocally and emotionally expressed by the pilgrims who participate in the *glendi* vernacular ritual singing. The entire improvised singing dialogue centres artfully round the saint, his church, and his pilgrimage. The pilgrims thank, pray, and promise in verse to come back and to fulfil their vows. At the same time, they discuss, consolidate, and revitalize old bonds of kinship and friendship. They remember together the past, express their feelings of nostalgia, loss, and pain, and they make plans for the future together.

In the preceding analysis, we focused on the behaviour and roles of the descendants of the Olymbitan families of Saria concerning their care for Saint Panteleimon's church and pilgrimage site. They expressed their commitment as a debt owed to the saint that transcends generations and is transmitted from father to son in the form of a vow to be implemented by the latter with the help of the community. We have examined the discourse developing between returning diaspora and local Olymbitans as regards the former's claims to being part of the community, and the latter's positive response to these claims. We witnessed the respect and prestige attributed to the donors and benefactors of Saint Panteleimon, and the encouragement for more people to contribute in similar ways, as expressed through *mantinádes*. Above all, we have attempted to show how individual thoughts, feelings and approaches to life are communicated and shared in the philosophical but also practical and realistic poetic discourse of the *glendi* with reference to the overarching symbol of the saint. The *glendi* marks the time frames within which the Olymbitan community reflects on its collective identity and expresses its worldview.

Saint Panteleimon and his pilgrimage function both as a summarizing/sacred, and an elaborating symbol for the community of Olymbitan pilgrims, providing them with the opportunity to reflect on the past and plan for the future of their collective identity and community life. The Olymbitans use the vernacular ritual of the *glendi*, to revitalize their roots on the now depopulated island of Saria. Thus, they reclaim it as part of their heritage, while also honouring Saint Panteleimon, its guardian Saint.

*I would like to thank Marita and Horst Hundemer for Fig. 2 and Fig. 4.

References

Anna Caraveli, 'The Symbolic Village: Community Born in Performance', *Journal of American Folklore*, 98 (1985), 259–86.

Arjun Appadurai, *Modernity at Large. Cultural Dimensions of Globalization* (Public Worlds, vol. 1, Minneapolis, London: University of Minnesota Press, 1996).

Βασίλης Νιτσιάκος, *Χτίζοντας το χώρο και το χρόνο* (Αθήνα: Οδυσσέας, 2003).

Βασιλική Χρυσανθοπούλου, 'Οι Χατζήδαινες της Πέρθης', *Λαογραφία*, 33 (1982–1984), 130–54.

Βασιλική Χρυσανθοπούλου, 'Ο τόπος της πατρίδας στο λόγο και στις εθιμικές τελετουργίες των Καρπαθίων της Καμπέρρας Αυστραλίας', in *Κάρπαθος & Λαογραφία, Γ΄ Διεθνές Συνέδριο Καρπαθιακής Λαογραφίας [Κάρπαθος, 21–26 Μαρτίου 2006]*, ed. by Μηνάς Αλ. Αλεξιάδης (Αθήνα : Πνευματικό Κέντρο Δήμου Καρπάθου & Νομαρχιακή Αυτοδιοίκηση Δωδεκανήσου – Επαρχείο Καρπάθου, 2008), pp. 1027–74.

Βασιλική Χρυσανθοπούλου, 'Ενδύοντας τις εικόνες: Συμβολικές και κοινωνικές διαστάσεις στα γυναικεία τάματα ("σκέπες") της βόρειας Καρπάθου', in *Κάρπαθος & Λαογραφία, Δ΄ Διεθνές Συνέδριο Καρπαθιακής Λαογραφίας [Κάρπαθος, 8–12 Μαΐου 2013]*, ed. by Μηνάς Αλ. Αλεξιάδης and Πόπη Κ. Ξανθάκου (Σειρά Αυτοτελών Εκδόσεων, Αρ. 9, Αθήνα: Ινστιτούτο Λαϊκού Πολιτισμού Τμήματος Φιλολογίας, Ε.Κ.Π.Α. – Καρπαθιακός Οργανισμός Πολιτισμού, Άθλησης, Παιδείας Δήμου Καρπάθου, 2016), pp. 1029–55.

Βασιλική Χρυσανθοπούλου, 'Από τη λαϊκή λατρεία στην τελετουργία και τη θρησκευτική συμπεριφορά: Η "μεταβαλλόμενη συνέχεια" των λαογραφικών προσεγγίσεων', in *Λαογραφία και Ανθρωπολογία. Μια συμβολή στον διάλογο*, ed. by Βασίλης Νιτσιάκος and Παρασκευάς Ποτηρόπουλος (Αθήνα: εκδόσεις Ι. Σιδέρης, 2018), pp. 263–319.

Charles Stewart, *Demons and the Devil: Moral Imagination in Modern Greek Culture* (Princeton Modern Greek Studies, Princeton, New Jersey: Princeton University Press, 1992).

David Sutton, 'Ritual, Continuity and Change: Greek Reflections', *History and Anthropology*, 15 (2), (2004), 91–105.

Δημήτριος Σ. Λουκάτος, *Τα καλοκαιρινά* (Λαογραφία-Παράδοση 3) (Αθήνα: Εκδόσεις Φιλιππότη, 1981).

Ευδοκία Ολυμπίτου, ''Ένα οδοιπορικό στη Σαρία της Καρπάθου: Ο χώρος και οι άνθρωποι', in *Κάρπαθος και Λαογραφία. Β΄ Διεθνές Συνέδριο Καρπαθιακής Λαογραφίας (Κάρπαθος, 26–29 Σεπτεμβρίου 2001)*, ed. by Μηνάς Αλ. Αλεξιάδης (Αθήνα: Πνευματικό Κέντρο Δήμου Καρπάθου, Νομαρχιακή Αυτοδιοίκηση Δωδεκανήσου – Επαρχείο Καρπάθου, 2003), pp. 511–27.

Ευρυδίκη Αντζουλάτου-Ρετσίλα, 'Το ελληνικό τάμα στο πέρασμα των αιώνων', in her book, *Πολιτιστικά και Μουσειολογικά Σύμμεικτα* (Αθήνα: Εκδόσεις Παπαζήση, 2005), pp. 21–29.

Ευάγγελος Αυδίκος, *Εορταί και πανηγύρεις. Σύνορα, λαϊκά δρώμενα και τελετές* (Θεσσαλονίκη: Επίκεντρο, 2017).

Ελένη Ψυχογιού, *'Μαυρηγή' και Ελένη. Τελετουργίες θανάτου και αναγέννησης* (Αθήνα: Δημοσιεύματα του Κέντρου Ερεύνης της Ελληνικής Λαογραφίας 24, Ακαδημία Αθηνών, 2008).

Jill Dubisch, *In a Different Place. Pilgrimage, Gender, and Politics at a Greek Island Shrine* (Princeton, New Jersey: Princeton University Press, 1995).

Juliet du Boulay, *Cosmos, Life, and Liturgy in a Greek Orthodox Village* (Limni, Evia, Greece: Denise Harvey (Publisher), 2009).

George Marcus, 'Ethnography in/of the World System: The Emergence of Multi-sited Ethnography', *Annual Review of Anthropology*, 24 (1995), 95–117.

Γεώργιος Σ. Αμαργιανάκης, 'Εντυπώσεις από μια μουσικο-λαογραφική αποστολή στην Κάρπαθο το 1970', in *Κάρπαθος και Λαογραφία. Πρακτικά Α΄ Συνεδρίου Καρπαθιακής Λαογραφίας (Κάρπαθος, 26–27 Μαρτίου 1994)*, ed. by Μηνάς Αλ. Αλεξιάδης (Αθήνα: Έκδοση Επαρχείου Καρπάθου, 1998–2001), pp. 63–69.

Γιώργος Η. Ζωγραφίδης, *Άλα πούππα να πάμε στη Σαρία* (Διαφάνι Καρπάθου, 2008).

Γιώργος Η. Ζωγραφίδης, *Τυπικό και δεοντολογία των παραδοσιακών διασκεδάσεων στην Όλυμπο Καρπάθου* (Ρόδος: Έκδοση Αδελφότητας Ολυμπιτών Ρόδου "Η Βρυκούς", 2020).

Laurie Kain Hart, *Time, Religion, and Social Experience in Rural Greece* (Lanham, Maryland: Rowman & Littlefield Publishers, Inc., 1992).

Leonard Primiano, 'Vernacular Religion and the Search for Method in Religious Folklife', *Western Folklore* 54 (1), (1995), 37–56.

Μηνάς Αλ. Αλεξιάδης, 'Do ut des', *"Δωδώνη", Επιστημονική Επετηρίς του Τμήματος Ιστορίας και Αρχαιολογίας της Φιλοσοφικής Σχολής του Πανεπιστημίου Ιωαννίνων*, 16 (1), (1987), 253–65.

Marcel Mauss, 'Essai sur le don. Forme et raison de l' échange dans les sociétés archaiques', *Année Sociologique*, I (1923–1924), 30–186.

Margaret Alexiou, *The Ritual Lament in Greek Tradition* (Greek Studies: Interdisciplinary Approaches, Washington, DC: Rowman and Littlefield, 2002).

Margaret E. Kenna, 'Icons in Theory and Practice: An Orthodox Christian Example', *History of Religions*, 24 (4) (May 1985), 345–68.

Μαρία Γ. Ανδρουλάκη, 'Να πούμε για την Παναγιά σήμερο στην Αυλή της, Ξενιτεμένοι ήρθασι και Φίλοι στη Γιορτή της …: Δεκαπενταύγουστος στην Όλυμπο Καρπάθου', *Τύπος της Κυριακής*, 13 Αύγουστος 2000, pp. 12–14.

Μαρία Γ. Ανδρουλάκη, 'Το γλέντι στην Όλυμπο Καρπάθου, Τεχνικές Συλλογικής Έκφρασης και Επικοινωνίας', in *Κάρπαθος & Λαογραφία, Δ΄ Διεθνές Συνέδριο Καρπαθιακής Λαογραφίας [Κάρπαθος, 8–12 Μαΐου 2013]*, ed. by Μηνάς Αλ. Αλεξιάδης and Πόπη Κ. Ξανθάκου (Αθήνα: Ινστιτούτο Λαϊκού Πολιτισμού Τμήματος Φιλολογίας, Ε.Κ.Π.Α. – Καρπαθιακός Οργανισμός Πολιτισμού, Άθλησης, Παιδείας Δήμου Καρπάθου, 2016), pp. 178–91.

Μανόλης Γ. Βαρβούνης, *Θεμελιώδεις έννοιες και μορφές της ελληνικής θρησκευτικής λαογραφίας* (Αθήνα: Στρατηγικές εκδόσεις Ι. Φλώρος, 2013).

Marion Bowman, 'Vernacular Religion, Contemporary Spirituality and Emergent Identities. Lessons from Lauri Honko', *Approaching Religion*, 4 (1), (May 2014), 101–13.

Marilena Papachristophorou, *Myth, Representation, and Identity. An Ethnography of Memory in Lipsi, Greece* (London: Palgrave Macmillan, 2013).

Μυροφόρα Ευσταθιάδου, *Ταξιδεύοντας στον Πόντο. Τουρισμός της νοσταλγίας* (Αθήνα: Μένανδρος, 2018).

Maurice Godelier, *L' énigme du don* (Paris: Librairie Arthème Fayard, 1996).

Maurice Halbwachs, *Η συλλογική μνήμη*, edited and with preface by Anna Mantoglou (Αθήνα: Παπαζήσης, 2013) [original edition: *La mémoire collective* (Paris: Les Presses Universitaires de France, 1968)].

Μανόλης Μακρής, 'Τα 'Σαριάτικα' κωπηλατικά τραγούδια', Η΄ Πολιτιστικό Συμπόσιο της Στέγης Γραμμάτων και Τεχνών Δωδεκανήσου (Κάρπαθος 1993), *Δωδεκανησιακά Χρονικά*, 16 (1998), 265–84.

Monique Scheer, 'Are Emotions a Kind of Practice (and Is That What Makes Them Have a History)? A Bourdieuian Approach to Understanding Emotion', *History and Theory*, 51 (May 2012), 193–220.

Νικόλαος Γ. Πολίτης, 'Αναθήματα κατ' ευχήν', *Λαογραφία*, 2 (1910–1911), pp. 125–30.

Pavlos Kavouras, 'Glendi and Xenitia: The Poetics of Exile in Rural Greece (Olympos, Karpathos)' (unpublished doctoral thesis, New School for Social Research, Ann Arbor, Michigan, U.M.I., 1990).

Παύλος Κάβουρας, 'Αυτοσχέδιο διαλογικό τραγούδι και γλεντικός συμβολισμός στην Όλυμπο Καρπάθου', *Εθνολογία*, 2 (1993), 155–200.

Sophia Handaka, 'Anthropological Reflections on Greek Orthodox Votive Offerings (Tamata), with Reference to the Mikes Paidousis Collection' (D. Phil. Thesis, University of Oxford, 2005).

Sherry B. Ortner, 'On Key Symbols', *American Anthropologist* 75 (5), (1973), 1338–46.

Stephen Pepper, *World Hypotheses* (Berkeley and Los Angeles: University of California Press, 1942).

Vernacular Religion in Everyday Life: Expressions of Belief, ed. by Marion Bowman and Ülo Valk (New York & London: Routledge, 2012).

Victor Turner and Edith Turner, *Image and Pilgrimage in Christian Culture. Anthropological Perspectives* (New York: Columbia University Press, 1978).

Walter J. Ong, *Orality and Literacy. The Technologizing of the Word* (London and New York: Routledge, Taylor & Francis Group, 2002 [first edition, 1982]).

GEORGIOS KOUZAS

From Pilgrimage to Festival and Commerce

Changes in the Use of Space in the Pilgrimage to the Church of Saint Barbara in the Municipality of 'Aghia Varvara' in Attica, Greece

Introduction and Aims of the Study

Although to most people the term 'pilgrimage' means something completely religious in nature, today, particularly in urban areas, the procedure involved in pilgrimages is not merely religious.[1] Much more than this, it is a process that is linked to social and economic processes that take place as part of religious festivals.[2]

My aim in the present article is not of course to consider all the various functions of urban religious festivals, which would require a complete study. My basic research questions here are threefold: (a) How far today do pilgrimages in urban areas possess merely religious aspects? (b) What are the other aspects – social, recreational and commercial – involved in pilgrimages today? (c) How, above all, is the space in which the festival takes place involved in process of change from the sacred to the secular?

The purpose is to examine the meaning of the change in the Saint Barbara pilgrimage to what is ultimately a commercial process. I will therefore look at the following matters: Initially, I focus upon the social importance of the space involved, which is a multi-facetted area that starts from the main boulevard of the municipality and ends at the church of Saint Barbara. This constitutes a transition or passage from the secular to the sacred, which however, becomes desanctified and secularized in urban space. This space, which bears the faithful towards the church, is a commercial space and above all the space in which the festival is conducted. Secondly, I will examine

---

1 Jill Dubisch, 'Golden Oranges and Silver Ships. An Interpretative Approach to a Greek Holy Shrine', *Journal of Modern Greek Studies*, 6 (1988), 128–85; Μανόλης Βαρβούνης, *Εισαγωγή στη θρησκευτική λαογραφία. Λαϊκή θρησκευτικότητα και παραδοσιακή θρησκευτική συμπεριφορά, πρώτος τόμος* (Θεσσαλονίκη: Σταμούλης, 2017), pp. 150–53.
2 Γιώργος Βοζίκας, 'Οι υπαίθριες αγορές των θρησκευτικών πανηγυριών στην πρωτεύουσα', *Λαογραφία*, 41 (2007–2009), 195–214.

Georgios Kouzas • PhD, Assistant Professor of Urban Folklore, Faculty of Philology, National and Kapodistrian University of Athens, Greece

Pilgrimage in the Christian Balkan World: The Path to Touch the Sacred and Holy, ed. by Dorina Dragnea, Emmanouil Ger. Varvounis, Evelyn Reuter, Petko Hristov and Susan Sorek (Turnhout, 2023), pp. 279–290.
BREPOLS PUBLISHERS   DOI 10.1484/M.STR-EB.5.132411

how emotions are created in the participants and how such emotions structure the predisposition and inclinations of the participants and their actions. I am particularly interested in how people interpret this passage from the sacred to the secular and why the very same people participate in commercial activity at the fair accompanying the religious festival. Lastly, in regard to the multi-facetted significance of urban religious pilgrimage: the urban area in which the pilgrimage activity takes place does not possess a merely religious significance. It also functions as an area in which inter-personal relations are strengthened, as a space in which items are bought and as a recreational process, given that the festival, which is annual, is not a frequent phenomenon.[3]

Ethnographic Research

Such an overall approach naturally involves use of the ethnographic literature relating to the subject. I decided not to deal with the many churches located in cities and towns, since such an attempt would have led to excessive generalization and the inability to examine the pilgrimage as a phenomenon in any depth.

I therefore decided that we should deal with a single pilgrimage and with a single anthropological example,[4] that is, with the Saint Barbara pilgrimage in the town of Aigaleo in Attica, Greece, which every year attracted thousands of the faithful. Saint Barbara is considered to be a wonder-working saint. There are widely known oral traditions,[5] regarding the discovery of her wonderworking icon by a group of the female faithful a century ago. I decided, furthermore, to stress only certain aspects, rather than examine the whole procedure involved in the pilgrimage. I was particularly interested by changes in the feelings and emotions experienced by individuals and in their subsequent actions, whether in terms of society or commerce, as they progress from the main boulevard, the Ierá Odós along the road (Eleftheriou Venizelou Boulevard) that leads to the church of Saint Barbara.

Thus the research, which took place in December of 2019, centred on the two boulevards, the Ierá Odós and Eleftheriou Venizelou and on the courtyard of the church of Saint Barbara, whose feast is celebrated on 4 December. This was thus the most recent public celebration of the feast (at the time of writing). The memory of Saint Barbara was not celebrated in 2020 nor did the accompanying celebration take place, because of the pandemic. I relied on participant observation[6] and on my experience gained during time spent in the field in the past.[7] I also thought it worthwhile

---

3 See also Μανόλης Βαρβούνης, *Λαϊκή θρησκευτικότητα στον ελληνικό αστικό χώρο. Μελετήματα νεωτερικής θρησκευτικής λαογραφίας* (Θεσσαλονίκη: Σταμούλης, 2014), pp. 95–112.
4 Γιώργος Βοζίκας, *Η συνοικία της Αγίας Μαρίνας στην Ηλιούπολη και το πανηγύρι της. Η καθημερινή ζωή και ταυτότητα της πόλης* (Αθήνα: Δήμος Ηλιούπολης, 2009), pp. 118–19.
5 Linda Dégh, *Narratives in Society: A Performer-Centered Study of Narration* (Helsinki: Academia Scientiarum Fennica, 1995), p. 58.
6 Elisabeth Tonkin, 'Participant Observation', in Roy F. Ellen, *Ethnographic Research. A Guide to General Conduct* (London – San Diego: Academic Press, 2003), pp. 219–21.
7 See also Richard Dorson, 'Doing Fieldwork in the City', *Folklore*, 92 (2), (1981), p. 150.

to cultivate a network of contacts in the area, consisting of inhabitants, tradesmen and priests, whom I had initially not known. I also undertook group interviews with these persons, by means of focus groups. An approach employing multi-sited ethnography,[8] which involves following the movements of subjects proved to be useful.

Cultural and Social Aspects of the Saint Barbara Pilgrimage

The Passage from Road to Sacred Space and to Sacred Time

The pilgrim, who visits the church of Saint Barbara, as he or she approaches the church to pay his or her respects to the saint, becomes aware immediately that he or she is entering a different universe. This world that he or she has penetrated is that of the sacred. Initially the visitor experiences a difference sensation of space. He or she leaves behind the Ierá Odós, a noisy arterial road, gradually entering upon a smaller road, Eleftheriou Venizelou Boulevard. This, because of the fair, does not contain any motor traffic and the only movement is that of visitors to the festival. As Giorgos Vozikas[9] has noted, the festival, despite being a commercial event, remains connected to sacred space and to sacred time. The fair is an intermediary event, with religious, commercial and social aspects and is located in the centre of this nexus. It stands on the threshold between two worlds, between the secular, consisting of life in the city, and the sacred, which lies in the sacred function of the church.[10] The fair, being an intermediary event, forms the pilgrim's transition, so to speak, to sacred space.[11] The inhabitants themselves who attend the church to pay their respects note that:

> As I pass through the fair, even when my eyes are closed, I can tell when I get to the church. The sounds of the fair, the smells, everything is all mixed up with church hymns and bells – It's like crossing from one place to another, like passing over to paying our respects to the saint that will happen in the church.[12]

On the one hand, then, we have a festival taking place. However, the act of paying one's respects to the saint is characterized by a conceptual polysemy, that is to say, by a combination of images and symbols. Thus there are religious elements that clearly emphasise the sacred nature of the place that the visitor is gradually approaching. These are tied to the feelings of the visitor and are both material and intangible. Among the material aspects, we can put the church and among the intangible we

---

8 Robert Yin, *Applications of Case Study Research* (California: Sage Publications, 2003), pp. 12–13.
9 Γιώργος Βοζίκας, *Η συνοικία της Αγίας Μαρίνας στην Ηλιούπολη και το πανηγύρι της. Η καθημερινή ζωή και ταυτότητα της πόλης*, pp. 122–25.
10 Mircea Eliade, *The Sacred and the Profane: The Nature of Religion* (New York: Harcourt Brace, 1959), pp. 18–21.
11 Diane Goldstein, 'The Secularization of Religious Ethnography and Narrative Competence in a Discourse of Faith', *Western Folklore*, 54 (1), (1995), 23–36; Arnold Van Gennep, *The Rites of Passage* (London: Routledge-Kegan Paul, 1960), pp. 75–80.
12 D., 62 years old, female, pensioner, Aghia Varvara, December of 2019.

can place the chanting of psalms, the voice of the priest and certainly the smell of incense. Let us now look at these matters in more detail.

In terms of material aspects, the church itself is particularly important. As Dubisch notes, in Greece churches, that is, church buildings, represent the link between sacred and secular.[13] That is to say, the building represents religion and God. At the same time, however, the church is a building created thanks to the monetary contributions of all the faithful in the area. Thus the faithful are aware of this dual nature of the church, as a place for piety and faith and a place deeply familiar to them. This intimacy with the church and faith in the power of the saint strengthens all the procedure involved in the pilgrimage and the frequency with which it occurs. My fieldwork made it evident to me that the visit to the church for the feast of Saint Barbara does not occur only once, on the day of the feast itself. Rather, visits are repeated another two or three times, usually on the eve of the feast and in the morning and afternoon of the feast day. Notably, in the accounts of the faithful, such visits to pay respects to Saint Barbara do not form merely a religious process, set in a sacred context. In fact, it is an 'all-encompassing' process, as Varvounis[14] observes. That is, in the accounts offered by those who come to pay their respects to the saint, one comes across elements of oral and local history and we also frequently find notions of collectivity,[15] and shared belief in the saint held by the local population, who generally believe that they benefit from the activity connected with Saint Barbara. In connection with all this, I give a small extract from the account of an informant.

> Pilgrimage here is an honour to the saint, but it also reminds us of our ancestors who used to come here then to pay their respects. Saint Barbara is tied to this place. We have many local legends about women who found the wonder-working icon a hundred years ago and other oral stories about the shepherd who saw Saint Barbara in a dream and she showed him the place to build a church. These stories are alive today…[16]

A significant role is played by the intangible, but still important factors of religious sounds, such as the noise of bells, the singing of psalms and the voice of the priest emanating from the loudspeakers, and smells of incense and flowers that decorate the church and the icons inside and out. Yet how are they connected with the visit to pay one's respects to the saint? The reply is that, although they have larger symbolic role, they nevertheless possess another function, secondary but still substantial, in that such simple sounds form soundscapes. In the view of Murray-Schafer,[17] a soundscape consists of the link between aural elements and the system whereby these elements

---

13 Jill Dubisch, *In a Different Place. Pilgrimage, Gender and Politics in a Greek Island Shrine* (Princeton: Princeton University Press, 1995), pp. 14–18.
14 Μανόλης Βαρβούνης, *Λαϊκή θρησκευτικότητα και εθιμικές πρακτικές. Μελετήματα θρησκευτικής και κοινωνικής λαογραφίας* (Αθήνα: Ηρόδοτος, 2015), pp. 661–62.
15 Antony Cohen, *The Symbolic Construction of Community* (London: Routledge, 1989), p. 55.
16 L., 76 years old, female, pensioner, Aghia Varvara, December of 2019.
17 Raymond Murray-Schafer, *Our Sonic Environment and the Turning of the World. The Soundscape* (Vermont: Destiny Books, 1981, repr. 1994), pp. 24–25.

are perceived by a particular group, and cognitively accompany the members of the group, so adding to the process involved in the pilgrimage. As Garrioch[18] has noted, sounds connected with religious rituals are typified by polysemy and variety, since they symbolize religious faith and reproduce a religious system. In the space from the road to the icon of Saint Barbara in the church we have one such typical soundscape: First of all, there are sounds that function emblematically, such as the sound of bells or the voice of the priest from the loudspeakers, which stimulate feelings of awe through respect for the divine. Furthermore, the sound of psalms is heard constantly, in the morning, afternoon and evening. We thus have an indivisible ensemble of sounds, in which the existence of each depends on all the others and all, when heard together, create emotions.[19] The existence of such emotions helps the faithful invest this space with symbolism and meaning. Such a sacred soundscape, in which the visit to the saint takes place, is of course strengthened by the mesh of smells of incense and flowers.

In the view of Turner,[20] odour forms one of the fundamental symbols of daily life, linked to the social and cultural conditions that create it. Smells help us at once to comprehend the surrounding space and to understand its functions and is a powerful mechanism for recall, in that it brings to mind images and memories from the past. The smell of incense, for example, immediately calls the sacred to mind, since it is associated with sacred matters and tends to predispose the individual to behave with respect and circumspection. At the same time, as our informants maintained, it instantly recalls memories from previous pilgrimages to Saint Barbara from their childhood years.

Here one may make two observations. First, the pilgrimage procedure has become extremely secularized in recent decades, since it has been subject to the potent influence of the commercial fair that everywhere in Greece accompanies the celebration of the memory of saints.[21] Secondly and equally important is the fact that despite the powerful influence of financial and commercial factors involved in the commercial fair, the pilgrimage itself has not lost its sacred character.[22] The procedure that informs it has not been secularized. Instead, its sacred and secular aspects complement each other even in today's urban environment.[23] It is interesting, so it seems to me, to look at the reversal of the process during the next phase, that is,

---

18   David Garrioch, 'Sounds of the City. The Soundscape of Early Modern of Early Modern European Towns', *Urban History*, 30 (1), (2003), pp. 22–24.
19   Manolis Sergis, 'Sounds of the Cities: Soundscapes of Music Echoed in Michael Mitsakis' Literary Works about Athens (1880–1896)', *Erytheia*, 34 (2013), pp. 248–49.
20   Victor Turner, *The Forest of Symbols: Aspects of Ndembu Ritual* (New York – Cornell: Ithaca, 1967), pp. 35–42; Michel De Certeau, *The Practice of Everyday Life* (Berkeley: University of California Press, 1988), pp. 11–12.
21   Μανόλης Βαρβούνης, *Εισαγωγή στη θρησκευτική λαογραφία. Ο κύκλος του χρόνου – ο κύκλος της ζωής – ο κύκλος της λατρείας*, δεύτερος τόμος (Θεσσαλονίκη: Σταμούλης, 2017), pp. 332–33.
22   Manolis Varvounis, 'Religious Folklore. Between Tradition and Modernity', *Jahrbuch für Europäische Ethnologie*, 15 (2020), 29–56.
23   Cf. Μανόλης Βαρβούνης, 'Μορφές του ελληνικού δημόσιου τελετουργικού και ελληνική λαϊκή θρησκευτικότητα. Μικρή σπουδή στη λαογραφική υπόσταση των δημόσιων τελετών στην Ελλάδα', *Θεολογία*, 86 (3), (2015), 231–50.

at how a purely religious practice, such as pilgrimage, both coexists with commercial and financial processes and at how at the same time it actually encourages individuals towards buying objects from the stalls of the commercial fair.

The Opposite Direction: From the Sacred to the Secular and Back Again

In the previous section, we examined some components of pilgrimage relating to the sanctity of space and changes in the uses of space between the public highway and the courtyard of the church. In this part, we will look at how the sacred is entwined with the secular and how the faithful as part of the pilgrimage process are channelled towards buying items at the fair. The spatial arrangement of the stalls is not fortuitous. The traders are aware that the closer they are to the church and, of course, to the icon of Saint Barbara and the church services, the closer they are to the sacred. And so, it is usually considered appropriate for stalls selling religious items to stand nearest the church, while towards the middle of the fair and particularly towards the exit there are stands selling items connected with daily life and household needs. Antonis, 65 years old, who sells plastic items for kitchen use, said the following:

> We people who sell things for the house, we arrange to be a bit further from the church. It's not respectful for somebody to go and pay their respects to the saint and to see outside the church plastic bowls and knickers. That's why we go down a bit further, to the beginning of the street and the people who sell religious things go nearer the church.

The stalls are arranged in similar fashion at fairs in the Greek countryside. Here, at the start of the road to the church, one finds not only financial activities, in the form of the buying and selling of objects, but also patterns of behaviour – shouting, bargaining over prices, laughter and joshing – that are not suitable for religious space. To speak in symbolic terms, we have here a progress along the road to the church from the secular to the religious world and the opposite, when respects have been paid to the saint and the faithful leave the church.[24] That is, after honour has been paid to the saint, one can discern a progress on the part of the faithful from sanctity, which extends symbolically as far as the religious objects sold at the stalls outside the church, back to the world, secular life and the stalls that sell purely commercial objects. Albeit symbolically and metaphorically, we have a circular pattern that informs the constant switching both between the situations and states of the visitors to the fair and between their moods and disposition, too.

The market at the fair is, first of all, an important open-air place for the purchase by the faithful of religious items. There they can purchase religious items, such as icons, lamps and censers, and consumable religious objects, such as incense, charcoal used in censers, lamp oil and holy oil. The object in the greatest demand, however, consists of the icon of Saint Barbara herself, whether these icons are of wood or plastic, to be

---

24 Setha Low, *Theorizing the City. The New Urban Anthropology Reader* (New Brunswick-New Jersey-London: Rutgers University Press, 2005), pp. 47–51.

placed on the domestic icon-stand or to be hung on the wall, or whether they are printed on mugs, key-rights, badges and diaries. As Dubisch[25] notes, the icon is centre of all religious behaviour. It is the reason why the faithful visit the church, it is the motive for the pilgrimage and it is the centre of all religious rituals. And, of course, the significance of the icon of the saint is both festal and symbolic. In terms of the latter, it is a key symbol and particularly a symbol that summarises things, as Ortner[26] suggests, and it is therefore prominent as the centre of the process of pilgrimage.

As for the road on which the fair is held, the icon of Saint Barbara in the church is, as it were, multiplied many times, since the saint appears both in pictures and on objects. Interestingly, I found that respects were paid to this sort of icon, too, found on the stalls of the traders at the fair. Many of the faithful, even in front of the icons on the stalls kiss the image of the saint or make the sign of the Cross, which is certainly an unusual way of paying one's respects to Saint Barbara. As an informant put it to me:

> Of course, I make the sign of the Cross even here, in front of the market stall, and of course I bow and kiss the icon. And this, too, for me is an icon of the saint and for me it's like seeing the wonder-working icon that's in the church.[27]

Vozikas[28] touched on the matter, in his study of the self-adhesive emblem of the fair, as did Kouzas,[29] who examined posters for such fairs. Both conclude that the depictions of the saints that appear on the posters or on the stickers are certainly for the faithful a symbolic depiction of the actual icon that they can keep on their person all the time. Such icons are accorded the same respect and honour as the real icon in the church.

Finally, there is another aspect that Beverly Stoeltje[30] notes in connection with fairs in America. As he notes, a fair offers a 'landing mechanism' back in reality, after the strict religious section of the proceedings connected with the divine and transcendent. In other words, Stoeltje is making the point that the fair is as much a place of work (for the sellers and those seeking work, albeit only temporary) as a space where visitors to the fair, who are not merely those who have come to pay their respects to the saint, are in quest of cheap goods. These include toys, kitchen tools and household items, together with clothes and disposable items, such as paper or plastic objects, all of which they need for daily life. At this point one may ask why, in such a large city as Athens, do so many of the inhabitants feel the need to buy basic

---

25 Jill Dubisch, *In a Different Place. Pilgrimage, Gender and Politics in a Greek Island Shrine*, p. 19.
26 Shery B. Ortner, 'On Key Symbols', *American Anthropologist* 75 (5), (1973), pp. 1339–40.
27 M., 86 years old, female, pensioner, Aghia Varvara, December of 2019.
28 Γιώργος Βοζίκας, 'Το αυτοκόλλητο σήμα στο θρησκευτικό πανηγύρι της πόλης. Σχόλιο επάνω στα όρια και τις πολιτιστικές διαστάσεις των αντικειμένων', *Επετηρίδα Κέντρου Ερεύνης Ελληνικής Λαογραφίας*, 29-30 (2004), 349–80.
29 Γιώργος Κούζας, 'Θρησκευτικότητα και αστικός χώρος: νεότερες μελέτες για τη θρησκευτική ζωή στις πόλεις', *Λαογραφία*, 43 (2013–2016), pp. 518-19.
30 Beverly Stoeltje, 'Festival', in *Folklore, Cultural Performances and Popular Entertainments*, ed. by Richard Bauman (New York: Oxford University Press, 1992), pp. 261–63; Cf. George Warshaver, 'Urban Folklore', in *Handbook of American Folklore*, ed. by Richard Dorson (Bloomington: Indiana University Press, 1983), pp. 162–71.

items at such fairs? Susana Narotzky[31] offers an answer. She notes that the informal economy functions constantly in western societies and complements the formal economy. She also notes the existence of the concept of 'economic reproduction' of similar phenomena in capitalism, such as uninsured workers and the absence of tax receipts or other means of tracking exchanges, that do not fulfil basic legal and formal requirements. Such phenomena continue in open-air markets because they cater to the needs of both traders and workers and of clients.

Thus, the road from the church, in addition to forming a transition from the worldly to the sacred for the pilgrim as he or she passes along it and in addition to being a space in which the icon is carried in procession, is also a space purely commercial in function. In Greece, such a space always accompanies religious feasts, and its point is to cater to basic needs.

The Co-existence of Sacred and Secular. The Hidden Aspects of Paying One's Respects to the Saint

In many conversations, during the course of my fieldwork, I found that the process of paying one's respects to the saint had other functions that complemented the religious and commercial aspects and were no less important. I start with a typical statement from an informant:

> For many people who live round here, the feast of Saint Barbara is the event of the year. But the thing is not just religious. For us it's much more a wonderful opportunity to see people from the area we don't often see, because with so many things to do every day you just don't get to see the people you'd like to and, besides, it's fun for us. Do you really think that everybody comes here just to pay their respects to the icon? They do come here for that, but it's much more, so that they can have a good time and buy things.[32]

I recorded many other similar statements from pilgrims to Saint Barbara. I realised that during the period in which respects are paid to the icon there are other social functions in play that are not as obvious as those associated with religion. First of all, the visit to the church to pay one's respects to the icon is closely tied to the meaning inherent in the unique event that occurs annually on 4 December. The feast is an important moment in 'cyclical time', which breaks the constant flow of daily life, that is, 'linear time' that typifies the life of the city-dweller.[33] My informants regarded 4 December as a notable break in their daily existence, since the events, involving religion, commerce and the reestablishment and reconfirmation of an urban local community, that make up this different period of time are structured over three days. Indeed, the multiple redefinitions and reinterpretations of the space where the

---

31 Susana Narotzky, *New Directions in Economic Anthropology* (London-Chicago: Pluto Press, 1997), pp. 131–37.
32 M., 58 years old, female, employee, Aghia Varvara, December of 2019.
33 Βασίλης Νιτσιάκος, *Χτίζοντας το Χώρο και το Χρόνο* (Αθήνα: Οδυσσέας, 2003).

festival is held bring about its symbolic and metaphorical metamorphosis. It is not merely the sacred space in front of the church. Rather, it is now a polyvalent space that draws to itself social processes that are clearly positive, such as entertainment for many of the faithful. The concept is extremely wide-ranging and linked both to the concepts of free time and to collectivity. Let us now look at how these two notions are tied to the process involved in paying one's respects to the saint.

Entertainment is linked with free time, which today is no longer identified either with the lack of employment or with leisure. For social scientists, entertainment is a social construct, albeit one that is a basic necessity directly linked to the social conditions, to the way of life and to the structure of employment prevailing at any one time. In the view of Koronaiou,[34] free time is above all social time, is linked with social processes and is to be differentiated from working time. It thus becomes an independent field of social activity, in which individuals enjoy and entertain themselves, so escaping from the commonplace nature of daily life in the attempt to see and experience something different to the norm. At the feast of Saint Barbara, a pleasant stroll, in a place with crowds, with sellers of merchandise, with unusual sights and various sound pictures, such as the cries of those selling their wares, songs and the sound of the conversation of those at the fair, makes for something different. Not in itself religious, this experience is an indivisible aspect of fairs in Greece.

At this point we may look at the matter of collectiveness, an aspect of the process of paying one's respects to the saint that is frequently overlooked. Collectivity at the fair and therefore in the whole process of paying one's respects to the icon has two aspects, namely, collective experience and collective memory. The pilgrimage to the icon is both an individual and collective experience. The individual pays his or her respects individually, although at the same time the whole of the local community takes part in the process. What, however, do we mean by the term 'community' in the context of a religious feast and indeed in a city? The term is certainly an inclusive concept with multiple meanings. Above all, at such a religious fair, the local community, which in town and cities is called the 'neighbourhood', once more reunites and reconstitutes itself.[35] The strengthening of bonds is achieved in multiple ways, through meetings and encounters at the fair, through conversation in the queue for the icon, through participation in religious rituals and of course through commercial interaction. There is also the matter of collective memory, that is, the memory of the collective past that returns to the present through participation in mass religious practices. Memories of the past, tales of revelry at the fair and, of course, stories of the miracles performed by the saint are just some of the aspects of the collective memory of the inhabitants of the area. Both the collective memory of the present and of the past are triggered by the process of paying one's respects to the saint and by everything that goes with this process in terms of space and human movement.

---

34 Αλεξάνδρα Κορωναίου, 'Κοινωνιολογία του ελεύθερου χρόνου' στο *Κοινωνιολογία του Ελεύθερου Χρόνου*, επιμέλεια από την Αλεξάνδρα Κορωναίου (Αθήνα: Νήσος, 1996), pp. 15–127.

35 Ευάγγελος Αυδίκος, 'Τελετουργία και "πρόσωπο" στην Αθήνα. Η περίπτωση των ορθόδοξων τσιγγάνων από το Διδυμότειχο', *Η Θράκη και οι άλλοι. Ιχνηλατώντας τα πολιτισμικά όρια και την ιστορική μνήμη* (Αθήνα: Οδυσσέας, 2007), pp. 157–65.

Conclusion

The chapter reflects the polysemy of the pilgrimage in the town of Aigaleo and the dialectical relationship between sacred and secular that resides in this process in terms of the use of space. In particular, I make use above all of a particular ethnographic example to make clear the significance of space and more especially of the road involved, as a cross-over point from the secular world of the city to the sacred space and time of the religious fair. This transition occurs in both material and non-material terms, through a combination of feelings, sentiments, sounds and movement.

As well, the commercial aspect of the celebration was attempted, since the procedure involved in this paying of respects to the saint, which is directly linked with the world of the secular, nevertheless has certain sacred aspects, such as the multiple depictions of the saint, whether religious icons or representations printed on household objects. These pictures assume a role analogous to that of main icon and many of the faithful pay their respects to these representations and treat them with honour, although the pictures stand on market stalls in the middle of the fair. Thus, the pilgrimage to the icon of the saint acquires new aspects in the space where the fair is held that are as important and as notable as those involved in the paying of respects to the icon in the church.

Another aspect that I have attempted to highlight lies in the invisible aspects of the pilgrimage to the icon that lie midway between religion and commerce. Such aspects are the entertainment inherent in the whole procedure, since for many of the faithful the process of the pilgrimage to the icon is not merely religious nor is their attendance at the fair solely commercially driven. Much more, for them it means involvement in a remarkable event that breaks up the monotony of everyday life and is for them a moment of entertainment.

These aspects of the pilgrimage to the icon make it clear that the event is not purely religious. It is, much more, a totally social event, with social, economic and entertainment aspects, in addition to the religious sides, these, of course, being a given. As a total social event, it is related to various aspects of daily life, to human feelings and certainly to sacred and secular time and space. Characteristic of this is the fact that sacred and secular space and time here, rather than conflicting with each other, actually complement each other. Lastly, this chapter hopefully makes clear that pilgrimage to icons as a procedure in Greek towns and cities is still alive even today, albeit admittedly not in the form that it had in traditional folk culture. It now displays dynamic new manifestations that confirm the point that cultural phenomena, rather than remaining untouched over time, change continually. Although these cultural phenomena are moulded by contemporary social and historical changes, they do not lose sight of the reasons why they came into existence, which here is the desire to render respect to Saint Barbara.

References

Antony Cohen, *The Symbolic Construction of Community* (London: Routledge, 1989).
Αλεξάνδρα Κορωναίου, 'Κοινωνιολογία του ελεύθερου χρόνου' στο *Κοινωνιολογία του Ελεύθερου Χρόνου*, επιμέλεια από την Αλεξάνδρα Κορωναίου (Αθήνα: Νήσος, 1996).
Arnold Van Gennep, *The Rites of Passage* (London: Routledge-Kegan Paul, 1960).
Beverly Stoeltje, 'Festival', in *Folklore, Cultural Performances and Popular Entertainments*, ed. by Richard Bauman (New York: Oxford University Press, 1992), pp. 261–71.
Βασίλης Νιτσιάκος, *Χτίζοντας το Χώρο και το Χρόνο* (Αθήνα: Οδυσσέας, 2003).
David Garrioch, 'Sounds of the City. The Soundscape of Early Modern of Early Modern European Towns', *Urban History*, 30 (1), (2003), 5–25.
Diane Goldstein, 'The Secularization of Religious Ethnography and Narrative Competence in a Discourse of Faith', *Western Folklore*, 54 (1), (1995), 23–36.
Elisabeth Tonkin, 'Participant Observation', in *Ethnographic Research. A Guide to General Conduct*, ed. by Roy F. Ellen (London – San Diego: Academic Press, 2003), pp. 216–23.
Ευάγγελος Αυδίκος, 'Τελετουργία και "πρόσωπο" στην Αθήνα. Η περίπτωση των ορθόδοξων τσιγγάνων από το Διδυμότειχο', *Η Θράκη και οι άλλοι. Ιχνηλατώντας τα πολιτισμικά όρια και την ιστορική μνήμη* (Αθήνα: Οδυσσέας, 2007).
George Warshaver, 'Urban Folklore', in *Handbook of American Folklore*, ed. by Richard Dorson (Bloomington: Indiana University Press, 1983), pp. 162–71.
Γιώργος Βοζίκας, 'Το αυτοκόλλητο σήμα στο θρησκευτικό πανηγύρι της πόλης. Σχόλιο επάνω στα όρια και τις πολιτιστικές διαστάσεις των αντικειμένων', *Επετηρίδα Κέντρου Ερεύνης Ελληνικής Λαογραφίας*, 29–30 (2004), 349–80.
Γιώργος Βοζίκας, 'Οι υπαίθριες αγορές των θρησκευτικών πανηγυριών στην πρωτεύουσα', *Λαογραφία*, 41 (2007–2009), 195–214.
Γιώργος Βοζίκας, *Η συνοικία της Αγίας Μαρίνας στην Ηλιούπολη και το πανηγύρι της. Η καθημερινή ζωή και ταυτότητα της πόλης* (Αθήνα: Δήμος Ηλιούπολης, 2009).
Γιώργος Κούζας, 'Θρησκευτικότητα και αστικός χώρος: νεότερες μελέτες για τη θρησκευτική ζωή στις πόλεις', *Λαογραφία*, 43 (2013–2016), 518–19.
Jill Dubisch, 'Golden Oranges and Silver Ships. An Interpretative Approach to a Greek Holy Shrine', *Journal of Modern Greek Studies*, 6 (1988), 128–85.
Jill Dubisch, *In a Different Place. Pilgrimage, Gender and Politics in a Greek Island Shrine* (Princeton: Princeton University Press, 1995).
Linda Dégh, *Narratives in Society: A Performer-Centered Study of Narration* (Helsinki: Academia Scientiarum Fennica, 1995).
Manolis Sergis, 'Sounds of the Cities: Soundscapes of Music Echoed in Michael Mitsakis' Literary Works about Athens (1880–1896)', *Erytheia*, 34 (2013), 235–58.
Manolis Varvounis, 'Religious Folklore. Between Tradition and Modernity', *Jahrbuch für Europäische Ethnologie*, 15 (2020), 29–56.
Μανόλης Βαρβούνης, *Λαϊκή θρησκευτικότητα στον ελληνικό αστικό χώρο. Μελετήματα νεωτερικής θρησκευτικής λαογραφίας* (Θεσσαλονίκη: Σταμούλης, 2014).
Μανόλης Βαρβούνης, 'Μορφές του ελληνικού δημόσιου τελετουργικού και ελληνική λαϊκή θρησκευτικότητα. Μικρή σπουδή στη λαογραφική υπόσταση των δημόσιων τελετών στην Ελλάδα', *Θεολογία*, 86 (3), (2015), 231–50.

Μανόλης Βαρβούνης, *Λαϊκή θρησκευτικότητα και εθιμικές πρακτικές. Μελετήματα θρησκευτικής και κοινωνικής λαογραφίας* (Αθήνα: Ηρόδοτος, 2015).

Μανόλης Βαρβούνης, *Εισαγωγή στη θρησκευτική λαογραφία. Λαϊκή θρησκευτικότητα και παραδοσιακή θρησκευτική συμπεριφορά*, πρώτος τόμος (Θεσσαλονίκη: Σταμούλης, 2017).

Μανόλης Βαρβούνης, *Εισαγωγή στη θρησκευτική λαογραφία. Ο κύκλος του χρόνου – ο κύκλος της ζωής – ο κύκλος της λατρείας*, δεύτερος τόμος (Θεσσαλονίκη: Σταμούλης, 2017).

Michel De Certeau, *The Practice of Everyday Life* (Berkeley: University of California Press, 1988).

Mircea Eliade, *The Sacred and the Profane: The Nature of Religion* (New York: Harcourt Brace, 1959).

Raymond Murray-Schafer, *Our Sonic Environment and the Turning of the World. The Soundscape* (Vermont: Destiny Books, 1981, repr. 1994).

Richard Dorson, 'Doing Fieldwork in the City', *Folklore*, 92 (2), (1981), 149–54.

Robert Yin, *Applications of Case Study Research* (California: Sage Publications, 2003).

Setha Low, *Theorizing the City. The New Urban Anthropology Reader* (New Brunswick-New Jersey-London: Rutgers University Press, 2005).

Shery B. Ortner, 'On Key Symbols', *American Anthropologist* 75 (5), (1973), 1339–46.

Susana Narotzky, *New Directions in Economic Anthropology* (London-Chicago: Pluto Press, 1997).

Victor Turner, *The Forest of Symbols: Aspects of Ndembu Ritual* (New York - Cornell: Ithaca, 1967).

EVELYN REUTER

Conclusion

The path to touch the sacred and holy is a metaphor referring to certain features of pilgrimage. A 'path' has a start and an end, symbolizes mobility to move from one point to another. 'Path' symbolizes physical and metaphorical mobility, i.e. it implies motivations and a strategy to reach a target. The result is a transformation: Persons change with each step they take, and do not return like they started. The target is twofold, and includes the activity of 'touching' and the object to be touched. 'Touching' enables physical experiences, and thus is an attempt to ascertain what someone believes in, but maybe cannot see or understand. Consequently, the sacred and holy are the targets to reach, the objects to touch, and the reasons to hit the road. Furthermore, the contact with the 'sacred and holy' results in the transformation and shapes it.

This volume takes a cross-disciplinary approach to evaluate the topic of metaphor. For this purpose, the authors investigate case studies to point out local and temporal features of pilgrimages in the Balkans. The social and cultural anthropological overview of pilgrimages in Christian communities of the Balkan also reviews theories. Especially the theories of Turner and Eade/Sallnow are still an important point of reference. However, while most of the contributions follow them, some (Lubańksa, Dugushina and Novik, Giakoumis, and Reuter) critique these theories and offer innovative theoretical approaches.

All contributions mention features that indicate a spatial dimension. Thus, a spatial theory can offer an appropriate approach to reflect these features. Especially, Kim Knott's spatial theory (2005) suits for this enterprise because she offers a constructive definition: 'place is that nexus in space in which social relations occur, which may be material or metaphorical and which is necessarily interconnected (with places) and full of power'.[1] Furthermore, according to Knott, places are 'perceived', 'conceived', and 'lived', i.e. people build places according to their needs and ideas,[2] which matches

---

1 Kim Knott, *The Location of Religion. A Spatial Analysis* (London, Oakville: Equinox Publishing 2005b), p. 134.
2 Cf. Kim Knott, 'Spatial Theory and Method for the Study of Religion', *Temenos - Nordic Journal of Comparative Religion*, 41 (2005a), pp. 162–63.

Evelyn REUTER • PhD, Collaborative Research Fellow at Sophia University Tokyo, Japan

Pilgrimage in the Christian Balkan World: The Path to Touch the Sacred and Holy, ed. by Dorina Dragnea, Emmanouil Ger. Varvounis, Evelyn Reuter, Petko Hristov and Susan Sorek (Turnhout, 2023), pp. 291–295.

perfectly with the conclusions of the chapters. Applying this spatial theory to the case studies of pilgrimage leads to a better understanding of pilgrimage dynamics. The following concluding remarks present some major results of this volume from the perspective of Knott's theory.[3] This volume examines physical as well as metaphorical places and spaces. However, most of the case studies refer to certain places that should be reached physically. Mainly these places are monasteries and churches, but this category includes other meaningful sites like prisons, private houses, or cities. All these locations are parts of broader spaces considered as geographical or political entities. In the volume, smaller entities are mentioned such as villages, cities, and regions, plus transregional or transnational entities like states, Europe, or more specific the Europe like Ladić and Hrovatin exemplify.

Among the metaphorical places, saints are the main places, because they played a significant role in the region, they established physical places or are reasons to establish them. Thus, saints also initiated the cults of pilgrimage directly or indirectly at physical places (cf. Giakoumis). Furthermore, metaphorical places include even objects such as relicts, icons, and statues of saints as well as natural occurrences like water and stones that are not obviously religious.

Physical and metaphorical places cannot always be sharply distinguished from each other. Thus, Gumenâi exemplifies the interconnection of a monastery and an icon, i.e. of physical and metaphorical places. The plurality of pilgrimage places is what Victor and Edith Turner (1978) have called 'polycentrism'. The interconnection of places results even in the production of new places and Giakoumis calls this as 'diffusion' to complement the Turnerian theory.

The connection between the considered places can take various meanings and shapes. In her chapter, Dragnea illustrates the path to the 'sacred and holy' as connection of two worlds, i.e. the 'mundane' here and now on earth and the other world of the divine. Moreover, Lubańska concludes that 'live-giving energy' is what people in Bulgaria are looking for at pilgrimages, i.e. a kind of divine power, miracles, feelings, and experiences. At the same time, the author proves that to gain this energy people have to give or to do something at the places, for the saints, and/ or with the objects. Thus, gaining energy seems to be the result of exchanging goods between human beings and the divine, while the physical and metaphorical places are supportive vehicles.

The perception of places depends mainly on the actors. Reuter shows in her chapter that the religious perception results from the entire context too. She concludes this from the differentiation of the actors' motivations and activities. Pilgrimages are completed by religious activities such as praying, celebrating feast days of saints, lightning candles, etc. Relevant to the findings of Reuter is the study of Necula who mentions that some of these visits are organized explicitly by parishes or dioceses. Thus, according to the author, the church as an institution is a main actor that uses pilgrimage as pedagogical method for educating people and

---

3 The authors indicated in this concluding chapter mainly refer to the participants of this volume. Therefore, the source will not be indicated unless required.

building a faithful Christian community. Beside the church, Necula mentions even teachers and children to emphasis the religious-educational function of pilgrimage. Furthermore, Hrovatin connects the educational dimension of pilgrimage also with the influence on European culture. Among the church staff are bishops, priests and pastoral teams organizing pilgrimages. In another chapter, Varvounis concludes, clerics are responsible for preserving the religious character. Monasterial residents, monks and nuns, control if practices, behaviour, or even clothing on-site are acceptable, and keep the official traditions. Further tasks might be documenting pilgrimages, or even creating people's needs for pilgrimages as concluded by the results of Anđelković. Accordingly, intended consequences of pilgrimages are the religious transformation of people and the influence on their lives. Thus, pilgrimages organised by church aim a spiritual revival as Dragnea states in her chapter.

Religious interpretation includes even perspectives of lay persons that do not belong to the church staff. Lay persons' religious practices and perspectives are often called vernacular, folk, or lived religion in contrast to the official religion controlled by the church (cf. Varvounis). Nevertheless, for the term 'energy' Lubańska concludes that some ideas of lay persons match with Eastern Christian theology, New Age spirituality and in her case teachings of Petŭr Dŭnov, a Bulgarian theosophist.

The volume illustrates that besides the religious connotated perception of pilgrimage there are other, non-religious meanings. The meanings of pilgrimages and visited places always depend from the actors' needs. Hrovatin concludes this for political, cultural, and religious aspects. In contrast to local communities, diaspora communities inscribe their own meanings to pilgrimages. As Chryssanthopolou concludes, the descendants of immigrants visit places of their ancestors' origins to reassure themselves of their own roots. This emphasis and revitalisation of their origins proves their patriotism, i.e. their political interests. At the same time, pilgrimages for diaspora communities connect their past with their future plans to visit places of their origins again.

Pilgrimages and their targets as physical and metaphorical places are consciously 'conceived' by actors, but they are also contingently formed by certain issues. As Dugushina and Novik conclude in their chapter, pilgrimages are always shaped by historical, political, and social circumstances. Historically, pilgrimages became very popular in the Middle Ages (cf. Ladić and Gumenâi). In that time, pilgrimage established cultural and economic connections, and enabled peaceful learning about various aspects of different cultures and civilizations. Nevertheless, even today pilgrimages in Moldova include pre-Christian traditions as Dragnea shows in her study. These pre-Christian traditions are what Varvounis defines as the current popular religiosity that is expressed in contemporary pilgrimage in Greece. According to Pantea, at the beginning of the twentieth century, pilgrimages have been connotated quite politically due to wars and border demarcations. During socialism, often the lay persons' religiosity continued, while religions were banned (cf. Giakoumis). The impact of socialism transformed pilgrimages and places, e.g. into visits to touristic spots. Since the 1990s and due to the new granted religious freedom, the establishment of the official church perspective is a rediscovery of tradition depending on the socialist politics of the individual states. Thus, regarding to post-socialist states, continuities and discontinuities become obvious.

Closely linked to the conception of places is the way actors live them, i.e. how they behave there and how they use them. This aspect refers for instance to the negotiation of religious differences at pilgrimages as another religio-political conclusion of this volume. While Pantea examines this issue for Orthodox and Catholic Christian communities in Romania, Dugushina and Novik illustrate the negotiations of interfaith coexistence between Christian and Muslim communities in Kosovo and Albania. In both cases, the borders between religious groups overlap with those of different ethnic groups.

However, during pilgrimage, actors do not only live their religions, rather than all aspects that characterize them. The chapters of Anđelković and Kouzas illustrate this by the interdependency of pilgrimage with tourism and economy. In addition to traders, Anđelković explains even how the local community profits from tourists. Moreover, the needs manufactured by the brotherhood illustrate the economic meaning of pilgrimages for the monastery and its residents as the main occasion to get money. Kouzas concludes that pilgrimages are interdependent social and economic processes.

Of course, all mentioned categories of actors can overlap or interact. Moreover, the actors' reasons, interpretations, and influences are interdependent. Nevertheless, some categories need more research. Little attention is paid on the role of gender and age of the pilgrims (cf. Ladić or Chryssanthopolou). More investigation is also required on the role of journalists, and the media (cf. Anđelković), especially the social media. Finally, with respect to the feature of healing (cf. Lubańska), even the role of healers at pilgrimage sites and the perspectives from medical staff on this phenomenon are worth to be studied further.

The volume concludes that the investigated places are targets and symbols of a community with a specific meaning for the actors. Hitting the path to touch the 'sacred and holy' is not always religiously motivated. There are even touristic, political, social, or economic reasons that can motivate people what become evident by the differentiation of actors. Moreover, these reasons can be combined so that the results of transformation are quite ambiguous as Reuter concludes.

However, regardless of the actual motivations to come in contact with physical and metaphorical places, the original reasons to visit the places are based on religion. This raises the question of the relation between 'sacred and holy' and 'secular' that is also called 'profane'. Often, these attributes are defined as dichotomy. This volume offers two more perspectives: For Kouzas, the attributes complement each other with respect to time and space. In contrast, Reuter asserts that 'religious' and 'secular' refer to the meta level of how to interpret cultural patterns. Moreover, she applies this theory to the spatial structure of pilgrimage targets: the identification of an inner and an outer area reflect the ambiguity of meanings. These approaches to rethink the dichotomy open new perspectives for further research on pilgrimages in general and in Southeastern Europe in particular.

References

Kim Knott, 'Spatial Theory and Method for the Study of Religion', *Temenos – Nordic Journal of Comparative Religion*, 41 (2005a), pp. 153–84.

Kim Knott, *The Location of Religion. A Spatial Analysis* (London, Oakville: Equinox Publishing 2005b).

Pierre Nora, 'Zwischen Geschichte und Gedächtnis. Die Gedächtnisorte', in *Zwischen Geschichte und Gedächtnis*, ed. by Pierre Nora (Frankfurt am Main: Fischer Taschenbuch Verlag 1998), pp. 11–42.

General Index

Aghia 279; *Aghios* 206
Akathist 8, 136, 137, 139, 196, 225, 227, 232
Albania 7, 17-18, 20, 21, 49, 50, 51, 52, 53, 56, 58, 62, 63, 64, 69, 70, 73, 76, 77, 78, 79, 80, 82, 83, 84, 91, 94, 97, 100, 103, 104, 106, 109, 294
Alms 225, 226, 227
Aloysius Stepinac, Cardinal 171, 180
Anthony of Padua, Saint 56, 110, 119, 128
Archimandrite 23, 131, 136, 137, 138, 140, 141, 142, 227
Athos, Mount 17, 73, 74, 75, 78, 81, 187, 196, 210, 216, 231, 254, 265
Ayasmo 35, 43, 44; *Agheasmă* 9; *Hagiasma* 9, 28, 35

Barbara (Varvara), Saint 21, 22, 279, 280, 281, 282, 283, 284, 285, 286, 288
Basil, plant 39, 97, 263
Basilica 27, 145, 170, 180, 195
Healing bathing 28, 234
Blagodat 9, 35, 41, 42
Blaise, Saint 112, 117, 118
Blessed objects 24, 42, 137, 149, 174, 202, 207, 208, 209, 210, 211, 212, 213, 214, 236, 284, 285, 288
Body sufferings 40, 44, 136, 235
Bosnia and Herzegovina 18, 58, 166, 170, 174, 179, 180
Bulgaria 7, 9, 12, 14, 15, 20, 21, 27, 28, 30, 31, 33, 34, 35, 36, 39, 42, 44, 45, 79, 96, 106, 133, 147, 196, 292

Catholic 16, 18, 19, 21, 23, 29, 31, 50, 54, 57, 58, 59, 60, 61, 62, 63, 64, 80, 101, 134, 145, 146, 148, 149, 150, 151, 154, 155, 157, 158, 159, 160, 161, 171, 173, 174, 175, 177, 179, 180, 191, 194, 265, 294

Chris Hann 14, 33, 223
Communitas 10, 11, 21, 29, 249
Communist regime 23, 51, 54, 58, 69, 80, 81, 82, 83, 84, 85, 171, 185, 191, 192, 197, 244
Constantinople 31, 109, 133, 139, 143, 187, 196
Croatia 7, 18, 20, 23, 109, 110, 111, 112, 115, 119, 123, 165, 166, 168, 169, 170, 171, 173, 174, 175, 176, 177, 179, 180
Crusade 114
Cult, of 110, 116, 117, 119, 135, 149, 158, 191, 241, 244, 245, 248, 253

Devotional, religious objects 9, 24, 33, 80, 82, 155
Diaspora 13, 24, 25, 84, 85, 177, 186, 196, 197, 260, 261, 266, 267, 275, 293
Dionigi Albera 11, 49, 93
Divine Liturgy 96, 97, 98, 100, 101, 150, 191, 192, 193, 225
Dŭnovism 28, 34

Ellen Badone 13, 24
Eulogiai 22, 31, 39, 41, 42, 43
Exorcism 40, 227, 228

Folklore 20, 195, 201, 203, 213, 214, 228, 231, 241, 259, 264, 266, 267, 268, 270, 271, 272, 273, 274
Folk Art 202, 207, 208, 209, 210, 211, 212, 213, 214, 215, 216
Francis, Saint 110, 116, 117, 119, 121, 194

Galia Valtchinova 12, 15
Glendi 9, 258, 260, 261, 262, 263, 264, 265, 266, 268, 269, 272, 273, 274, 275, 276
Glen Bowman 11

GENERAL INDEX

Greece 7, 17, 19, 20, 21, 24, 25, 31, 79, 82, 83, 84, 196, 201, 202, 203, 204, 207, 208, 209, 214, 215, 257, 258, 265, 266, 267, 275, 279, 280, 282, 283, 286, 287, 293
Gregory Palamas 33

Hagiography 133, 134, 135, 230; *see also vita* 72, 73, 74, 75
Healing 14, 21, 22, 25, 27, 28, 30, 32, 33, 34, 35, 36, 37, 39, 40, 43, 45, 49, 54, 59, 60, 92, 106, 136, 149, 160, 168, 180, 226, 227, 228, 229, 230, 231, 232, 234, 235, 236, 239, 242, 245, 248, 251, 262, 263, 265, 294
Hegumen(ia) 98, 132, 138, 139, 140, 142, 152, 156, 230, 233, 240, 241, 243, 244, 245, 247, 248, 250, 251, 252
Hermits 232, 236
Hermitage 36, 231, 241, 242, 247, 249, 253
Hesychasm 36, 232, 236
Hodoș-Bodrog, monastery 146, 148, 151, 152, 155, 156, 158, 159, 161
Holy Communion 137, 170, 216, 225, 226, 227, 253; *see also* Eucharist 98
Holy Mass 174, 178, 179
Holy oil 39, 263, 284; *see also miro* 39
Holy Unction, sacrament of   137; *see also* Anointing 228, 231
Holy water 9, 39, 42, 136, 137, 138, 174, 212, 234, 236
Holy places 7, 11, 187, 189, 246, 253
Holy spring 9, 35
Holy Land; *see also* Jerusalem 17, 71, 109, 110, 112, 114, 115, 116, 118, 120, 124, 133, 179, 187, 196, 201, 202, 205, 216
Hymn(s) 8, 73, 76, 77, 82, 195, 196, 225, 263, 264, 281

Ian Reader 13, 240
Incense 193, 236, 260, 282, 283, 284
Islam 53, 56, 63, 74, 75, 175, 176

Jill Dubish 32
John Cassian, Saint 190, 196
John Eade 10, 11, 50, 93, 173, 232

Kim Knott 21, 291
Kolivo 39; *see also colivă* 226
Kosmas and Damian, Saints 21, 37, 40, 43, 44, 50, 52, 53, 62, 63, 77, 84
Kosovo 21, 50, 51, 52, 57, 58, 59, 60, 61, 62, 63, 64, 240, 241, 254, 294
Kuklen, monastery 22, 27, 40, 41, 42, 43, 44
Kurban 9, 34, 39, 55

Loreto, pilgrimage to 110, 119, 121, 124, 128, 155

Mantinádes 25, 258, 260, 264, 265, 266, 267, 268, 269, 273, 274, 276
Mario Katić 14
Marian shrine 58, 110, 119, 122, 128, 165, 166, 167, 169, 170, 177, 179
Marian pilgrimage 8, 167, 177, 178
Maria Couroucli 11, 12, 49
Maria Radna, monastery 145, 146, 147, 149, 150, 151, 152, 153, 154, 155, 158, 159, 160, 161, 162
Martyr (s) 69, 76, 83, 84, 134, 135, 136, 139, 140, 186, 189, 205
Martyrdom 74, 75, 76, 83, 188, 189, 265
Medjugorje 179
Michael J. Sallnow 10, 11
Mina, Saint 22, 36, 37, 38
Miracle-working icon 23, 37, 42, 132, 139, 149, 222, 228, 229; *see also* wonderworking icon 131, 137, 139, 280
Moldavia, Medieval 23, 131, 132, 133, 135, 136, 138, 139, 140, 142, 143, 192
Moldova, Republic of 20, 22, 131, 143, 221, 222, 223, 225, 227, 228, 230, 231, 232, 236, 293
Montenegro 18, 58, 121, 245, 254
Mother of God 76, 143, 148, 149, 150, 156, 165, 166, 170, 171, 179, 180, 192, 224, 225, 227, 228, 230, 233, 236, 249; *see also Theotokos* 148, 188, 190; *Bogorodits(c)a* 42, 43, 95
Mother of God, Bistrica of 18, 23, 165, 166, 167, 168, 169, 170, 171, 172, 174, 175, 176, 178, 179, 180

GENERAL INDEX 299

Mother Teresa 60
Muslims 19, 20, 21, 49, 50, 51, 53, 54, 55, 56, 57, 58, 60, 61, 62, 64, 71, 74, 75, 79, 91, 93, 94, 98, 99, 100, 106, 194, 202, 294

Naum, Saint 21, 77, 78, 91, 94, 95, 99, 101, 103, 105, 106
Neamț, monastery 23, 131, 132, 133, 135, 136, 137, 138, 139, 140, 141, 142, 143, 189
Nectarios of Aegina, Saint 232, 247
Nicholas of Bari, Saint 117, 196
Nicodemus of Berat, Saint 20, 69, 72, 73, 74, 75, 76, 77, 78, 80, 81, 82, 83, 84, 85, 90
North Macedonia, Republic of 7, 11, 18, 21, 57, 60, 91, 94, 97, 99, 105

Obradovsky, monastery 22, 27, 36, 38, 39
Offerings 9, 21, 28, 38, 98, 105, 145, 149, 225, 263; *see also* votive offerings 28, 30, 37, 38, 55, 98, 263
Ohrid, Archdiocese of 78, 94, 96
Orthodoxy 14, 19, 20, 21, 23, 24, 27, 28, 30, 31, 32, 33, 34, 35, 36, 42, 44, 45, 50, 52, 53, 54, 57, 58, 61, 62, 63, 64, 74, 75, 79, 80, 83, 84, 93, 94, 95, 96, 97, 98, 102, 105, 106, 134, 136, 139, 140, 141, 143, 145, 146, 147, 148, 149, 150, 151, 152, 153, 154, 155, 156, 158, 159, 160, 161, 162, 175, 179, 185, 186, 188, 191, 193, 194, 196, 201, 206, 207, 208, 216, 221, 222, 229, 231, 234, 241, 245, 247, 266, 294
Ostrog, monastery 18, 245, 246, 248, 250, 254
Ottoman Empire 34, 146, 166, 167, 169, 175, 180

Paisius Velichkovsky 133, 138, 139, 140, 141, 188, 189
Palestine 71, 109, 123, 124, 139, 202
Panteleimon, Saint 25, 257, 261, 262, 263, 264, 265, 266, 268, 269, 270, 276
Paraskeva of Epivates, Paraskeva of the Balkans 133, 134, 143, 189, 191; *see also* Saint Petka 27, 95, 103, 133

Pecherska Lavra, Kyiv 136, 196, 230
Peregrinatio 29, 32, 112, 114, 118, 123, 186
Peter and Paul, Apostles, Saints 77, 84, 121, 167
Poklonnichestvo 7, 21, 27, 29, 30, 35
Protestantism 19, 31, 159, 175, 177
Pre-Christian beliefs and practices 23, 62, 165, 177, 180, 226, 231, 237
Psalms 8, 216, 282, 283

Reformation 32, 165, 176, 177, 180
Relics 8, 9, 15, 18, 19, 21, 22, 28, 30, 33, 35, 39, 40, 42, 69, 77, 78, 79, 81, 82, 83, 84, 85, 116, 123, 133, 134, 135, 136, 137, 191, 205, 211, 212, 224, 230, 231, 236, 243, 244, 245, 247, 248, 249, 251, 253
Religious Tourism 15, 96, 191, 202, 207, 208, 253
Magic 40, 224, 229
Reliquary 40, 77, 78, 80, 81, 82, 84, 85, 90, 135, 140, 212, 244, 248, 249
Ritual bread 39, 79, 97, 98, 148, 225, 227, 263
Robert M. Hayden 12
Romania 7, 16, 20, 23, 25, 131, 134, 145, 146, 147, 154, 155, 158, 161, 185, 187, 188, 189, 190, 191, 192, 193, 194, 195, 197, 241, 294
Rome 109, 115, 116, 117, 118, 121, 123, 124, 128, 135, 139, 150, 186, 196

Sabor 9, 246, 247, 248, 249, 250, 251
Sacrifice 34, 40, 55, 56, 60, 98, 225, 229
Sacred time 22, 281
Saint Catherine on Sinai, monastery 109, 132
Saharna, monastery 228, 230, 231, 233, 234
Sanctuary 51, 52, 53, 54, 55, 57, 58, 59, 60, 62, 63, 239, 253
Serbia 7, 16, 20, 21, 22, 58, 60, 79, 94, 152, 239, 240, 241, 242, 243, 244, 246, 247, 248, 250, 252, 254
Sick people 39, 40, 42, 149, 228
Simon Coleman 10, 13, 29

Slava 246, 247
Slovenia 174, 175, 176
Synod 134, 157, 228, 230
Pilgrimage stations 172

Terra Sancta 109, 114, 118, 123, 124
Therapeutic 22, 64, 232
Tumane, monastery 22, 239, 240, 241, 242, 243, 244, 245, 247, 248, 249, 250, 251, 252, 253, 254
Țipova, monastery 226, 231, 232, 235

Veliko Tarnovo 133
Vespers 79, 96, 216, 257, 262, 264
Via Crucis 29
Victor Turner and Edith Turner 10, 29, 71, 224, 231, 260, 283, 291, 292

Yugoslavia 19, 57, 58, 62, 94, 95, 97, 103, 106, 161, 171, 173, 244

Zosim, Saint 241, 242, 244, 245, 247, 248, 250